Also by Tom Bissell

FICTION
God Lives in St. Petersburg and Other Stories

NONFICTION
Chasing the Sea:
Being a Narrative of a Journey Through Uzbekistan,
Including Descriptions of Life Therein, Culminating with an Arrival at the Aral Sea,
the World's Worst Man-Made Ecological Catastrophe, in One Volume

HUMOR
Speak, Commentary:
The Big Little Book of Fake DVD Commentaries,
Wherein Well-Known Pundits Make Impassioned Remarks
About Classic Science-Fiction Films
(with Jeff Alexander)

THE **Father** OF **All Things**

THE **Father** OF **All Things**

A Marine, His Son, and the Legacy of Vietnam

Tom Bissell

PANTHEON BOOKS

NEW YORK

9/09

Pantheon Books and colophon are registered trademarks of Random House, Inc.

Portions of this book have appeared in *Best American Travel Writing 2005* edited
by Jamaica Kincaid (Houghton Mifflin, New York), *Columbia, Harper's Magazine,
Lost,* and *The Old Town Review.*

Owing to limitations of space, acknowledgments for permission to print
previously published material may be found following the index.

Library of Congress Cataloging-in-Publication Data
Bissell, Tom, [date]
The father of all things : a Marine, his son, and the legacy of Vietnam / Tom Bissell.
p.   cm.
Includes bibliographical references and index.
ISBN 978-0-375-42265-2
1. Vietnam War, 1961–1975.   2. Vietnam—Description and travel.
3. Bissell, John.   4. Bissell, Tom, 1974–   5. Veterans—United States—
Family relationships.   I. Title.
DS557.B57 2007
959.704'3—dc22   2006049427

www.pantheonbooks.com

Printed in the United States of America
First Edition
2 4 6 8 9 7 5 3

Of course, for my father: all things

For my friends Gary Sernovitz, Jeff Alexander,
Dan Josefson, Matthew McGough, and Andrew Miller

And for my Vietnamese friends,
who showed me their country

War is the father of all and king of all.
Some he shows as gods, others as men.
Some he makes slaves, and others free.
—HERACLITUS

last night i flew with a division of three helo's out over the western side of taqaddum. it is low light level over here which just means there is now moon light, very dark. it is hard to tell the ground from the air. we went for a landing and decided it was too dusty so we headed back in to the airfield and practiced lands on the runway. while we were doing our touch and goes there was alot of small arms fire east of us about 3 to 5 miles in the city of . . . well i can't say cause i can't spell it. anyways i thought it was cool. on the nvg's (night vision goggles) you can see all the tracers shooting high in the sky. but i don't know what they are shooting at there was nothing over there.
—FROM A U.S. MARINE'S 3/17/04
E-MAIL FROM IRAQ

Contents

Author's Note

More than thirty thousand books on Vietnam are currently in print. *Why another?* one might (and probably did) ask. Especially a book written by someone who was not even alive in March 1973, when the last of the U.S. combat troops returned home. I bring to what the Vietnamese call the American War only this: I have spent most of my life thinking about it. Vietnam has occupied a larger portion of my mind than perhaps any other topic. The reason for this is as simple as it is elemental: like 3 million other Americans, my father served to prevent the Republic of Vietnam's collapse to the forces of a largely Communist insurgency aligned with a neighboring nation known as the Democratic Republic of Vietnam. Like an estimated 800,000 other Americans, my father saw combat during his service. What I could not know about my father because of his experience has always fascinated and troubled me. When the opportunity arose to travel to Vietnam with my father, I accepted instantly, unaware that the magazine piece I intended to write would prove so consuming that I would have no choice but to address our trip and its personal reverberations at much greater length.

I say the war "occupied" a huge portion of my mind but would not dare claim any real suffering because of this. The war did not torment or haunt or injure me. Rather, Vietnam was an abstract shadow that rarely left my other thoughts undarkened. Why might this be? As the literal and spiritual children of veterans who fought the only war in which the United States failed to enact its will, many of us came of age with a view of warfare virtually unknown in the United States since the aftermath of Appomattox, when Confederate children saw their own fathers stumble home in defeat. Many of us grew up ashamed of our fathers' war—and sometimes of our fathers themselves.

This book is thus my attempt to speak for myself while confronting something I believe many younger Americans feel. I wanted to write a book that was specific to my own experience but also engaged with the universal. In this spirit, I have included a fair amount of what I found to be the more fascinating aspects of, and questions about, recent Vietnamese history. I realized early on that, though I had read a number of books about the Vietnam War, I knew dishearteningly little about its indigenous contexts and historical determinants. (Or that Ho Chi Minh loved volleyball.) Conversations with numerous otherwise knowledgeable people around my age led me to conclude that I was far from alone in my ignorance. I open this book with an account of the Republic of Vietnam's last few weeks of existence, a story that is told alongside my attempt to re-create, as my parents experienced it many thousands of miles away, the night of Saigon's fall in 1975. The Republic of Vietnam was not the only thing terminated on that day. A certain kind of American experience ended on April 30, 1975, while another, more benighted experience began.

Allow me now to anticipate, and put a stake through the heart of, one inevitable charge: There is nothing "new" in this book about the Vietnam War. What this book contains, I very much hope, is an emotional experience interwoven with established historical facts of the Vietnam War—an experience that I hope is and feels new. Let me say too that I address the historical record with great respect for the historians whose work I have read and used. I fully acknowledge that nonhistorians dwell upon historical events at their own risk. I have nevertheless attempted to read the secondary English-language literature of the war widely and carefully, though I realize that I have probably missed many important works. Vietnam is a massive topic, its history massively contended, and one could literally devote one's life to it. Encyclopedism was not my goal while researching this book.

But this is not really a book about the nation of Vietnam, or even the Vietnam War. It is, instead, a book about war's endless legacy. I did not intend to write a book about the legacy of war, but how could it have been otherwise? War is a force of influence above all else—the most purely distilled form of partisanship ever devised. Yet war's energies and dark matter are too complicated to allow anyone the certain physics of right and wrong. When war begins, leaders inevitably frown as they promise courage and bravery, guarantee tragic sacrifice, yet vow, all the same, to see it through. What any war's igniters rarely admit are the small, terrible truths that have held firm for every war ever fought, no matter how necessary or avoidable: *This will be horrible, and whatever happens will scar us for decades to come.* Indeed, even necessary wars can destroy the trust of a people in their leaders, just as war destroys human beings on both sides of the rifle.

War is appetitive. It devours goodwill, landscape, cultures, mothers, and fathers—before finally forcing us, the orphans, to pick up the pieces. These pages are, I hope, a few such pieces.

T.C.B.
November 28, 2005
New York City

A Brief Note on Spelling

Vietnamese words, save for those clearly borrowed from other languages (for instance, *oto,* or "automobile") and a few compound-word phrases, have one syllable. Thus it is not Vietnam but Viet Nam (pronounced *Vyet* Nam), not Hanoi but Ha Noi, not Danang but Da Nang, not Saigon but Sai Gon—and this is not even to include the various diacritical markings that indicate the tonal emphasis of each vowel. Our familiar Western corruptions occurred during the first years of U.S. involvement in Viet Nam, when newspaper headline writers smashed together alien place names in order to conserve front-page acreage. For Vietnam's most recognizable cities I have continued this somewhat embarrassing tradition and used the compounded form. For less well known cities, such as Nha Trang and Da Lat, and other Vietnamese terms, such as Viet Cong and Viet Minh, I have opted for usage appropriate to their language of origin.

ONE

The Fall

The waters returned and covered the chariots and the chariot drivers, the entire army of Pharaoh that had followed them into the sea; not one of them remained.

—EXODUS 14:28

I

It would have been spring. The neighborhood yards still yellow and concrete hard, the side panels of the cars you pass on the way home from work spattered with arcing crusts of road salt, the big oaks and elms that loom along Lake Shore Drive throwing down long pale rows of shadow. These trees are covered with stony gray bark, their naked branches black lightning against a deepening indigo sky. Everywhere winter's grim spell still holds.

A midwestern spring at the Forty-sixth Parallel is a different sort of season than the spring one finds even five degrees lower, in Milwaukee, say, or Chicago. In Michigan's Upper Peninsula spring never truly arrives. It passes through for a few weeks, shrinks and smoothens the filthy fringes of snow that sit packed against the curbs, finishes with a fine icy sheen the misshapen islets of snow out in the yard that stubbornly refuse to melt, but spring does not arrive. It does not come. One receives only the suggestion of spring here, followed by a hot, windy summer. You are thinking of this as you circle around your huge yard (which takes up half the block), noting its lumpy archipelago of remaining snow, before finally pulling into the driveway. There is something exhausted about the way your station wagon's engine sputters and dies. For a moment you sit there in the car looking at the remaining mounds of snow. On bright days, when the sunlight angles down on the ice crystals just right, the reflection can be difficult to look at. But on this cloudy late afternoon there is but little light. Your eyes ache anyway, the silvery imminence of evening hovering above you. *Where is spring?* you think, now standing in your driveway, gazing upon your house, its coldly reflective windows, its closed doors. Today you have left work early and driven the long way home. It is 5 p.m. on April 29, 1975.

The lights come on in the empty kitchen. You keep your hand on the circular plastic knob, fiddling with and turning the adjustor. Darker, lighter, darker. You cannot find the proper setting, going from break-room bright to dinner-party mild to opium-den dim at the speed of light. But what is the speed of darkness? The cabinetry is all chocolaty wood, the countertops a hard Formica blaze of orange, a room that seems dark even when it is blazingly illumed. At last (fuck it) you switch off the overhead light, the sound of your own heart more audible while you stand in charcoal shadow.

You stare at the kitchen table. Two ashtrays, one on each end of the table, form twin pyres of your wife Muff's lipsticked butts. An empty baby bottle, its sides still cloudy with clinging milk. A tall red, white, and blue can of Budweiser, its top-popped aperture keyhole-shaped. You know it is urine warm and half full before you even touch it. Your live-in younger brother Paul's, no doubt. (Muff claims to see Paul only when he is "drunk, sleeping, or hung over." He is twenty-four. What can you do?) The lazy Susan and its cargo of gift-shop jetsam, souvenirs from trips you no longer remember: expensive glass salt and pepper shakers Muff had to have, the floral-patterned porcelain sugar dish, the toothpick holder shaped like a rotund little monk, the plastic tray freighted with a yellow slab of room-temperature margarine. A neatly planed pile of mail awaits you on the table's corner. All of it adding up to life, one little corner in a seven-year repository of marriage. You do not even look through the mail.

When I asked you what this time was like, you said only, "I was a young guy, working hard. Always pissed off. Always." You were a trust officer at the First National Bank, managing other people's money. They *save* up here in the woods. From the millionaire widows living in fire-place-heated homes to the couples sitting on $700,000 portfolios while driving rusty Ford pickups, you were learning all about the strange camouflage and various neuroses of rural wealth. What made many of your customers' mattress stuffing so frustrating was that you were broke. Every morning that you parked your used Chevy station wagon beside your boss's long cream Cadillac reminded you of this. The Bissells, of course, were reputed around town to have money—how faces in Escanaba changed when the name *Bissell* came flying back at them!—but over the last seven years you had watched it all go up in the low fires of your various new responsibilities.

JOHN AND JOHNO BISSELL

Broke. Such a hard, simple, declarative word. You dreamed of making $20,000 a year, three times and more your current salary. Twenty thousand dollars: the number itself was talismanic, as beautiful as a finish line. It would bandage these seven years of hemorrhaging marital wounds and keep them stanched forever. Because now things were not well. "Your mother," you told me once, without bitterness, "wanted a better life." Everything at this time felt to you cold and dead, as though your touch itself were warmth-draining, death-contagious. Every room of the house was dark and angry that spring, unwarmed and unloved, but there were few places for blame to gather. Nor was there any place to hide.

You walk through your family's ancestral seven-bedroom house looking for your wife and sons, a journey of several minutes. To many visitors, the Bissell house, one of Escanaba's biggest, always felt less like a home than a series of pastel caverns linked by massively arched throughways. You drift across the canary-wallpapered dining room (the chandelier so huge and gaudy it was vaguely embarrassing to pass beneath it), the green-carpeted living room (most of its antique furniture having not known human weight in years), and pass into the final and most spacious—the television room. The Bissell house's placement on the littoral edge of town allows the television room's four massive bay windows to look out onto Ludington Park, beyond which spans the seascape tundra of still-frozen Lake Michigan. Today the lake is a surface storm of twirling snow devils. As expected, here you find Muff and your sons. Your little sister Alicia is upstairs, in her room, listening to the Monkees (she still refuses to acknowledge that they did not play their instruments), while your brother Paul, you can guess, is out with friends, most likely attached to a keg hose.

Muff is watching television with your son Johno, who at five resembles nothing so much as a pudgy, thin-haired Buddha. Muff looks beautiful, of course. How could she not? She once bested her classmate Farrah Fawcett in a junior high beauty contest in Corpus Christi, Texas. The hair your wife has bleached platinum blond every week for the last decade achieves gravity-defying proportions, a hair-spray skyscraper. She wears slightly too much powder blue eye shadow that is carefully matched to the color of her thin turtleneck sweater. She holds Johno on her knee, lightly bouncing him—though he is too big for this—her long hard white fingernails mildly alarming whenever she pushes his hair across his forehead. She looks at you and nods hello, already expecting the worst.

At the room's far edge, across a bay of orange carpet, almost swallowed by her recliner, Aunt Grace sits knitting. She is white-haired and thick-calved, wearing big nunnish brown shoes, a solid blue dress, and a red shawl so tasseled and incomplete-looking your initial thought is that

MUFF AND JOHNO

she is knitting it upon her own shoulders. You know that amid the needles' steady clicking Grace is waiting for the inevitable flare of discord
between you and Muff, whereupon she will quietly stand to leave and,
later in the evening, offer neutral comfort to you both. With age comes
wisdom: the sort of bromide one hears all the time, even as less and less
clear evidence seems to support it. Grace is welcome proof that—at least
sometimes, in some people—with age comes wisdom. But Grace is not
much help with what vexes you today. Her own husband Herb died of a
heart attack in his forties, still wracked by the horrors of World War I's
battlefields. Herb never spoke of the war to Grace, and thus, in your
mind, she never truly knew the man she loved. War, then. Always war. In
regard to the war, your war, you could very much use some human wisdom right now. You are thirty-three years old, and the events of the last
few weeks have not made much sense. Or rather, the events have made
sense, but nothing else has.

Vietnam is a dream to you. It has been eight years since you took in its
scents, felt its Asian sunlight on your white skin. The war comes to you
now not as whole memory but in pieces and fragments as ragged and
drifty as ash. Up half the night, turning in the wet-flannel heat, checking

on sentries, checking on your gunner placements. Up early in the morning for patrols, still hot. Or sleeping all day for night patrols, hot again, these night patrols the worst, always the worst, feeling like four-hour-long panic attacks enacted within a nightmare. Your clothes rotting, your feet rotting. The ankle sores that never healed and remained as bright and wet as fresh raspberries. The sweat that was like another layer of clothing. Your smell, that deep swampy smell of your body. The mold you picked from between your toes and flicked lightheartedly at whoever was nearest. The smell of twenty Marines' unwashed asses and unbrushed teeth all around you, the olfactory orchestra of the jungle itself, the warm, buttery smell of a cleaned M14, the firecracker stench of gunfire. You still smell it, sometimes, when you wake up sweating, Muff having been driven to the couch hours before by your kicking. You smell it when the remnant of the malaria banished to the depths of your cells catches you with a chill that almost takes you to your knees, when your limbs thrum with a ghostly soreness, when the shrapnel wound on your neck glows with a sudden inner fire.

You left Vietnam in late 1966, a time when the word "quagmire" was just abandoning *Roget's* as its most natural habitat. The war then was still tenable, winnable—or so it was thought. But now it was *la fin de la guerre,* the real *fin,* not the "peace with honor" that extricated the Americans in 1973, only two years ago, but the final campaign. A headline you saw only seven days ago: HOPE THINS FOR MILLIONS ADRIFT ACROSS INDOCHINA. Your hope has thinned, too, and your very body aches of its thinning. You feel incomplete, as though within you some crucial girder of emotion has gone missing. That part of you is still in Vietnam. That part never left.

II

In late March 1975, the Saigon newspaper *Chinh Luan* published an article, now known as the "Fare Thee Well" dispatch, that had been written in the midst of fierce combat between the armies of North and South Vietnam as South Vietnam was unraveling. The author was the

South Vietnamese war correspondent Nguyen Dinh Tu. Through "the outstanding initiative and very strong leadership of the United States," Tu wrote, "the Paris Peace Agreement was signed on the 27th of January 1973 to international applause of our friends, especially in the United States, leading to 'Peace with Honor' in accord with the desires of former President Nixon, the present Secretary of State Henry Kissinger, Congress, and the entire American people. The fact that these friends have been able to return to the warmth of their families is something for which I personally, with all my heart and soul, rejoice." But Tu went on:

Now, after two years of "Peace with Honor[,]" through the reports of newspapers, wire services, radio, and television all over the world, those friends are now observing the disintegration that is spreading daily across my homeland. Thousands of my country's soldiers have continued to fall throughout the two years of "Peace with Honor." Thousands of my people, including many children, have continued to die throughout these two years of "Peace with Honor." Hundreds of thousands of my people are homeless, hungry, cold; and furthermore and even more important, without hope, without even the dream of a life worth living for these two years of "Peace with Honor," and for the coming days, the coming months, and perhaps even the coming years. And everyone in Vietnam, including me, my friends, we now ask ourselves, how long will the "Peace with Honor" continue, and where will it lead? . . . [A]ll of my people, and I personally, have understood that our friends, especially our American friends, the American Congress and the American people . . . look upon the war in Vietnam from which they have drawn so far away, as if it were a nightmare that must be pushed completely away from their minds in order for them to live peacefully and happily in the warmth of their families. No one, in psychological terms or any other terms, can continue forever to retain the affection and assistance of the person next to them, be that a single person, a friendly country, or an ally in a desperate situation. The soldiers of my country, my people (please understand "people" here to mean the overwhelming majority, the poor, the war victims, and not the rich and fat minority in Saigon and a few other cities in Vietnam and in some foreign countries), and I myself, we understand all of this. . . . Out of a feeling of help-lessness, because I cannot find any words of my own with which to express my deep gratitude and bid a respectful farewell to the allies, especially to the Americans in the United States Congress, in the United States government, to the American soldiers and the Amer-ican people who cherish "Peace with Honor," let me with a heart that is completely sincere quote a line of poetry from Lord Byron to send to all these friends:

> FARE THEE WELL! AND IF FOREVER,
> STILL, FOR EVER FARE THEE WELL.

When the Paris Peace Agreement—officially known as the Paris Accords for Ending the War and Restoring Peace in Vietnam—was signed in Jan-uary 1973, many regarded it as the virtual surrender of South Vietnam to the Communists. Nguyen Van Thieu, South Vietnam's tough, soft-spoken, intelligent, perpetually dapper, and moderately crooked presi-dent at the time of the accords' signing, certainly never saw the terms imposed by the Paris Accords as anything but "an inhumane act by an inhumane ally," as he later put it. He even wept in Henry Kissinger's pres-ence when shown an early version of the agreement. While the accords' terms were still being debated in March 1972, North Vietnam launched its biggest offensive in four years—a series of attacks almost Swiss in their synchronization. Several tank-backed battalions of North Viet-namese soldiers charged southward over the Seventeenth Parallel, which had divided North Vietnam from South Vietnam since 1954. They were quickly joined in battle by the Viet Cong. ("Viet Cong," from "Viet Nam Cong San," or "Vietnamese Communists," was invented in the mid-1950s by either the South Vietnamese government or its American advis-ers—accounts differ—in order to blanket the resistance movement with purely Communist motives. Viet Cong also refers only to insurgency forces operating within South Vietnam; the Viet Cong's proper name was the National Liberation Front, or NLF. The People's Army of Viet-nam, or PAVN, refers to North Vietnam's professional soldiers. The groups were in league but not always mind-melded, as was often assumed at the time.) The North's surprise Easter Offensive was finally broken by a fearsome use of American airpower officially known as Line-backer I.

The North was not only plotting offensives and being bombed while it contemplated the terms of the Paris Accords; it was also being prod-ded toward the signing table by its putative allies the Soviet Union and the People's Republic of China. Both nations were sick of shoveling rubles and yuan into the bottomless furnace of the Vietnam War and were eager to follow President Richard Nixon's lead along the first tenu-ous cobblestones of détente. If the South felt abandoned by the United States, the North felt in some ways equally abandoned by its Soviet and Chinese allies, both now publicly softening their views of the West. To have been a Vietnamese of any political inclination during the early 1970s was to have felt a dire sense of sudden, unfamiliar friendlessness.

What terms, then, did the Paris Accords impose upon the long-fighting nations of North and South Vietnam? Then–National Security Adviser Henry Kissinger convinced North Vietnam's chief negotiator, Le Duc Tho, to release U.S. prisoners of war in both North Vietnam and Laos and to withdraw all PAVN troops from Laos. The North also agreed to the establishment of an Administration of National Concord ("what-ever that meant," Kissinger notes humanely in his memoirs), to be set up by the Thieu regime, and a coalition of southern Communists called the Provisional Revolutionary Government (PRG), which had recently been known as the Viet Cong and whose negotiation duties would largely consist of dismantling Thieu's regime. Two of these concessions (those of the American POWs and Laos) were of little use to Thieu, one (the PAVN withdrawal from Laos) was helpful, and one (the coalition gov-ernment) reduced Thieu to rage. Partaking of any coalition government at all with Communists had been the most signal of Thieu's "Four No's," a public relations campaign the Saigon regime launched shortly before the Paris talks began. The three remaining forbidden contingencies were (1) no negotiation with the Communists, (2) no Communist activity in South Vietnam, and (3) no territory belonging to South Vietnam to be ceded to the Communists.

What follows is the buffet of allowances from which Thieu and his countrymen were forced by Kissinger to dine. While the North pledged that its armies would vacate the parts of South Vietnam controlled by the South's Army of the Republic of Vietnam (ARVN), it was allowed to retain up to 145,000 troops in all areas "liberated" by the North and NLF, which meant a hostile standing army in South Vietnamese territory and, in effect, placed the NLF on equal political footing with the South Vietnamese government. Meanwhile, the South was not allowed to increase its ARVN troop strength and was forbidden to accept additional weapons from the United States, except as replacements for weapons falling under the forgiving designation of "worn-out" or "damaged." Any and all American offices and military bases throughout South Vietnam, with the exception of the U.S. Defense Attaché Office (known as "Pentagon East") and the U.S. Embassy in Saigon, were to be shuttered. The South would additionally have to honor and obey an independent international coalition that would oversee "free and democratic" elections in South Vietnam.

President Thieu did receive various sweeteners, secretly and otherwise. For instance, the leases of American military installations were quickly transferred to South Vietnamese holders to allow their continued operation, and several billion dollars' worth of "replacement" weapons were speedily shipped to South Vietnam from Taiwan, South Korea, and Israel, an operation known as Enhance Plus. This gave South Vietnam, quite suddenly, the fourth largest air force in the world. Most important, in one of three private letters Nixon had written Thieu, the U.S. president promised his Vietnamese counterpart that the United States "will respond with full force should the settlement be violated by North Vietnam."

Kissinger and North Vietnam's Le Duc Tho were jointly awarded the Nobel Peace Prize for coming to terms in Paris. Only Kissinger accepted the prize, though he did not attend the ceremony for fear of attracting protestors. Le Duc Tho proceeded from the sensible premise that the only peace earned at Paris had been for the United States. He still had a war to fight. Tho would later be central in urging the North Vietnamese to proceed with the final, all-out offensive on South Vietnam.

Even though the South's army, which numbered almost one million soldiers, had been augmented by two decades of American aid and the North's army had been literally decimated after its surprise offensive of 1972, it was clear to most that the Paris Accords seriously undermined Thieu's government. Without huge tactical support from the United States, the South's armies were in most cases haplessly commanded, dangerously underpaid, and utterly corrupted. Not a few ARVN soldiers took to the old practice of selling arms and rice to the Communists to support their families. In other regions, ARVN officers demanded payment to authorize medevacs for the wounded and outright bribes to call in artillery strikes for their pinned-down comrades. However weakened, cautious, and hungry, the North's army and the NLF were growing in strength and determination in the early 1970s.

Not surprisingly, the Paris Accords' cease-fire was quickly broken by both sides, nullifying the promised elections that would unify Vietnam. President Thieu called this outbreak of new hostilities "the Third Indochina War," but for the first time in modern history the people of Vietnam were fighting without the direct presence of foreign intermediaries. Within a year of the Paris Accords' signing, the South's army had lost 40 percent of its soldiers to desertion and death, and, in the words of the historian Larry H. Addington, "the corruption so endemic to South Vietnam had caused much of the war matériel that the Americans had lavished on the [South] to be drained away to improper uses." This finally amounted to $200 million of "misplaced" and "lost" equipment and weapons. President Nixon's May 1974 request to set the ceiling of aid to South Vietnam at $1.6 billion was rebuffed by Congress. Nixon resigned three months later, to the shock of President Thieu, who had been assured that nothing amid Watergate's circus of illegality was an impeachable offense. The House-Senate conference committee that agreed to cap aid to South Vietnam at $1 billion gave Nixon a last kick by lowering the amount to $700 million.

Arguing for a return to the "revolutionary violence" of the late 1960s, North Vietnam's hard-liners advocated a full assault against the weakening Thieu regime. As the North's General Vo Nguyen Giap later wrote, "our people now had the historic opportunity to liberate South Vietnam totally. . . . [T]he time had come when the enemy was facing complete failure while we were in a position to win complete victory." On January 7, 1975, the North Vietnamese, having patiently planned their move, finally attacked the South in force and quickly took the province of Phuoc Long, which was located a mere fifty miles from Saigon's suburbs. This most flagrant violation of the Paris Accords so far was also "a carefully calculated experiment," in the words of one PAVN major general, to see whether President Gerald Ford would reengage the United States in the conflict. The collapse of Phuoc Long province was not a staggering military loss by any means, but it did demonstrate to the North Vietnamese that the "massive and brutal retaliation" Nixon had promised President Thieu would simply never occur. Nixon himself was on his way to the memoir-enabling sunshine of San Clemente, California, and Ford's war powers had undergone congressional vasectomy.

Many South Vietnamese units initially fought well during the North's 1975 offensive, but when it became clear to the South's people that no emergency aid was forthcoming from the United States, the ARVN's morale, fragile at the best of times, began a last disintegration. "There was a kind of sickness that infected them," one ARVN general later said of his fellow soldiers to the historian Larry Engelmann, "the sickness of an idea. . . . They wanted to depend on America, and when they could not depend on America they ran away."

On March 10, after sending out numerous false radio messages and leaking decoy troop movement schedules, North Vietnam marched 10,000 soldiers down the newly paved Ho Chi Minh Trail into a region of South Vietnam known as the Central Highlands, a strategically invaluable area due to its miles of elevated ground and the terminus of the Communist supply network that smuggled men and weapons into South Vietnam. For the North, the once-terrifying ordeal of journeying down the Ho Chi Minh Trail—a veritable autobahn now that it was no longer being cratered by American B-52s—was no more. Furthermore, the enemy the North met in the Central Highlands was galaxies from its ideal fighting condition. A large percentage of the South's soldiers in the Central Highlands were badly undersupplied (there are numerous stories of ARVN soldiers scrounging in the dirt for unspent rifle rounds and buying grenades with their own money) and, by one account, strung out on heroin, which had become newly affordable once South Vietnam was emptied of America's lotus-eating soldiers in 1973.

Within two days of its offensive in the Central Highlands, the North captured the important mountain town of Buon Me Thuot and sealed off the majority of the ARVN's supply routes in the region. On March 14, a straw-grabbing President Thieu ordered an ARVN retreat from the Highlands, which he claimed was part of a strategy to "lighten the top so as to keep the bottom." Thieu's decision was so militarily baffling that many of the North's generals feared it was a trap. They were not the only ones caught unawares: the total evacuation of an important area under fierce enemy attack was unforeseen even by Thieu's most craven generals.

The ARVN retreat, which under the best of circumstances would have taken months to plan, instead got under way in hours. President Thieu's hope was that the Central Highlands' retreating divisions would be met and reinforced at the coastal city of Tuy Hoa, whereupon some would turn around to wage a counteroffensive and others would form a heavily armed human moat around the Mekong Delta and Saigon. The retreating ARVN columns never reached their destination of Tuy Hoa. These soldiers had one route of escape from the Central Highlands— the thin, badly paved, and heavily mined Route 7B, an old logging road that had hitherto been abandoned as unfit for transport. When Thieu's withdrawal order reached the ears of the region's general populace, riots erupted. Soon Route 7B was jammed with 60,000 troops and 400,000 civilians. An ARVN colonel later described to Engelmann how the tanks and armored personnel carriers and trucks had been covered with desperate refugees and members of many soldiers' families: "Sometimes they would fall off, and the convoy kept moving and they screamed and were crushed. . . . It was a nightmare." Yet it got worse. Some ARVN soldiers in this "convoy of tears" (a phrase coined by the war correspondent Nguyen Dinh "Fare Thee Well" Tu), driven mad by fear and hunger, began killing and raping people. South Vietnamese A-37s accidentally bombed one retreating ARVN armored unit that had radioed for air support. When it rained, the road became a river of boot-swallowing, tire-stopping mud. By the time the North's armies reached the bogged-down, civilian-hampered battalions of ARVN soldiers, there was open revolt. Three quarters of the 25,000 troops were wiped out. The few who escaped fled to the sea, and the ARVN general responsible for transmitting Thieu's withdrawal order soon shot himself.

A North Vietnamese spy in South Vietnam's Central Intelligence headquarters now began to provide his unwitting comrades with false maps indicating the Communists' attack plan. The air advantage the South had long held, already sorely weakened by a lack of American aid, was now fully obliterated. Empty forests were bombed as the North's untouched armies gobbled up South Vietnam's countryside. The coastal cities of the South began to fall in mid-March. The city of Hue then fell on March 24, Danang on March 30. All "nonessential" American personnel were secretly told by the U.S. Embassy to begin their evacuation the next day.

By the end of March, eight provinces had fallen to the Communists. The beginning of April was no better. In its first days Qui Nhon, Nha Trang, and Da Lat fell into PAVN and NLF hands. Thanks to looting ARVN soldiers, Nha Trang burned for almost a week before being formally occupied. Early April also saw the attempted assassination of President Thieu when a South Vietnamese F-5A jet, feigning engine trouble, broke away from its formation and dropped a bomb on the Presidential Palace in Saigon. The F-5A's U.S.-trained pilot, Nguyen Thanh Trung, was a long-scheming defector to the North whose Communist father had been killed by the Saigon government years before.

On April 4 an American cargo plane filled with hundreds of Vietnamese war orphans and various Defense Attaché Office personnel left Saigon for the United States. This "orphan airlift" was the unofficial beginning of the evacuation of all Americans and those South Vietnamese particularly vulnerable to Communist charges of collaboration. Some U.S. Embassy officials in Saigon hoped that the arrival of so many Vietnamese orphans on American soil would provide a catalyst for public sympathy and win more aid for the South. But one of the plane's rear doors had not been properly latched and was torn from its hinges shortly after takeoff. The C-5A Galaxy (then the world's largest aircraft) crash-landed in a rice paddy outside Saigon, killing 135 and making the orphan airlift, at that point, the second worst disaster in aviation history. More than half of the dead were orphans, and most did not die during the crash itself but drowned while trapped in their seats. Those who survived, in the words of one rescuer, were "so frightened they couldn't even cry" and had to be hosed down to wash the mud from their bodies. On April 10, President Ford made a final attempt to convince Congress to appropriate $1 billion in emergency military assistance to South Vietnam, saying in a speech before the House that the "situation in South Vietnam . . . has reached a critical phase . . . and the time is very short." At least two members of Congress stood and walked out in the middle of Ford's speech in what was (then) an unprecedented display of contempt for a sitting president.

III

I have before me a letter, undated. My mother, who gave it to me, says my father probably wrote it to her in the mid-1970s, when things between my parents, who divorced in 1977, were especially toxic. The letter is handwritten and badly folded (it looks like a blindfolded attempt at a paper airplane) and stained mysteriously pink along its top edge. But the ink still leaps off the page, as bright and resonant as a week-old tattoo. Obviously written after an argument, it reads:

My Dear Sweetheart,

Muffin, this is no poem, it can't be. I want you but you're too beautifully asleep. Muffin, you look so pretty tonight! I love you so much—so very much.

I honestly don't know what I would do, or where I would be, without you. Thank you for being here—with me; for now and forever.

The wind is blowing—I can hear the waves crashing onto the beach. In a way it reminds me of us. The storm comes but always you and the calm settles, both upon nature and us.

My darling, I love you and need you. Tonight you're in a flat calm and you're the most peaceful, beautiful thing I have ever seen. I have lived, died, laughed, cried, reveled, and moped with you for years now. I want to continue to do so for two thousand more.

I love you, Muffin.

Any glimpse we get of our parents prior to our incubation is liable to haunt and astound. It is hard to accept that your parents were once young, uncertain people, driven by passions and miscalculations. The first time I read this letter of my father's, it sat me down with damp, scalding eyes. This was not a sepia snapshot of two smiling strangers in superannuated clothing who somewhat resembled my parents. This was a narrow psychic tunnel into the subterranea of their marriage.

What was it about this letter that hit me so roughly? Perhaps the weird personal recognition I found in it. My father's letter does not sound terribly unlike the gut-torn missives I have written to the objects of my own reckless love. Or perhaps it was the discovery that these two human beings who treated each other so awfully when I was growing up once loved each other so much, and so indisputably.

I was lucky. I was three when my parents divorced, and they wound up living only blocks from each other. Unlike the children of most divorced parents, any questions of custody were for my brother and me ridiculous. I am not even sure which of my parents was granted custody (what an unfriendly word!) or what the terms of visitation were. My brother and I simply drifted back and forth between parents, as calculating as thieves. My clearest memories of my mother and father's early interaction are of my father standing out in the cold of my stepfather's house, waiting while we put on our shoes or finished breakfast, so he could take us to church. My mother would not allow my father inside the house. She would not even answer the door or speak to him. "Your father's here," she would say coolly when the doorbell rang. When I opened the door, my father's expression was always the same, every morning, a host of multitudes. Embarrassment, pain, stoicism, anger—somehow his long, thin face contained all of them. His hands would invariably be stuffed in his pockets, his hair superbly combed. He would smile when he saw us and never said a word about having had to wait outside. Something about the way he stood out there in the dark cold— he seemed so *wronged*—made me unfairly blame everything that had gone bad between my parents on my mother. I was probably twelve or thirteen before she finally let him into the house. This letter of my father's provided my first real glimpse of the invisible wreckage that lay beneath those awkward mornings.

After Vietnam, my father wound up on a military base in Beaufort, South Carolina, where he traded his rifle for a clipboard and ran a motor transport and aviation gas company for the Marines, garrison duty he describes as "absolutely, totally boring." But soon after arriving in Beaufort he met the daughter of Colonel Frank C. Thomas, chief of staff for the First Marine Air Wing, who had been in and out of Vietnam since 1964 and who was known to everyone as Colonel T. My father claims not to remember the first time he met my mother. If what my mother says is true, it is little wonder. She met him at the Marine Corps's Officers' Club in Beaufort. "He was obnoxious, drunk, and crude," my mother reports. "I dated a bunch of other guys before I finally went out with him. I guess he wouldn't take no for an answer. He kept bugging me. But he was funny. I loved his sense of humor—when he was sober. He was so dark when he was drunk, but when he was sober he was the most wonderful man. He also had a lot of integrity. I liked that."

They married in 1967. My mother was nineteen, my father twenty-five and still limping, in every sense, from injuries he incurred in Vietnam. My father's father had died several years before, and his mother had struggled with, and after a stay in the Mayo Clinic was thought to have beaten, tongue cancer. Nonetheless, my grandmother was concerned enough about her health to have sat down with my mother shortly before she married my father. Of that day my mother particularly remembers the bright red scarves worn by my grandmother that hid gruesome surgical scars on her throat. My grandmother, after some general overtures, made my then-teenage mother promise that, if anything happened to her, she would raise her children Paul and Alicia, aged sixteen and twelve. My mother remembers feeling overcome by a great gust of shocked concern, then blurting, "But you're fine now!"

ALICIA AND JOHN BISSELL, SR.

"All the same," my grandmother said, looking evenly at my mother, "can you promise me that you will do this?" My mother, still stunned, promised my grandmother that she would. Colonel T., at the same time, made my father promise him two things: that he would never quit the Marine Corps, and, more important, that he would never take his little girl, a true daughter of the South, back north to Michigan with him. My father, then up for major and beginning seriously to plan for his career in the Marine Corps, made these twin promises to Colonel T. with equally puzzled surety.

Thirty days after my parents were married, my grandmother died of the cancer that had unexpectedly spread to her lymph nodes. She was fifty. My nineteen-year-old mother found herself the custodian of two children only a little younger than she. While her promise shakily held, my father's was instantly broken. Over near-unanimous resistance from his fellow jarheads, Colonel T., and his new wife, my father resigned his

Marine Corps commission and moved my mother to his hometown of Escanaba, Michigan, to take care of his brother and sister, whom he did not want to uproot. The move especially devastated my mother, a woman who proudly flew a Confederate flag off her front porch throughout my childhood. The sum of my mother's worldly experience to this point, other than partying her way out of the University of South Carolina, was the South and the Marine Corps, and now both had been cleaved from her. There was no anodyne for this severance, only the cauterizing assurance of the man she loved. But she loved him, I suspect, and in no small part, *because* he was a Marine. She once admitted to me that her fondest wish as a young woman was to be a Marine Corps wife. The seasonal balls, the crispness of the uniforms, the hot, orderly calm of military-base housing in the great American South: this is what she knew, all she wanted, and now it was gone.

Colonel T. was especially hard on my father about his decision to leave the Marine Corps. A letter from December 14, 1967, addressed to "Capt. & Mrs. John Bissell," has my grandfather telling my father:

Quite frankly, I am not surprised by your actions. Do not misunderstand me, I am not speaking of potential, I think you have all the potential in the world to make the Marine Corps a career[,] I just don't think you have or have ever had the basic motivation and understanding of the requirements to do so. . . . My only concern is your and my daughter's stability and happiness. I expect you to provide stability, responsibility and maturity of an adult male regardless of your vocation. And the best way not to do this is to live your life like a feather on the wind, blown in whatever direction happens to offer the path of least resistance and appears most desirable. I have seen too many attempt this little game and then seen them at age 45–50 still looking for the career that will give them what they want. . . . John, I have known you a year now and have observed a complete switch in thought. To be able to change courses is fine, it indicates flexibility and adaptability, so long as it's based on logical rational reasoning and *all* factors and facts. . . . But a constant hopping from one field to another that looks greener

indicates only insecurity, lack of self-confidence and a tendency to
wallow in self-pity.

This letter was written to my parents from Danang in coastal Vietnam, a
city referred to by Colonel T. as "the pearl of the Orient." It ends with
this: "Do not worry about the rockets. They pose practically no danger
and if they hit you, you are either stupid or extremely unlucky, neither
of which you can do a thing about. So if the poor little blighters want to
lug them 400 miles on their back, for two seconds of *whoosh*, then I feel
sorry for them. . . . So don't worry about me, I'm living high on the hog
and am quite secure. Like a bug." I imagine that my grandfather, a
thoughtful analyst of military history, was familiar with Dien Bien Phu.
This horrific, weeks-long final battle of the First Indochina War in 1954
had seen the "poor little blighters" of the Viet Minh dragging nearly
eighty antiaircraft guns for two months through mountainous jungle in
their triumphant effort to overwhelm the supremely confident French
Expeditionary Corps, whose French, Vietnamese, Moroccan, and Algerian soldiers were dug tick-deep into the tactically worthless encamp-
ment of Dien Bien Phu. While the men and women of the Viet Minh
hauled pieces of these one- and two-ton armaments on old carts and
bicycles through the forest, this is what they sang: "The mountains are
steep, but the determination in our hearts is higher than mountains. /
The chasms are deep and dark, but what chasm is as deep as our
hatred?" Two seconds of *whoosh*, indeed.

I never knew my grandfather. I imagine that Colonel T. and I would
have disagreed on many things, possibly everything, but from reading
his letters I can discern an acute intelligence. This moves and saddens
me, because it is intelligence in the service of the same blindness that in
Vietnam shut the eyes of so many men. From a letter to my mother and
father of October 1967: "Well here I am, another war, the same stupid
faces with different names. . . . Things have changed a great deal since
the last time I was out here. At least there are a helluva lot more Marines.
In fact the place is fairly breathing with them. Lots of traffic and lots of
gooks, on bicycles, water buffalo and bare feet. . . . It's interesting now,
John, in the way everything is so closely tied together and the fantastic
response time that we are now capable of in all kinds of situations."

COLONEL T.

What the U.S. military was capable of seemed markedly less won-drous to Colonel T. only a year later: "I suspect the little brown gooks will continue to get pretty mouthy until the election in the U.S. is set-tled, but now while the idiots are mouthing off they will respond in any way they can . . . to influence American opinion in ways they think will help them most. So I don't look for any real cool off on their part, they will continue to kick up dust and a lot of people will still have to die. Mostly gooks but each time it does cost us Marines. I wish I could figure out a way it could end but I can't." On February 9, 1968, shortly after the North launched the Tet Offensive, the sudden-ness and ferocity of which stunned everyone in the United States from LBJ down, Colonel T. (who by this point, according to family legend, had an NLF bounty on his head) wrote again from Danang. "I seem to have gotten a tad behind in my writing but I have been out on some rather sporty evenings lately," he begins, jauntily alluding to the fact that during Tet, Danang had been hit repeatedly by 122 mm NLF rockets. After some irritated analysis of the surprise offensive, Colo-nel T. begins to reveal what one can only surmise is his growing despair about the war:

I do not think there is enough natural drive and courage to do much except talk. Not enough of us understand the problem and of those who do too many I'm afraid do not have the gumption or nerve to do anything about it. It takes an awful long and completely unselfish view to lay it on the line now for the benefit of coming generations. It's much easier, and safer, to, a la the hippies, only consider your own happiness in your life, dodge all responsibility and let those coming later try to take care of the situation. But I really don't believe that this mental and moral condition will apply in the U.S. too much longer, because as I've said before I think the generation starting about with [his son] Bo's time will revert, and from them will come those archers of the El Dorado who will stand tall and strong among all men and sit coequal and in peerage with Crockett, Washington, Lee, Sherman, and Jackson.

Two weeks after Colonel T. wrote these words, Walter Cronkite, on live television, publicly opposed the Vietnam War for the first time by saying, "It seems now more certain than ever that the bloody experience of Vietnam is to end in a stalemate. . . . The only rational way out . . . will be to negotiate, not as victors, but as honorable people." Many of the proudest sons of the System, not only my grandfather and Cronkite but Lyndon Johnson himself ("If I lost Cronkite, I've lost Middle America"), could no longer abide the wasteful, destructive path upon which the System had confidently placed itself, only to be strangled by the vines of Vietnam.

My grandfather's casual use of "gooks," his dismissal of hippies, and his odd placement of Davy Crockett along the mantelpiece of American military history all suggest that Colonel T. was a man of the South, and a product of Marine Corps thinking, in many if not most ways. He was also, by all accounts, a profoundly honest and decent man. As my father once told me, Colonel T.'s formidable sense of ethics had led him to the professional Waterloo of opposing a new plane the Air Force was attempting "to cram down the Marines' throat." The guilty plane ("one of the Fs") had been designed for ground-based use and was thus too heavy for aircraft-carrier landings. But warlocks in Air Force Research and Development insisted the plane's weight would not compromise its performance. Colonel T. disagreed and effectively killed the plane's deployment. "Some of the generals and admirals never forgave him," my father told me. "That was big money. When you get up in the armed forces, any rank above colonel is the result of politics. From colonel on only the politicians win." Colonel T. thus never became General T., a rank many of his friends and acquaintances had long anticipated for him. He made his embattled return home from Vietnam in 1969. In March 1970 he wrote my mother to wish "my little blonde girl a happy 21. . . . Age is turning out to be a really relative thing. I know that I'm getting older rather fast but so far I can't find very many things that it affects. I really don't feel any different now than I did when I was 21." Five months later my grandfather died in his sleep of a heart attack. Within a few weeks occurred the one thing Colonel T. had been most looking forward to, the upcoming event he mentions in every letter: his first grandson, my brother, was born.

My mother did not take his death well. *Her* mother took it even worse, and within months she moved in with my mother and father in Escanaba. What followed my spectacularly southern grandmother's widowed arrival in one of Michigan's snowiest redoubts is among my family a matter of considerable *omertà*. Put simply, my grandmother and my father did not get along. Put perhaps more simply yet, my grandmother would not have pissed on my father if he were on fire. My grandmother was once a promising Hollywood ingenue—she very nearly married the actor Jackie Cooper—and like most of the women in her line (my mother included) was extraordinarily beautiful and emotionally extravagant. The very few people my grandmother's considerable powers of emotional seduction proved unable to win were no doubt regarded by her with frustrated suspicion. But my father did something far worse than fail to succumb to my grandmother's Division One charms: he married a southern woman's child, a crime for which there is no easy forgiveness.

PRETTY GRANDMA

Moreover, losing her husband so early and unexpectedly could not have been easy. As a southern military wife, my grandmother had little to prepare her for life alone. Midwestern small towns are trying homes even for those of us who love them; to have been transplanted to such a place in a state of irreparable grief must have been dreadful. But my grandmother was almost surreally vain, forbidding, for instance, her grandchildren from calling her "grandmother," the existential implications of which upset her. "PG," or "Pretty Grandma," was what we came up with in its stead. This lovely human orchid was now quite far from her steamy native soil and many admirers, and was cast instead to the affections of the unlettered, dipthong-shunning rubes of the high rural North. She lasted in Michigan only a few years, partly because of a many-thousand-dollar loan my father made to her, which she neglected to repay (or, eventually, remember). By the the early 1970s, when she left Escanaba for Los Angeles, where she lived until the months before her death in 1989, my parents' marriage had taken on enough emotional bilge to capsize it.

Nowadays even to bring up the matter of my grandmother's Michigan sojourn with either of my parents—as I recently did when I came across a letter of PG's that referred repeatedly to "Sean," to whom my mother had, apparently, given birth—is to splash kerosene all over smoldering deposits of resentment. So who is "Sean"? "Sean" is what my grandmother called my brother John for months after his birth. ("I will get off a present for Sean this week. What a smile that boy has!") John, not coincidentally, is also my father's name. PG's insistence upon "Sean" continued until my mother finally caved in and gave John Clement Bissell II a nickname: not Sean but "Johno," use of which my grandmother cheerfully took up. As did, for whatever reason, my father. In the end, my parents never really recovered from my grandmother's stay with them. Their marriage was nudged ever closer to the chasm.

Sometimes I wonder if when my father looked at my mother he saw PG—as if that would provide some causal explanation for the death of their marriage. The women looked startlingly alike, and not in the watered-down manner in which children usually resemble their parents. Their resemblance was rather a matter of photocopied enzymes, laboratory surreality, clone magick. They both had the same disarming smile, with its perfect teeth-to-gums ratio; the same elaborate coif of unnaturally white blond hair; the same dollishly too-big head, thin though fit limbs, and wonderfully trim figure. They even shared the same *aura,* some faded Old South glow that a mere parasol or colonnaded backdrop could have reenergized.

I can only wonder what you were thinking when you sat down on the couch beside Muff in late April 1975. The helpless anger you felt—the war, your marriage, the money you had lost to PG—I know about from having talked to you. But where did all the rage you were feeling go? In your anger, of course, you were far from alone.

The orphan airlift crash had benumbed everyone still paying attention to Vietnam. The pointless deaths of so many innocents took the more general pointlessness of the war and italicized it, capitalized it, underlined it in flame. Combat deaths, even defeats, meant something. But a plane crash in a war zone was barren of meaning. On the news you had glimpsed footage of the burned and muddy little bodies covered by

Red Cross blankets—and some part of your mind neatly switched Vietnam off. You stopped caring. But now, three weeks later, you find you *do* care again, care deeply and totally, and you simply cannot believe what has been brought down upon Vietnam during the three-week leave of your concern.

Yesterday you read a piece in the *Chicago Tribune* written by a journalist who had previously served in the Marine Corps in Vietnam. He wrote of staring at a map of Vietnam: "places marked in grease pencil and the names of certain places underlined. . . . Hoi-Vuc, Binh Thai, Hill 270 and Charlie Ridge and Purple Heart Trail. It was difficult to accept the idea that they were now in enemy hands." How difficult it was to accept this. The roads down which you had once commanded convoys are now the parade grounds of whole divisions of North Vietnamese armor. The thatched huts you had often held off your men from burning—how tender your heart went when confronted by the peasants of Vietnam—now happily fly the red, blue, and yellow flag of the NLF, the Viet Cong. Saigon itself is about to fall. On the radio during the ride home from work you learned that, a few hours ago, the American evacuation was completed. The latest predictions are that the city will not last the day. You stare at the television with Muff and Johno next to you. What is on is not of interest. Nothing is of any interest. Your reddened, open eyes see nothing, and your ears are immune to all sound but the black throb of your thoughts.

You are thinking, *What a horrendous, lost effort.* What, you wonder, will happen to your South Vietnamese friends? Not the cowards who have been losing the war faster than the North can win it but the ARVN Marines and Special Forces commandos who shared with you their fears of the Communists. These men had lost fathers and uncles to the Communist slaughter in Hue. Their cousins and grandparents had evaporated during the North's murderous land reform campaigns of the 1950s. You know that these men, and their families, will pay in blood for this day. As you stand and make your way to the humming couch-sized television, you feel at your core a great windy emptiness. You turn the television's knob, cycling through the same thirteen channels, hoping one of the networks has broken into regularly scheduled programming with a special report from Vietnam. Nothing. Nothing, nothing. Sometimes over the last few days the screen has been filled with *All in the Family* and sometimes with the nightmare of collapsing South Vietnam as narrated by Walter Cronkite. Coverage from South Vietnam has been like video incoming: upsetting, irregular, bracketed by a kind of strangely attentive silence. All the people at your bank claim to be unable to watch the news when Vietnam fills their screens. Too painful, they say. But it is all you want to watch. Or perhaps you want your pain to be everyone's.

IV

To say that this or that city fell to the Communists on such and such a date cannot begin to encapsulate the bedlam that was South Vietnam in the spring of 1975. Colonel T.'s old coastal haunt of Danang is a case in tragically awful point. A month before it was taken over, Danang's streets were barricaded, curfewed, and quiet; a nervy, impotent vigilance had taken root in every household. Many in Danang took to watching the sea, not out of any expectation of rescue—most realized they were too unconnected for such an exalted fate—but rather out of simple longing for its blue vastidity of potential escape. (Many Vietnamese would try to escape by sea; many who did so died—of thirst, disease, starvation, drowning, tiger sharks, and something as sixteenth century as pirate attack.) By the time March literally and figuratively reached its ides, 30,000 PAVN soldiers were closing in on the city, and the first of an eventual million refugees had floated into Danang and transformed its shatteringly beautiful beaches and Buddhist temples into shantytowns. Some of the traffic jams into the city—containing "cars, jeeps, trucks, buses, motorbikes, bicycles, pushcarts . . . literally anything that can roll," one American journalist observed—were ten miles long, making it difficult if not impossible for ARVN forces to move about the region and redeploy as battlefield circumstances dictated.

On March 19, President Thieu addressed the South Vietnamese people on national television. Although his audience did not realize it at the time, the address had been taped much earlier in the day. In an unusually steady voice, Thieu promised that the old imperial capital of Hue, then suffering rapid Communist encirclement, would be held to the last man. But Thieu had already transmitted secret orders to his generals authorizing Hue's virtual abandonment. This Thieu did partly to protect Danang and partly to transfer his best soldiers to Saigon to protect him in the increasingly likely event of a coup. Albert Francis, Danang's U.S. consul general, was asked by a visiting U.S. Embassy colleague how long he felt the city could withstand the Communists. Francis replied, "At least a month, I think." It perhaps did not bode well that the USAID-operated hotel in Danang was called the Alamo.

Hue fell, as expected and dreaded, on March 24. The battle at Hue, General Vo Nguyen Giap wrote, was "very quickly fought. We gave the enemy no time to organize any resistance. . . . So they were quickly and neatly wiped out. Our strategic offensive thus became a lightning onslaught." By this point the PAVN divisions were traveling so fast that, as one American described it, "they couldn't keep up with their own gasoline." The next morning several PAVN artillery shells landed in Danang's clogged city center, wounding a dozen and killing six. Following this salvo came a downpour of rockets that struck the city's ARVN military outposts. This was part of North Vietnam's "blooming lotus" tactic, whereby intentional civilian deaths were used to incite panic, which in turn allowed a city to be quickly taken over. The visiting U.S. Embassy official told by Albert Francis that Danang would last a month was forced to flee for his life less than four days after arriving.

At 4:30 a.m. on March 28, a motor-driven barge pulled alongside Danang's U.S. Consulate, located on the Han River. The plan was to ship out of the city as many Americans and politically imperiled Vietnamese as quietly and secretly as possible. The street on which the consulate building was located had been blocked off, but the Vietnamese asleep along the nearby docks woke up and panicked. Within minutes the barge was under siege by as many as 5,000 terrified Vietnamese. David Butler's *The Fall of Saigon* tells us what happened next:

Then people started tossing small children from the pier up onto the barge. Some missed, the children falling into the black water between the dock and the barge, which rolled with the wakes of other traffic on the river and the surges of the several thousand people on board.

At five-thirty, there was a rush of ARVN troops. From the shore [U.S. Consul General Albert] Francis ordered the barge to depart.

But . . . the other Americans on board were unable to free a thick rope that ran from a bitt on the barge down to the dock. And the Vietnamese mob on the dock was not about to free the cable on that end. In fact, lithe young men used it to scramble up onto the barge.

Without realizing what he was doing, the captain of the tug let the barge drift back into the dock. The men scrambling up the rope like monkeys were crushed. The tug strained to break the rope. More young men and boys clambered up the rope. The barge swung back toward the pier and they were killed. . . . The ghastly scenario was played out twice more and then something finally gave way and they were free and that particular roundelay of death ended.

In the chaos, hundreds of Danang's consulate workers and CIA informants and their families were abandoned.

In Saigon the news from Danang, essentially a second capital in terms of its military and economic significance, was grimly received. It in fact threatened to unravel the quickly dwindling remainder of South Vietnam still controlled by Saigon. The U.S. ambassador to South Vietnam, Graham Martin, had for the last several weeks been attempting to preserve a sense of calm among U.S. officials and South Vietnamese. He has since been both loathed and admired, but Martin faced one of the least enviable situations in the history of U.S. diplomacy, and widespread panic was never more than a spark away from ignition. One of the last issues of *Stars and Stripes* to be published in Vietnam, for instance, carried a screaming headline promising the slaughter of "AT LEAST A MILLION" South Vietnamese if the North triumphed. Martin kept a fragile but certain calm in the last months and weeks largely by secrecy and studied, quotidian ceremony. The U.S. deputy ambassador, Wolfgang Lehmann, later recalled to Larry Engelmann that Martin "did things like keeping all our pictures hanging on the walls [of the embassy], because the moment you start packing—'Oh, the Deputy Ambassador is packing up!'—spreads like wildfire."

Previously the U.S. ambassador to Thailand and Italy, Graham Martin replaced Ellsworth Bunker as ambassador to South Vietnam in June 1973, despite having never passed the Foreign Service exam. Vietnam had come to Martin long before he came to Vietnam: his helicopter-pilot nephew Glen, whom Martin had adopted, was slain during some of Vietnam's earliest fighting. The war was a highly personal matter to Martin, and he once attacked *The New York Times* journalist David K. Shipler in a blistering 4,600-word cable to the State Department wherein he all but called Shipler a Communist propagandist. Many of the journalists in Vietnam returned such antipathetic favor, especially when Martin routinely split hairs over the number of Communists and political prisoners held, and often tortured, by the Thieu government. While Amnesty International put the number at 200,000, Martin maintained that the number was more like 30,000. Martin made things no better for himself when he attempted to illume the bright side of Thieu's corrupt government by explaining, "A little corruption oils the machinery." Knowledgeable estimates hold that anywhere from 20 to 40 percent of the U.S. aid received by South Vietnam was routinely raked off the top by knaves in its government and military. One popular South Vietnamese racket wound up stuffing the pockets of ARVN officers with $100 million a year. The racket in question? Washing GI clothes.

Yet Martin had opposed the Vietnam War, saying, "We should have never gone in there with American soldiers." Years after the fall of Saigon, Martin told Larry Engelmann that he "never really had any great attachment to the Vietnamese, North or South. I don't particularly like any of them. I love the Thai. I think they're the most marvelous people in the world." Martin's fondness for the Thai could no doubt be traced to his success as ambassador there: "We had the same sort of insurgency in the Northeast [of Thailand] that they had in the beginning in [Vietnam], and I kept insisting that I didn't see any white faces on the other side. . . . [N]o Americans in combat or any combat advisors, even. . . . I wouldn't let the Americans even carry sidearms on the bases out there." The insurgency in Thailand was ultimately defeated by the Thai people themselves—and, Martin added, "We didn't have any My Lai massacres either." As for Vietnam, a nation torn to pieces by a war he did not support, Martin had only one goal. As he told Henry Kissinger in February 1975, "There is absolutely no way that I am not going to be held responsible for the fall of Saigon. From beginning to end, it's going to be me. So I am not interested in doing anything except what makes sense right now to get the Americans out alive and as many of our Vietnamese friends, to whom we have committed ourselves, as we can."

But Martin's notion of what the U.S. commitment to Vietnam amounted to had its limits, as Ed Daly learned when he barged into Martin's office on March 28, 1975, the day of Danang's disastrous barge evacuation. Daly was the president and founder of World Airways, a charter airline, often in government employ, that had profited during the war by running rice and weapons to South Vietnam, as well as delivering copies of *Stars and Stripes,* which was printed in Japan, to Saigon. A former Golden Gloves boxer, the paunchy, bearlike Daly had a fondness for drama and bluster, as evidenced by his tendency to stroll around Saigon in flowered Hawaiian shirts and a shoulder holster crammed with a loaded .38. He was wearing the holster when he walked into Martin's embassy office, along with a many-galloned cowboy hat. A nervous Marine guard trailed after Daly. "Give the gun to the Marine if you want to talk to me," Martin insisted. "I can get in to see popes," Daly complained, "heads of state, generals, with one or two days' notice. Why do you make me wait ten days to see you?" That he was commonly armed and routinely foulmouthed did not apparently occur to Daly as possible explanations for why Martin resisted meeting with him, nor the fact that Martin had been out of the country for several weeks.

Under the auspices of a U.S. Embassy contract, World Airways had over the previous few days flown three flights into Danang to evacuate Americans and South Vietnamese refugees. The evacuations, though harried, had been successes. Why, Daly now asked Martin, was World Airways being denied a last flight into Danang? Because, Martin explained, the situation was too volatile. Indeed, the embassy had just lost contact with Danang's U.S. consul general, Albert Francis, who would soon be beaten senseless and left for dead by score-settling ARVN soldiers. The South Vietnamese officials at Saigon's Tan Son Nhut air base had additionally threatened to shoot Daly's 727 down if he attempted to fly to Danang from there. "What," Daly demanded, "are those bastards at Tan Son Nhut going to do if I take off without their goddamned clearance?" Martin said he imagined that they would hold true to their guarantee and take down Daly's plane. Daly asked Martin what he would do if they did that. "Applaud them!" Martin said. "Who the hell do you think you are?" Daly told Martin that he was "nothing but a used-car salesman."

Jan Wollett, a World Airways flight attendant, described to Larry Engelmann being awakened in her Saigon hotel room at 6 a.m. the day after Daly and Martin's meeting. She went down to the lobby to find Daly and some others waiting for her. They were going to Danang. Wollett found it ominous that the flight had not been catered and that there were no guards or interpreters along. Inexplicably, some USAID people had assured Daly that the situation in Danang was "fine" and that guards would not be needed. A United Press International journalist named Paul Vogle, along for the ride, spoke fluent Vietnamese, so Daly believed they were covered. At 8 a.m. the 727 took off, carrying Daly, three flight attendants, five journalists ("Hey, the more the merrier," Daly had said), the pilot, and the copilot. Another World 727 followed Daly's into the sky twenty minutes later.

Daly's recipe for heroism was to land the first plane, remain on the ground for "ten or fifteen" minutes, load up with passengers, and take off. The other World 727 would then do the same. Coming into Danang, Daly's pilot tipped the 727's wings to semaphore friendliness. The plane landed and taxied down Danang's spookily empty tarmac without incident—but the rescue quickly went bad. Wollett knew "something really bizarre was going on" when a small truck loaded with ARVN soldiers pulled up alongside the taxiing aircraft. One man jumped out of the truck brandishing a pistol, which he began to empty into the airplane's fuselage. As the 727 moved on down the tarmac, refugees hiding behind blast barriers and concrete revetments at the tarmac's far edge began a dash toward the plane. Those aboard the 727 place their number anywhere between 1,000 and 4,000. (One says it was 20,000.) David Butler tells us that the refugees "poured out in jeeps and trucks and armored personnel carriers and even in an old bulbous-nosed black Citroën taxi from the late 1940s." There were many women and children in the onrushing mob, but they had the misfortune not to have been armed. The soldiers among them faced no such disability, and Darwinian improvisation went to work. The soldiers began shooting women and children, then other soldiers, in the back. A pickup truck loaded with civilians pulled abreast of the plane before nearly anyone else had made it there. An evilly quick-thinking ARVN soldier "sprayed it with an M-16," according to one observer, "and the jeep flipped over and everybody went out of it."

Daly was standing at the bottom of the plane's aft stairs waving his pistol when the shooting began. In response he fired several rounds into the air. Joe Hrezo, Daly's second in command, was also packing a .38 snubnose, but "figured if I started shooting . . . I'd have gotten the shit shot out of me." The journalist Paul Vogle was next to Daly at the base of the stairs, shouting in Vietnamese, "One at a time, one at a time. There's room for everybody." But there was not. A British journalist named Tom Aspell had jumped off the plane early to photograph the rescue and quickly realized his error. He attempted to make his way back to the 727 but could not fight his way through the crowd. Joe Hrezo, too, left the plane and was similarly unable to get back on board; he sprinted for the airport's control tower, where he established radio contact with Daly's pilot.

On the plane itself, the first soldiers had begun to board. One ran up and down the aisle screaming, "Take off! Take off! They're rocketing the field!" Jan Wollett, the flight attendant, shouted at this hysteric, "Shut up and sit where I tell you to sit!" and then went to the door. Outside, at the base of the stairs, she saw Ed Daly being clawed by panicking Vietnamese; blood poured from the deep scratches on his arms, and his shirt and pants had been all but ripped off. Wollett then saw a "family of five . . . running a few feet from me, reaching out for help to get aboard. It was a mother and a father and two little children and a baby in the mother's arms. . . . I reached back to grab the mother's hand, but before I could get it, a man running behind them shot all five of them, and they fell and were trampled by the crowd." Wollett, too stunned for any emotion, immediately reached for another woman, but "a man behind her grabbed her and jerked her out of my arms, and as she fell away he stepped on her back and her head to get up and over the railing." Daly, who witnessed this, hit the offending brute in the face. (Daly would leave Danang with a broken hand.) A "sheet of blood" splashed "across everything," and the man fell off the stairs and was crushed by the crowd.

The plane, designed to carry a little more than 130 people, quickly filled up with more than 250. All but eleven of the rescued passengers were ARVN soldiers—and not only soldiers but members of the Hac Bao (Black Panthers), "the toughest, most elite unit in the 1st Division," David Butler writes. The two members of the flight in who had not been able to reboard, Tom Aspell and Joe Hrezo, now attempted to jump back onto the plane. Via the tower radio, Daly's pilot told Hrezo that he would circle back to pick him up. The problem was that the pilot had to wend through the assortment of stalled and burning vehicles strewn across the runway. He also had to travel fast enough to elude those still chasing the plane and slowly enough for Aspell and Hrezo to board. He also had to find enough room to take off. The 727's problems increased one-thousand-fold when an ARVN soldier rolled a grenade under the plane, the detonation of which, in Paul Vogle's words, "jammed the [wing] flaps full open and the undercarriage in full extension." Other abandoned soldiers began to shoot at the departing plane. One bullet struck the fuel tank (the 727 would leak fuel from Danang to Saigon) but miraculously failed to trigger an explosion.

Soon after North Vietnamese rockets began to hit the tarmac, Joe Hrezo made it aboard while Daly was still beating people off with his pistol. Tom Aspell was not as lucky. "Grab me!" he yelled as he ran alongside the aft stair, now warped and broken from the weight of so many passages. Aspell, "in the very best tradition of the business," again according to Paul Vogle, threw his camera on board before attempting to climb the stairs himself. When he did, several Vietnamese lampreyed onto him. As the plane accelerated, Aspell lost his grip and fell, along with all the Vietnamese who had counted on his strength to ensure their escape. Aspell would be evacuated by an Air America helicopter several hours later, and his footage would be broadcast around the world the next day. It says something about the day's moral tumult that Vogle could congratulate Aspell for saving his footage, however historically valuable, when Aspell seems to have made no similar effort on behalf of his fellow human beings.

Daly's pilot, who had judged a runway takeoff impossible, opted to take off from the taxiway. But the taxiway ran out of cement, and soon the plane was rumbling along the grass. On liftoff, the 727 struck a vehicle and a fence pole and pulled from its pilings a long stretch of concertina wire. Yet people were still hanging on to the aft stair. One by one they were sucked away. "One guy," the CBS journalist Mike Marriott recalled to Larry Engelmann, "managed to hang on for a while, but at about 600 feet he let go and just floated off—just like a skydiver. I watched him fly away." Several men had stowed themselves in the 727's wheel wells. Others grabbed hold of the landing gear. As it retracted, one was crushed, rendering the gear inoperable. Another was photographed by a UPI photographer aboard Daly's accompanying plane (which never landed in Danang) losing his grip and tumbling thousands of feet to his death in the South China Sea. Marriott, for his part, had two thoughts. The first was "This is the start of the fall of the country. This country is gone." The second was his "very strong" doubt that the bullet-pocked, grenade-wracked, fuel-leaking 727 would be able to land in Saigon. They were all going to die.

Airborne now, Jan Wollett confronted her passengers. People were sitting three to a seat, bleeding and crying. Wollett pushed the intestines of one injured man back into his stomach. Another man, bleating for help, began to pull on Wollett's pant leg. It was the scoundrel who had pushed the woman Wollett had earlier attempted to help before Daly smashed him in the face and sent him to the tarmac. Wollett aided the man to a seat, discovering only then that his "head was laid wide open, and I could see inside his head and it was just a bloody, pulpy mess." Wollett tore open a flak jacket and used its sawdust innards to stuff the man's head wound and stop the bleeding.

Somewhat unbelievably, the plane landed safely in Saigon, though the normally forty-five-minute-long flight took more than two hours. Everyone cheered when it was clear that the damaged landing gear had held, despite the fact that, in Wollett's words, the "shock of what [the ARVN] soldiers had done to their friends and families seemed to be destroying them slowly. . . . They had run over each other and shot each other to get on this plane. Now the panic was disappearing and the realization of the horror of what had happened—of what they had done—was beginning to sink in." All of the soldiers were arrested as they exited the plane. "They deserved it," Paul Vogle wrote. Vogle's vivid UPI account of the flight—a piece of post-traumatic-stress journalism if there ever was one—has been described as "the single most memorable news story of the 1975 offensive." One of Vogle's most chilling lines concerns the mangled body pulled out of the landing gear bay by Tan Son Nhut crewmen. The dead soldier's "M-16 [was] still strapped to his shoulder. . . . He got his ride to Saigon, but being dead in Saigon is just the same as being dead in Da Nang."

Later that night, at a restaurant in a Saigon hotel, shortly before an exhausted Joe Hrezo "went across the street to a bar and found a girlfriend," Daly tried to describe the trip to some journalists. But the journalists kept jabbering and drinking. Daly unholstered his pistol and said, "I want to have your attention here or somebody's going to get shot." Daly, who died of a heart attack in 1986, would be depressed for years that his rescue mission had managed to save so few civilians. As World Airways' official history relates, "Daly flew back to the U.S. with 218 Vietnamese refugees—including 57 orphans whom he took personal responsibility for. The U.S. Department of Immigration and Naturalization was none too pleased with the orphan airlift and attempted to fine World $218,000 for violating immigration rules. No fine was levied as public outcry in Daly's favor changed the government's mind."

Most of these orphans wound up in the care of various fundamentalist Christian churches in California.

Another man was troubled by Daly's rescue mission. After seeing Aspell's appalling footage, President Gerald Ford publicly lamented the "immense human tragedy" of Danang's collapse and privately said to an aide, "That's it. It's time to pull the plug. Vietnam is gone."

On March 30, several trucks crammed tight with North Vietnamese soldiers moved into Danang, which the Communists would later call the most "gigantic development" in their push toward Saigon. Most of the soldiers were women. To the people of Danang they were an unfamiliar blur of pith helmets, green fatigues, rubber sandals, and Russian rifles. The women formed into units, hit the streets, and fanned out, shouting dogma-enriched instruction in high-pitched northern accents over their handheld bullhorns. The actual "liberation" of Danang did not, as the Communists boasted, "see a single shot fired"—or rather, the only shots fired were self-inflicted, into the skulls of terrified, left-behind ARVN soldiers who feared slaughter at Communist hands. But that particular roundelay of death ended as well. The next day it was Easter.

V

While you stand before the television fruitlessly changing its channels, Muff finally asks what you are doing.

Your response comes softly. —Looking for news.

—*John,* Muff says. That is all she says, a word containing an entire month's worth of frustration.

—There's nothing you can do about it, Johnny. This is Grace, speaking from the other side of the room. You have almost forgotten she is there. Slowly you turn. She is twenty-five feet and a universe of understanding from you. Her knitting needles are still. She is looking at you with small bright eyes, the face that surrounds them loose-skinned and kind. —You have to go on.

You look away and say nothing. You are choking on your anger, your simple human desire to be understood.

Muff is bouncing Johno, who has started to mewl and fidget, more roughly now. —Have a drink, she says, looking at Johno, the floor, her index fingernail. Anywhere but you.

A drink. It has been a bad month for that as well. The less you cared about Vietnam, the more necessary it became to forget everything else. The point man in your quest for amnesia was Pfc. Johnnie Walker. You have been leaving home, as though hypnotized, in the small of the night, wandering into bars, getting in fights. You had not remembered how easy getting into a fight was. Merely look at someone so hard they are finally obliged to inquire, *What are you looking at?* The answer: "You're pretty fucking ugly, you know that?" There is your fight. The last two you lost and came home laughing, your face a bouquet of bruise blooms, your lip seeping, your gums lined in red. Muff refused to take care of you those nights. She could not abide violence. But what did she think her father did there in Danang? The man was not eating prawns all day. He sent B-52s on bombing runs, a mass murderer from 17,000 feet.

Within you violence still prowls, and lately it has needed very little encouragement to slip through the bars of its cage. For instance: Dennis, your other brother, the second oldest, visited home a few months ago. Dennis was in the Air Force. This had been what had made it so easy for you to resign your commission. Dennis's Air Force service—in Thailand, primarily, building roads—meant that the Bissell family was contributing its share to the war effort, and your final clearance came through quickly. But you did not like how easily Dennis parlayed having flown over Vietnam, however hazardous this was, into having "fought" there. Over this very issue the two of you nearly came to blows—until Muff, cradling your son, inserted herself between the two of you, screaming, "Stop it! Stop it!"

Of course you know that if you keep behaving this way you are going to lose Muff forever. You know that as you stand before the television and stare at her as she tries to prevent Johno's small, explosive whimpering from turning into an emotional mushroom cloud. She looks so pretty tonight! You honestly don't know what you would do, or where you would be, without her. You have lived, died, laughed, cried, reveled, and moped with her for years now. You want to continue to do so for two thousand more. Yet running contiguous to this certainty are rivers of far inkier thought. They flow through the black, treeless landscape of your mind and feed into your heart, changing its electricity, coarsening it. *Fuck her. She does not know. She cannot know.* And your mouth is so dry. You need a drink. You pacify yourself by thinking of that drink, the way the scotch-soaked slivers of ice will melt against your teeth. You breathe and wait until the darkness passes through, but before it can do so Muff stands and walks out of the room, dragging Johno by the hand, both of them suddenly allied in tears. Grace goes after her, throwing a disappointed look your way before disappearing around the corner.

GUENELLA

You are standing triumphantly alone in the middle of your television room, listening to the spectral sound of the windows deflecting the wind, when your black Labrador Guenella comes trotting up to you, her tail sweeping happily back and forth. You named her after a young woman with whom you fell in love in Georgetown, during college. She spurned you for a Washington Redskins tackle, which at the time had seemed both remarkable and not at all remarkable. Naming your dog after her had been a crude form of revenge, but you now love this dog so much you cannot imagine what, at the time of its naming, you could have possibly been thinking. You crouch and run your hand over Guenella's sleek black brow. Her coat feels as soft as mink, and her long bologna tongue drops contentedly from her mouth. The tongue steals to your face, runs pink and frictionless up your cheek. Your eyes close, and your forehead presses against hers. She is a beautiful dog, the best you have ever had. You love the totality of her loyal ignorance. After a long while you look outside onto frozen Lake Michigan, the horizon beyond it preserving a fading hem of candied red light. Everything else is a different hue of dark, the snow low mounds of gray against endless black lawn. The room itself fading but for the blue flicker of the television. Darkness upon darkness, and nothing but this faint cathode fire to hold it back. You are sitting there with Guenella when the news, at last, comes on. *In Saigon,* you are told, *it is morning.*

What finally ended my parents' marriage? Neither claims to remember the precise event that drove them both toward the false rescue of infidelity, and there the matter hangs. My birth, in January 1974, a little more than a year before the fall of Saigon, was, as they say, an accident. My mother had always had irregular periods and had no idea she was pregnant with me until a routine checkup. At the time my mother was on a hard-boiled-egg-and-wine diet, which was, according to her, "the big guru fad diet" of the day. When told the news, she exclaimed, "I'm going to deliver a pickled egg!" Neither she nor my father wanted or expected another child. As if to embody their apprehension, I was born a sickly, tiny thing and contracted pneumonia immediately. At one point a priest was summoned to give my days-old Catholic soul its last rights. My father spent that night in the hospital's chapel, praying. During the first, frail year of my life, I kept them together. When my condition improved, my mother remembers a near rebirth of goodwill between her and my father, then its sudden inexplicable collapse. But what caused this collapse? Again, neither remembers.

Once, after an argument of considerable megatonnage, my father gave my mother a charm bracelet. She still has it and sometimes even wears it. Attached to this bracelet are a poodle, a Labrador retriever, a sailboat, a tandem bicycle, my brother's and my birthstones, two baby boots, a diaper pin, a thimble, two enjoined hands, all of them references to the secrets and shared enthusiasms of a relationship neither much wishes to recall anymore. My father gave my mother the bracelet's first charm in a full champagne glass. She almost accidentally swallowed it. This first charm, my father's desperate attempt to mend what was clearly and hopelessly coming undone, was the pair of enjoined hands. He presented it to her on her birthday. My mother recalls this as one of the last truly happy moments in their marriage. She also recalls how soon things degenerated afterward. My father had engraved upon the charm my mother's birthday, followed by the year. My mother's birthday is March 20. The year is 1975.

VI

On April 3, 1975, Saigon was closed to all Vietnamese but those who could prove they lived there, a measure taken to slow the influx of refugees and prevent NLF guerrillas from establishing terrorist cells within the capital. On the day Saigon was sealed, officials in the U.S. Embassy, beginning to ponder the possibility of emergency evacuation, finally got together a list of all the 6,000 Americans known to live in Saigon and its environs. This number was arrived at by, among other methods, poring over records at the embassy's commissary that tracked liquor purchases. In Saigon's Presidential Palace things were relatively quiet. One of President Thieu's few formal orders in the first weeks of April decreed the closure of Saigon's plentiful saloons and whorehouses, apparently to encourage Saigon's men to save money for ammunition. The Western journalists recently dispatched to Saigon by magazines, newspapers, and networks left the city's hotels awash with more correspondents than at any time since the United States had withdrawn its soldiers. In the meantime, as the journalist David Lamb notes, the insurance premiums covering the lives of these journalists had increased by 1,000 percent.

Ambassador Martin did not believe Saigon would fall. He was certain that Vietnam's recently discovered offshore oil deposits would convince Congress to come to its senses and allow aid to South Vietnam. (When the local employees of two Western oil concerns, Esso and Shell, asked for embassy permission to be evacuated, Martin forbade them to leave, fearing it would render one of South Vietnam's most important industries inoperable overnight.) The ambassador's optimism was incurable, and possibly demented. As David Butler writes, Martin "spoke [to an NBC journalist] with evident sincerity about the prospects of holding a truncated South Vietnam, from Nha Trang south, living off the riches of the Mekong delta." Martin diagnosed the disastrous retreat from the Central Highlands as "a minor problem" and boasted that in a year's time he would take a leisurely tour of one captured city.

Martin—along with Henry Kissinger, who was similarly doubtful of the prospect of Saigon's fall—had something resembling an excuse in the person of Saigon's CIA station chief, Thomas Polgar, who throughout April fed Martin and Kissinger selective intelligence that turned out to have a crippling effect on the embassy's ability to operate under what no one could bring himself to realize fully was siege conditions. The balding, bespectacled Polgar had been born in Hungary, escaped to the United States, and posed as a Nazi for U.S. intelligence during World War II. Although a committed anti-Communist, Polgar paid undue attention to the talk making its way around Saigon in the spring of 1975 that the North would allow a "transitional government" in South Vietnam, albeit one dominated by Communists, rather than conquer Saigon outright. This would permit the Communists a period of months, even years, to take over slowly, without alienating their longtime enemies. For this to happen, however, President Thieu would have to resign and preferably be replaced by Duong Van Minh, an ARVN general considered a neutralist—he was known to have argued against bombing the North, for instance—in South Vietnamese politics. Polgar held firmly to this *ignis fatuus* and used it to seed the stories of his chosen journalists, particularly Malcolm Browne of *The New York Times*. Polgar's deeply conjectural reading of the situation thus wended its way up to presidents Ford and Thieu, among many others, with seeming authority, creating what is called in intelligence circles a "false confirmation." This helps to explain a high-ranking NLF officer's postwar comment that the Communists found that their "infiltrations of the American Embassy and the Central Intelligence Agency were not that important, because they really didn't know much about what was going on."

Initial talk of a transitional government mainly came through French intermediaries, though the North's leadership, especially Prime Minister Pham Van Dong, had hinted for years that a transitional government after North-South negotiations was possible. (Whether a negotiated end to the conflict was ever possible is still being debated by scholars. By the 1970s, however, any talk from the North about its willingness to "negotiate" was a calculated untruth.) It is fitting that the French, the authors of so much disaster in Vietnam, would appear, as the curtain fell, with another garland of woe. Apparently it was not enough for the French to have essentially created the Communist insurgency by assailing the Vietnamese people's long-standing Confucian traditions, imposing ruthless taxes on staples such as salt, banning the distillation of Vietnamese rice into alcohol, forcing the Vietnamese to import pricey French wine, introducing the Brazilian rubber plant to Vietnam's ecology, throwing up dozens of brutally managed rubber plantations, establishing among the Vietnamese an impressive 5 percent literacy rate in what had previously been one of the most literate cultures in Asia, and designing a colonial policy that by design ensured that the Frenchmen who emptied the trash bins of Vietnam's leading universities were paid more than the Vietnamese professors who taught Zola and Hugo. (In neighboring Laos the situation was even worse. After the better part of a century of French rule, Laos, by 1960, had three Lao engineers, two Lao doctors, and one telephone for every 4,300 Laotians.) The French mission was so confident about the inevitability of a transitional government in South Vietnam that the 10,000 French citizens in Vietnam were told to stay put. This as many foreign embassies—among them the United Kingdom's, New Zealand's, Canada's, South Korea's, and Taiwan's—were burning their files and leaving.

In early April, sixteen PAVN divisions, or about 150,000 soldiers, were bearing down on Saigon—except for the single PAVN division that had been left behind to guard Hanoi, an attacking force that constituted North Vietnam's entire military. Only two years before, the ARVN had been one million strong. Of that million, a half-dozen infantry divisions, an airborne brigade, an armored brigade, and some harum-scarum ranger units were all that was left. Fewer than 90,000 ARVN troops remained to defend South Vietnam—others put the number as low as 60,000—almost none of whom had much spleen for fighting.

The leader of the assault on Saigon was General Van Tien Dung. Among the mummies of North Vietnam's Politburo, the fifty-eight-year-old Dung cut a dynamically youthful figure. He was also pragmatic and took orders well. This was especially crucial, as the North's policy as how best to deal with the South was never a settled matter within the Party. Le Duan—arguably the most militant member of the Politburo, a southerner by birth, and the leading Hanoi light after Ho Chi Minh's death in 1969—had long demanded an attack-dog course of action toward South Vietnam, which many of Duan's more moderate comrades opposed.

In October 1974, while the North's final offensive was being hatched, the Party issued an internal document known as the "Resolution for 1975." Widely viewed as a compromise between the North's hard-liners and moderates, the resolution established a fluid plan of attack that would allow the North's policy to be made on the fly, according to battlefield developments. Although the Resolution for 1975 allowed for moderation, Le Duan made sure its intentions were heavily tilted toward all-out military victory. To this end the North began to draft every male up to forty years of age. Even Communist Party members, many of whom had been able to tiptoe around the war's hotter edges, were assigned combat units. Le Duc Tho, Kissinger's co–Nobel Peace Prize winner, was sent to Saigon in early April. In *Decent Interval*—written by Frank Snepp, an analyst of North Vietnam in Saigon's CIA station, and arguably the finest account of the fall of South Vietnam—we learn that North Vietnam's president (as in the USSR, largely a figurehead position) pulled Tho aside as he was setting out. "You must win," President Thang told the Nobel Peace Prize winner. "Otherwise you should not come back."

Through April, the Communists had seen only white flags and what General Giap fondly refers to as "big, very big, annihilation battles" during their campaign (though General Dung did have one genuinely frightening encounter—with a herd of stampeding elephants). Thirty-five miles away from Saigon, however, at the city of Xuan Loc, the North Vietnamese finally ran aground. Xuan Loc was a rubber-plantation bulwark and provincial capital of 100,000 that served as the gateway to Saigon and the nearby city of Bien Hoa, where 60 percent of ARVN's diminishing matériel was now held in a munitions dump. Because of Xuan Loc's location at a triple intersection of roads, including a highway that streaked south to the coast, Saigon could not be held without Xuan Loc's capture.

President Thieu sent to the imperiled city his best remaining divisions. After an artillery attack on April 8, the city emptied of civilians. The ARVN head of Xuan Loc's defense, General Le Minh Dao, who had set up his headquarters upon the grounds of an old French plantation, breathed fire days before the North arrived in force. "I vow to hold Xuan Loc," General Dao said, according to *The Fall of Saigon*. "I don't care how many divisions the other side sends against me, I will knock them down."

On April 9, Dung's and Dao's armies met in what would perhaps be the most horrific battle of the war. "Our troops," admits the official Communist history of the People's Army of Vietnam, "fought the enemy for control of every section of trench, every house, every city block. . . . Enemy aircraft, taking off from Bien Hoa, Tan Son Nhat [*sic*], and Tra Noc airfields, pounded Xuan Loc with bombs. The battle turned into a hard, vicious struggle. Our units suffered heavy casualties." One PAVN division saw 1,100 men killed in the first two days, its artillery was "seriously depleted," and half its Soviet tanks were turned into red-hot scrap. In response General Dung sent the majority of his soldiers around Xuan Loc to outflank its defenders and, in some cases, bypass the city completely and move on. Even this proved costly to the PAVN assault. On the doorstep of their capital, the ARVN ceased to be what one writer had dismissed as "a collection of individuals, all of whom happened to be carry-

ing weapons" and became an army. Aware that they were literally fighting
for their children's lives, the abysmally outnumbered soldiers defending
Xuan Loc would hold off the Communists for two sanguinary weeks.

At Saigon's Defense Attaché Office, Vietnamese and "nonessential"
Americans had been seeing evacuations for many days now. The DAO
was a gigantic complex located on Tan Son Nhut air base, which was
itself among the largest U.S. bases in the world. Four thousand Americans had once worked in the DAO, and its (air-conditioned, swimming-
pooled, bowling-alleyed) operation had cost upward of $30 million a
year. The evacuation protocol available to the Americans was found in a
booklet two inches thick. "All of a sudden," one U.S. Marine major
recalled to Larry Engelmann, "people were dusting off plans that had
been written in 1973 for emergency evacuation, and they were looking
at them and saying, 'Oh, Jesus, this is bullshit; now what do we do?' "
    The original evacuation plan had envisioned only two embassy air-
lifts, which would chopper out "between twenty and forty people."
Everyone else would be driven in buses to Tan Son Nhut, from which the
evacuees would be flown out in fixed-wing aircraft rather than helicopters. By mid-April it became clear that this was not an adequate plan. So
many Vietnamese had been tainted by their involvement with the Americans that a much larger evacuation plan was needed, and quickly. A
scenario was gamed up to figure out how many Vietnamese could realistically be flown out of Vietnam. It was determined that 921,000 could be
evacuated. However, this would require eight days, involve the participation of an astounding percentage of U.S. vessels in and around the
waters of Vietnam, and "would only be practical assuming the following: No interference by either the NVA [North Vietnamese Army] or the
VC; full cooperation by the Government of Vietnam; reasonable degree
of crowd control." Unfortunately, there was virtually no public support
in the United States for such a massive and expensive airlift of Vietnamese, and the rules determining which Vietnamese could leave their
country remained nebulous and often cruelly arbitrary.
    The embassy found itself paralyzed with visa requests. As Wolfgang
Lehmann, Ambassador Martin's second in command, told Larry Engel-

mann, "The categories of Vietnamese at risk were virtually endless. . . . It's not true we had no plan. We missed people; yeah, that's perfectly true. But there was a plan and there was a system. But again, we had no . . . formal authority to send any Vietnamese to the United States until the twenty-fifth of April." A young American named Ken Moorefield was not satisfied with such spinelessness. During his first few hours working out of the DAO, Moorefield let through two hundred Vietnamese. Talk began to circulate among the Vietnamese at the DAO that Moorefield was softhearted, and they besieged him. Many families were unwilling to obey when Moorefield asked them to pull from the evacuation line their draft-age sons or elderly parents in the interest of creating space for others. "No, Mr. Moorefield," one family said to him, "don't ask us to make those decisions. You make them for us." As often as not, Moorefield was unable to do so. Once the officials within South Vietnam's Ministry of Interior arranged for their own departure, the Vietnamese no longer needed exit visas, and the rubber-stamping proceeded apace. Moorefield's heroics probably led to the evacuation of 10,000 people, and soon Vietnamese were flowing out of the DAO "around the clock," a hundred people at a time, on both government and commercial flights, according to one U.S. official. Faced with this pressure, immigration officials in Washington were forced to relax visa requirements. Eventually all that was needed to escape was a piece of paper bearing the U.S. Embassy seal and the easily forged names of a Vietnamese beneficiary and American sponsor. There are stories of Americans adopting twenty Vietnamese at a time. One American adopted an eighty-year-old Vietnamese Catholic priest. When asked, "What in the hell is this?" by an Air Force officer at the DAO, the American replied, "Well, that's my adopted son."

On April 11, Kissinger gathered together his senior State Department staff for a "pep talk" on Vietnam. "This thing," Kissinger began, "is now going to run its course; its course is reasonably predictable. And what we are trying to do is to manage it with dignity and to preserve a basis for which we can conduct the foreign policy in which people can have some confidence in us. . . . I think people are going to feel badly [*sic*] when it's over. I don't think there are going to be many heroes left in this."

In Saigon, rumor fed rumor. The city, Frances FitzGerald once wrote, "breathed rumors, consumed only rumors, for the people of Saigon had long since ceased to believe anything stated officially as fact. Rumor was the only medium." Thus: President Thieu was actually an agent of the North. Thus: American B-52s were again seen prowling the sky—haven't you heard? Thus: General Nguyen Ngoc Loan, the Saigon police chief infamous for being photographed executing an NLF prisoner during the Tet Offensive, promised that if the Americans did not help evacuate more Vietnamese, the men under his command would kill every American they saw. As the military situation worsened, the Saigon regime broadcast shocking news that, in Hanoi, First Secretary Le Duan had murdered a Party rival, and that thousands of Chinese troops had consequently invaded North Vietnam. This last was a rumor that, for once in Saigon, no one took seriously—except for American journalists.

By now the forever-bubbling talk of a coup d'état against President Thieu had been brought to a full boil. Those responsible for adjusting the thermostat included CIA Director William Colby and *The New Yorker* journalist Robert Shaplen. Colby argued that the United States should "jettison" (Kissinger's word) Thieu in exchange for the "unimpeded evacuation of Americans," an idea for which Kissinger had harsh words: "[T]hose of us who were meeting daily in the White House Situation Room faced real, not theoretical, choices." The influential Shaplen took a less theoretical view, pressing upon all who would listen the wisdom of replacing Thieu with Nguyen Cao Ky, the former prime minister of South Vietnam, with whom Shaplen was friendly.

A northerner by birth and trained by the French (and married, for a time, to a Frenchwoman), Air Marshal Ky had been made the first Vietnamese air squadron leader when France allowed Vietnam an independent military in the 1950s. He had been one of South Vietnam's most popular—which is not to say beloved—political figures. (Many young men in South Vietnam, for instance, grew jaunty mustaches in imitation of Ky.) The presidential age requirement initially written into South Vietnam's constitution had been lowered from forty to thirty-five explicitly for Ky. But his fighter-pilot arrogance—and he was, by all accounts, a brilliant pilot—had turned many of the Americans in Viet-

nam against him. It did not help that when Ky was once asked by a journalist which historical figure he most admired, he instantly answered,
"Hitler." Thieu finally tore power away from Ky and made him his vice
president in 1967. Ky began plotting to remove Thieu, but many of his
fellow malcontents were killed during the Tet Offensive, forcing him to
abandon his plans. He spent the next few years stewing and flying
around the country in his silver jet. Of the South's staggering surrenders
in the spring of 1975, Ky in his memoir writes, "Ho Chi Minh couldn't
have done it better."

Emboldened by Shaplen and other allies, Ky was hosting luncheons
shortly after Danang fell in which he discussed with equally outraged
ARVN officers the prospect of deposing Thieu. Word of this instantly
got back to the Presidential Palace, distracting Thieu at the moment he
could least afford to be distracted. In early April, Ky approached General
Le Minh Dao, commander of the 18th ARVN Division and the man who
would later lead the stand at Xuan Loc. General Dao refused to help Ky
("Too busy fighting the communist, cannot participate"), and Ky was
informed by Thomas Polgar that if he attempted a coup there would be
no CIA support for it. For a man who had come to believe that Vietnam
was merely an unloved puzzle piece in a Cold War jigsaw, this was too
much.

"If only we had had time," Ky writes in his memoir, "if only the Americans had not stopped us, we might have done something. Even if we
had not lost Saigon, we still had the Mekong Delta. My plan was really to
make Saigon a Stalingrad. All the women, all the children, all the old
people would be evacuated. The only ones to remain in the city would
be volunteers, but there would be half a million of us to defend our capital as the Russians had defended Stalingrad." Lest one think that Ky is
unaware that his plan was to replicate one of the bloodiest slaughters in
world history, he goes on, "An American correspondent said [to Ky], 'If
you try to turn Saigon into a Stalingrad, thousands will die. Finally you
will die. Do you really consider that to be a useful act?' " Ky's response?
"You mention the word Stalingrad. Do you realize after all these years
people still know that name? That is enough for me." Ky does not much
bother to contemplate the possibility that South Vietnam's incessant

political instability had more to do with its defeat than anything the Americans did.

Ky was growing so flamboyant in his coup plans that Ambassador Martin finally had to go see him. Ky's memoir is generally to be taken with a metric ton of salt, and it is not likely, for instance, that Martin really said to Ky things such as "I know you are extremely well-informed" and "I am inclined to think you are right." Martin himself said, "[T]he whole point of that trip was to talk about a bloody coup that wouldn't have served any purpose on God's green earth at that stage except bolstering Ky's ego. So I just talked around the subject." Martin walked out of the air marshal's house having succeeded in suggesting that while the embassy might conceivably support an *eventual* coup, it would be a good idea to hold off on such attempts for now. The chapter of Ky's memoir in which Martin's visit is discussed is titled "Graham Martin: Formula for a Double Cross."

On April 17, President Thieu had what was likely the worst morning of his life. First he was told that his ancestral graves in a village outside the city of Phan Rang had been accidentally destroyed during an ARVN retreat. Ancestor worship is practiced by many Vietnamese, even those, like Thieu, who were nominally Catholic. Upon receipt of this news, David Butler writes, Thieu's face "writhed with agony. He walked from the room as if in a trance, retreated to the basement bomb shelter and was not seen again for twenty-four hours." But he did not go into his bomb shelter before being told by his aides that he should probably resign. Three days later Ambassador Martin, under strong pressure by Kissinger, Ford, and Martin's contacts in the South Vietnamese military, dropped in on President Thieu in the Presidential Palace. There Martin made the tactical claim to "speak as an individual only, not as the representative of the President or the Secretary of State, or even as the American ambassador." In David Butler's account, he then said, "Mr. President, I have reason to believe that if you do not step down, the [ARVN] generals will ask you to." Thieu inquired of Martin whether, if he resigned, Congress might finally be persuaded to allow aid to South Vietnam. Martin said he did not think that was likely. Later that night,

Martin returned home and wrote a dispatch to Ford and Kissinger detailing the completion of his distastefully passive-aggressive chore. He ended with this: "I went home, read the daily news digests from Washington, took a shower, scrubbed very hard with the strongest soap I could find. It didn't help very much."

The next afternoon, Thieu resigned. During his lachrymal, hourlong speech, Thieu openly defied the United States. "You ran away," he said, "and left us to do the job that you could not do. We have nothing and you want us to achieve where you failed." He also said: "The three hundred million dollars that the Congress won't approve is what they used to spend to support their troops here for ten days." And: "Kissinger did not see that the Paris Peace Accords led the South Vietnamese people to death. Everyone sees it and Kissinger does not see it." Aware that the United States wanted the supposed neutralist General Minh to replace him, Thieu decreed that his replacement instead be his vice president Tran Van Huong, who was seventy-one years old, and blind. The negotiations that would supposedly begin with Thieu's resignation did not open up. From their headquarters at Tan Son Nhut's Camp Davis, the Communists' Provisional Revolutionary Government (whose water, somewhat pathetically, Thieu had shut off) said that nothing was changed. There would be no negotiations. Thieu escaped to Thailand, where his brother served as South Vietnam's ambassador. It was also as far as Thieu's DC-6 plane could fly without refueling. Thieu had to escape for many reasons, not the least among them Air Marshal Ky's pledge to kill him. Henry Kissinger would later write, with considerable understatement, "Thieu had every reason to resent America's conduct. . . . [H]is country deserved a better fate." Thieu himself would lament, "It is so easy to be an enemy of the United States, but so difficult to be a friend."

At Xuan Loc, as the Communists were pushing from the city the last of the ARVN's stubborn remnants, the leaders of South Vietnam's military unleashed weapons so horrible they had only rarely been used in combat. The first were five-hundred-pound "daisy cutter" bombs designed to annihilate not human targets but Vietnamese jungle. A daisy cutter detonated above ground, evaporating everything within hundreds of yards, resulting in a charred, barren area perfect for Hueys to set down on. When the daisy cutters did not deter the Communists, a weapon called the five-ton cluster bomb unit was dropped. It was the first time that the five-ton CBU—called by Frank Snepp "one of the most lethal non-nuclear weapons in America's arsenal"—had ever been used in Vietnam. When the decision was made to deploy the "earthquake bomb," it was discovered that not one of the South's ancient C-30 planes had bomb racks big enough to carry it. But Air Marshall Ky, "working throughout the night with Vietnamese maintenance men," rigged up a new bomb rack. The five-ton CBU was then dropped. Anyone near its blast radius was perforated by the many thousands of fléchettes and pieces of shrapnel the bomb hurled in every direction for half a mile. It also sprayed an eight-foot-thick wave of burning kerosene that traveled nearly as far. Those who did not perish from the shrapnel or kerosene wave were asphyxiated within the deoxygenated vacuum created by the five-ton CBU's apocalyptic detonation. "The destruction was so enormous," Ky writes, "that for three days there was no fighting." Despite the devastating effectiveness of the CBU, the South Vietnamese military command resisted using more of them. Air Marshal Ky then called in a favor with an old friend. The result? "No problem. Use the bombs when you need to." Ky: "It did not change the outcome of the war, but perhaps some of us found a modest sense of achievement, of satisfaction, in being able to hit back at the hated enemy, even if it was now too late." There were numerous international protests at the use of the five-ton CBU, and the Communists finally responded by destroying the runway of Bien Hoa's nearby airfield, from which the CBU-carrying C-30s were taking off.

Xuan Loc fell on the morning of April 21. Six hundred South Vietnamese soldiers voluntarily stayed behind to provide cover as the survivors of the remaining ARVN units were evacuated by helicopter. These courageous souls peered over their barricades to see 40,000 North Vietnamese troops rushing at them across a cratered, gray, altogether lunar city. They were quickly done away with, finally allowing the Communists to cut off Saigon from all incoming and outgoing land routes. The city could now be left to starve or suffer invasion from all sides.

Events now gathered a dreadful momentum. After a week in office, Thieu's replacement resigned and was replaced by the neutralist Duong Van Minh, also known as "Big" Minh. The literally though not figuratively toothless General Minh was said to have ordered the murder of South Vietnam's president Ngo Dinh Diem and his brother after the coup that deposed Diem in 1963, and Minh's personal bodyguard is believed to have been one of the killers. (The bodyguard later committed suicide in highly suspicious circumstances.) But that was all hieroglyphically ancient history now, and General Minh became president on April 27. His first act was to put off his inauguration because his astrological chart was not promising. In his eventual inaugural speech the neutralist promised that in "the days ahead we will have nothing but difficulties, terrible difficulties. The positions to be taken are grave and important[;] our position is a difficult one." Minh read robotically from a prepared speech that for the first time in the history of South Vietnamese politics acknowledged the existence of the Communists' Provisional Revolutionary Government. He spoke of negotiation, of implementing peace on the basis of the Paris Accords, the need for "reconciliation" and ending "the coercive system imposed on the press." Those listening to Minh are said by David Butler to have felt their hearts shrivel. Minh then paused and looked out upon his Presidential Palace audience. "In these difficult hours," he said, no longer reading, "I can only beg of you one thing: Be courageous, do not abandon the country, do not run away. The tombs of our ancestors are here, it is here that we all belong." "The room," Butler writes, "applauded emotionally." Minutes after the applause ended, the North launched a rocket attack and aerial assault on Tan Son Nhut air base—the final proof, if any were needed, that there would be no negotiation, no cease-fire, with or without President Minh, between North and South Vietnam.

The air attack on Tan Son Nhut was led by Nguyen Thanh Trung, the same defector to the North who weeks earlier had attempted to assassinate President Thieu by dropping a bomb on the Presidential Palace. (Trung now flies friendlier skies for Vietnam Airlines.) The North's General Dung called the attack on Tan Son Nhut "the most perfect joint operation ever by our armed forces and branches." Much of the equipment used to attack Tan Son Nhut belonged to North Vietnam's enemies. During the North's drive on Saigon, billions of dollars' worth of U.S. and ARVN equipment had been scooped up. Among the haul were 550 tanks and more than 1.5 million rifles. The planes Trung and his fellow pilots used to strafe Tan Son Nhut were almost all captured American warplanes, many of them picked up on the runways of the cities PAVN forces took without struggle. At Pleiku more than sixty working aircraft were captured, and at Phu Cat the North picked up fifty more.

Ken Moorefield was at the Defense Attaché Office near Tan Son Nhut when the American-made bombs began coming down. "I remember thinking throughout how ironic this was," he told Frank Snepp. "How many times in my two years as a combat officer in the delta had I called in air strikes against the VC! Now I knew what it felt like to be on the receiving end, and totally defenseless." For those at the DAO that afternoon, the attacks were more terrifying than deadly. "We were grinding away," Henry Hicks, the man in charge of evacuating the DAO, told Larry Engelmann, "flying people out, when all of a sudden there come these goddamned airplanes and they bomb us." (The next morning Hicks was shot at by the "goddamned" South Vietnamese guards guarding Tan Son Nhut's entrance gate.) The people of Saigon, however, panicked. It was the first time they had ever been bombed in force, as the North had lacked offensive airpower for the vast majority of the war. In response President Minh declared martial law and followed that order by asking Hanoi for a cease-fire. The request was refused. Minh then demanded that all Americans in Saigon leave within twenty-four hours. This was a godsend. As Martin put it in a cable to Washington, "President Minh's request will permit the announcement of [our] departure to be by request, not from our panic." In his memoir Kissinger takes a similar tack: "Since this coincided precisely with our withdrawal schedule, it in fact helped our extrication by avoiding the charge that America was abandoning its friends."

In the early hours of April 29, the full last day the world would know the Republic of Vietnam (though few realized this: Thomas Polgar had a May 1 lunch date), we find one of the sadder episodes in the grief-sodden epic of the Vietnam War. Lance Corporal Darwin Judge and Corporal Charles McMahon were the only two Marines guarding a lonely sentry point near the Defense Attaché Office. The Marines were "buddies," in the words of their sergeant, and had been sent to Vietnam as reinforcements—their unit's only reinforcements. Neither had been to Vietnam before. They had been given sentry duty because it was thought the least dangerous assignment available. Three days before, McMahon had sent his mother a postcard: "After this duty, they may send us home for a while. . . . I'll try to write when I have time and don't worry Ma!!!!" At four in the morning on April 29, a half-dozen 122 mm PAVN rockets—Soviet-made projectiles famous for their inaccuracy—struck the DAO complex and Tan Son Nhut in rapid succession, one landing less than two feet from where McMahon and Judge were standing. McMahon caught the brunt of the rocket and was reduced to what one witness described as "a charred stump." Judge's body was in better repair; one of the first Marines to arrive at the scene believed Judge might still be alive. Darwin Judge and Charles McMahon were the last two uniformed American soldiers to die in the Vietnam War.

After the rocket attack, South Vietnamese Air Force pilots scrambled for their planes, unloaded their missiles and bombs, left them on the runway, and made for Thailand. Some pilots shot others for particularly contested planes. Soon after the rockets stopped, Nguyen Cao Ky writes, "the Communists started pounding the runway of the air base with their big Russian 130mm guns. Within minutes thick, oily smoke spread into a huge cloud as the enemy scored a direct hit on the main fuel depot. Several planes on the ground exploded in gigantic orange flashes." A huge portion of Saigon's remaining air force was thus destroyed on the ground. Graham Martin would later claim that Tan Son Nhut had been attacked because the South had in previous days been flying too many of its planes to safer havens. A PAVN general disagreed when he addressed the matter with Engelmann: "The real reason we shelled the runway of Tan Son Nhut was not because the Air Force had withdrawn their airplanes. We shelled the airport simply because that is when the artillery units arrived within shelling distance of Tan Son Nhut."

A few braver Saigon pilots took to the air of their own volition. Air Marshal Ky himself had spent a portion of the previous day taking out batteries of rocket launchers in an F-5. Now, with the airfield of Tan Son Nhut under attack and that of Bien Hoa in flames, many pilots were surreally refueling at abandoned Shell stations around the city. In some areas the line of planes waiting for gas stretched for blocks. Ky, who hours earlier had announced on the radio, "I will stay here until my last blood, until I'm dying," flew himself in a chopper to South Vietnam's military headquarters. It was deserted but for one lieutenant general. "I don't know what to do anymore," the man told Ky. "Come along with me, then," Ky said. Ky flew to the USS *Midway* off the coast of Vietnam, where the ship's American commander "very touchingly" allowed Ky the use of his private quarters, in which Ky spent half an hour weeping.

On the morning of April 29, "departure envelopes" (diplomatic emergency kits stuffed with money and the addresses of various embassies throughout Indochina) were prepared for embassy officials in case anyone was separated during the evacuation—the imminence of which no one any longer had reason to doubt. When Ambassador Martin learned that Tan Son Nhut had been adjudged an impossible launching point for the evacuation, he demanded to be taken there in his bulletproof limousine, an errand that squandered two precious hours. At Khe Sanh earlier in the war, Martin later argued, planes had landed at and taken off from its bombarded airfield all the time. Martin would tell Larry Engelmann that he knew "a great deal about what flies and what doesn't fly. . . . Out at Tan Son Nhut . . . they were telling me they couldn't land the planes. That didn't make any bloody sense. I went out there to see and it still didn't make any bloody sense. You could have taken a jeep and cleared the runway of debris in thirty minutes." The "debris" Martin spoke off included hundreds of live munitions, burning fuel tanks, partially exploded planes, and, in Frank Snepp's words, "one F-5 jet, its engine still running . . . abandoned just in front of the loading ramp." It was finally impressed upon Martin that an evacuation from Tan Son Nhut's devastated runways would not be possible.

It had not yet been determined whether to keep a small staff in the U.S. Embassy after the Communists moved into Saigon. Martin felt strongly that the United States should; it was a matter of international dignity. Complicating matters was Article XXI of the Paris Accords, which required the United States "to contribute to healing the wounds of war." If the United States had a diplomatic presence in Saigon after its government's collapse, it would likely be held accountable for Article XXI. During the Paris peace talks, Kissinger and Nixon had promised, but had not committed to paper, a $4.25 billion aid package to North Vietnam, the awarding of which they neglected to mention would depend on congressional approval. Hanoi's Liberation Radio had the temerity to keep bringing this up and on the morning of April 29 asked "whether the U.S. imperialists agree to compensate for and heal the deep and extensive wounds they have caused the Vietnamese people." If the United States stayed, it would not only lead to a diplomatic relationship but the promise's violation, since Congress would never authorize such an aid package. It would also mean that the United States would have no standing to hold North Vietnam to Article VIII(b) of the Paris Accords, which concerned the return of U.S. soldiers designated as missing in action. The inevitable decision was made: full evacuation.

The evacuation's code name was initially Operation Talon Vise. When that code name was compromised, another, unintentionally flatulent code name was settled upon: Operation Frequent Wind. It was also called Option IV. Options I, II, and III all involved fixed-wing aircraft, whereas the last-resort Option IV called for an evacuation exclusively reliant on helicopters. The one helpful aspect of Option IV was how much more difficult it would be for the Vietnamese to storm helicopters. Among the many unhelpful things about Option IV was the design of the embassy grounds, likened by more than one pilot to a well. As a Marine put it to Larry Engelmann: "They [the helicopter pilots] had about a seventy-foot vertical descent to get into the embassy. They had to come over, hover, then descend seventy feet into this hole, and there wasn't that much room." For these overloaded helicopters to lift off would be no easier. "[I]nstead of doing what they call a 'translational' maneuver, where you get the bird off the ground and then lean it forward, they had to go straight up. There was no room. . . . They literally had to go straight up seventy feet." If one helicopter failed to execute this midair slalom, Option IV would be over. There was no Option V.

The morning's one beam of sunlight was news from Moscow, which

Kissinger received. The Soviets let it be known that the North would let the U.S. evacuation continue until midnight of that day, with the strong insinuation that it did not mind if many thousands of South Vietnamese were also evacuated. (Later the North's leaders would admit, with disturbing honesty, that the expatriation of so many southerners had helpfully prevented them from having to reeducate them later.) The Soviets' note mirrored an earlier note from April 22, which read, "The position of the Vietnamese side on the question of evacuation of American citizens from South Vietnam is definitely favorable. . . . We are told that the Vietnamese do not intend to damage the reputation of the United States." In those final words stands the colossal folly of the Vietnam War. The most powerful nation in the world, hotfooting it out of one of the poorest, being assured that no one intends to "damage" its reputation.

VII

In Saigon it is morning. But in Michigan it is night. What connects these places across mountains and seas, you feel certain, is a cord of bright endless pain that happens to feed directly into your collapsing nervous system. You sit staring at the television. Around you and within you everything ends, yet Escanaba itself is a cocoon of maddening stillness. Muff is upstairs, bathing the boys. You can hear, over the television's low volume, the sloppy, glorious sound of children in water. It is just after 9:30 p.m. Aunt Grace is long asleep. Your little sister Alicia, wearing an untucked red gingham shirt and knee-torn blue jeans ratty with denim tendrils, had wandered downstairs, taken one look at you on the couch, and retreated back up to her room. Your younger brother Paul has not yet come home. As usual these days, you find yourself all alone. You hate solitude until you have drunk past it, drunk until your grief becomes purely, endurably chemical and a mysterious chorus of conversation fills your skull. Then you cherish your solitude. Protect it. *Get away from me.*

But tonight solitude will not do. You begin calling your old Marine buddies, the only people who will understand why something happen-

ing a dozen time zones and 12,000 miles away can hurt you so profoundly. After three tub glasses of Johnnie Walker, your dialing finger
feels as large and clumsy as a foot, and you mash apelike at the numeric
keypad before finally getting your first call through. It is to R—— in
Chicago, not your closest friend in Vietnam, but okay, he will do, as a
start. The phone rings and rings. He should be home. You want him to
be home, doing what you are doing, suffering what you are suffering. Or
perhaps he wishes, this night above all others, not to talk. *Get away from
me.* But suspecting he is there, and is listening to these rings, angers you.

You feel very lonely sometimes, stranded here upon Michigan's Upper
Peninsula—a part of the country tacitly impossible to pass through by
accident. Anyone who finds himself in the U.P. meant to find himself in
the U.P. Yet you never intended to wind up back here. Your own cruel little paradox. The shabby churches, the clusters of prefab roadside homes,
the gas stations on the brink of foreclosure, the shoppes whose hand-
painted signs offer some staple (souvenirs, driftwood, smoked fish) of
Escanaba's garage-sale economy. Sometimes you feel a hopeless, land-
locked dementia take hold of you, and you long for Vietnam. For all its
dreads, in Vietnam you never lost your simple human awareness of
being alive. It was a young man's land, covered in a dew of terrifying possibility. But among these mute forests of the Upper Midwest it is as
though the future never happens. You once believed that a young person
growing up here had three options: to go mad, devote oneself to sub-
stance abuse, or develop a sense of humor as harsh as a drill bit. The last
gambit was a great consolation to those who knew they would one day
leave and a great annoyance to those who knew they would not. You
seem to have managed all three, a hometown boy after all.

You are dialing G—— in New Jersey when you see Muff descend the
stairs and without a word or glance turn at their base and imperially
head off to your ground-floor bedroom. It could be that she did not see
you. Television flicker sends sputters of color around the room, and you
can almost believe that you are invisible in this odd darkness. But you
know she saw you, or sensed you, and recoiled. When did you begin this
long, impotent slide toward estrangement? In self-defense you have
both formed new emotional jurisdictions, access to which requires pass-

words that change from day to day. You misconstrue the rawness of Muff's need as her loss of faith and know she believes your remoteness to be indifference. Every word you exchange has become an encrypted ultimatum. So you do not speak for days, and then, without warning, you make sudden, detoxifying love, begging for each other's forgiveness. But now, for the first time, your truces refuse to take. You have suffered some massive dislocation. In response Muff has been going on one retail tear after another, trusting that more possessions will form the simplest route to salvation. She wants a better life, a life you are beginning to see you are powerless to give her, because for her "better" means something quite simple: not with you.

You reach G——, a man who in boot was given to dumping an entire box of cornflakes into a huge salad bowl and pouring over this carbohydrate mountain a half gallon of milk. Like you, like all of you, a volunteer. He is sickened by the day's events, which are still being relayed only sketchily by the news. He is not nearly as drunk as you are. In fact, he claims to have not been drinking at all. This seems to you incredible. Before you know it G—— is speaking of betrayal, of how personally he took President Ford's widely noted remarks of April 23, six days ago, in a speech at Tulane University. Ford said this:

> Today, America can regain the sense of pride that existed before Vietnam. But it cannot be achieved by refighting a war that is finished as far as America is concerned. As I see it, the time has come to look forward to an agenda for the future, to unify, to bind up the Nation's wounds, and to restore its health and its optimistic self-confidence. . . . We can and should help others to help themselves. But the fate of responsible men and women everywhere in the final decision rests in their own hands.

Decent, sensible, utterly obtuse words. President Ford ("the weakest president in U.S. history," in the words of North Vietnam's prime minister Pham Van Dong) spoke of the war as some misadventure roughly as regrettable as a bounced check, not the scorching trip through the vortex by which an entire generation was third-degree-burned. "Optimistic self-confidence"? You and G—— know that, in hours, you will be veterans of the only war the United States has lost—about which there is, apparently, some glee. When Ford said the word "finished," Tulane's applauding students got to their feet.

There is no national confidence to be restored after this war, after that self-satisfied applause. Where to begin? You and your fellow warriors proved unable to find, with any consistency, an enemy hiding in an area less than half the size of New Mexico. You and your fellow warriors were unable to defeat an enemy outnumbered in active combatants by a margin thought to be five to one. You and your fellow warriors could not crush an enemy with a per capita income of $160, an enemy whose nation's gross national product was one four-hundredth that of your own. "Self-confidence"? In whom? In *what*? You sought to counter an insurgency and wound up activating a larger insurgency, in effect proving that everything the Communists said about the United States and its "puppet government" in Saigon was right, even though it was not. That is what you did: you made a lie true.

None of which Ford could admit, even if he believed it. Apparently, he did. Robert Hartmann, Ford's counselor, described to Larry Engelmann how the president had "conversationally" mentioned before the Tulane speech that he didn't "know why we have to spend so much time worrying about a war that's over as far as we're concerned." "Well," Hartmann replied, "then why don't you just say that?" At the last minute, the fateful Vietnam interlude was added to the text of Ford's speech. Kissinger called the insertion into Ford's speech "a typical inside-the-Beltway bureaucratic victory," one "masterminded" by gutless "gloaters" who had not had the decency to consult Kissinger about the last-minute addition. ("I don't think Henry would like it," Ford had worried to Hartmann. Hartmann: "You're the President, and if that's the way you feel, say it.") Kissinger was angry because the speech signaled with no ambiguity that the United States was done with Vietnam. As Kissinger later argued in his memoirs, "ambiguity about how far we were willing to go [in saving South Vietnamese] was the sole bargaining card left." In Kissinger we have a man who would strategize how best to escape from a burning skyscraper or issue a position statement from the cabin of a jetliner in free fall. (In fact, Kissinger had already stupidly shown his cards. After the Paris agreement was signed, Pham Van Dong asked him if the United States, like the Mongols, would return to attack Vietnam again. "Once is enough!" Kissinger responded.)

But neither you nor G—— blames him, exactly, for the collapse of all you fought and suffered for. You blame fifteen years of inexplicable decisions. You blame the war planners who forbade firing on any enemy boat larger than fifty feet or smaller than twenty feet. The colonels who on Monday would order that a Communist hill be taken, suffer a dozen Marine casualties in the doing, order its abandonment on Friday, and upon news of its recapture on Sunday order its takeover again. The Air Force majordomos who decreed that no U.S. pilot could shoot at North Vietnamese surface-to-air missile sites until they fired; meanwhile the patient American flyboy was ejecting from a burning metal comet. You blame John F. Kennedy. You blame Lyndon Johnson. You blame President Thieu. You blame Richard Nixon. You blame the American people for not understanding war. You blame the journalists for blowing the My Lai massacre out of all reasonable proportion and turning the public against what was a noble and just cause. You could have won the war, you know, if it had been fought the way war was intended to be fought. And for all that, you almost won. But Kissinger? "Had I thought it possible that Congress would . . . cut off aid to a beleaguered ally," Kissinger wrote, "I would not have pressed for an agreement as I did in the final negotiations in 1972." The man was a fly on the manure pile of war, believing above all else that the manure was *his.* You hang up with G—— even angrier than you were before you called him. Jesus, where is Muff? You want to tell her how goddamned *angry* you are. Then you realize that, in all likelihood, this is why she has avoided you tonight and will be avoiding you for the foreseeable future.

Next you call C——, your closest friend from Vietnam and the man you made the godfather of your second son. C—— wound up in the Marine Corps because of several early indications of his promising career as a hoodlum. In 1963 he had stolen a car or some approximate last-straw offense. The sentencing judge offered C—— a choice of jail or the Marine Corps, a post–Korean War innovation of jurisprudence known as "alternative sentencing." He wound up surviving three tours in Vietnam. Now, thanks to you, he works in Escanaba, in your own bank. C——'s lakefront home is only blocks away from where you now sit and dial. He answers after one ring.

—You watching?

—Clusterfuck.

—Jesus Christ.

—I feel ill.

—Nothing we can do about it now. *Dang di* fucking good-bye, Vietnam.

—I'm ashamed of my country. For the first time in my life I'm ashamed to be an American.

—We hung those people out to dry. Every last one of them.

—Thing was *won* when I left, for Christ's sake. It was practically *over*. The VC were almost all dead. You could walk through VC villages in 1969 and there wouldn't be a single shot fired. There were roads I wouldn't even bother carrying a weapon on anymore. How did this happen?

—We didn't have the balls to see it through. It's politicians. Journalists. You can't fight a war if you're afraid of photographs. Or if you're listening to some goddamn poll.

—Where were the photos of the hospitals we built? The medicine we gave out?

—You know what we should have done. Invaded the North. Bombed Hanoi. I mean really bombed it. The Big One. War over. If the Russians and Chinese wanted to take issue with that. . . . The thing is, we never defined *what* we were going to do.

—It was defined. If you were in the Army, you were killing Communists. If you were in the Marines, you were trying to pacify the families of the Vietnamese guys the Army killed.

—Which means there was nobody with enough guts to define anything.

—You watching alone, or is she with you?

—She won't watch. She went to bed. Says she's sick of it. Says she hopes it really is over.

—That sounds familiar.

—She said the same thing to you?

—If we were on speaking terms, yeah. She might have said something very much along those lines.

—What do you suppose Caputo is doing right now?

—I don't know. Getting the hell out of there, I hope.

Philip Caputo, who before becoming a journalist had gone through Officer Candidate School with you and served a tour in Vietnam, was in Saigon in late April, wondering whether or not he should flee. "[H]ow would we, American correspondents," Caputo wondered, "be treated by the Communist victors? In the final moments of chaos, would the South Vietnamese, feeling betrayed by Washington, turn their weapons on every American they saw?" On April 28, Caputo found himself on South Vietnam's main artery, Highway 1, outside Long Binh, writing "a personal account of what must be one of the great tragedies of modern times. . . . A hundred yards away, North Vietnamese mortar shells and rockets are slamming into government positions guarding the bridge over the Dong Hai River."

Caputo was covering the long, desperate march of South Vietnamese peasants from the North's blitzkrieg toward Saigon. Many of these peasants were "refugees two and three times over—people who ran from Xuan Loc, from Da Nang and Ham Tam and Qui Nhon. Now they are running again, but this is their last retreat." Caputo described the procession: "They shambled in the rain and heat: barefoot civilians, soldiers whose boots were rotting on their feet, some still carrying their weapons and determined that their little bands would stick together, most without weapons, broken men determined only to escape." The previous night, Caputo could hear in his Saigon hotel room the crackle of small-arms fire, rockets hitting the airport, the thunder of field guns. He wrote that through his hotel's top-floor window, "I could see the flames of a burning fuel dump. Gekko lizards clung to the room's white walls, the walls quaking from the secondary explosions set off by the bombs, the lizards immobile in their reptilian indifference." Seeing everything so obviously falling apart moved Caputo to reflect on the deaths of his friends: "Those men had died for no reason. They had given their all for nothing."

—I feel like—

—I know what you feel like.

—Can you honestly tell me what we really did?

—We fought. We did our duty. We were Marines, and we did what Marines do. And sometimes Marines die.

—All so we could sit here and watch this.

—It's over. It doesn't have to mean anything.

—It has to mean something.

—Then it means what you want it to mean.

—You know what? I have no idea, no clue, what that could be. I think I want . . . my God. I want my friends back. I want the men I saw die to be alive again. I want every letter I wrote the parents of my boys to have never been sent. I want to walk around with normal thoughts in my head and not all this—

—Look. Drink.

—I have been. I am.

—Drink more. It's easier. And quit crying.

—It's not any easier.

—Then you haven't been drinking enough.

—It's less painful. That's not the same thing.

—Semper fucking fidelis.

—God, we bled. We bled so much.

—We're still bleeding. And we'll bleed a lot more before this is over.

VIII

On President Ford's order, the evacuation of Saigon was implemented at 10:25 a.m. local time. The choppers were supposed to have begun arriving in Saigon one hour after Ford's order. But on the U.S. ships awaiting orders in the South China Sea there was berthing confusion. Many of the Marines assigned to certain details found they were not berthed on the same ships as the helicopters in which they were intended to fly to Saigon. Not until half past noon did the initial wave of thirty-six helicopters depart. The flight to Saigon took forty-five minutes, and the first helicopters did not arrive at the DAO—pegged for earlier evacuation than the embassy—until 2 p.m., almost four hours after Ford's evacuation order. The tense Marines sitting within their ocean-skimming gunships were not the only people feeling confused. In Saigon the Western journalists, civilians, and Vietnamese promised evacuation were equally perplexed as to how they would find their way to their departure points. The plan held that everyone would gather at preassigned points, where buses would pick them up and take them to the DAO and the embassy. But the streets were already filling up with panic-stricken Vietnamese. The journalist Ken Kashiwahara, of ABC News, described for Larry Engelmann the morning of April 29 as "an island of one kind of insanity in a world of another kind of insanity. Nothing made sense anymore. Adding to the general insanity was the fact that the signal for the evacuation was the playing of Bing Crosby's 'I'm Dreaming of a White Christmas' over the Armed Forces Radio." If playing a Christmas standard in April did not seem a clear enough indicator that something was afoot, the deejay announced at the song's conclusion, "It's a hundred and five degrees in Saigon and the temperature is rising. Mother wants you to call home." The decision to play "White Christmas" was that of an Armed Forces Radio employee named Chuck Neil. "Why not play a recording of something that every American will recognize in a split second?" Neil later explained. Even this went awry. Neil learned that morning he did not have Bing Crosby's recording of "White Christmas" on hand. Instead he played Tennessee Ernie Ford's.

Among the people picked up by bus that morning was Philip Caputo. He arrived at the DAO to find rockets hitting the complex and the DAO's security detail emptying their clips into the sky. *The New York Times* journalist Fox Butterfield, traveling in the same convoy as Caputo, told Larry Engelmann that as they passed Tan Son Nhut air base "a C-119, a 'flying boxcar,' a South Vietnamese Air Force plane . . . took off to about 600 to 1,000 feet and a rocket hit it and it just came apart. It was filled with people." After disembarking from the buses, Caputo and his fellow evacuees ran toward the DAO's tennis courts. With shells exploding all around them, Americans, journalists, Vietnamese civilians, ARVN officers, and "even a few old French plantation owners" scrambled for the CH-53 helicopters, known alternately as Jolly Green Giants or Sea

Knights. Giants, knights. A story holds that when the first French warship wandered into Vietnamese waters in the early 1800s, it was thought by the Vietnamese to be a dragon. So the colonial experience rode into Vietnam on the back of a dragon and now left via giants and knights. Caputo steeled himself against the choppers' ninety-mile-an-hour propeller wash and climbed aboard. Shortly after his CH-53 lifted off, Caputo noticed on the ground a smoke puff, which was instantly followed by the uniquely terrible corkscrew trajectory of a heat-seeking missile spiraling up at him. A decoy flare was released by the chopper, and the incoming missile went lost in an orb of false heat. Caputo's chopper also took small-arms fire from ARVN soldiers until it cleared Vietnam's beaches and floated over the South China Sea, where Caputo saw "thousands" of fishing junks loaded with refugees. When the blocky silhouettes of the U.S. armada hardened above the watery horizon, he knew: "We've lost."

"Well," Caputo was told by a seaman when he climbed off the chopper, "that's one country we don't have to give billions of dollars to anymore." He walked across the deck as Vietnamese—pilots, civilians, and generals—were frisked at gunpoint. The choppers that were no longer in use had their rotors locked and were pushed over the carrier's edge into the sea. Some Vietnamese, shocked into the realization that they were not going back to their homeland, attempted to jump after the drowned helicopters. An officer aboard the USS *Denver* took a long look at Caputo. He was wearing a dirty shirt and a beard he had not trimmed for days; his only possessions were some maps and his notebooks. He was assigned his berth in the ship, to which he quickly retired. He had been awake for thirty hours. He found other men in the berth, who paused as he entered, then nodded at him. As Caputo climbed into his cot, they resumed talking. Ambassador Martin was "nearly certifiable" for delaying the evacuation, they said. Did anyone else know he was walking his dog around Saigon as recently as yesterday? Did they realize how many classified files had fallen intact into North Vietnamese hands at Danang and Nha Trang? Caputo then realized that his bunkmates were CIA field agents. The deck officer had assigned Caputo to what he assumed was his fellow agents' room. Caputo said nothing. Eventually he was too tired to listen and fell asleep.

———————

Back in Saigon, Ken Moorefield was driving one of the evacuation buses. It says something about Operation Frequent Wind that although Moorefield had never driven a bus before, this somehow did not disqualify him for bus-driving duty. Moorefield quickly lost his patience with the journalists he was picking up, many of whom, he later told Frank Snepp, "were getting all tangled up in their equipment. 'Leave it!' I yelled to them. 'For chrissakes, leave it!' But not one of them would part with his precious tripods or tote bag—or raise a hand to help with the Vietnamese." Later in the evacuation, as Snepp writes, one journalist "tried to elbow aside an old Vietnamese woman and push his cameras and tripods" into a helicopter. An embassy official walked up behind the journalist, "tapped him on the shoulder, flattened him with a roundhouse in the jaw, and threw his cameras into the bushes."

The journalist Ken Kashiwahara, also on a bus, told Engelmann he saw "a Vietnamese man . . . running up alongside the bus. He was carrying a baby. And he held out the baby and was pleading, 'Please take my baby! Please take my baby! Please take my baby!' And the bus kept moving. And the man fell. And the baby fell, too, obviously. And the man dropped the baby. And the rear wheels of the bus ran over the baby." Kashiwahara then had the bewildering thought that he and the rest of the bus's occupants might not escape the country. (Elsewhere in Saigon, others had been coming to identical conclusions. An American husband-wife team employed by the CIA as analysts made the decision that if Saigon filled up with pith-helmeted North Vietnamese before they escaped, the husband would put a bullet through his wife's brain and then turn the gun on himself.) Many of the buses traveled in circles, their drivers having no idea how to navigate Saigon's roadblocked streets. The journalist Ed Bradley, trapped on one bus, described to Engelmann how "every time our driver turned a corner with his bus he wiped out about three restaurants. This went on for seven hours!"

In the streets, Saigon policemen beat American "big noses" and when that grew tiresome opened fire on buses and cars carrying evacuees. *The New York Times*' Malcolm Browne, who three years earlier had been expelled from South Vietnam by President Thieu, reported finding "a blanket on the sidewalk next to the Continental Hotel, in the heart of the downtown foreign quarter. On the blanket lay a sleeping baby, beside it a small plastic bag containing ragged clothing and some toys." Browne wrote of Americans wandering the streets in search of old Vietnamese friends, then abandoning their searches when set upon by angry Vietnamese for whom no one was looking. Eventually Browne had the thought to call his contacts at the Provisional Revolutionary Government headquarters "after a particularly heavy shelling" of Tan Son Nhut air base. He asked how they were doing. "I cannot tell you how grateful we are for asking," his PRG friend responded, "especially considering the circumstances. We hope you all get through this somehow." Before boarding his designated bus, Browne was told by a weeping Vietnamese man, "You may hear after you leave that some of us here have died, perhaps even at their own hand. You must not spend the rest of your lives with that guilt. It is just a part of Vietnam's black fate, in which you, all of you, became ensnared for a time."

The journalist Keyes Beech, of the *Chicago Daily News,* drove around Saigon in a packed bus after having been turned back at Tan Son Nhut's first checkpoint, where security conditions "were out of control." The scene beyond his window was incomprehensible. The American PX had been broken into, its protective layer of barbed wire torn away while men with raked and bloody arms carried away refrigerators in rickshaws. Bicycles and scooters tore down wide avenues shedding contraband soap and candy bars at every turn. One witness described ARVN soldiers walking around with wristwatches "strapped all the way up to both elbows." Some children were armed with pistols. "You could find almost anything that night," Andrew X. Pham would write years later. "The defeated army discarded guns, ammo, helmets, knives, uniforms, boots, water tins. . . ." Looters were stripping every American business of carpets, sofas, faucet fixtures, filing cabinets, and rolling chairs. The sharp stench of smashed whiskey cases blew through the streets. Through these Boschian tableaux Beech's bus journeyed. "We were a busload of fools," he wrote, "piloted by a man who had never driven a bus [not Moorefield] and had to wire the ignition when it stalled because the Vietnamese driver had run away with the keys the night before." A number of cars began trailing Beech's bus in the vain hope it would find some way out of the bedlam. "At every stop," Beech wrote, "Vietnamese beat on the doors and windows pleading to be let inside. We merely looked at them. We already had enough Vietnamese aboard. Every time we opened the door, we had to beat and kick them back." The bus—"our prison and our fortress"—was nevertheless overrun. "I found myself pushing a middle-aged Vietnamese woman who had been sitting beside me on the bus and asked me to look after her because she worked for the Americans and the Viet Cong would cut her throat." At last, out of options, Beech's bus drove down Thong Nhut Boulevard (today Le Duan Boulevard) and stopped at the U.S. Embassy, around which 10,000 Vietnamese had formed a violent, writhing bracelet of grief.

The six-story embassy had been built in 1967. A year later, during the Tet Offensive, it was widely (and erroneously) reported that several shoeless NLF commandos had made it as high as the embassy's upper floors, which the CIA occupied, but apparently none had made it beyond the first. Since then its already fearsome armature had been considerably strengthened. The embassy's concrete artillery shield was possibly the strongest in the world, and in the last few days its ten-foot-high wall had been dressed in barbed wire. A break had been made in the wire, which eight Marines were guarding. This was essentially the only way inside, as the embassy's front gate had been reinforced with steel bars that, for good measure, were welded into place. The embassy's 160-Marine security force had set up in the courtyard a .30-caliber machine-gun nest, its barrel trained on the gate in case the Vietnamese broke through. The compound's inner concinnity had been equally disturbed. The embassy restaurant was in the alpha stages of being ransacked, and its swimming pool was doing double duty as a toilet and dumping site for whatever bullets and firearms any Vietnamese had managed to get inside, as there were rumors that NLF "assassination squads" were intent on killing American officials.

After the Vietnamese woman he had sat next to on the bus announced she was going home to poison herself, Beech and his fellow journalists beat and pushed their way through the crowd toward the wall. They "ceased to be correspondents. We were only men fighting for our lives, scratching, clawing, pushing ever closer to that wall." Beech, at the time, was sixty-one years old. And this thought occurred to him: "Now . . . I know what it's like to be a Vietnamese. I am one of them." The Marines at the wall had their orders: grab and pull up Americans first, third-country nationals second, and then, only then, approved Vietnamese. How anyone was to communicate his or her approved status is difficult to imagine, and there are many stories of ethnic-Vietnamese American citizens futilely waving their passports at the Marines. Ken Kashiwahara, as an Asian, was particularly worried about his chances of getting over the wall. He screamed the only thing he could think of that would convince the Marines he was an American: "The Dodgers won the pennant!" Luckily, he was recognized and pulled up.

Despite one American general's belief that there was "something about a United States Marine that demands respect from the Vietnamese people," many Vietnamese climbed atop the wall and exchanged blows with the Marines before being heaved back into the crowd. The Marines did not treat only Vietnamese ruthlessly. One went so far as to smash an American journalist's television camera after the journalist caught on film a particularly brutal repulsion. When another Marine was pulled into the crowd by the Vietnamese, the journalist Bob Tamarkin wrote, "the mood . . . turned from bare tolerance to fitful rage." The Marines broke children's noses with their M16 butts. They beat old women. The wall became so chaotic that other embassy officials were forced to pitch in. Tamarkin wrote, "One official drew his revolver, stuck it point-blank in the face of a young Vietnamese boy and screamed: 'Get down, you bastard, or I'll blow your head off. Get down!' " And: "One official who had thrown a young girl from the wall three times finally gave in. 'I couldn't take it anymore. I feel sorry for her.' " (The man was named Jeff Kibler. He was a twenty-four-year-old embassy accountant.) This is from Frank Snepp: "[O]ne Vietnamese woman, in an effort to climb over the surrounding fence herself, had become pinioned on a metal upright. Now she hung there like a speared fish, blood slowly oozing across the front of her [dress]."

Families who had arrived at the wall watched as one or two members of their group were selected from the crowd—acts of charity that never-theless obliterated these families for decades. It is little wonder that while reading about the fall of Saigon, one repeatedly comes across the trope of Americans unwilling to look into Vietnamese eyes. Butler: "On the walls and at the gates, it was hard to look anyone in the eye." The pull quote from a *Harper's* cover story entitled "Last Days in Saigon," written by Dennis Troute, was "Don't Look in Their Eyes." The scholar Neil L. Jamieson writes of his experience during Saigon's fall: "[O]ne man mut-tered to his companions: 'Don't look in their eyes.' The advice was unnec-essary. We left with our heads down, confused, frustrated, and ashamed."

Keyes Beech still had not made it in. In the scrum Beech's briefcase hit the face of a Vietnamese baby in its mother's arms. The baby's father began to punch and attack Beech, who "tried to apologize as he kept on beating me while his wife pleaded with me to take the baby." Beech was finally pulled up the wall by a Marine with "long, muscular arms," while others pushed and punched the Vietnamese attempting to scale the wall alongside him. Beech had arrived at the wall safeguarding the lives of some Vietnamese and Japanese friends. They were not pulled up. By 3 p.m., things had somehow gotten worse. It took Bob Tamarkin an hour and a half to move three yards through the crowd before he was finally pulled up. Meanwhile, French Embassy officials stood watching from the walls of their own next-door compound. All of those who approached the French Embassy begging for help were ignored.

The bus convoy system broke down late in the afternoon. Ken Moore-field arrived at the embassy at five and was pulled over the wall while some Vietnamese, as he later put it, "were waving documentation I myself had stamped the day before." Moorefield found 2,000 people in the embassy compound, mostly Vietnamese but also many third-country nationals and journalists. He armed himself with an M16, hor-rified by how easily a saboteur could have lobbed over the wall a satchel of C-4. Not a single chopper had yet arrived at the embassy. The DAO, with its more implicated Vietnamese population, many of them high-ranking military people who had been waiting for weeks to be evacu-ated, was still the first priority. Sometime after 5 p.m., however, the first helicopters arrived. The larger CH-53 landed in the embassy parking lot, with the smaller CH-46 coming down on the roof.

At 6 p.m. what Tamarkin called the "rampage" began. Those Vietnamese lucky enough to have gained entrance into the embassy and observant enough to suspect that there was no way all of them would be evacuated began to pillage. It began innocently enough, with several hundred cases of soda being stolen from a storeroom, which was emptied, Tamarkin wrote, "within minutes." The embassy restaurant's freezer was next, and when the looting spread to the storerooms containing cartons of American cigarettes, the Marines finally began beating Vietnamese in the halls and along the embassy's staircases, in some cases stuffing the dropped cartons of cigarettes into their own pockets and duffels. Outside now, it was quiet. The thousands of Vietnamese who crowded every embassy gate were sitting quietly, hopelessly. If any looked up at the roof of the embassy, they would have seen smoke gushing from the chimney of the embassy's rooftop incinerator. Every piece of paper generated since the embassy's founding twenty-one years ago was being burned. As Frank Snepp notes, the Saigon CIA station alone had more than fourteen tons of material to put to the torch. In the days leading up to the evacuation, thousands of laminated name cards for high-risk Vietnamese had been printed up, reserving seats for them on outgoing evacuation planes. They had never been distributed. Now they, too, were being incinerated.

"[N]either Ford nor I," Henry Kissinger writes in his memoir, "could influence the outcome any longer; we had become spectators. So we each sat in our offices, freed of other duties yet unable to affect the ongoing tragedy, suspended between a pain we could not still and a future we were not in a position to shape." Kissinger describes an "almost mystical stillness" in the White House. He also describes what was tormenting him: namely, his "role in the next-to-last act: the acceleration of negotiations after Le Duc Tho's breakthrough offer of October 8, 1972. What has torn at me ever since is whether the demoralization of the Saigon structure which led to its collapse in 1975 started with the pace of negotiations we imposed . . . on the verge of both an honorable end of the war and national reconciliation."

Kissinger had been in a "position to shape" so many nations' histories, not only that of Vietnam but those of Cambodia, Chile, East Timor, Cyprus. It is a parade of such consistent misery that it is hard to believe that the baton leader could possibly allow himself a backward glance, much less a "pain" he would care to "still." The men whose professional acquaintance Kissinger had made during the Vietnam War—Nixon, Thieu, Ford—fared well only by comparison. In fact, only one species of humanity seemed to emerge with consistently full sails after dealings with Henry Kissinger: Asian Communists.

IX

Standing beside Johno's bed, you reach through a pure stillness so dense and soundless it seems to you almost mystical. Your cupped palm comes to rest upon your son's tiny forehead, his skin blood warm, vaguely humid. You marvel at how this hard shield of young bone only millimeters beneath Johno's flesh gives way to an impossibly soft edging of fine black hair. You rub a bit of his hair between your fingers. The inexplicable reality of Johno stuns you. This small, sleeping mass of tissue, growing as you gaze upon him, is your five-year-old son. You know how terribly fragile tissue is, how prone it is to tear and bleed, how inadequately scaffolds of bone protect their sinewy cargo of heart and lung and liver. You touch this intact and whole little body, knowing only that he is yours. Your son.

Sometimes you want to crush your boys, to hold them so close that everything damaged inside you is pressurized into nothing but love. Your love is an inferno that, miraculously, destroys nothing. You are in awe of this ferocious yet harmless love, and you pledge, as you needlessly fuss with Johno's blanket, that your boys will never doubt your affection, ever, under any circumstances. Your own father firmly withheld his affection, and did so without apology. Manhood, for him, began at twelve, and a few years after you had passed this magically transformative age he proved it to you by dying. You have never been able to quite believe the men and women around Escanaba who approach you with stories of your father's munificence. The doorman at the House of Ludington describing the Christmas Eve your father handed him the gift of a transistor radio. The woman whose rent your father covered during a hard time. The waiters who fondly recall his extravagant tips. These people are only a little younger than you and, unaware that you have few similar memories of your father, always seem to expect something more than your pained smile and clumsy retreat. But he was a good man. So good. This you recognized, then and now. You wish merely that he had not been so indirect in his goodness. Even in death he is stingy, for what are your memories of him now but deficits he still refuses to cover?

You stagger down the hallway while walls and doorjambs leap out at you and picture frames jump from their nails. You stop to rub your battered shoulder as the floor beneath you pitches and sinks. What is wrong with this house? Why is it attacking you? Your little sister Alicia's door: locked. You worry about her—such a stubborn girl!—and remember the night she looked icily at Muff, who was basting a roast. "My mother," Alicia announced, "didn't do it that way." Muff's head fell and quietly hung there for several moments. "I'm not your mother, Alicia," Muff finally said, looking over at her. "I'm never going to be your mother. And I'm sorry, but I can't do a thing about it." Stubborn, stubborn girl, arguing with an equally stubborn girl about a surpassingly stubborn woman. Jesus! You move down the upstairs hallway—a long dark space that deserves to be haunted—doorways passing you on the right, a solid bank of windows on the left. Your brother Paul's door is open. And there he is. He must have come in through the back and taken the narrow, rarely used staircase off the kitchen. His room smells like a brewery filled with sweaty socks next to a barnyard. Paul lies faceup on his bed, his open mouth emitting one chainsawlike snore after another, his arms flung out from his body and one foot still in its shoe. You stare at him, thinking, *All these people in my care. All these eyes that keep me informed of how often I disappoint them.*

They would not care to know the many beachheads of your concern. This house contains a multiplicity of futures for you to worry over. You can feel the future sometimes, moving through the passageways of the house, each version of it as distinct as an odor, each impossible to assign to its bearer. Like poltergeists of possibility, they drift by you, spin you around, and turn to mist as they pass through your spatulate fingers. And now another future seems to stir in the darker, more sinister quiet at the end of the hallway. You look through the floating shadows at this unknowable future—or is this something from the past? You are still outside Paul's bedroom and feel a sudden need to be elsewhere. You are only thirty-three, and already you have ghosts coming at you from every temporal direction. You go down the stairs (since when did they get so fucking steep?), stumbling once, near the bottom, turning your ankle and feeling it merely as the idea of pain—just as a ghost is merely the idea of a person, just as the future is merely an idea of the present.

Muff, promisingly, has left your bedroom door open, but you hesitate before going in. You know you are not ready for sleep. You are, in fact, horribly awake, your eyes so wide and raw they feel held open by tooth-picks. You stand a single step outside your bedroom's threshold, staring into the thick breathing blackness at the just-visible foot of your bed, its comforter aglow in moonlight. You are awake, but is she awake? Is she waiting for you to slip beside her? Two rooms away the television still murmurs, splashing the room between you and it with inviting color. The momentum of looking over at the adjacent room sloshes your body's weight to the right. You list, slowly begin to fall, regain some modicum of balance with two thunderous steps, and fall into a nearby chair so elderly its springs audibly break beneath your weight. Much better. You have begun to come to grips with the fact that your inability to stand up straight is not so much a matter of the house attacking you but more that you are afloat on a wave of alcohol.

Still: how *nice* it is to be drunk. Much better than getting drunk, which took so much alienating effort. But *being* drunk required no effort, and by the time you were drunk everyone was gone. But now, for some reason, you are tired. You sit there, enjoying this room in which no one ever sits. The room feels different from other rooms. The absences are lighter, a pleasantly unexciting novelty not unlike sitting in a car no one has yet owned. Nothing obligates you here, and the feeling is shiver-ingly unfamiliar. You feel cold. So many rooms in this house, and within them so many different kinds of warmth. Moments ago you wanted only to hold your boys. But your wife, the woman you love more than anything, you want only to avoid. Once you have convinced yourself that this, too, is a form of love, you stand. Your hand closes around your bedroom door's glass knob and pulls it shut. The door catches with a snap. You know if she is awake she has heard this. You are making as much noise as a convoy. She has heard the whole thing.

In the kitchen, you prepare to wash up the dishes left over from lunch. You remove your tie. You scrape various tidbits off the plates into a mangy brown paper bag, to be given eventually to Guenella. You prepare a bubble bath in the sink for the plates and silverware, and with infinite care you lower an aquamarine bowl into the tepid foam. Its resonant flint glass emits a sound full of muffled mellowness as it settles down to soak. You work very slowly, with a certain vagueness of manner that might be taken for a mist of abstraction in a less methodical man. You grope under the bubbles, around the glasses, and under the melodious bowl, for any piece of forgotten silverware—and you retrieve a nut-cracker. You rinse it, and are wiping it, when the leggy thing somehow slips out of the towel and falls like a man from a roof. You almost catch it—your fingertips actually come into contact with it in midair, but this only helps to propel it into the treasure-concealing foam of the sink, where an excruciating crack of broken glass follows upon the plunge. You hurl the towel into a corner and, turning away, stand for a moment staring at the blackness beyond the threshold of the open back door. You look very old, suddenly, weathered by emotion, until a film of tears dims your blank, unblinking eyes. Then, with a moan of anguished anticipation, you go back to the sink and, bracing yourself, dip your hand deep into the foam. A jagger of glass stings you. Gently you remove a broken glass. The beautiful bowl is intact—but of course, this is not my father. It is Nabokov's Timofey Pnin. This late scene from *Pnin* stands as perhaps the saddest few pages I have ever read. They have nothing to do with my father, of course. But neither does much of what I have written here. I am done trying to imagine how my parents experienced April 29, 1975. I scavenge Nabokov as I have scavenged all of my information about that night.

For the weeks and months I have been writing of this evening, for instance, I have been looking at a photograph of my mother. It is an old photo, white-bordered, its once-vivid colors now dim and tannic. She is sitting at the kitchen table of the Bissell house, a house I have no memories of her ever living in, a house in which I last slept when I was twelve. She is staring past my highchair-trapped brother, whose impish face is turned toward the camera. In the photo she wears too much eye shadow and a blue turtleneck, the costume in which my imagination has dressed her here. This photo is not from 1975. In fact, I have no idea when it was taken. (Neither does she.) The half-full can of Budweiser that my father discovers when he arrives home has its origin in this photo, as do the lip-sticked cigarette butts, as does the centerpiece loaded with knickknacks. I have ransacked this photo because it is virtually the only visual reference point I have for this time I could not experience and these events I did not witness. The Bissells were never a photographical family. Whatever photos were taken have been scattered by the various winds of divorce. About that I never much cared—until now.

While there is much I cannot know, I have come upon an equal amount I am unable to establish. My father says he came up with the name "Johno," yet my mother makes an identical claim. My Uncle Paul tells me he was married in 1974 and by 1975 was no longer living with my parents, yet both my mother and father initially remembered him being there in 1975. And although my mother says she has "no vivid memories of Saigon falling," she does "remember the day Elvis died." (I am sure, too, that I was demandingly underfoot for much of April 29, 1975, but the inanity of writing about myself as a sixteen-month-old baby made itself clear after one quickly abandoned sentence.)

The relentlessness of all this uncertainty is not local only to the story of my family. A party was held at the residence of the Polish ambassador to Vietnam, for instance, the day President Thieu resigned. Some present at the party claim it took place in the afternoon, others at night. When Thieu slipped out of the country later that day, some put forth the notion that he was carrying a suitcase filled with gold ("The clink of metal on metal broke through the stillness like muffled wind chimes"), while others argue he was not ("That story is just bullshit"). A disserta-

tion's worth of discrepancies exist between what Kissinger remembers and what Polgar remembers, between what Nguyen Cao Ky remembers and what Ambassador Martin remembers, between what Wolfgang Lehmann remembers and what Frank Snepp remembers. "I was appalled at what he told me," Snepp writes of Lehmann. "His version of the truth, as he spun it out . . . bore little relation to what I remembered."

Among other things, history is the arrangement of memory. History is an argument with the past. The United States could have won the war in Vietnam if its soldiers had not been forced to adhere to disastrously protracted battle plans when it was clear by 1967 that simply killing huge numbers of the enemy was not a realistic path toward victory. The war in Vietnam was unwinnable due to the historically empirical difficulty of stifling insurgencies toward which a sizable portion of the indigenous population feels sympathy. The war was won in Vietnam by 1971 and lost in Washington. By 1971 it was clear to those fighting in Vietnam that the losing U.S. effort had passed beyond all moral solvency. Or: My parents' marriage fell apart because of the emotional collapse my father suffered after the fall of Saigon in 1975. The marriage was over by 1972. "The reason we got divorced is because we got divorced. And frankly, it's none of your damned business." "Your dad could be the kindest, gentlest, most wonderful man." "I put a tremendous yoke upon her with Paul and Alicia, you know." "Things were bad for the last three or four years." "I think she wanted the marriage to be over, so she found someone else." "He did the best he could do. We all did. But I fell out of love with him."

Nothing is so impossible to imagine as disaster—until it is upon you. My father wrote my mother that he wanted to be with her for two thousand years. At the moment he wrote those words, any other fate must have seemed inconceivable. Henry Kissinger wrote that "the total Communist takeover" of Vietnam was a disaster that "four American administrations had resisted so strenuously for two decades." Indeed, defeat in Vietnam, the columnist Joseph Alsop wrote in 1964, would signify the surrender of "all that we fought for in the Second World War and in the Korean War." Secretary of State Dean Rusk wrote to President Johnson in 1965 that he was "convinced it would be disastrous for the United States and the Free World to permit Southeast Asia to be overrun by the Communist North." The unthinkably disastrous occurred nonetheless, and I—we all—live in the paradoxical normalcy of aftermath. Of course, I do not intend to equate the destruction of my parents' marriage with the collapse of South Vietnam, yet in my mind they are endlessly connected, just as the largest house can be entered through its smallest door.

Why do disasters demand such constant revisitation? Perhaps the first human being to delineate yesterday from today was not acting upon any natural observation but was instead seeking to commemorate some previously unthinkable event. *Where were you when? Do you remember?* We employ so many signifiers to hallow our larger, shared disasters that memory itself collapses beneath the weight. *I was there. I remember.* But all one truly remembers of most disasters is having forgotten what existence was like before they occurred. Disaster does not change one's world so much as narrow its parameters. Futures once as boundless as pastures shrivel into tunnels. What is lost in a disaster is never innocence. What is lost is a different sort of knowledge.

On April 29, 1975, my father was losing something of himself. He was losing what was at that time possibly the largest part of himself. This was his certainty that what he had suffered in Vietnam was necessary. In other words, he was losing his past and future all at once. He would lose much more. We all would. We would lose so much we would forget, perhaps, what it was we had lost.

X

With night falling over Saigon, sedans belonging to the U.S. government, their headlights shining, were arranged in a circle around the embassy's courtyard. Thomas Polgar, who by this time had likely begun to realize the Brobdingnagian nature of his analytical blunders, went to the wall to look for his beloved Vietnamese chauffeur, Ut, who had gone out earlier in the day to look for people Polgar himself had inadvertently stranded and now was unable to get back into the embassy. Polgar—who may have been drunk at this point—proved powerless to get Ut pulled up. "I think I saw him in the crowd," Snepp reports Polgar as murmuring, "but I could not reach him. I simply could not." Polgar now sank into what he himself called an "emotional coma." It is little wonder. The betrayals of so many Vietnamese—a series of careless American shrugs that tore lives in two—were growing apparent to all by the minute.

Hundreds of translators working for the CIA—men and women who were, in Snepp's words, "the best acquainted with CIA operations and personnel"—were left behind because the officer in charge of their evacuation took an early chopper out. Snepp also writes of the loyal U.S. Embassy guards of Nung descent—the Nung are one of Vietnam's eternally oppressed aboriginal people—with whom he exchanged words on April 29: "Remember us," one Nung guard said to Snepp. It was "one of his few English phrases. That was the last I saw of him. He and all the rest would be left behind." The embassy's switchboard could scarcely handle the number of calls coming in. Lacy Wright, a State Department officer, picked up one call. "We've been up here all day and nobody has come to get us," the caller said, through heavy sobs. Wright swallowed hard, offered some useless advice, and hung up. More calls. One hundred and fifty people were trapped here. Two hundred more were trapped there. "We were told to come here. What do we do?" "I'm a Vietnamese, but I got my American citizenship in 1973. I've got three kids. What can I do?" Eventually, the embassy phone was simply not answered. Meanwhile, according to Snepp, Graham Martin overheard this exchange over the walkie-talkie in his office: "Hey, there's another gook climbing over the wall. Shoot him!" "I can't shoot him. For chris-sakes, let him over."

Later in the evening, President Ford's chief of staff, a man named Donald Rumsfeld, cabled Martin about a pressing matter: "I understand that 154 IBM employees, including their families, are still awaiting removal from Saigon. I further understand they are now standing in front of the IBM building awaiting instructions where they should go for evacuation. I ask you to do your utmost to see that they are evacuated with the current helicopter lift." One's heart goes out to these stranded souls. But it is a scenario of depressing familiarity that, among a metrop-olis of identical desperation, the only people our future secretary of defense felt any urge to look after were employed by a major U.S. corpo-ration. Despite Rumsfeld's efforts, the IBM employees never made it out. Nor did the employees of Esso and Shell, whom Martin had earlier counseled to stay for the good of the country. None of the Vietnamese working for Western corporations received payment for their last few weeks of work. It has been estimated that the unpaid back salaries owed to Vietnamese by Western companies amounted to almost $1 million.

At the Defense Attaché Office complex, 2,700 Vietnamese and Amer-icans were suffering occasional, nonspecific potshots from disillusioned ARVN snipers. The specter of dying at the hands of South Vietnamese soldiers grew so dire that one American joked that "we were going to lock ourselves in a room . . . and pray for the arrival of the North Viet-namese Army." One sniper was finally shot by Air Force officers. Another firefight, in the words of Sergeant Kevin Maloney, took place "right outside Tan Son Nhut. They made a big deal at the time about us getting out of there without firing a shot—well, I'm telling you what, the people who were saying those things weren't in Saigon." This was not the only instance of fighting between the United States and Vietnamese. As President Ford later sheepishly admitted to Congress, U.S. and North

Vietnamese forces engaged in combat at several places on Saigon's out-skirts. PAVN missiles were fired at U.S. Phantom jets, for instance, and the jets responded with missile barrages of their own.

Frank Snepp wrote that, as the DAO evacuation neared completion, one U.S. official took "one final look" at Tan Son Nhut air base: "As far as he could see, the airfield was littered with fireballs, each going from blue to green to brilliant white as it rolled its way through rows of parked air-craft. He stared out at these Disneyesque images for a few moments, unable to believe that they, and everything else he had witnessed this day, were now part of the irretrievable past." Shortly before midnight, the last of the Marines guarding the DAO were extracted, and the explo-sives placed throughout the complex were detonated by remote control from the DAO evacuation's final helicopter. The sky filled with magne-sium-fed fire. Five miles away from the DAO, those within the steel wombs of Marine helicopters rising from the embassy's roof and court-yard felt their eyes fill with flames. Keyes Beech: "Tan Son Nhut was burning. So was Bien Hoa." Lacy Wright: "[Y]ou could look out to the west and see Long Binh Base burning. A huge, huge fire. . . . Everything that we had tried to do was going up, literally, in flames." Ken Kashiwa-hara: "It looked like the entire countryside was exploding in flames. . . . It really looked like all of Vietnam was burning."

Two hours before the DAO was destroyed, Ambassador Martin, his hair (in the journalist Bob Tamarkin's words) "perfectly combed," appeared to survey the damage done to his embassy. He said nothing, was not recognized, and vanished back inside. By now those at the embassy were waiting as long as fifty minutes between helicopter land-ings. When the White House asked if Martin might not be able to speed things along, he responded by cable: "Perhaps you can tell me how to make some of these Americans abandon their half-Vietnamese children or how the President would look if he ordered this. For more than 50 minutes there have been no CH-53s here. And only one CH-46." The ambassador never lost his barbed nature, removing a photo of Henry Kissinger from an embassy wall and replacing it with a map of Hanoi. "May as well let them feel at home," Martin said. Two hours after his previous cable, he was again hectoring the White House: "There is now a long lull. Nothing in last twenty minutes. . . . I sure don't want to spend my May Day here." The North's evacuation deadline of midnight had now passed, which General Dung, waiting on the edge of Saigon, equated with the raising of "a divine hammer." ("Once the bamboo is notched," PAVN soldiers were told by their officers of the assault on Saigon, "one blow is enough to break it.") By 12:30 a.m., the approaching rumble of PAVN artillery could be heard within the embassy's reinforced walls. Parties of eighty Vietnamese at a time were slowly making their way upstairs to the embassy roof "like toothpaste through a tube," in the words of one American. On the roof itself, a few Marines, no doubt driven to something resembling madness by the day's activity, began to "conduct" the crowds of Vietnamese to sing. The Marines, CIA agents, and embassy factotums not on the roof were going through the embassy destroying everything of possible use. One Marine was seen reading a copy of *The Fall of Rome*. Frank Snepp himself found a book: Don Oberdorfer's *Tet!* Snepp left the book where he found it, believing the embassy's next tenants "might be somewhat amused to learn what the Americans had thought of that last great offensive." By 3 a.m., the evacuation was twelve hours behind schedule.

At 4:15 a.m., Martin cabled the White House for the last time: "Plan to close mission at about 0430 30 April local time. Due to necessity to destroy commo gear, this is the last message from embassy Saigon." Minutes later, the embassy's communications officer whacked the "commo gear" with a sledgehammer, and Marines destroyed the rest with explosives. Martin made his way to the roof, which was, in Snepp's account,

> a vision out of a nightmare. In the center of the dimly lit helo-pad a CH-47 was already waiting . . . its engines setting up a roar like a primeval scream. The crew and controllers all wore what looked like oversize football helmets, and in the blinking under-light of the landing signals they reminded me of grotesque insects rearing on their hindquarters. Out beyond the edge of the building a Phantom jet streaked across the horizon as tracers darted up here and there into the night sky.

After an aide checked the courtyard to make sure he didn't "see any white faces," Martin climbed aboard the *Lady Bird 9* carrying the American flag. It was 4:47 a.m. With Martin were various embassy personnel, including Ken Moorefield, and two missionaries. The chopper rose into a morning sky filled with monsoon-spawned lightning and headed for the USS *Blue Ridge,* the Seventh Fleet's flagship. Only months later, in a Hanoi museum, Ambassador Martin's departure from the embassy roof would be depicted in a primitive diorama, to the delight of Vietnamese children.

Unfortunately, anywhere from 400 to 420 Vietnamese were still in the embassy waiting for their promised evacuation. Army Captain Stuart Herrington was with some of them. As Martin's helicopter left, Herrington screamed at them in Vietnamese, "*Khong ai se bi bo lai!*" Nobody's going to be left behind! "And I believed it," he later told Larry Engelmann. Among those left behind were Vietnamese firemen who had been providing crowd control (their families had gone out earlier), a gaggle of drunk and unconscious South Korean diplomats, and a German priest, who, in Herrington's words, "helped out." Before they could board choppers, the evacuation was terminated by White House order. The remaining Americans were told to be on the next flight out. Herrington argued, but it was no use. He informed the Vietnamese waiting with him that he was going to the bathroom and ducked away for the roof. On his way there he passed the embassy plaque that was inscribed: "In memory of the brave Americans who died defending this Embassy during the Tet Offensive, 1968." Such was Herrington's bitterness that he said to himself, "To hell with the plaque." It was later salvaged by an American journalist who had stayed in Saigon to cover the Communist takeover.

By 5 a.m., Herrington and three American civilians were the only non-Marines left in the embassy. One was the journalist Bob Tamarkin. The others, an American man and an American woman, refused to give Tamarkin their names. History will know them only for their deluded bravery, as they had come to help their Vietnamese friends escape the country before realizing the situation was hopeless. "You know," Tamarkin heard the man say, "I had ordered $100 worth of tailor-made clothing yesterday when I arrived, and I paid for it in advance." The last civilian helicopter left the U.S. Embassy with only four people on it. Herrington: "I was sickened, naturally. I never in my life felt worse, never will feel worse than at that moment walking away from those people. . . .

I just couldn't stop crying." In his memoir, Henry Kissinger would claim that he had no idea how the roughly four hundred Vietnamese had been abandoned. This is strange if only because the military officials present at the embassy said the evacuation had been terminated "by presidential order" *after* it had been made clear that many Vietnamese were being left behind. As he was borne aloft, Tamarkin looked down into the embassy courtyard. There, "hundreds of Vietnamese looked up," waiting for the next helicopter.

In *Decent Interval,* Frank Snepp mentions "the legacy and shame of total defeat" that many Americans felt while abandoning Saigon to its fate. "There is a simple truth," Aleksandr Solzhenitsyn once wrote,

> which one can learn only through suffering: in war not victories are blessed but defeats. Governments need victories and the people need defeats. Victory gives rise to the desire for more victories. But after a defeat it is freedom that men desire—and usually attain. A people needs defeat just as an individual needs suffering and misfortune: they compel the deepening of the inner life and generate a spiritual upsurge.

Operation Frequent Wind was not, by any metric, a victory, despite its success in extracting from Saigon 1,373 Americans, 5,595 South Vietnamese, and 85 third-country nationals. The largest helicopter evacuation in history, Frequent Wind saw only two fatalities, when exhausted pilots were forced to ditch their helicopter over the South China Sea and were never found. Even General Dung, in his memoir, marveled at the success of the evacuation, the last thirteen hours of which were far from the entire story. Over the month of April, 51,888 people (45,125 Vietnamese and 6,763 Americans and other foreigners) had been airlifted from South Vietnam. Another 6,000 left by barge, and an unknown number thought to be in the low thousands escaped on unrecorded "black flights" engineered mainly by the CIA. Another 65,000 South Vietnamese escaped on their own. But the number of Vietnamese abandoned must exceed this total number by factors of five, ten, fifteen. In a war of such endless ambiguity and suffering, it is somehow fitting that even the stunning success of the evacuation was qualified with so many dismal failures and betrayals.

Nor was it over. Shortly after Herrington and Tamarkin's helicopter cleared the roof, Kissinger learned that "elements of the 9th Marine Amphibious Brigade protecting the evacuation—comprising 129 Marines—had been left behind for some inexplicable reason." The airlift was resumed. Major Jim Kean, the commanding officer of the Marine unit responsible for protecting the evacuation, later told Larry Engelmann that he knew the Marines' withdrawal could trigger "a big donnybrook in front of the embassy door." After slinking away from their posts unnoticed, many of the Marines in Kean's command were thinking, "My God, we're only thirty seconds away from pulling this thing off without a fight." Of course, "all hell broke loose. The crowd outside realized what was happening . . . and they panicked." The Marines retreated deeper into the embassy, locking out the Vietnamese charging after them and littering the stairway to the roof with "big old fire extinguishers" to slow any who made it past the bolted doors. A CH-46 arrived, and the Marines were forced to leave behind their flak jackets and helmets in order to squeeze more men on board. Soon only eleven Marines were left. They were, as Major Kean notes, the last U.S. ground forces in Vietnam.

For a dismayingly long time no more choppers arrived. My father in Michigan was just returning home from work as dawn arrived in Saigon, where some Marines slept on the embassy rooftop as the sun came up. Others watched President Minh's "cavalcade of cars" pass by the embassy on its way to the palace. Before driving away, a few of Minh's guards shot at the looters tearing apart the open floors of the U.S. Embassy. While some Marines were counting ammunition in case they had to make a stand against the sixteen PAVN divisions driving into Saigon, Major Kean did "something kind of funny," which was to whip out his .45 and pump into the embassy's satellite dish antenna every bullet he had. Eventually the Vietnamese smashed through the barriers the Marines had established and were now pounding against the locked rooftop door. "An arm smashed through the window of the door under the helipad," David Butler writes. One Marine "got to it fast and pulled the arm into the broken glass, and it was yanked back with a cry. . . . More arms reached through the broken window. So they kept a man there to grab the arms and jam them into the glass." This Marine also sprayed the intrusive Vietnamese with Mace. One Vietnamese man had succeeded in crawling up the side of the embassy, but someone dropped something heavy and knocked the man off as though he were nothing more than a barnacle. The final chopper set down on the roof at 7:53 a.m. Major Kean ordered that the helipad be teargassed as they lifted off. The last Marines to leave Vietnam thus caught a rotored-up miasma of gas while keeping their weapons fixed on the Vietnamese still trying to break through the rooftop door. The last words spoken by a Marine in South Vietnam: "Hey, Major, they want to know what kind of pizza you want in Manila!" Kean was not sure if he would be court-martialed for using tear gas. "Ultimately," he told Engelmann, "they gave me a medal."

The last, fiercest fighting of the war occurred on the northern edge of the city, near Tan Son Nhut air base, as the Marines were leaving. "I really had no idea we were fighting the last battle of the war," one PAVN colonel would tell the journalist David Lamb years later. "We had been fighting for so long it was hard to believe the war would not go on forever. That morning the enemy fought well. The fighting was very heavy. There were dead on both sides. Then just like that the firing stopped and the war was over."

As the war ended, a thirty-year-old Australian journalist named Neil Davis was eating a croissant on his hotel's patio. Davis was a beloved figure in journalistic circles. He had given thousands of dollars of his own money to war orphans throughout Southeast Asia and secretly paid for an operation that corrected the crippled leg of an eleven-year-old Saigon girl. He had been in Cambodia as Phnom Penh fell to the Communist Khmer Rouge earlier in the month, an experience that had hardened his determination to stay on in Saigon. "No more running," he had said, according to David Butler. "It's fucking humiliating." After finishing his coffee, Davis walked over to the Presidential Palace. Save for a few looters, the city around him was as empty and silent as an asteroid. Throughout their efforts to conquer the South, the Communists had counted on a popular general uprising or, in Communist argot, a Popular General Uprising, that would throw off Saigon's puppet government. The Tet Offensive had been the North's first major attempt to trigger the general uprising. Its failure was total. The Communists tried again during the Easter Offensive of 1972. Again the only southern response was acrimony, directed toward both the Communists and the Saigon government. Even on this day, with the Communist victory complete, there was in Saigon—"always the home of the entrepreneur and the collaborator," in Frances FitzGerald's words—no uprising, only silence. On the radio were twelve-hour-old broadcasts from the Voice of America. At the U.S. Embassy, amid the shells of scorched sedans, people were still waiting to be evacuated. Snepp's Nung guards were there. In a few hours they would all be rounded up and many of them shot. As the morning progressed, a message recorded by President Minh began to play throughout the city over loudspeakers that had previously been used as air-raid sirens: "I believe firmly," Minh's voice announced to the quiet city, "in reconciliation among all Vietnamese. To avoid bloodshed I ask the soldiers of the Republic to put an end to all hostilities. . . . I also call on our brothers, the soldiers of the Provisional Revolutionary Government, not to open fire."

Meanwhile, PAVN tanks and Chinese-built trucks were filling up central Saigon, many covered in foliage to ward off the air attacks that never took place. Some of these tanks' occupants climbed out into the sunshine and were approached by worried, curious Saigonese. The soldiers were mostly bumpkinish boys. They were surprisingly friendly, though one witness to the liberation noted that most of these short, pale young men were wearing ill-fitting uniforms: "You know what they looked like? They looked like tourists who were lost." Faced with the wonders of Saigon, many of the Communists had questions for their defeated countrymen. According to David Butler, one question was "How could an army from a city like this not fight for it?" Another was "Why did you let us win? It will be terrible now."

Neil Davis wandered into the Presidential Palace, which within days would be renamed Reunification Palace. There, in a "wide, carpeted marble stairway," he ran into President Minh. Again, David Butler's *The Fall of Saigon:*

> [Minh] was dressed in a dark-tan safari suit, and was unshaved and red-eyed. Davis was certain that the new president had not slept that night. He was almost as certain that he had recently been weeping.
>
> "Oh, Mr. President," Davis said, not in commiseration but in the tone of voice with which one says, "Oh, fancy meeting you here." The two men had known each other for years. They shook hands. And then Davis' mind went almost blank as he wondered what one said to a president, and a general, who had just surrendered after thirty years of war. Finally he asked, "What are you doing?"
>
> "I'm waiting for the other side," Minh answered.
>
> "Are they going to come here?"
>
> "Yes, very soon."
>
> Davis now could think of no way to carry the conversation forward. He initiated a parting handshake. Minh turned and walked toward the president's office down a long, open passageway colonnaded with marble columns along the front of the building. Davis filmed the retreating figure, thinking it was one of the saddest shots of his career.

Minh had an abundance of circumstance over which to weep. Waiting for the Communists to arrive at the Presidential Palace was not what the South's leaders had envisioned. They had recently remodeled a penthouse in the riverfront Majestic Hotel, which they had planned to use as a negotiation room. On April 24, the penthouse was destroyed in a PAVN rocket attack. As David Lamb notes, Minh also had trouble summoning his cabinet due to the fact that all of the palace's switchboard operators had fled. In a final indignity, the general who had that morning transmitted President Minh's cease-fire order, Nguyen Huu Hanh, was a secret Communist agent.

Davis drifted back outside. It was a beautiful, blue-skied day. Dragon-

flies, hundreds of them, floated about in the air. About fifty ARVN soldiers were lounging beneath the many trees on the palace grounds.
None was holding a weapon, and some were in their underwear, having
shed their uniforms in the optimistic wish that they would be mistaken
for civilians. Then Davis noticed a T-34 tank—which he initially believed
was an ARVN tank—coming down the street toward the Presidential
Palace's front gates. Its treads clapped harshly against the pavement, and
it fired one artillery round—the last such round fired during the war—
over the palace. A few blocks behind the lead tank was a T-54 that contained Colonel Bui Tin. Colonel Tin was the only member of the 203rd
PAVN Armored Brigade who had ever been to Saigon. He had with him
a photo of the Presidential Palace, "so I knew what we were looking for,"
as he would tell Larry Engelmann. The tankers did have orders, however,
that read: "Cross the Thi Nghe Bridge. Proceed straight ahead on Hong
Thap Tu Street. Go seven blocks and turn left. [The palace] is right in
front of you." Despite this, the 203rd had gotten lost in Saigon's streets.
The lead tank had overshot the palace by a block on its first attempt to
find it, and its crew sheepishly accepted the guide services of a UPI-
employed Vietnamese photographer, who would later wind up in a
reeducation camp. The lead tank, Tank 844, was driven by Bui Duc
Mai. Emblazoned on the helmets of Mai's crewmen: "Onward Saigon!"
Davis, fumbling to get his sixteen-pound camera up onto his shoulder,
hurried over to the palace's entrance in order to get a better shot of Mai's
tank as it bore down upon the heavy iron gates. The world suddenly
shrank to fit within his camera's lens.

So much would happen, not only in the coming moments but also in
the coming weeks, months, and years. Neil Davis would not get the shot
he wanted, for the gates were opened before Tank 844 reached them.
The indelible image of 844 triumphantly crashing through the gates was
a minutes-later reenactment—so attuned were the victors, even at the
instant of their victory, to the power of propaganda. Colonel Tin would
find President Minh in his office. Minh would say, "I have been waiting
since early this morning to transfer power to you," to which Tin would
answer, "There is no question of your transferring power. Your power
has crumbled. You have nothing in your hands to surrender and so you

cannot surrender what you do not possess." The red, blue, and yellow National Liberation Front flag would in twenty minutes be flying from the Presidential Palace's flagpole. Saigon would be renamed Ho Chi Minh City, despite the fact that apparently its eponym's most vivid memory of his brief time spent there was his discovery of ice cream. President Minh would be arrested, consigned to a reeducation camp for a short time, and then, in 1983, be allowed to leave the Socialist Republic of Vietnam for France, where he would never speak of the war. General Le Minh Dao, who at Xuan Loc had vowed to be the shore against which PAVN's human waves would break, would perish in a reeducation camp in 1984. Nguyen Dinh Tu, the author of the "Fare Thee Well" dispatch, had numerous connections that would have allowed him to leave Saigon in the war's closing days, but he stayed to cover the Communists' arrival, belatedly realizing that there was no one left to publish his dispatch, and would die in a Saigon prison in late 1975. Air Marshal Ky would open a liquor store in California that would go bankrupt. Ambassador Martin would suffer rumors among Washington's chattering classes that he had gone insane, retire from active State Department duty in 1977, and not get as much as a good-bye luncheon thrown for him. Communist Vietnam would invade Communist Cambodia, Communist China would invade Communist Vietnam, and there would remain Americans compelled by the logic of the Domino Theory. One million Vietnamese would abandon their country during Vietnam's first decade of reunification, despite the fact that the two Vietnams had suffered no significant exodus (other than the Catholics' mass departure from North to South Vietnam in 1956) in three previous decades of more or less continuous war.

In 1975, you did not live in the world as it is today. There was no cable news, no live feed or satellite phone that would have allowed you to experience Saigon's final, inarguable fall while you sat in your Escanaba, Michigan, living room. There were only reports. Uncertain news from Indochina. Sketchy details emerging from Saigon. The most recent update. The last anyone had heard. Was living any easier when disaster was routinely secondhand? Were we all more able to relax? Or did you know, somehow, what was happening? Had you felt it? Are you feeling it now, as you rise from your couch, leave your unlit home without telling Muff, and wander out into the chilly spring night? What are you thinking as you start your car? How do you feel as the cold, ninety-proof vapors of your breath vanish in the car's gradually warming interior? Does the road look any different to you now as your headlights spill whitely over it? When you pass out of Escanaba and into the timbered silence of its surrounding woodlands, do you think at all of what will happen to you, your family, your children? You ride your chariot through two tall closing walls of darkness. At 11:10 p.m. Eastern Standard Time, when the gates of the Presidential Palace in Saigon are finally bashed from their stone pillars, do you flinch? And if so, is there any place for this sharp pain to go? The trees keep coming, the darkness beyond them never ending. Does the darkness have any bottom? Will it swallow you whole or crash down upon you? You are not sure. All you know is that now the darkness stands before you. You cannot go back. Your only choice is to drive right into it.

TWO

An Illness Caused by Youth

OR

A Few Queries About the Vietnam War

My father, it was your sad image,
so often come, that urged me to these thresholds.
My ships are moored on the Tyrrhenian.
O father, let me hold your right hand fast,
do not withdraw from my embrace.

—VIRGIL, *THE AENEID*

I

While sitting next to my father on the All Nippon Airways flight from Tokyo to Ho Chi Minh City, I finally grasped what had been bothering me. It was not the odorlessness of the processed cabin air, or the tidally sustained roar of the engines, or even the handful of tranquilizers I had gobbled. What bothered me was the increasingly unsettling sensation of simply being beside my father. Somehow he made me feel physically diminished. Perhaps fathers could not help but make their sons feel smaller. What was a father if not the one man who would always wield power over his son? One did not have to love (or even like) one's father to sense this essential inequality. I loved my father very much, but I was suddenly a little too reminded of him, which is to say, a little afraid.

I studied the hairy hands that held open the Vietnam guidebook I had bought for him: thick fingers, big knuckles, huge glossy nails. I then regarded my father's head. It seemed something out of a circus tent. I could not even look at it all at once. His round, wet eyes, Kilimanjaran nose, lost-cavern nostrils, and geological chin dimple belonged to separate facial ecosystems. The westernmost edge of the United States' mainland was eleven hours behind us, and his striking physiognomy occurred to me now because during the previous legs of our trip I had been seated one row ahead of my father, not next to him. I had also tired of the book I had brought aboard and was actively searching for something to think about, since, while flying, if I was not vigilant, my thoughts tended toward the macabre, such as, for example, the imminence of my own death.

Maybe all I really felt was simple filial humility. I recalled the famous schoolyard question: Can God create a boulder so large that even he cannot move it? Similarly, could a child ever feel bigger than his parents? I was not thinking of size. Rather, could a child feel *existentially* bigger? I did not believe so. I doubted it. And with that the various sleep aids I had ingested began, once again, to bring on the ugly process of manufactured sleep: eyelids as heavy as anchors, mind blown out like a candle, head in free-fall. . . . My nose smooshed hard against my father's shoulder. I sparked upright.

My father adjusted himself in his seat, still reading. Then, in an instructive singsong voice: "If you sleep now you're going to spend the first few days completely jet-lagged."

Moments before our first flight this morning, I had taken an Ativan, an antianxiety medication. I took another Ativan right after we lifted off. A few hours later I took another. In Tokyo's airport I washed down another with a Diet Coke. I had taken a Sominex about an hour ago. I had also drunk a Sapporo. None of this was so I could sleep. The odds of my falling asleep on an airplane were cosmologically long. The reason I had taken the pills was to relax.

I was now touching my head with fascination. "I think my hair has lost its curl."

My father looked over at me and asked, almost fondly, "How can anyone who travels as much as you be so afraid of flying? It's ridiculous."

"*Of course* it's ridiculous. *All* pathological fear is ridiculous. It's not as though I'm afraid of much. Flying, sharks, snakes. The classics."

My father shook his head, the overhead light igniting around his head a dandruffy nebula. Thankfully, he changed the subject. "Do you know that today is the Marine Corps's two-hundred-and-twenty-eighth anniversary?"

"No kidding?"

A single nod. "November tenth."

"Are you thinking this is a good omen or a bad omen?"

"I'm not thinking anything. I just thought it was a neat coincidence."

He returned to his reading. I stared out my window at a moon so close and bright I could count the dark wrinkles around its craters. Flying to Vietnam on the 228th anniversary of the United States Marine Corps: "a neat coincidence," indeed. While growing up, I had associated nearly everything about my father with the Marine Corps and Vietnam.

There were two types of Vietnam veteran: those who talked about the war and those who did not talk about it. My father talked about the war, though, if anything, this only deepened the abyss between us. I had learned something from discussions with those who had veteran fathers. This was that our fathers seemed remote because the war itself was impossibly remote. Chances were, the war had happened pre-you, before you had come to grasp the sheer accident of your own placement in time, before you recognized that the reality of yourself—your bedroom, your dolls and comic books—had nothing to do with the reality of your father. This strange, lost war, simultaneously real and unimaginable, forced us to confront the past before we had any idea of what the past really was. The war made us think theoretically long before we had the vocabulary to do so. Despite its remoteness, the war's aftereffects were inescapably intimate. At every meal Vietnam sat down, invisibly, with our families.

Inspired, I pulled out my handheld tape recorder. "Hold on. I'd like to get some stuff down." I pushed the plastic brick toward my father's mouth.

His dubious eyes took their time traveling from me to the tape recorder before they returned to his guidebook. "All right."

"I don't think we've ever really talked about why you joined the Marines. Why *did* you join the Marines?"

He did not look up and spoke very softly. "I'd always wanted to be a Marine, so I enlisted after I graduated from college. It was that simple. I couldn't get any other job."

"But you went to Georgetown. You couldn't get a job after Georgetown?"

"Do you plan on letting me read?"

"You can read in a minute. Let's get this down."

"What was your question?"

"Georgetown. You couldn't get a job."

He sighed and looked straight ahead. "Well, there was a huge recession then. I suppose I could have worked in a department store or something. But I liked the Marines, I enlisted, and once they found out I could spell 'college' they sent me to Officer Candidates School."

"You did this knowing Vietnam was coming."

"We all knew it was coming. Keep in mind we did not train for Europe or the desert or mountain warfare. We did not go to northern California. We went to the swamps of Virginia. We knew exactly where we were going. Our drill instructors told us. Our officers told us. 'We are headed for Vietnam. You and me, brother.' "

"Did it ever bother you that Johno and I didn't join the Marines?"

His face scrunched thoughtfully. "I don't know if I would say it *bothered* me. . . . It could have been something for me to feel some pride in, yeah. I don't know." Back to reading.

"Let me ask you about these Marine Corps commercials they have nowadays."

He looked tired. "Which commercials?"

"The one with the knight defeating an evil sorcerer, getting hit by lightning, and turning into a Marine. Or the one with the guy fighting a magma monster in a volcano, getting hit by lightning, and turning into a Marine."

His hand moved in an oblique, conjuring manner. "I've seen them."

"But have you ever seen Soviet propaganda? One major difference is that Soviet propaganda had some connection, however deranged, to reality. Is being a Marine *at all* like fighting sorcerers?" No response. "Doesn't seeing those commercials bother you, as a Marine?"

"Absolutely not."

"Come on. You don't find it a little bit weird?"

"It's an honorable career."

"That's not what we're talking about."

He held out a flattened hand, palm up. "What is a Marine's job? A Marine is a professional soldier, trained to kill. He's not trained to do anything else except kill, sustain himself in a horrible situation, do whatever good he can, and accomplish what he's told to do by his superiors. Or her superiors. Like it or not, that's a Marine's job. It's not always right, or correct, but that's what Marines are sworn to do."

At this he retreated back into his guidebook. I decided I would leave him alone, switched off the recorder, and watched our bunned and kerchiefed Japanese stewardesses wander up and down the 777's plastic corridors. Finally I was left staring into the blank shallows of the television screen mounted in the seat before me.

As a boy, I dreaded those evenings my father had had too much to drink, stole into my bedroom, woke me up, and for an hour at a time would try to explain to me, his ten-year-old son, why the decisions he had made—decisions, he would mercilessly remind himself, that had gotten his best friends killed—were the only decisions he could have made. Other nights, he would remember fondly the various women he had courted in Vietnam, of which there seemed an extraordinary number, giving over my still-unformed imagination to bizarre thoughts of myself as an Asian boy. With my school friends I would tell elaborate stories about my father. How he had single-handedly fought off an entire company of "gooners." The day he had gotten lost rafting down a river and survived a waterfall plunge. The time he had been multiply shot and how a kind black soldier had dragged him to safety. Some were true; most were not. The war had not ended for him, and soon it was alive in me.

Sometimes it felt as though Vietnam was all my father and I had ever talked about; sometimes it felt as though we had never really talked about it. Oddly, the Vietnam War had given me much for which to be thankful, such as the fact that my father's friend and fellow Vietnam veteran Philip Caputo ultimately became my literary mentor. My father makes a brief appearance in Caputo's *A Rumor of War,* which is commonly regarded as one of the finest memoirs of the conflict and was the first Vietnam book to become a major bestseller. When in *A Rumor of War* Caputo learns of the death of his and my father's friend Walter Levy, who survived all of two weeks in Vietnam, he remembers a night in Georgetown when he, Levy, and some others went to a bar "to drink and look at girls and pretend we were still civilians." And then this: "We sat down and filled the glasses, all of us laughing, probably at something

Jack Bissell said. Was Bissell there that night? He must have been, because we were all laughing very hard and Bissell was always funny." I still remember the first time I read that sentence—I was twelve, thirteen—and how my heart had convulsed. Here was the man of whom I had never had as much as a glimpse. Here was the man whose life had not yet been hewn by so much death, whom I did not find in bluish, 2 a.m. darkness drinking wine and watching *Gettysburg* or *Platoon* for the fortieth time. In *A Rumor of War* I saw the still-normal man my father could have become, a man with the average sadnesses.

I used to stare at his framed purple heart ("the dumb medal," he always called it) and, next to it, a photo of him taken during his training at Quantico: BISSELL stenciled across his left breast, friendly Virginia greenery hovering behind him, my smirking father looking a little like a young Harrison Ford, holding his rifle, his eyes unaccountably soft. How I had wanted to find that man. A dinner with a magazine editor, during which we were supposed to come up with ideas I might write about, led me to talking about my father and, inevitably, about Vietnam. The magazine editor, having regarded my earlier ideas as "terrible," looked at me, leaned back, and said, "*That's* what you should write about." I was almost thirty years old, my father just past sixty. It staggered me, suddenly, how little relative time we still had left together. I knew that if I wanted to find the unknown part of my father I would have to do it soon, in Vietnam, where he had been made and unmade, killed and resurrected. Months ago I told my father over the phone that a magazine was willing to send us to Vietnam. He was quiet, as quiet as I had ever heard him. "Gosh," he said.

Now, on the plane, the Japanese captain made the announcement that we were "making our final approach" into Ho Chi Minh City, his English pronunciation that of a man whose tongue had been injected with codeine.

My father's head tilted at a doglike angle. "What did he say?"

"I think he said we were 'baking our final perch.' "

"I thought he said we were 'making our finer porch.' "

We laughed, and then my father's large hand clamped down on my knee. He squeezed too hard and for too long. "You okay?" I asked him.

He nodded, then smiled. "Nervous."

"Well. I'm nervous, too, if it makes you feel better."

He thought about this far longer than I had intended, which was not at all. "That does not make me feel better."

I had decided I would not learn any Vietnamese before going to Vietnam. At one point or another this had seemed like a good idea. At one point or another most bad ideas seem like good ideas. Language is culture, and the particularities of Vietnam's seemed at the time beyond the ken of whatever I might wrest from my father's and my trip. I was also not that interested. The war interested me, as did much of Vietnam's history, as did how entangled both had become in the double helix of the American psyche, but to me the only striking thing about Vietnam's language and culture was how unmitigatedly foreign they were, and, I suppose, part of me wanted to keep them that way. While I would eventually realize exactly how idiotic this was, the lesser stupidities of the idea were already clear to me by the time my father and I passed into Tan Son Nhut airport's wide, yellow-walled customs area.

I could not read a thing. Of course, most of the important signs had an English translation beneath them (how excellent of the world to accommodate its cheerful monoglots, its English speakers), but these translations did nothing to lessen the sensation of utter illiteracy that came over me. This preemptive awareness was so sudden and powerful that my father would later ask me why it was I had stopped cold when we walked into the customs area. I stopped because I realized I had never before traveled in a place where I was so thoroughly unable to communicate. During my previous travels I had always been at least able to fake a greater awareness than that which I actually had. Faking awareness was immensely useful in Communist and former Communist countries, as most are police states. The mere appearance of awareness was often garlic to secret-police vampires. But I could not say a single word in Vietnamese. Not one. I could not even say "one." Gamma rays of cluelessness emanated from my body.

I had not expected this. My last six months had been spent doing little but reading about Vietnam. Only in the past few weeks had I felt as though I was beginning to know something of the place. (That feeling, I now knew, was illusory.) Rigging me to Vietnam were some powerful but extremely gossamer connections, all of them traceable to my father's service. Vietnam also subtended many of my more abstract interests: the legacies of colonialism, the theory and practice of revolutionary Communism, the various forms of moral suicide committed by intelligent people in search of a consistent worldview. Now I was in the place I had been reading about and anticipating for months—and within my chest were fluttering streamers and within my head an absent white glow.

My father, on the other hand, was smiling as he helped an elderly Vietnamese woman with her luggage. Blinking, stunned, I followed him through customs and straight out into the humid facewash of the Ho Chi Minh City night. It was not that hot, but it was a wet and energy-stealing tropical heat. The representative from the tour service we had hired—a short, squat-faced young Vietnamese woman wearing glasses that looked like a sideways 8—coolly directed us toward a white four-door Toyota. I had not been ecstatic about procuring the services of tour guides, but I had known we really did not have a choice. We jumped in back, and the car began to move. I was in Vietnam with my father, and all around us was Ho Chi Minh City. All around us was Saigon. My father had been to Saigon only once, as a junior officer, for an hour, in 1965, to pick up some movies to show his troops. My mind, bludgeoned by sleep aids, worked out its new parameters while my father leaned forward and spoke to the young woman from the tour service in a very clear tone of voice, each word as distinct as it was loud: "Does anyone still call the city Saigon?"

"Most people," she said.

My father waited for more, a pleasant, inviting look on his face. This look faded as the silence continued. "Right," he said finally. He then asked, for still puzzling reasons, "And what street is this we're on?"

The woman took her time saying something to the driver before she bothered to answer my father. "Nguyen Van Troi."

My father gave her a long look, then sat back. "Okay," he said quietly.

I could tell he was hurt. This young woman was not a guide, though; she was simply the person who was picking us up, taking us to the hotel, and once again driving us to the airport in the morning for our flight to Hue. We were not staying long in Saigon, and we were not her responsibility. Still, I decided I did not like this young woman. Perhaps she was sick of Americans, who had been coming to a unified Vietnam in large numbers for only about a decade now. The biggest, most concentrated rush of Americans began in 1993, as the economies of Asia began to expand during what was called the Asian Miracle. Most of these incoming Americans were businesspeople and their various shield bearers. In 1995, the United States and Vietnam began to normalize relations. More Americans came. Then, in 1997, the prosperous economies of Asia once again began to obey the laws of financial gravity, and many of the American businesspeople left Vietnam. Next to go were the Americans who enjoy traveling to places rumored to be undiscovered by other Americans, a hard attribute to square with Vietnam, considering that in living memory it had been home to the most massive American incursion in history, but, all the same, they moved on to wherever it is such people go. So now in Vietnam you mainly had that happily unendangered species known as the American Tourist. Retired American tourists want to come to Vietnam and see everyone courteous and friendly and smiling and let bygones be bygones and stuff their faces with delicious Vietnamese food. Younger Americans want to come and buy a Ho Chi Minh T-shirt, and this is if they have brains, but most young Americans do not, in which case Vietnam is fucking *awesome.* Then there is the slightly older American male tourist traveling to Vietnam. Often he is alone. There are two types of these. The first is a veteran, who has simply no idea how to deal with you. The second, who will likely have a mustache, probably just wants to have sex with you.

None of it was any excuse for hurting my merely curious father's feelings. Thankfully he already seemed over it, squares and orbs of Saigon's primary-colored light moving across his still, watchful face. How to describe Saigon, the awesome unreality of Saigon? To imagine Saigon, for more than a decade the American capital of Asia, one must first consider that after 1975 the city had been forced to wear Marxist handcuffs for fifteen years. Once released, it had enjoyed throughout the 1990s one of the most steroidal economies in Asia. Today Saigon was responsible for consuming a third of Vietnam's entire state budget. This was only fair, as it provided 80 percent of Vietnam's tax revenue. It was the richest, biggest city in the region (some say 60 percent of all Indochina's money sits in Saigon banks), a place where the Citibank logo now glowed with iconic confidence on the side of a modest skyscraper. It was also an extremely poor city in which many gainfully employed Vietnamese lived two, three, four to a very small room and shared toilets by the dozen. "Saigon is no longer the charming mix of colonial grace and 1960s kitsch," Robert Templer writes in *Shadows and Wind: A View of Modern Vietnam,* "but a late twentieth-century urban disaster-in-waiting with many of the failings of other cities in the region." A city of the future, then, a city of the past. And it was the best of times, it was the worst of times. Saigon was amazing, it was vaguely disappointing, and in it one could imagine every kind of life making its home here, every kind of experience. It was a city of people who moved through it looking slightly stunned.

Saigon was also louder than a tractor pull in an aluminum stadium. Flowing through its streets, as quickly as platelets through veins, were approximately 3 billion scooters. "My *goodness,*" my father said as a versicolor flash flood of beeping little scooters overtook us on all sides. "Look at them all!" Thanks to these scooters—a sort of half-moped, half-motorcycle hybrid—we were now learning about one of Vietnam's more extraordinary innovations. This was the incredibly busy intersection that did not have a stoplight. What happened at the incredibly busy intersection that did not have a stoplight was this: fifty scooters and three cars came from the north, forty scooters and five cars came from the west, and then without stopping they all passed through the intersection at the same time. This went on all day, at all hours, all over the city. It sounds impossible. But then fish do not collide, flocks of birds do not collide. Phenomena of the type we were witnessing are not unknown to nature. It all seemed to work phenomenally well and would continue to seem that way until I read a report about Greig Craft, the founder of an advocacy group known as the Asia Injury Prevention Foundation. The report noted that 40 percent of the world's road deaths occur in Asia and that Vietnam has the most road deaths in Asia. Thirty-seven people a day were killed in Vietnam in traffic accidents. As the report noted, this is the equivalent of a 767 fully loaded with Vietnamese crashing thirty times a year. (It is also a little more than half the number of civilians who used to die every day during the American War.) "No one saw it coming," Craft is quoted as saying in the report. In one generation, "Vietnam went from buffalo to bicycle to motorbike." The leading cause of death for U.S. tourists in Vietnam? Road crashes.

I began to pay close attention to the way people here handled themselves on the road. Few Vietnamese wore helmets, and in many cases entire families (father, mother, two children) were riding on a single scooter. How better to shear away an entire branch of one's family tree? Despite how much the Vietnamese adore children (the nation has one of the highest childhood inoculation rates in the world, and nearly every Vietnamese child can read), numerous smiling and horrifically imperiled children were riding draped over the handlebars of their families' scooters. One father smoked a cigarette while steering his scooter with one hand. With his other hand he held a cell phone to his ear. Nestled in the crook of his arm was what looked to be a several-month-old baby.

We were coming upon District 1, which provided Ho Chi Minh City the same deeply unrepresentative mask that Midtown provides Manhattan. District 1 was where many worked and few lived, where less adventurous visitors came to base the entirety of their impressions, where the night sky's every star was consumed by terrestrial light. Here in the updated Babel of District 1's confusion there was an overabundance not of language but of product. Citibank was the least of it. Around us were doors and awnings emblazoned with names such as the American Board of Cosmetic Surgery. There was a bar called Heart of Darkness and a club called Apocalypse Now. Here was an Isuzu showroom, there a L'Occitane boutique. Yamaha, Kentucky Fried Chicken, Sheraton, Sanyo, Bulgari, HSBC, Ford, L'Oréal. Across the streets and upon the people fell the softly invincible radiance of all this neon.

The common thing to say after noting the incorporated roll call of Saigon billboardry was that the Communists of North Vietnam won the war but lost the peace. But any Communist regime that stayed in power after the dissolution of the Soviet Union had some idea of what it was doing. It should be recalled that Vietnam's Communist leaders had attempted to apply the tenets of formal Marxism as long as they could, though there were Party members who questioned the logic of Marxism as early as the late 1960s. In its insistence on implementing Marxism, though, the core leadership of the Communist Party of Vietnam nearly accomplished what thirty years of warfare could not: the unconditional destruction of the country.

The Vietnamese Communist Party was not known for its quick studies. Hanoi erected its first statue to Lenin in 1985, and three years later parts of Vietnam were afflicted with famine despite First Secretary Le Duan's 1975 promise that after ten years, every full-tummied Vietnamese family would have a television and a refrigerator. To have abandoned formal Marxism by the late 1980s was not particularly surprising or any kind of hangdog admittance; it was dire necessity. For all the reform the Party had allowed, it maintained a rigor mortic grip on most of Vietnam's industries. Its current leadership was a colorless, anonymous lot at best. Its prime minister had a third-grade education, a deputy in its equivalent of our Drug Enforcement Agency was convicted of drug smuggling, and its minister of trade was caught with more than $1 million in cash taped to the bottom of his dining room table. Frustrating masters, certainly, for what was, by most accounts, one of the planet's most resilient and hardworking populations.

The squat-faced woman from the tour service dropped us off, established the implausibly early time she would be back in the morning, and lickety-split drove away. I picked up my big red duffel and began to walk toward our hotel's glass doors to check in. But my father hooked my arm in his and asked if we might just stay here for a moment. So we stood on the curb outside our hotel, looking around at Nguyen Hue, District 1's main drag. A huge, busy, bright, vibrant, vaguely seedy city center. And Vietnam. No use minimizing the psychic impact of this, or blowing it off. As wildly unrepresentative as this may have been, it was Vietnam. "Tremendous," my father said after a while. "Just tremendous."

"I know. You wake up, take a couple plane rides, and suddenly the trees are tropical and the urinals have different shapes."

My father squinted at something down near the end of the street.

"What's that over there?" He was pointing across a clogged traffic circle at a large, beautiful palace, formerly a French hotel, now "the most photographed building in Saigon" (I was basically reading the guidebook aloud to him), that, of course, the Communists had commandeered and made the People's Committee Building of Ho Chi Minh City. The Vietnamese flag—yellow star, red field—hung with humid limpness from the pole fixed atop the palace's highest, most central tower. The People's Committee Building, which on the outside was as fancy as a wedding cake and on the inside was reputed to be breathtaking, was of course closed to all actual people.

"Why would they take such a beautiful building like that and close it off?" My father shook his head. "Communism is funny stuff."

He intended this as a friendly jab at me. For many years now my father had operated under the belief that his youngest son was a Communist. The evidence: at seventeen I had announced I was a socialist and adamantly carried in my back pocket a copy of *The Communist Manifesto* that I occasionally attempted to read. Years later there was apparently nothing I could do to convince my father that I was not a Communist, not even publishing a book that was essentially a 353-page attack on Communism's horrible legacy in Central Asia.

"That's nothing," I told him, passing back his guidebook. "Stalin had Moscow's Temple of Christ the Savior—a thirty-story-tall building that took sixty years to build and was probably the greatest architectural achievement in Russian history—razed to the ground. Its foundation for years was a public swimming pool."

"Speaking of Stalin . . ." Again he was pointing, this time at a granitey black statue that stood at the center of a small park before us. Among all the lights the shape of the stone was easy to make out: Ho Chi Minh, an adored child in his lap.

The book I had been reading on the plane was William J. Duiker's biography *Ho Chi Minh*. (Professor Duiker, in speaking of his Penn State students over the years, once uttered some of the truest, most memorable words ever about the Vietnam War: "They still cannot grasp that the war had something to do with other people.") That his Communist son was reading a book about Ho Chi Minh had greatly bemused my father. All day he had been asking for updates—*How's Uncle Ho? What's he doing now? Oh, yeah? Now where is he?*—and then sadly shaking his head. Here on the streets of Saigon I looked at my father and said, "You're equating Ho with Stalin?"

He put up his hands and smiled. "Oh, of course not. I wouldn't dream of it. Oh my goodness, no."

"Because I'm not sure that comparison holds water, actually."

"Oh, I know. Absolutely not. Charming man." Again he shook his head, smiling at me as though I were, at most, seven years old. "Come on, you twerp. Let's go check in."

A little later, electrically awake thanks to sleep-aid blowback, I lay clothed atop a tightly made bed, thinking about the Ho Chi Minh statue. It had replaced an earlier statue that honored ARVN soldiers slain in battle, which was yanked down by Communist lassoes soon after the 1975 takeover. The position of the Communist Party of Vietnam, essentially unaltered since 1975, is that South Vietnam never existed. What existed was a "puppet" state. What of ARVN? ARVN never really existed either. Puppet army. Also, there was no Vietnamese civil war. What happened in 1975 was not a violent takeover but a revolution against this puppet state.

Despite the Party's obfuscation, many people believe that North Vietnam and South Vietnam still exist. Some Vietnamese, once you have come to know them, may even tell you that the divisions between North Vietnam and South Vietnam are deeper, the wounds more profound, than those that exist between Vietnam and France, between even Vietnam and the United States. There are many reasons for this beyond the war. Due in part to the south's historically heavier French presence, the scholar Neil L. Jamieson writes, "Southern villages have always been more open, less corporate, more tolerant of individual initiative and cultural heterodoxy"—a land of easygoing Buddhism. Others are blunter: life for those in the sterner, more Confucian north, whether because of its climate, its generally poor soil, or its closeness to China, has been much harder, historically speaking, than life for those in the south. People who lead hard, mentally blunting lives are typically more vulnerable to—and tolerant of—the devices of dictatorship. Prior to 1945, however, Communist insurgency was a far more powerful force in the southern part of Vietnam, particularly among Trotskyist Communists, most of whom would ultimately be killed by the Viet Minh. In the north of Vietnam the French were far more repressive when faced with political agitation, and the north's peasants were too poor to put much faith in Marxist abstractions. The south's major social problem was landlordism, making it a fecund breeding ground for revolutionaries.

Of course, what eventually became South Vietnam had not been in any sense free; it had been run by a series of nasty and horrendously corrupt regimes. But was it a literal dictatorship? One barometer of dictatorship is freedom of the press, freedom of information. In North Vietnam there existed one official newspaper, *Nhan Dan* (The People), which was (and today is) the Party paper; one television station, which was the Party television station; and one radio station, which was the Party radio station. In South Vietnam more than twenty-seven popular, inconsistently censored newspapers competed for large weekly readerships, and its three television and twenty radio stations "were free," in Richard Nixon's admittedly qualified words, "to express dissenting opinion within certain bounds." The one untrammeled dictator South Vietnam was unlucky enough to have, Ngo Dinh Diem, wound up shot to death in the back of a truck.

Shortly after Saigon's fall, a Communist official exhorted the city's worried masses not to worry, that the only people who had been defeated were "the American imperialists. . . . Anyone with Vietnamese blood should take pride in this common victory of the whole nation. You, the people of Saigon, are now the masters of your own city." But Truong Chinh, one of North Vietnam's most bloodthirsty ideologues, soon announced that the Party would "level" all differences between the North and South. The "poisonous weeds" of capitalism had to be pulled up and burned. In this way the long and ongoing process of Communist refurbishment began.

One can guess with minimum imagination most of what the Communists did after reunification. First they banned all books whose titles did not include the words "Ho," "Lenin," "Marx," or "Communism." Then they emptied the libraries. Absolutely. This was done right away. Then they got to work on the schoolbooks. Some Soviet educators were brought in to help out, since properly removing all the facts from history can be challenging. Next the Communists closed all Buddhist pagodas. Every single one of them. Then, in every city but especially in Saigon, the Communists renamed many of the streets and parks and buildings and schools. Freedom Street was renamed General Uprising Street (leading to the common Saigonese joke "After the General Uprising we lost our Freedom"), and so on. In Saigon, though, the Communists did keep a few of the French street and school names. Pasteur, for instance. He was a nice man. And Marie Curie. She won the Nobel Prize. But the rest had to go. Then came the reeducation camps. The Party has always stressed that it never carried out the "bloodbath" promised by the U.S. and Saigon governments and that it "treated with clemency not only the Vietnamese who collaborated with the enemy, but also military prisoners." That would depend on how one defined "clemency." It would also depend on how one defined "bloodbath." Most scholars believe that 5,000 South Vietnamese military and civil officials were executed outright for "crimes against the people" in the aftermath of reunification. Considering the length and viciousness of the war, this is not a shocking number. The number of people sent to reeducation camps is another matter. Despite Ho's statement during the war that the "puppet soldiers are also sons of Vietnam," the first year of the South's liberation saw at least 300,000 Vietnamese being told to report for a month of *hoc tap,* or political reeducation. Bags were meagerly packed, families kissed goodbye—but none of these people returned after a month. Most did not return after a year. While a relatively small number of people were killed in the camps and surprisingly few were tortured, the conditions were brutal: starvation rations, no contact with loved ones, forced labor. These 300,000 reeducated souls, a chagrined former minister of justice was careful to stress, were all notable South Vietnamese officials. In other words, the figure did not "include people who were arrested in the sweeps by government organs and military authorities that terrorized Saigon and the provinces during that period." The number of these less prominent reeducated South Vietnamese may be more than a million.

Two kinds of people had it the worst in the camps: those employed by ARVN's psychological warfare department, and writers. Scholars inclined to forgive Vietnam's Communist regime claim that 90 percent of those who survived reeducation were released by 1978. This is debated. The Vietnamese offered to empty their reeducation camps in 1982 and send everyone to the United States, but when the United States could not promise that those released would not discuss reeducation camp conditions, the offer was rescinded. Throughout the 1980s, former ARVN generals were still being set free. In 1988 alone, eleven were released. At any rate, with reeducation fully under way, the Vietnamese Communists then decided to collectivize the country's agriculture. In the past many Communist countries had collectivized their agriculture, which is to say that many Communist countries had abolished the private ownership of land and turned it all over to the state. The end result of nearly every Communist collectivization known to history had been famine and misery. This was widely known by the time the Vietnamese were planning collectivization. Famine and misery followed the collectivization of Vietnamese agriculture.

The Party's vision for its reunified nation also had less classically dogmatic aspects. For instance, morning exercise. The Vietnamese Communist Party decreed that all people had to wake up at six, walk out into the street, and engage in morning exercise. The Communists also decreed that people everywhere in Vietnam had to sit through all movies until the very end. Then, for the fun of it, they banned all of South Vietnam's most popular musicians, even those who were not political, even some who had supported the insurgency. Then the Communists began to destroy the cemeteries of the 200,000 ARVN war dead. Yes, they destroyed cemeteries—just as the South Vietnamese had destroyed Viet Minh war memorials in the 1950s. These ARVN soldiers' names, units, and identities were lost forever, their bodies interred beneath stones engraved only with UNKNOWN or PUPPETS. The North's war dead, known as MARTYRS, were buried in grand cemeteries that government volunteers were instructed to keep meticulously clean. The mothers of these soldiers received lifelong pensions, free health care. The mothers of ARVN soldiers received nothing, and for years many were denied basic government services. Then the Communists banned the *ao dai*. The ao dai is a ceremonial, somewhat kitschy garment worn by Vietnamese women. Its roots are in the ancient past, but its modern design—swooshy silk pantaloons beneath a bright tight dress that is slit up the side so that it reveals a tiny triangle of waist flesh—comes from the 1930s. The ao dai, both extremely revealing and extremely discreet, is by general consensus one of the world's sexier garments. Nevertheless, the Communists banned that too. No ao dais. They also banned ancestor worship, the most important and widely shared form of religious devotion in Vietnam. That had to go. Then they tried preventing families from selling *pho*, the national dish of Vietnam, from homemade stalls. Most of Vietnam's traditional foods were frowned upon by the Communists for years. Instead eat this imported Bulgarian cabbage. Have this good Communist borscht. Then they banned martial arts.

On most of these forbiddances and edicts it took the Party a decade to lighten up. Amazing. It was truly amazing to me, as I lay there. Obviously, no one had been expecting reunification to be candy and sunshine. But rather than encouraging the most educated and highly trained remaining citizens of South Vietnam to work with them to lift up their devastated country, as most were prepared to do, the Communists, with their vindictiveness, drove a million Vietnamese away and ruined the lives of millions more. And that was not all. Just as no statues honor the puppets, none, astonishingly, honor the National Liberation Front—that is, the Viet Cong. Late in Frances FitzGerald's 1972 *Fire in the Lake*, one finds this passage:

> With North Vietnamese help the NLF has fought the United States for over a decade and remained undefeated. Standing in the place of all Vietnamese, it has carried on the tradition of [the fifteenth-century patriot] Le Loi and those other Vietnamese heroes who waged the millennium-long struggle against foreign domination. . . . Their victory would not be the victory of one foreign power over another but the victory of the Vietnamese people—northerners and southerners alike. . . . [I]t is possible that success might cause the revolutionary movement to disintegrate, just as it

all but dissolved the Liberation Front in Algeria. But it seems unlikely.

FitzGerald's somewhat disquieting enthusiasm for the NLF failed to foresee the possibility that what would dissolve the NLF would be not victory but the leadership of North Vietnam.

It is not out of fussiness that I refer to the NLF rather than the Viet Cong. Viet Cong, or Vietnamese Communist, is actually not correct, as the Front was not an exclusively Communist movement. Most NLF guerrillas would not have known the dialectic from a diacritic. The secret ruling core of the NLF was ardently Communist—its public ruling core was composed of various left-wing insignificants—but the Front was given its name by its masters in North Vietnam to avoid alienating South Vietnam's non-Communist nationalists.

Even Ho Chi Minh was sometimes irritated by the independent-mindedness of the South's insurgents, complaining in 1949 about their excessive individualism. The NLF also had many factions, which troubled the North's leadership. Many in the North believed that the NLF was undisciplined. Here the old men of Hanoi had a point. There are on record numerous NLF desertions to the South (overseen by the Chieu Hoi, or "Open Arms," amnesty program, which racked up an amazing 47,000 deserters in 1969 alone) but hardly any recorded desertions from the North Vietnamese Army. The NLF, for its part, never forgave the northern leadership for the Tet Offensive, the military failure of which nearly wiped out the NLF—particularly a useless second offensive Hanoi ordered months after it was clear that the first assault had resulted in a massacre.

So when in 1975 NLF members joyously rushed to fly the Front's colors from Saigon's Presidential Palace flagpole, it would prove premature. While Ton Duc Thang, Ho Chi Minh's elderly successor as president of North Vietnam, said publicly in Saigon that "the whole Vietnamese people will share a new happiness," it soon became obvious that the North Vietnamese intended no such happiness sharing. As Truong Nhu Tang, a prominent NLF leader who later went into exile, wrote, "our police and security were being handled exclusively by various [North Vietnamese] departments." Tang does note that this "was not a new development" but goes on to say that "before . . . we had been involved in a common struggle, in which our organizations had faced severe manpower and expertise shortages. Now, with victory, it was somehow different." North Vietnam's staunch Maoist Truong Chinh quickly made it known to NLF members that they "had no further role to play," in Tang's words. These NLF men and women, who had joined the insurgency out of belief and desperation, who had suffered and died by the hundred thousand, were no longer important. They were, Tang writes, an "obstacle" to what he bitterly calls the North's own "imperialistic revolution." Tang writes finally that "there was no way to swallow the gall in our mouths or to shrug off the shroud that had settled on our souls. We knew finally that we had been well and truly sold." Tang's NLF comrades would bring up the rear in the victory parade after the liberation of Saigon.

Only in the late 1980s did the betrayals of many who had aided the Party's long grasp for power begin to come to light in Vietnamese society. One Party veteran who had defected to the West while ostensibly getting medical treatment in East Germany wrote scathingly of how the "Le Duan clique" had betrayed Ho Chi Minh's revolution. Duan, a jug-eared neo-Stalinist who after Ho's death went to great lengths to encourage the Uncle Ho personality cult, had in actual fact worked to isolate Ho politically in the last decade of his life, even purging some of Uncle's allies. Other former Party luminaries—among them Bui Tin (the northern colonel who accepted President Minh's surrender in 1975), Hoang Minh Chinh (a war hero), and Nguyen Ho (an early comrade of Le Duan who memorably wondered how Vietnam could reconcile with the United States but not itself: "Are dollars the condition for reconciliation?")—emerged as critics both within and without Vietnam in the late 1980s and early 1990s. Former NLF Colonel Pham Xuan An (who doubled as a *Time* magazine correspondent during the war) spoke for many NLF veterans when he said, "All that talk about 'liberation' twenty, thirty, forty years ago, all the plotting, and all the bodies, produced this, this impoverished, broken-down country led by a gang of cruel and paternalistic half-educated theorists." Unfortunately, these critics were quickly brushed aside by the obedient Vietnamese press, occasionally jailed by the authorities, only fitfully noticed by the Vietnamese public, and largely ignored by much of the West.

Meanwhile, a block away, a frozen child lay across the frozen lap of the frozen icon who had founded this frozen government that my poor father had fought a doomed, misguided war in order to prevent. It was going to be an interesting trip.

Query: *Was Ho Chi Minh a Stalinist?*

In Ho Chi Minh we have a man playful enough to have sent messages to his staff members in the form of paper airplanes and ruthless enough to have said of his purged and executed friend Ta Thu Thao, "All those who do not follow the line that I have set out will be smashed." In the view of Ho's longtime comrade Pham Van Dong, "Ho Chi Minh is high but not far; new but not strange; great but does not make up greatness. . . . Seeing him for the first time, one has a feeling that one knew him long ago." One American agent of the pre-CIA Office of Strategic Services (OSS) remembered Ho this way: "If I had to pick out the one quality about that little old man sitting on his hill in the jungle, it was his gentleness." The French diplomat Jean Sainteny, who unsuccessfully negotiated with Ho to prevent the outbreak of the First Indochina War, claimed his Vietnamese counterpart was a man "of the highest caliber . . . [with] his intelligence, his vast culture and total unselfishness." A description of Ho Chi Minh from a French intelligence dossier: "Fearless, sly, clever, deceptive, ruthless—and deadly." As an American psychological warfare expert in Saigon once complained to a journalist, "You know, it's damned difficult to go out and tell people to hate a guy who looks like a half-starved Santa Claus."

Ho Chi Minh: Che Guevara with an epicanthic fold? Who else has been compared to Lenin *and* Gandhi? Probably the most rhapsodic mainstream Western appraisal of Ho remains David Halberstam's 1971 biography: "In his lifetime Ho had not only liberated his own country and changed the course of colonial rule in both Africa and Asia, he had done something even more remarkable; he had touched the culture and soul of his enemy." The least favorable recent look at Ho (which angrily cites the above passage) comes in Michael Lind's fiercely argued 1999 polemic *Vietnam: The Necessary War,* in which Ho Chi Minh is "Stalin's Vietnamese disciple."

Ho Chi Minh (Chinese for "he who brings enlightenment") was the final identity of a complicated man. Like the wispy beard he would make famous, the name was initially taken up as a disguise. He was born Nguyen Sinh Cung, renamed by his parents Nguyen Tat Thanh, left Saigon on a French steamship in 1911 as Van Ba, made his revolutionary name abroad as Nguyen Ai Quoc, attacked the French in pamphlets as Nguyen o Phap, traveled to the USSR as Chen Vang, served as a Soviet translator as Ly Thuy, wrote articles for the Soviet press as Nilovsky, infiltrated rival Vietnamese revolutionary groups as Wang Shan-yi, traveled in Siam as Father Chin, worked in Hong Kong as L. M. Vuong, was arrested in Hong Kong as T. V. Wong, was interrogated in Hong Kong as Song Man Cho, served China's People's Liberation Army as Major Hu Guang, wrote inflammatory anti-French articles as P. C. Line, chaired the Vietnam National Liberation Committee as Hoang Quojun, picked up in a Chinese prison the name Hu Lao Bo, fought the Japanese as Mr. Hoo, worked as a U.S. agent in World War II under the code name Lucius, attacked the United States in the North Vietnamese press as C.D., and finally wrote biographies of himself as Tran Dan Tien. There are more aliases, but one gets the idea. In a file somewhere there is an old visa request for one Ho Ting-ching, whom the U.S. Office of War Information wanted to send to San Francisco to broadcast pro-American propaganda in Vietnamese during the early 1940s. Just as Fidel Castro failed his tryout for the Washington Senators, this idea was rejected. Ho Ting-ching, or Ho Chi Minh, had a different appointment with fate.

Ho Chi Minh was born in 1890 in a three-room hut to a low-level imperial bureaucrat father and a literate storytelling mother in the central province of Nghe An. According to Ho's biographer William J. Duiker, Nghe An's people are "known as the most obdurate and rebellious of Vietnamese," and, in time, they would rebel against even Ho Chi Minh.

Educated in French schools in Vinh (a city whose population U.S. bombing would decades later literally reduce to zero) and Hue, Ho engaged in his first political activity when he offered his translation services to a crowd of peasants seeking redress from the French authorities. In return the young man received several wallops from an intemperate French policeman's baton. Ho got off easy: within hours the French opened fire into the crowd. The next day at Ho's school French officials turned up looking for a "tall dark student" who had been involved in the demonstration. Ho was expelled that day, wandered the countryside for months, earned money by teaching Chinese and martial arts, and, after taking a trade school course in pastry cooking, ultimately hopped a steamship out of Saigon and traveled around the world, eventually mastering seven of its languages. Whether he was in Africa, the Americas, Asia, or Europe, Ho Chi Minh noticed black and brown and yellow men laboring beneath European whips (he also claimed, somewhat dubiously, to have seen a KKK lynching in the American South), and those experiences created in him the realization that Vietnam was merely one flower in a planetary garden of human exploitation.

But was he a Stalinist? By the time Ho was thirty he was living in Paris and had become a founding member of the French Communist Party, the only group that took his critiques of colonialism seriously. As World War I ended, Ho wrote his first, fairly moderate tract, "Demands of the Annamite People" ("Annam" being the French protectorate that today corresponds to the central third of the Socialist Republic of Vietnam), and attempted to bring it before President Woodrow Wilson at Versailles. Despite what one historian has heartbreakingly described as Ho's "spiffy suit" (it was a rental), Ho failed to catch Wilson's eye. Ho went on to publish "Demands" in several Socialist magazines under the name Nguyen Ai Quoc, or Nguyen Who Loves His Nation. The French police figured out that Nguyen Ai Quoc was actually Nguyen Tat Thanh, the expelled radical from Hue who had disappeared several years before, and began to track him. (Ho sometimes left notes for his pursuers cheekily outlining his day's itinerary.)

Around this time Vladimir Lenin ordered the French Communist Party to join the international organization of parties known as the

Comintern. The FCP's radicals agreed, but its moderates did not. Ho Chi Minh sided with the radicals, even though he still knew so little about formal Communism at this point that he was heard to ask what Marxism meant. Ho's writings soon darkened considerably, and his letters to Vietnam became so revolutionary in tone that the colonial French authorities were soon monitoring their recipients. Yet, as a historian writes, "one can only be amazed at how *little* [Ho's writings] offer: most of them are polemic tirades about some obscure French official in some remote province who beat up his houseboy, raped the kitchen-maid's daughter, and closed the village school."

In 1923, one year before his idol Lenin's death, Ho made his first trip, by invitation, into the Soviet Union. How was Ho Chi Minh greeted in the young socialist utopia? He was arrested. Eventually Ho became a well-known foreign Communist in Moscow and grew close to the prominent Soviets Nikolai Bukharin and Grigory Zinoviev. Photos of Ho at this time reveal a young, tie-wearing man of Mormon intensity. Ho's first break came as Mikhail Borodin's translator in Canton, China, though he understood his real job to be setting the stage for Communist revolution in Vietnam. China at the time was home to several anticolonial movements of ethnic Vietnamese, few of them Communist but many violently opposed to the French. As often as possible, Ho Chi Minh infiltrated such groups and Marxified them from within. In 1930, working closely with Soviet agents, he founded the Vietnamese Communist Party, later the Indochinese Communist Party, later the Vietnam Workers' Party, and later yet again the Vietnamese Communist Party. In 1931, British authorities collared Ho in Hong Kong during a regional crackdown on radicalism, the first of his several arrests. A British official judged Ho to be "one of the worst agitators in the region" and went on to say that

> one's sporting instincts of course are in favor of letting the man go to Russia instead of in effect handing him over to his [French] enemies, but I think that this is a case for suppressing those instincts. Revolutionary crime in Annam is a really low-down dirty business, including every kind of murder, even burning public officers alive

and torturing them to death. For much of this crime Nguyen is personally responsible, and it is not in his favour that he has directed the affairs from afar instead of having the guts to go and take a hand in things himself.

But Ho was released, possibly because he agreed to inform on his colleagues to British intelligence, possibly because it was decided he was ineligible for extradition to French-controlled territory. By 1934, Ho Chi Minh was back in Moscow. This was a bad time to be in Moscow. Joseph Stalin's Great Terror—a scourge so fanatically thorough that even President Mikhail Kalinin's *wife* was arrested—was transforming from a storm into a whirlwind. Ho's old comrades Zinoviev, Bukharin, and Borodin were all purged and executed. According to Duiker, there is some evidence that Ho himself was investigated during the Great Terror, which if true means that Ho Chi Minh is one of the only human beings known to have emerged from the other side of Stalinist justice. By 1938, Ho was begging the regime that killed his friends "not to leave me too long without activity and aside and outside the Party." He was finally given a job lecturing on Vietnamese history at a Soviet institute. In other words, Ho Chi Minh walked into an evil insane asylum and made it out alive, apparently unshaken, and seeking the encouragement of mass murderers. Indeed, a file has a Soviet handler speaking of "special plans" for her Indochinese comrade.

Was he, then, a Stalinist? If so, Stalin is not believed to have been fond of Ho, nor Ho of Stalin. (Ho's relationship with China's Mao Zedong, despite Ho's early fervor in translating Mao's work into Vietnamese, was similarly tenebrous. Ho is said to have privately and caustically referred to Mao as the "Celestial Emperor," and Mao's regard for the Vietnamese in general was negligible.) It took Stalin five revealingly long years to recognize Ho Chi Minh's regime once it declared its independence, and Stalin treated Ho so poorly during his first state visit to Moscow (a highlight: "Oh, you Orientals—you have such rich imaginations") that Nikita Khrushchev later described Stalin's behavior as "disgusting." All of which would appear to argue against Ho's Stalinist credentials. Unfortunately for Ho's admirers, his Stalinist proclivities became discernible during North Vietnam's August Revolution in 1945, the purges of North Vietnam's government soon thereafter, and the infamous land reform campaigns of the mid-1950s.

Ho's behavior following the August Revolution is most easily defended. During World War II, Vietnam had been controlled by the Nazi collaborators of Vichy France and then by the Empire of Japan. With a small amount of covert U.S. assistance, Ho and the Viet Minh waged guerrilla war against the Japanese. (Another of Ho's duties was rescuing American pilots shot down over the South China Sea. Virtually none of the U.S. agents or soldiers Ho worked with or rescued was later contacted by the U.S. government for their insights into Ho's motivations.) The orphaned colonial nation of Vietnam emerged from the chaos of World War II with no clear master and in the midst of a Japanese-caused famine that would kill one to two million Vietnamese. In August 1945, Ho Chi Minh filled the power vacuum by walking into Hanoi's Ba Dinh Square and taking his perch on the balcony of the French municipal theater building. Before 400,000 people, Ho proclaimed the founding of the Democratic Republic of Vietnam—"probably the swiftest and most bloodless Communist takeover on record," according to the historian Bernard Fall. It was the first time Ho, who was now fifty-five, had ever been in Hanoi and one of the first times he publicly used the name Ho Chi Minh. Ho could not use the name Nguyen Ai Quoc, as Quoc was a known Soviet agent, and Ho was aware that the Party did not yet have the support of the masses. For similar reasons Ho had formally dissolved the Indochinese Communist Party to create the illusion that a nationalist rather than a Communist party was coming to power. As Ho was founding his nation on purely nationalist pretenses that even Duiker admits were false, the forces of Free France rushed en masse into the similar vacuum left in Saigon to the south.

France's ultimate refusal to recognize the legitimacy of Ho's Hanoi-based government created numerous problems. While Ho attempted for appearance's sake to cobble together a representative government, some of Ho's colleagues within the Viet Minh were less solicitous and began murdering those who opposed them; there are references at this time to "Ho and his gang of cutthroats." Nevertheless, given his precarious situation, it is hard to imagine that Ho was giving overmuch thought to which class enemies should be shot. One of the non-Communist nationalists assassinated by the Viet Minh was Ngo Dinh Khoi, the older brother of South Vietnam's future president Ngo Dinh Diem. Khoi's crime was having collaborated with the Japanese against the Viet Minh, and his son was killed alongside him. In Stanley Karnow's telling, Diem was brought before Ho six months after his brother's death. When Diem accused Ho of having murdered Khoi, Ho said, "I knew nothing of it. I had nothing to do with your brother's death." To his face Diem called Ho "a criminal who has burned and destroyed the country." Ho Chi Minh, far from being a merciless Stalinist, offered Diem a job. When the offer was refused, he let Diem go.

The purges of Ho's representative government in the years leading up to the First Indochina War are less easily defended. The first results of Ho's August Revolution were not promising: a nation split in two, standing foreign armies all over the country, an unstoppable famine devastating the population, and no diplomatic recognition. The Japanese, despite their surrender to the United States, were taking their time in leaving Vietnam. To Ho's horror, the war's victorious Allied powers gave the (not yet Communist) Chinese the duty of occupying the northern half of Vietnam while the Japanese withdrew, and the British were charged with overseeing the Japanese withdrawal from Vietnam's southern half. Skirmishing among these forces, the Viet Minh, and various other indigenous Vietnamese political groups (one a scurvy gang of river pirates) inevitably broke out. All the while, the French were attempting to once again don the colonial mantle, forcing Ho to negotiate with the French while attempting to placate the Chinese while attempting to earn the amity of the British while attempting to downplay his own Communism with his friends in the United States while attempting to keep open channels with a now extremely distrustful Stalin—to little avail, forcing Ho to conclude, famously, that Vietnam stood "quite alone." Not even Ho's old allies in the French Communist Party (who were far more Stalinist than Ho) would help him, as they did not wish to harm their chances in the imminent national election by appearing to support colonial independence, an unadmired position among the average French. "We cannot trust Ho," said the chief of France's Communist Party. "He is a Trotskyite at heart."

In 1945, Ho found himself at the helm of Vietnam during its pivotal point in history—and his fledgling showpiece government was falling apart. North Vietnamese Communist ideologues such as Truong Chinh were arguing that not enough blood had been spilled, non-Communist nationalists were complaining of being bullied, Trotskyist factions hostile to Ho were gaining in strength, the French were unyielding.... "Independence is the thing," runs one of Ho Chi Minh's more amoral maxims. "What follows will follow."

While Ho was in France in late 1945, attempting to prevent war and rid Vietnam of all occupying forces, his friend and colleague General Vo Nguyen Giap began to annihilate all who might oppose the Communist line within the ranks of Hanoi's government and beyond. Thousands were executed, imprisoned, or forced into exile. Whether Ho gave the actual order for this purge is doubtful, but the purge would have needed his consent. That Ho made sure he was out of the country suggests some awareness on his part of the deed's blackness, especially after he had urged against similar measures in the past. (While in France, Ho ran into David Ben-Gurion, the future first president of Israel. Ho liked Ben-Gurion so much that he offered Hanoi for the Israelis' use as a government-in-exile home base.) In March 1946, Ho, wishing above all else to avoid war, returned to Vietnam and argued for his political life in favor of allowing the French a temporary reentry into Vietnam. While the purge had presumably rid his government of those who would have opposed this strategy most strongly, many of Ho's closest allies, even General Giap, were alarmed by Ho's concession. "Can't you understand what would happen if the Chinese stayed?" Ho asked them. "You are forgetting our past history. Whenever the Chinese came, they stayed a thousand years. The French, on the other hand, can stay only a short time. Eventually, they will have to leave." To the Vietnamese people themselves, Ho said, "I swear I have not betrayed you."

The French did leave, ultimately, though at dreadful cost, after the battle of Dien Bien Phu in 1954. At roughly the same time, the Chinese, whose Communist Party had come to power in 1949, flooded into Vietnam to help along little brother's revolution. The arrival of Chinese Communists in North Vietnam would create a lasting split within Ho's party, due in large part to the disaster of North Vietnam's various land reform campaigns, which had begun in 1953.

What was land reform? Land reform—the product of men inclined to think in terms of the "middle peasantry"—was supposed to rid Vietnam of its putatively wealthy landowners and turn their holdings over to the people. Some type of land reform was badly needed in North Vietnam, as a tiny percentage of its people, many of them Catholic, owned a huge portion of its land. "Landlords" had been despised in Vietnam long before the social abacus of Communism slid them over into a distinct class. The North's Communist Chinese advisers were adamant about implementing land reform. Ho Chi Minh resisted, saying he was "in no hurry" to redistribute land. But the reform went ahead anyway. The first step was something called "thought reform," wherein the peasants were taught why the landlords deserved what they had coming to them. Communist cadres worked Vietnamese peasants into furies against the landlords, who owed them, they were told, "blood debts." The second step was confronting the landlords.

Land reform initially involved a few dozen villages; it then spun out of control. The peasants quickly ran out of landlords and turned on the next richest class, and the next, then one another; mock trials and bloody executions speedily became land reform's major distinctions. This was all likely by design. The North Vietnamese Maoist Truong Chinh believed fervently in the historical necessity of class war. (One Vietnamese joke has it that Truong Chinh understood only one part of Ho Chi Minh's most famous dictum, "There is nothing more precious than freedom and independence." The part Chinh understood was "There is nothing.") Ho rejected class war, mindful of the fact that even the wealthiest farmers barely made a living. Still, Chinh argued that at least 5 percent of the population had to be eliminated. Apparently he did not care which 5 percent: a landowner who had once sheltered Chinh was sentenced to death, and Chinh did nothing to interfere. Duiker writes, "Although Ho Chi Minh may have been appalled at the indiscriminate violence that accompanied the campaign, in the view of one Vietnamese observer, he had been intimidated by Mao Zedong and was afraid to contradict Chinese officials." Indeed, already China's "advisers" in Vietnam had liquidated several Vietnamese Communists for complaining about excessive Chinese influence.

By 1956, thousands of people had been executed during North Vietnam's experiment with land reform. How many thousands? Duiker calls this magic number "highly controversial," adding that even "sympathetic observers" concede that at least 3,000 people were killed. Others put the number at 15,000 or 30,000. CIA propaganda of the time claimed it was 50,000, and Michael Lind says it could be as high as 100,000. What finally soured the Party on the campaigns was sobering reports that many honored Viet Minh veterans were being denounced and killed.

It has been written that Ho Chi Minh's famous post–land reform apology to the Vietnamese people was "a remarkable achievement," that the "equivalent in the West would be for a president or prime minister to confess that he committed treason against the nation." While this view seems overly marvelous, it is true that Ho Chi Minh's was the first unambiguous apology—and remains one of the only—made by any Communist leader to his people. Ho claimed, in part, that the land reform abuses had occurred "because I lacked a spirit of democracy, I didn't listen and didn't see." General Giap also apologized and admitted that the Communists had "executed too many honest people. . . . [S]eeing enemies everywhere, we resorted to terror." Real action was taken by Ho, from removing the vicious revolutionary Hoang Quoc Viet from the Politburo to the spontaneous release of 12,000 prisoners to Truong Chinh's dismissal as general secretary (though Chinh would years later avenge himself). Unfortunately, the apology did not mark the end of the killing. In Ho Chi Minh's home province of Nghe An an antigovernment protest erupted, the first in North Vietnam since the end of the First Indochina War. The unrest came from a Catholic region that had traditionally supported the Viet Minh and was purged anyway. This brief resistance was crushed.

The final disaster of land reform was the resulting abandonment of the Party by most of North Vietnam's intellectuals, who until the debacle had been ideologically moderating influences. As a result, Ho Chi Minh, a man capable of great mercilessness (in 1958 he urged that "rightist" writers in North Vietnam be destroyed and once spoke of "hatred" as being his most powerful weapon), would serve as the Party's main ideological ballast until his death in 1969.

Was Ho Chi Minh a Stalinist, then? Almost everyone who met Ho, with the exception of Joseph Stalin and the Indian Communist Manabendra Nath Roy, found him a man of genuine warmth. Many Chinese diplomats living in Hanoi wished that the gentle, learned Ho were their leader instead of the dour, crude Mao. The stories of Ho's personal kindness (such as when, in the middle of the jungle, in the middle of a war zone, he found champagne for some OSS officers) are more numerous than those of his occasional political brutality. He was also largely unmoved by strict ideology: "No peasant will understand this," he once said when handed an impenetrably Leninist broadside. Tellingly, the most militant of Vietnam's Communists—men brutal enough to have purged the author of North Vietnam's national anthem—came largely to ignore Ho, and Ho came to distrust them, particularly Le Duan. By the end of his life Ho had little political power; he was, as he put it, a "flag" for Vietnam.

Ho once maintained that after his service to the Soviet Union in the 1930s (which, it is quite possible, *did* disillusion him), he was no longer committed to the cause of world Communism. Long after lying about it would have served any purpose, many of Ho's comrades spoke of his lasting disappointment at falling out of the United States' favor, and until the United States dispatched its advisers to South Vietnam, anti-American sentiment was virtually unknown among North Vietnam's Communists, much unlike their fellows in China and the USSR. Meanwhile, freedom lovers in the U.S. government delayed the publication of a memoir by Archimedes Patti, one of Ho's OSS handlers, until the 1980s, for the high crime of containing a positive portrait of Ho Chi Minh.

Perhaps simple nuance is what the life of Ho Chi Minh rather fruitlessly argued for. For instance, the basic *Communist* is a rank-and-fileist who may or may not be violent but is unlikely to see much broad success due to incurable mental rigidity. The *Commuleftist* is sympathetic to Communist causes but not doctrinaire, operates mostly under nonviolent banners, almost always lives in a democracy, and can be highly principled. The *Communationalist* believes in the sometimes violent liberation of oppressed people under a Communist pretext, despite being unmindful of or ill educated about the particulars of Communism. The *Commufascist* may or may not believe in doctrinaire Communism and is distinguished primarily by an absolute willingness to engage in (or assist those engaging in) all manner of violence in order to retain power.

Holders of such disparate philosophies are often unified by opposition rather than finding one another naturally, which can be discerned by how poorly Communist countries have generally gotten along. (In many cases not even republics within the Soviet Union had good relations with one another.) Ho Chi Minh had the ill luck to be a moderately reasonable Communationalist at a time when the vanguards and moneylenders of Communism were monstrous Commufascists. The tragedy comes when one attempts to reckon how the story could have gone any other way. The leap of American imagination needed to come to Ho Chi Minh's aid was almost certainly too far. If, however, Americans could remember a war that had allied them with the Commufascist Stalin, they could surely imagine stranger bedfellows than a Communationalist such as Ho Chi Minh.

But perhaps this is letting Ho off the moral hook too easily. Here is a story Duiker has pulled from one of Ho's two self-penned biographies:

> One day, a Chinese nurse who was assigned to care for Uncle [Ho's name for himself] asked him secretly: "Uncle, what is communism?" . . . The nurse knew that Communists were not smugglers, thieves, or murderers, so she couldn't understand why Communists were arrested.
>
> "To put it simply," Uncle replied, "Communists hope to make it so that Chinese nurses will not have to take orders from their British superiors." The nurse looked at Uncle with wide eyes and replied, "Really?"

No doubt Ho believed this, and perhaps as time went on the self-slavery of Communism remained less odious than any kind of foreign domination. The often cited point that Communism was itself a foreign ideology is too facile an observation, and it begs the question of why every other political vision available to Ho had the associative venom of a wicked colonial legacy flowing through it. (André Malraux: "It is difficult to conceive of a courageous Annamite being other than a revolutionary.") During the Vietnam War, *The New York Times* interviewed some young South Vietnamese about why Communism appealed to them. One responded that he took "note of the fact that on this side we have half a million foreign troops while on the other side there are none." When one takes into consideration the universal appeal of self-determination, the lengths to which foreigners were willing to go to prevent it in Vietnam, and the liberating promises (however qualified) of Communism, Ho Chi Minh was a Stalinist, certainly—and maybe the only Stalinist who can be forgiven it.

II

My father looked crumply-eyed over my shoulder, his mouth cast in the same emotionally undecided frown that I had noticed, with increasing frequency, in recent photographs of myself. My back to the street, I whirled around in my crackling wicker chair to have a look. Simultaneously a group of German (or perhaps French) tourists entered the café and crowded around its entrance while waiting for a hostess to escort them to a table. The men were red-faced and abdomenous, the women coltish and slim, sandals with socks all around. I turned back to my father with a querying look. "What is it?"

After a small, distracted shrug he said, "Nothing" and returned to the lightly oiled row of circular squid tubes arranged Olympic-ring-style upon his oval plate.

We were in Hue and had been here a little more than an hour. We had arrived at a small regional airport, in fact an old French airport, to meet Truong and Hien—our driver and guide, respectively. We had been told that Hien specialized in touring veterans of the American War, and with him we would spend the next twelve days. Both were friendly and, I thought, clearly touched by the nature of my father's and my trip. Hien had been shocked to learn that we lived so far apart in the United States and wondered whether we saw each other much. My father had answered, "I see him just enough not to dislike him." Hien had then asked if we were hungry, brought us to this café, and then, with Truong, promptly disappeared.

Truong and Hien. In Graham Greene's *The Quiet American,* Fowler observes that it was difficult to assess the age of Vietnamese men because "they are boys and then they are old men." Truong had a shaggy bowl haircut, a small mustache, long gangly arms, and a disarmingly goofy smile. Hien, only a few inches over five feet, was as compact and solid-looking as a dwarf male gymnast. He was additionally in possession of the single longest facial hair I had ever seen. It grew out of a mole on his cheek and was capable, literally, of being thrown over his shoulder. (Long mole hair is considered good luck in the Vietnamese culture.) Hien looked to be about thirty-six. He was fifty-two. Truong looked to be about twenty-two or twenty-three. He was thirty-six.

My father's tour of Vietnam had never taken him to Hue, and I had suffered from no particular mania to visit this city. But it was impressed upon us that a trip to Vietnam was not a trip to Vietnam without Hue, we had to see Hue. So now we ate in one of Hue's many small French-style cafés, sitting on wicker chairs covered with plush red cushions, our table draped with a velvety red tablecloth, large frondy plants lurking in every corner, while Jimmy Buffett's "Cheeseburger in Paradise" played at a low but nevertheless unacceptable volume. As my father sipped from a tiny cup of Vietnamese coffee—"Hooo, that'll curl your toenails"—I saw, over his shoulder, through one of the café's windows, the wide brown motionlessness of the Perfume River. Long, narrow wooden boats vaguely reminiscent of crocodiles floated along with ominous quietude. My eyes ached. The little sleep I had managed to get had been like slipping a grit-lined pillowcase over my brain. Jet lag had clipped off my nerves at their sparking ends.

A few minutes later my father was again peering over my shoulder.

His expression this time was small-eyed, considered, more thoughtful. "They're about the right age. Don't you think?"

I turned again. By now the tourists had been escorted to their seats, leaving the café's spacious and doorlessly sunlit entrance clear. A few feet from the jamb huddled a one-legged Vietnamese man, clad in a dirty yellow poncho to fend off the rain that had not yet fallen but would, today and every day. This man was, among other things, a dead ringer for Manuel Noriega. Just beyond the Vietnamese Noriega was an even older shirtless man whose left hand was a freakishly withered twig of bony flesh. In his right hand was his beggar bowl. They had not been there when we entered.

I swiveled back to my father, sobered, and stared at my plate of spring rolls. After a few moments I looked up. "Do you think they're veterans?"

He was still staring at them, his forehead deeply lined. "What else would they be?"

"I wonder which side." But I probably did not need to wonder. Veterans from the NLF and PAVN were said to have some right to hospital beds and other shelter. These men were almost certainly ARVN. Already this morning—outside the airport, inside the airport, beside Hue's hotel while we dropped off our luggage—we had met so many Vietnamese men who claimed to have fought with the Americans that my father finally muttered, "If all these people were with us, then why the hell did we lose?"

My father continued to stare at the beggars, his eyes bulging in helpless concern. He shook his head and then began to fork away at his squid. "When we leave, we should give them something."

This astounded me. My father's politics are best described as Orthodox Midwestern Independent, irritated by the moral superiority of the Left and uncomfortable with the moral certainty of the Right. But his fierce antipathy for those who did not, in his mind, *work hard*—street people, Europeans, his Communist son—coursed through the ironworks of his mind like a vein of molten slag. Were my father himself not a hard worker, this attitude would have been infuriating. But he was one of the hardest-working men I had ever known.

As for me, beggary made a hash of my conscience. Give it a face, render it helpless, place it before me, and my pockets were emptied. With beggars I was a hopeless enabler and not to be trusted. We finished eating (each of our bites requiring thirty preoccupied chews), settled the bill, tipped heavily, looked at each other, rose, pushed our chairs back under the table, and moved across the tourist-crowded restaurant like long-striding bureaucrats of munificence. At the entrance my father turned and whispered, "You take the other guy," by which he meant the withered-handed man. I went over to him and caught a sidelong glance of my father handing to Noriega a 10,000-dong note. This was about seventy cents. Noriega took the money with a quiet nod. The withered-armed man was without expression as I searched through my bills for a 10,000-dong note. All I seemed to have were 20,000-, 50,000-, and 100,000-dong notes. No matter the denomination, a different-colored portrait of Uncle Ho stared kindly up at me. I caved in and gave the withered-armed gentleman 50,000 dong—a little over the considerable sum of $3.

Suddenly, a legless crablike man wearing a flip-flop sandal on each hand scuttled out from the shady interior of an across-the-street convenience shack. He moved with the disarming, skittering quickness of a longer-armed primate. As an image it was fairly nightmarish, as a biophysical display nothing short of astounding. The crabman had for some reason dead-reckoned upon my father and scrambled right past me. By now a little crowd had gathered. They were mainly young Vietnamese who took in the unfolding and no doubt daily drama with smirking but not hostile amusement.

The crabman reached my father, whose clean khaki pants had never looked cleaner, whose blue shirt had never looked bluer. With heartrending proficiency the crabman extricated his begging hand from his filthy flip-flop's homemade webbing and held it up to my father. My openmouthed father stared down at the crabman. But I too had more supplicants. They were emerging from the hibiscus and palm trees lining the street and from all the shacks and alleyways. A little boy in a wheelchair came rolling up to me and practically skidded to a stop inches from my Nikes. "What's cooking, bub?" he asked. I gave him money to make him go away, which he did. In fact, he wheeled on, directly toward my father.

My father and the crabman were still regarding each other, the crabman's tongue unfurled with canine extravagance and my father's expression simply unprecedented. One would think that after nearly three decades of surprising, disappointing, pleasing, and worrying him, I would have seen all his possible permutations of facial expression. But this one was new. It was not a look of sadness or fear or anger or guilt. His face asked no questions and expected no answers. It was a face looking deeply into that of another human being and seeing no possibility but that of mercy. He gave the crabman a 50,000-dong note, the smallest bill, I gathered, that he now had. He turned away from the crabman, and though he had been trying to ignore the wheelchair boy he handed over some money to him as well. My father then walked on. Where he was headed in this city he had never visited I had little idea, but he was certainly in a hurry to get there. I moved after him, but after two steps another beggar latched on to my hand and softly tugged.

Hien materialized with panic-widened eyes and rushed up to my wandering-away father. When Hien grabbed him by the arm, it took my father a moment to turn around, and he looked down at Hien with a face simultaneously lost and thankful. Just as suddenly as Hien had appeared, the car pulled up to within two feet of the café's doorless front entrance. With Secret Service efficiency Hien pushed my father down into the backseat. The car went into sideways reverse, squirted forward, and was suddenly beside me. I handed out several more 50,000-dong notes before retreating into the car's air-conditioned interior. Hien slammed my door shut, a sound that seemed inordinately harsh. As we began to pull away, I looked out the window. What had felt like an invading army of the scrofulous and maimed I now saw as six or seven peaceful if insistent beggars sensibly plying their trade at one of Hue's major tourist arteries. The boy in the wheelchair was laughing, and the crabman dragged himself back toward his darkness. Only Noriega waved goodbye. Some tourists—an older couple, clad in white—were now emerging from the café. The remaining and extremely keyed-up beggars quickly gathered around them. I turned away. We had made this couple's egress from lunch much more difficult.

We drifted along in silence. My father's head lolled back against the seat. His glasses were off, his eyes open, his hands in his lap. It did not even seem as though he was breathing.

"Dad?"

Months later I would share with a friend the story of my father's run-in with the beggars of Hue. My friend was something of a Vietnam hand and would respond by telling me that such a collision was becoming a stock scene in the literature of Americans in the new Vietnam. My friend would not say this to be snide or dismissive. Even as I was watching my father and the crabman there had seemed a ghastly familiarity to it, an easy fatedness.

"Hey, Dad?"

My father's eyes were fixed on the car's ceiling. He was as oblivious to my voice as he was to Truong and Hien's respectful silence. It did not matter on which side those men had battled, who had wounded them, what had wounded them, or that the only people that boy in the wheelchair had likely ever fought were his brothers and sisters. As a young man, something in my father had compelled him to come to Vietnam, to engage in what he knew was war. Now he had come back to see what his youth's passion had contributed to. The reason this was becoming a stock scene in the literature of Americans in the new Vietnam was that a confrontation with the lingering costs of war was inevitable for every American who came here. It was inevitable and, for those who fought here, incalculably painful. Even a broken heart is a cliché.

"Dad?"

His mouth opened. "That was . . ." His voice was thick, throat-tightened. "I think that . . ." The sluice of his reddened eyes' underrim glowed with moisture. He cleared his throat—a revving, strangely formal sound. "I think maybe that was probably a mistake."

The rainy-season fog seemed to enhance rather than obscure the mossy, stony mystery of many of Hue's beautiful buildings. Around the taller structures' square shoulders the fog looked like grand stoles of smoke or mist. Hue, the city of children, scholars, and kite flying, was the ne plus ultra of Vietnam's tourist industry and as such fiercely minded. While freelance tour guides were allowed to work in relative freedom throughout most of Vietnam, a tour guide caught without a proper license in Hue was given a commission-erasing fine of 2 million dong (about $140).

The omnipresence of the Perfume River gave Hue's streets the busy maritime feeling of long, wide docks. In the past the banks of the Perfume had been repositories for what Communists usually refer to as Vietnam's "social evils": drugs, prostitution, gambling, and fun in general. The government was said to have cleared away much of this six or seven years ago during one of its remindful crackdowns. As we drove along the Perfume's edge my father and I silently observed skinny brown men in shorts and sandals squatting on the bows of their sampans. Large tourist "dragon boats" painted a cheerfully ugly mixture of blue and yellow and green chugged down the Perfume's center, leaving a wake that looked as though the river were being unzipped. Hue's riverfront alternated between pretty restaurants, elegant colonial buildings, a latex mattress factory, and what were little more than bamboo lean-tos with rusty metal roofs. We passed a lonely-looking Catholic church, the old French Cercle Sportif building (now Hue's tourist center), and a neighborhood said to be populated by such beautiful young women that it had often been raided by members of Hue's royal family in search of concubines. We finally stopped and spent a few minutes wandering around the grounds of the Quoc Hoc, or National School, the most prestigious secondary institute in all of Vietnam.

It was founded in 1896 by the emperor Thanh Thai, one of imperial France's less distinguished client rulers. The giggling orgy enthusiast's only lasting legacy was this academy, which, after Thai was sent into exile, was superintended for many years by his gloomy minister of rites, Ngo Dinh Kha, the father of future South Vietnamese president Ngo Dinh Diem, who himself studied here. Operated under French supervision, the school taught its economically diverse student body a sophisticated curriculum of French and Vietnamese subjects and was designed to educate a new generation of Westernized Vietnamese bureaucrats intended to replace the imperial court the French themselves had made useless by corrupting. The French thus wound up educating the generation that would throw their Gallic asses out of Indochina. Within the classrooms of the National School, Ho Chi Minh became well known among his schoolmates for asking too many questions and the quickness with which he picked up languages; Vo Nguyen Giap, the future general who would best the French at Dien Bien Phu, first developed his lifelong fondness for French language and history (and, ominously, his fascination with Robespierre); and Pham Van Dong, North Vietnam's future prime minister, studied like the proper nobleman's son he was and, unlike Ho and Giap, avoided being expelled.

To find in Hue at one time a conflux of such celebrated personalities was not unusual. In this way Hue is unique: Hanoi and Saigon, which have long battled with Hue for the distinction of Vietnam's flagship city, became areas of wealth and political significance only with the advent of colonialism, whereas Hue's significance predates the formal arrival of the French. Hue became the capital of Vietnam in 1802 after two hundred years of civil war, when the triumphant lords of the Nguyen Dynasty moved their throne here from northern Vietnam. This move of centralization was a signal to any remaining pockets of resistance that the whole of Vietnam was under Nguyen control. (The Nguyen Dynasty would nominally endure until 1945.) Despite its status of capital, Hue always remained relatively small. When Ho Chi Minh's bureaucrat father worked here in the late 1890s, it was home to fewer than 10,000 citizens. As a city of immense cultural importance, Hue was the recipient of several wartime gentlemen's agreements that it not be touched, no matter the chaos surrounding it. Yet it had also been the site of some of Vietnamese history's most wanton slaughter.

In 1844, a French missionary imprisoned by Vietnam's ruler became the first official justification France used to act militarily against this distant land of water buffaloes, small men, and green mountains. After a series of inconclusive confrontations (one somehow involved the USS *Constitution*) and a brief, violent battle, France was content for several years to allow merely its traders and missionaries to operate in Vietnam. The first French soldiers arrived in force in 1858, again under the pretext of protecting the Vietnamese Catholics its missionaries had managed to ensoul. France initially focused on capturing Hue, but local resistance, and the unexpected difficulty of traversing the jungle, stopped its forces en route. Instead the French invaders captured the insignificant fishing village of Saigon and over the next few years made highly one-sided deals with Hue's hapless Nguyen emperor, Tu Duc, who was in effect forced to trade land to ensure the security of his throne.

After Tu Duc's death in 1883, Hue's throne was occupied by a series of young monarchs—one ruled for a day, another killed himself within months of becoming ruler, one died mysteriously, another was all of twelve years old—which made conquering the remainder of Vietnam occasionally literal child's play for France. When China (the nation that in Vietnam's history plays the twin role of opportunistic ally and meddling kraken intent on extending its tentacles south) abandoned Vietnam to France's designs in 1885, Vietnam's native resistance was weakened considerably, though some clashes between insurgents and French soldiers remained fierce. One of the nastiest battles took place shortly after Tu Duc's death. As French warships sat anchored near Hue, a French official warned Duc's successor, "Imagine all that is terrible and it will still be less than reality. The word 'Vietnam' will be erased from history." Once the ships' cannons began to lay waste to Hue, the city quickly surrendered. Two years later, another burp of resistance led to Hue's second destruction at French hands. As for erasing Vietnam, the French were as good as their word: "Vietnam" did cease to exist, and a three-zoned colonial entity made up of regions known as Tonkin, Annam, and Cochin China replaced it. The brutal French promise of national erasure brings to mind U.S. Air Force General Curtis LeMay's thought from 1965 that, when it came to Vietnam, "We could bomb them into the Stone Age." These echoes abound. The following statements, for instance, both concern Vietnam—but who said them, and when?

"When our soldiers are again threatened, as they are today, we will be asked for more money and more men. We will not be able to refuse. And millions upon millions, fresh troops on top of fresh troops will lead to our exhaustion."

"The troops will march in, the bands will play, the crowds will cheer, and in four days everyone will have forgotten. Then we will be told we have to send in more troops. It's like taking a drink. The effect wears off, and you have to take another."

The first was said by Georges Clemenceau, then a French parliamen-
tarian, in 1885. The second was said by John F. Kennedy to Arthur
Schlesinger, Jr., in 1961.

Not a few historians regard comparisons between the French and U.S.
ordeals in Vietnam as only superficially illuminating. There are excep-
tions. The historian Fredrik Logevall believes that the French experience
in Vietnam is of "central relevance" to that of the United States and
laments the lack of thought U.S. officials gave to France's defeat. While
John F. Kennedy was apparently sobered by French President Charles de
Gaulle's warnings about Indochina ("For you, intervention in this region
will be an entanglement without end"), many others in the Kennedy
and Johnson administrations, particularly Secretary of State Dean Rusk,
believed that France had met with failure in Vietnam because it was a
faltering old power, relied too often on untrustworthy Algerian and
Moroccan soldiers, and as a colonialist nation was only seeking to
exploit the Vietnamese people.

So who said these things, and when? "We have had enormous difficulties in enforcing our authority. . . . Rebel bands disturb the country
everywhere. They appear from nowhere in large numbers, destroy
everything, and then disappear into nowhere." That was a French commander in 1862. "We kill scores and scores of them. But there are always
just as many left—in fact more. There's an inexhaustible supply. And
then it's not always the real, full-blown Viet that we kill. . . . Often they
are just villagers, people's militia." That was a French lieutenant in the
1940s. "[The people] have the impression that . . . we are fighting aim-
lessly without a clear objective. What is painful is not so much the fact of
fighting without accepting the sacrifices, it is that we are apparently
fighting without any goal." That was a French writer from 1953. By then
the French war in Vietnam had the nickname it deserved: *sale guerre*,
dirty war.

In the aftermath of Dien Bien Phu, a French journalist wrote of his
belief that "the Americans would never have fought as we did. They
would have fought a different war. And by crushing the country and the
people under a hail of bombs and dollars, they might very well have had
more success than we." Ho Chi Minh told a journalist in 1962 that the

"Americans are much stronger than the French, though they know us less well." Karl Marx famously said that history occurs first as tragedy, then as farce. But Marx was being characteristically dyspeptic. History occurs first as tragedy, then as needless tragedy.

We parked near a row of food stalls and walked over to Hue's ancient Citadel, the city-within-the-city of Hue and since 1993 a UNESCO World Heritage site. At one point the Citadel contained three separate cities, and within them lived and worked all the batteries of Vietnam's royalty, from its mustached emperor to its assiduous mandarins to its secluded and spoiled princesses. The outer wall that surrounded the Citadel was twenty feet tall and in some places thirty feet thick. Enclosed within these massive stone walls were five square miles of land. Some of the wall's bricks, watered by centuries of rain and humidity, were dark algae shades of gray or green; others, the clear product of restoration, were the dulled red of clay. We approached the Citadel across one of its surrounding grassy esplanades. These flat areas guaranteed that those seeking to attack the redoubt would enjoy little cover. Schoolgirls in white ao dais walked around the Citadel's perimeter, some selling flowers, others visiting with their friends, yet others having their pictures taken. A light, cool rain fell from a still-sunny sky.

"Wow," I said to my father as Hien rushed ahead to buy our tickets.

He nodded. "It's neat."

I punched him on the shoulder. "Come on. 'Neat'?"

He glanced at his shoulder, then at me. "What am I supposed to say? It's pretty neat."

"Did you know that Vietnam had things like the Citadel when you came here?"

"Why do you ask that?"

"Something I read. As French rule went on, a lot of the French, naturally enough, got interested in Vietnamese culture. Some realized that this culture was in fact hundreds of years older than French culture. It was humbling, and it made such people a lot more willing to negotiate when the war started."

My father looked around. "I suppose that's why the Marine Corps is

not known for its cultural understanding. To answer your question, no.
I knew very little about Vietnam when I came here. Few of us did. No
great emphasis was put on the culture. I had no idea, for instance, that
there were so many ethnicities inside of this country. When I found out,
I was flabbergasted. I had no idea, furthermore, as to the religious needs
of the people. I had no idea how much like the French we would seem to
them and how much that would determine whether they would like us
or hate us."

"Are you bitter?"

"About what?"

"How stranded you were by your training in understanding this
place?"

Before answering he sucked on his teeth thoughtfully. "Oh, I don't
know. These people just wanted to be left alone. Grow their crops, raise
their animals, love their children, live as good a life as they could."

"Dad? Topic sentence, please?"

His eyes again found mine and narrowed. "We quickly learned, when
we came in, that close to half of the children in rural parts of this country died before they were twelve—many of diseases that were unknown
in the U.S. Hardly anyone had a balanced nutritious diet. And they had
very little, if any, medical attention from the South Vietnamese government. That sure as hell didn't help the situation. Yeah, I wish we'd
known some of this. I also wish, in retrospect, that all the money that
was pouring in from the U.S. had been used more for humanitarian
purposes. That right there could have wreaked wonders."

"So are you bitter?"

His hands lifted, palms out. "I'm not bitter."

"Said so convincingly."

"I'm not bitter! I'm more just . . ."

Before my father could figure out what he was, Hien, holding our
tickets, waved us toward the entrance. On our way to him we passed
over the Citadel's moat. Resting upon its water was an inch-thick layer
of pond scum that looked like shredded mermaid and smelled like a
cross between chlorophyll and a yeast infection. A large sign listed all of
the activities we were not to engage in, such as "twig-breaking." We

entered the Citadel's main gate, a deep stone portal that retained many bullet gouges. My father removed his glasses and while cleaning the lenses with his shirttail leaned in toward the rough gray wall to have a look at one of the bullet holes. "Small-arms fire. A Kalashnikov, I bet."

"Do you remember the time you admitted to me that you actually kind of liked war?"

He winced and put his glasses back on. "Did I say that? I must have been locked and loaded."

"You said you loved war, you hated war, war scared you, you couldn't get enough of war."

"War," my father said finally, "is an illness caused by youth."

We emerged on one of the Citadel's huge brick patios. Vietnamese culture is notably Sinophobic despite its many similarities to Chinese culture, though within any cultural phobia lurks a good deal of furtive philia. The Citadel, then, was an assemblage of Chinese architectural clichés, though parts of it bore strong French influence as well. A major difference between the Citadel and the architecture of traditional China was how many trees the more countrified Vietnamese had planted throughout its grounds. Of course, the consequences of the finally ineffable Sino–Viet relationship can be overstated. Just as surely, they can be understated. Many historians have argued that the major explanation for Vietnam's soldierly culture is its relationship with China. When a mouthwatering nation exists directly south of a large and extremely hungry nation, militarism becomes a mind-set the former nation enthusiastically promotes among its people. A corollary argument has it that the long-held Vietnamese idea that a small force, cunningly operated, can defeat a larger one—in other words, the intellectual basis of all guerrilla warfare—is equally traceable to Vietnam's troubled proximity to China.

The Citadel's buildings were not its only Chinese element. The old Confucian system of governance administered from Hue was in key ways a Chinese replication, as were the clothes its emperor wore, as were the symbols festooned upon its architecture, as were the symmetrics by which the Citadel's three cities were arranged. The names of the Citadel's structures alone had Chinese aromas: the Temple of the Generations, the Purple Forbidden City, the Imperial City, the Palace of Supreme Harmony. Many of the Citadel's buildings had been destroyed—some more than once—and those standing today had been heavily restored, an ongoing, decade-old process begun only after Vietnam's leaders opened up to the possibilities of tourism and put to bed their Communist bugbear for anything that could be construed as a celebration of feudalism. Brightly painted and restored buildings existed alongside decrepit and unrestored shells, many of the latter's exposed, tree-branch joists rottenly infested with ants.

Soon Hien was no longer leading us. Instead he seemed pleased simply to stand amid the astonishments of such a storied place. It was clear he was proud of it, if a little bored, and I envied the closeness he felt to his culture. Even at an American site as splendid as the Lincoln Memorial, say, it would not have occurred to me to be proud of my culture. Why was that? I wondered aloud to my father. "Because you're an ungrateful little prick," he answered.

Alone I passed carp-filled ponds and potted bonsai trees, then journeyed across a wide stone walkway stained gray from the moss that had just been swept off it. On one patio I found an array of gigantic four-hundred-year-old bronze urns, a specialty of the Nguyen Dynasty. Many of these urns were scored with bullet strikes. Thanks to my father, I could now identify the little dings and dents as having been caused by small-arms fire. But also upon these urns were huge .50-caliber gashes that looked less like the product of impact and more like the result of a blowtorch.

We walked past the Royal Theater, stepped off a restructured portico, and walked amid an abrupt pasture of thigh-high grass and crumbling stone walls. Dragonflies swooped around us in the cold, clammy humidity. The grassy field we were standing in was all that remained of the Palace of the Queen in the Purple Forbidden City. Here was an occasional foundation, there the odd section of wall. From this empty field we could see two things. The first was the Imperial City's central bastion, also known as the King's Knight, a large though somehow squat-looking three-story tower from which, traditionally, the emperor's colors were flown. Today flying from the King's Knight, just visible over the treetops, was the Socialist Republic of Vietnam's flag, which had the additional interest of being the largest flag I had ever seen.

In 1945, the last Nguyen emperor, Bao Dai, abdicated his throne, turned control of his country over to the Viet Minh, and allowed the Viet Minh's red, blue, and yellow flag to be run up the King's Knight pole. There the Nguyen Dynasty terminates. Although Bao Dai had been looking for a way out of Vietnamese politics—his truest self was found at a blackjack table with two French hookers on his arm—he did not have much choice but to abdicate. His government was riddled with Viet Minh sympathizers. Bao Dai himself was agnostic on the Viet Minh, and though he suspected that the mysterious patriot Ho Chi Minh was actually the Communist Nguyen Ai Quoc, he accepted a brief role in Ho's government as an adviser. None of this lasted long. Bao Dai abandoned the Communists when he realized he was being used by them for propaganda purposes and was for a short time looked upon by the United States as a potential leader of South Vietnam. The "Bao Dai Solution," this was called. A thirty-two-year-old tennis-loving emperor who could barely speak Vietnamese was called by U.S. Secretary of State Dean Acheson a representative of Vietnam's "true nationalist spirit."

The second thing we could see was the Royal Reading Pavilion—the Citadel library—and the stunning rock garden that girdled it. This was the only structure in the demolished Purple Forbidden City that managed to survive the Tet Offensive.

The sudden sense I had in this place of being surrounded by ghosts felt thick and silencing. Today a number of people living within the Citadel's perimeter still found human bones in their backyards, and many claimed that their houses were haunted. This was not unusual in Vietnamese culture, in which the existence of ghosts typically went undebated. When I asked Hien if he gave the ghost stories any credence, his nod was instant and solemn.

"I don't know about ghosts," my father said, "but an Army buddy of mine got syphilis from a Citadel whorehouse."

"The Marines were here in the Citadel, too," I said to him.

My father looked at me. "Yes. Yes, they were." His face creased, and then, as he considered this further, became slightly stricken. "I'm finding out that this is a pretty emotional place for me. I have to say I didn't expect that."

In one of the many little museums scattered across the Citadel's grounds, I had noticed my father linger before a photo that showed General Vo Nguyen Giap visiting the Citadel to celebrate one of the innumerable holidays the Communists had concocted to commemorate themselves.

"Back there—I saw you staring at that photo of Giap."

"I was. I was thinking about him."

Hien, suddenly, spoke up. "And what do you think of General Giap?"

I sensed several responses solidify and disintegrate in my father's mind. "I think . . . he was very smart."

The brilliance of Giap was debated. It was easy to be a brilliant general, his detractors claimed, when you were willing to accept a catastrophic number of casualties. A typical example of this debate is the Tet Offensive—though, when Tet was first proposed by Hanoi's ranking general in the South, Nguyen Chi Thanh, Giap opposed the idea, as did Ho Chi Minh. (Thanh died before the attack took place, allowing Giap to take over its planning.) Nonetheless, Tet was both Giap's most audacious and brilliant attack and his biggest military disaster. The offensive was, in fact, what caused Giap's Politburo star its final dimming.

A triumph, a failure: the Tet Offensive seemed peculiarly Asian in its ying-yangedness. It began in the valley near the city of Khe Sanh, in 1967, in Quang Tri province, only miles south of the demilitarized zone between North and South Vietnam. Barricaded within a besieged base atop a plateau, U.S. Marines held out for months against the violent parries of what many anticipated would become a massive Dien Bien Phu–style assault. As the area around the Marines' plateau became what has been described as "the most heavily bombed target in the history of warfare," General William Westmoreland, the commander of the Military Assistance Command, Vietnam (MACV), waited for the NLF and PAVN forces skulking around the valley to bring the fight to the Marines. He had sought such a decisive confrontation for months and was certain it would occur at Khe Sanh. (PAVN soldiers had allowed the capture of false documents outlining a planned Khe Sanh assault. "The

Americans like captured documents," Pham Van Dong once said. "We made sure they got plenty.") Two months before the Tet Offensive, Westmoreland, still waiting for the Khe Sanh attack, announced, at President Johnson's urging, "We have reached an important point when the end begins to come into view." He claimed that the enemy's hopes were "bankrupt." Only days before the Tet Offensive commenced, Westmoreland boasted, "I hope they try something because we are looking for a fight."

The Tet Offensive—so named for the Tet holiday that in Vietnamese culture celebrates the lunar new near—began at 3 a.m. on January 31, 1968, and is believed to have been launched in order to win the war before the death of the fast-weakening Ho Chi Minh, who used the occasion to scribble out some of his last bits of poetry: "Forward / Total victory shall be ours!" Tet saw South Vietnam invaded by 70,000 PAVN soldiers and the activation of nearly every NLF guerrilla. It also involved the attack of virtually every major city in South Vietnam—with the notable exception of Khe Sanh. The months of testing assaults there had been a diversion to draw away the attention of Westmoreland and his medley of tacticians.

The offensive's purpose was to trigger a spontaneous uprising in South Vietnam. The execution itself was brilliant: in Saigon the firecrackers that marked the Tet holiday were used to cover the first bursts of machine-gun fire. For North Vietnam and the NLF, however, brilliance of execution and fulfillment of execution turned out to be quite different. The South's NLF guerrilla force was practically annihilated in Tet's various battles, though its infrastructure survived, and PAVN troops suffered at least thirty times the 3,000 military casualties they inflicted. (The North Vietnamese initially claimed to have inflicted 43,000 U.S. casualties.) Such reckonings have caused many to accuse the American media of misrepresenting the true result of the Tet Offensive and demoralizing the American public after what was, in actual fact, an enemy rout.

For three years, the U.S. military had been announcing to the American people its constant progress in Vietnam, the improving military situation on the ground, the ever-growing "light at the end of the tunnel."

Tet proved that this whipped and weakening enemy was capable of a massive, powerful, and superbly planned surprise attack. Indeed, Tet was followed by a year of the bloodiest and most vicious fighting of the war. Although Tet inspired 61 percent of the American people, as one Gallup Poll indicated, to describe themselves as "hawks," a few within the Johnson administration went from hawks to doves overnight. In the wake of Tet, General Westmoreland saw his request for 206,000 additional troops turned down by the White House for the first time (though only because his request was leaked and Johnson knew the public would not have stood for another escalation). Why did Westmoreland need more troops? Because, as Westmoreland explained, Tet was quite obviously "a diversionary effort to take attention away from . . . an attack on Khe Sanh."

"Yes," Hien agreed. "General Giap is very smart."

"But," my father said carefully, "I think he threw away the lives of too many North Vietnamese and VC."

Hien stepped forward slightly. "We consider the VC to be the Revolutionary Force."

"I'm sorry?"

"We don't distinguish between the North Vietnamese and the VC. We think of them together as the Revolutionary Force."

"Oh." My father turned to me, while behind him the Citadel's freely growing grass swayed like emerald corn. "Did you know that?"

I was sitting next to a rock mound swiss with bullet holes. I shrugged.

My father returned to Hien. "But they weren't really the same, were they?"

"We consider them the Revolutionary Force."

"I understand that. But they weren't the same. We Marines, at least, never regarded them as the same. We had a lot of respect for the North Vietnamese Army." My father made a demonstrative little fist and shook it. "Tough soldiers. Good fighters."

Hien's entire bearing changed. This little man suddenly appeared twice as tall. He threw his long growth of mole hair over his shoulder and said, with grim finality, "We consider them the Revolutionary Force."

My father, who now looked slightly frightened, turned to me for less dialectical conversation. "Did you do any reading about the battle for Hue? It was pretty much a Marine battle, you know."

I had done some reading. The struggle that emptied the grassy field we now stood upon was one of those battles in which every side emerged looking little better than blood-drinking berserkers. Most of the 5,000 to 8,000 NLF guerrillas and PAVN regulars who attacked Hue sneaked into position, using as cover the crowds pouring into the city for the Tet holiday. There was scarcely any U.S. military presence in Hue—a handful of advisers in the city itself and a unit of noncombatant Army decoders in nearby Phu Bai—but a fair number of U.S. civilians. While one ARVN division was headquartered within the Citadel, its infantry did not operate near Hue, and, in any case, most of its personnel had already taken holiday leave. Despite warnings that three enemy battalions were apparently headed toward Hue, no one was put on high alert since the American officer transmitting the information was known as a worrywart. When the offensive began, the city of Hue was attacked from all sides. The Citadel, for psychological reasons, was the main target. Perhaps a dozen ARVN sentries were standing guard at the Citadel when the attack came, and those who survived the initial enfilade ran off. Shortly after the Citadel's breach, the NLF flag was snapping in the breeze above the King's Knight, where it would remain for the next three weeks.

The Communist liquidation of Hue's hostile class elements then commenced. As Don Oberdorfer writes, the captured text of the NLF/PAVN plan for taking Hue "suggests that the leadership did not expect to be able to hold Hue for very long, for it emphasized destruction of 'the enemy' over establishment and consolidation of the new order." Like most such liquidations known to history, any logic intended to guide these deadly proceedings swiftly imploded; every foreign citizen in Hue but the French—whose "sympathy" the guerrillas were to try to "gain"—was targeted. Among the victims were two young U.S. foreign service officers, who were bound and executed; an American employee of NBC, who was cut down in the street while running from the NLF; a German pediatrician, his wife, and two other doctors, who were bound and executed; two French priests, who (apparently for their theism) were bound and executed. A popular Vietnamese Catholic priest named Father Dong, who prayed regularly for Ho Chi Minh because "he is our friend too," was buried alive. Thousands of Vietnamese with real and imagined ties to the United States and the Saigon regime or non-Communist nationalist parties were machine-gunned and left in mass-grave lime pits outside the city.

It should be noted that NLF terrorism had grown less selective as the war dragged on and would become truly ugly in the late 1960s and early 1970s, when the NLF was reduced to assassinating altar boys. Nothing quite as awful as the Hue purge would be repeated by the Communists during the war. Early in the conflict, the NLF was usually careful not to antagonize the local population and in most cases behaved toward the Vietnamese peasantry with greater respect than the Saigon regime's police and soldiers typically cared to show. By 1968, Ho Chi Minh's old warning that reckless terrorism was a "bourgeois" device had been disregarded by many cells, and in 1969 the NLF was shooting rockets into Saigon with no concern for the civilian population. Between 1957 and 1972, the NLF assassinated 37,000 people. During the same period, the United States killed, at the very least, 365,000 noncombatant civilians. To argue that there was a moral difference between these twin splurges of slaughter would be difficult. The overall lack of discrimination on both sides, the historian James P. Harrison has argued, left the people of South Vietnam to choose between the "revolutionary terror" of the NLF and the "counter-revolutionary terror" of the U.S. military. Toward which side the hearts of most Vietnamese listed is not hard to imagine. At any rate, the final number of Hue's victims is still frequently debated—an apparent inevitability for any massacre that involves Communist aggressors. The most reasonable estimate of those killed during the purge is 3,000 to 4,000.

For the same psychological reasons that the Citadel was attacked by the insurgents, the U.S. command determined that it had to be recaptured by the South Vietnamese. The ARVN forces ordered to retake the Citadel did what ARVN forces usually did, which was to advance within half a mile of the enemy, find a tall thick wall, hide behind it, and wait for reinforcements, who then did the same. On February 10, three battalions of U.S. Marines were ordered to do what the ARVN refused to do. The little progress made during ARVN's nine-day nonassault was mostly erased upon news of the Marine reinforcement, which ARVN forces celebrated by instantly withdrawing from the Citadel.

The battle for Hue marked the first time U.S. Marines had engaged in close urban combat since the fight to retake Seoul from the North Koreans in September 1950. Often Hue's fighting was less house-to-house than room-to-room. Marines have spoken of their unwillingness to pass through any doorway without first rolling a hand grenade into the adjoining room, which goes some way toward explaining why 10,000 civilians died during Hue's recapture. Even with this harsh caution, the Marines took approximately one casualty for every meter they were able to advance through the city. During the first days of combat, the Marines were under orders to preserve the Citadel's architecture— which must have been like staging a gunfight in the Louvre—but the tight streets, dense hedges, and courtyard walls made fighting effectively impossible. Tanks, for instance, could not fit through numerous Citadel streets unless many buildings were destroyed. Throughout the city NLF mortar shells descended with perfect silence and exploded in dirty flameless bursts. As casualties increased, patience fell. "We did our best to avoid malicious damage," one Marine said at the time. "Yet, when we had to destroy a house, we destroyed it." Some companies went lost in the Citadel's courtyards, and several Marines bled to death from treatable injuries simply because no one could find and evacuate them. From the beginning of the assault, the casualty rate was so high that if a Marine could walk he was ordered to keep fighting. "Although replacements routinely arrived during the battle," Edward F. Murphy writes in *Semper Fi—Vietnam,* a history of the Marine Corps in Vietnam, "too often they were chewed up by the killing machine of Hue before their squad leaders could even learn their names." As Murphy notes, many replacements arrived so fresh from Camp Pendleton in California that "there were Marine KIAs found still wearing their stateside fatigues and boots." There is a story of a Marine who in the bloody chaos was stuffed into a body bag while he was still alive, of a Marine with a blown-off arm weeping with childlike relief at being allowed to leave the fight.

After ten days of fighting, the United States' concern for the Citadel's architecture had evaporated. The more of Hue the Marines destroyed by air and artillery, and the more parts of the city that were scorched black with napalm (one Marine described inhaling the air around the Citadel as "eating death," and many walked around wearing surgical masks soaked in aftershave), the fewer places PAVN and the NLF had to hide. As the city was blown apart, desperation on all sides increased—and not only among combatants. This is from Michael Herr's *Dispatches:*

> A little boy of about ten came up to a bunch of Marines from Charlie Company. He was laughing and moving his head from side to side in a funny way. The fierceness in his eyes should have told everyone what it was, but it had never occurred to most of the grunts that a Vietnamese child could be driven mad too, and by the time they understood it the boy had begun to go for their eyes and tear at their fatigues, spooking everyone, putting everyone really uptight, until a black grunt grabbed him from behind and held his arm. "C'mon, poor li'l baby, 'fore one a these grunt mothers shoots you," he said, and carried the boy to where the corpsmen were.

Fittingly, the battle's end was empty of meaning and heroism. The PAVN soldiers and NLF guerrillas who had survived days of aerial and artillery bombardment slipped past snoozing ARVN guards the night before the Imperial Palace was finally retaken. When an ARVN unit charged inside the palace to capture it (the Marines had cleared the way up to the palace gate), it was discovered to be mostly empty. The Marines came in after the ARVN. One Marine found the body of a PAVN soldier and was photographed urinating into the corpse's mouth. On February 25, the battle for Hue was finished. Hue, too, was finished. Seventy percent of the city was rubble. Of Hue's 140,000 people, 90,000 had nowhere left to live. It is estimated that 7 percent of the city's civilian population was killed during the agonal three-week siege. Thousands of distended, broken-open bodies filled the Citadel's moat and lined Hue's streets. The Marines, Hue's liberators, lost almost 150. Only one U.S. Medal of Honor was awarded for conduct during the battle. It was posthumous.

"A lot of guys I went to basic with died in this place," my father said. "A lot of guys. Guys who joined up again. Guys who kept volunteering. All died right around here." He shook his head.

"Like who?" I asked.

"You don't know them."

"Well, what were their names?"

He looked at me queerly. "What do you care?" This was said with a brusque sort of inquisitiveness, not anger.

I got to my feet. "I'm sorry. You're right. Just morbid curiosity."

My father—the abrupt smile on his face false to anyone who knew him—turned to Hien. "What do *you* think?"

Hien regarded his shoes, which looked like small leather noses peeking out from beneath his blue slacks. "I think this is a special place for many people."

My father said nothing and stood there in the wind, amid the grass. When he closed his eyes, it almost looked as though he were listening to someone.

Query: *Why were the leaders of South Vietnam so corrupt and incompetent?*

In the early 1960s, the magnitude of the political problems in South Vietnam was growing apparent. Nonetheless, the American strategy in Vietnam was to stay the course, back the South Vietnamese government, and, in Secretary of State Dean Rusk's words, "play for the breaks" militarily. What follows are passages from a number of books that together summarize the problem of playing for the breaks militarily alongside the South Vietnamese:

About this time Lieutenant Colonel Utter radioed for the ARVN airborne to close the growing gap on Lindauer's left flank. To his surprise the ARVN commander refused. Try as he might, Utter could not get the South Vietnamese to join the fight.

We hesitated to use ARVN interpreters because their methods of questioning people was to slap them upside the head with a revolver or shoot their foot off and say, "You VC?" The guy says no and BANG. "You VC?" Sooner or later, after losing enough pieces, the guy would say yes and then he'd be shot because now he's guilty.

He radioed the [U.S.] division advisor, who reported that "the [ARVN] 5th Division is asleep. The division commander consulted with his astrologer, who told him this was not the right day to go on an operation."

He noticed that almost every time he heard the approach of what might be a bunch of Viet Cong walking down the trail and into the snare, one of the Saigon soldiers would give the ambush away by coughing, by snapping the bolt of a weapon, or making some other noise. This occurred too often to be accidental.

When his American adviser pointed out that across the stream seemed a better place to camp, the [ARVN] officer had said the area was already occupied by the V.C. The adviser asked, "Why don't you go after them?"

"As long as we don't bother them," the ARVN commander replied, "they won't bother us."

Before the introduction of U.S. ground forces into South Vietnam, the ARVN was receiving tens of millions of dollars a year for training and equipment, and U.S. advisers were appalled to learn that many ARVN soldiers had no idea how to use a rifle sight. Some ARVN commanders repeatedly refused to answer calls of radio distress. One shot from a sniper was sometimes enough to bring an ARVN battalion to a halt. An American adviser calculated that, during one six-month period, ARVN's 7th Division spent 74 percent of its time "resting." In 1966, it was discovered that only one ARVN officer had been wounded in action since 1954. While luckless ARVN conscripts and volunteers were killed by the thousand—the ARVN ultimately lost four times as many soldiers as the United States—in 1967 one particularly timid ARVN infantry division, the 25th, had more men killed in traffic accidents than combat. ARVN rolls routinely listed among their ranks what became known as "ghost soldiers"—that is, dead troops listed as still being on active duty and thus still being paid while their living commanders pocketed the wages. The wages were not much, which is surely one reason why the ARVN's morale was so awful. Many ARVN lieutenants earned as little as $18 a month.

There were honorable men within the South Vietnamese military, but they were a lonely minority. Many ARVN officers typically achieved their rank through bribery or nepotism. Not surprisingly, these men quailed during combat throughout the war. No matter how brave, strong, and physically tough the soldiers beneath them happened to be, loss of nerve on the part of a commanding officer can and did turn the tide of entire battles. While the ARVN contained a few men who had fought alongside the Viet Minh against the French, most of its personnel were the local military leavings of imperial France. Others hailed from Bao Dai's short-lived collaborationist army, formed in 1948. Many from such implicated backgrounds took easily to feelings of disdain for the Vietnamese peasantry, whom they called *nha que*, "country bumpkins." (These feelings linger in urban Vietnam today, as evidenced by the tendency of men to grow their fingernails long to prove they do not "work.") At their cruelest, such men did not blink at mowing down the livestock of peasants suspected of colluding with the NLF or tossing a village girl to their soldiers for some sporting rape. Consider that South Vietnam's army fought a less well equipped enemy that in numbers of armed combatants rarely approached even a third of its troop force and yet rarely got the upper hand. Beneath President Ngo Dinh Diem in 1963, 250,000 ARVN soldiers were battling roughly 30,000 NLF guerrillas—and losing roundly.

Ngo Dinh Diem is arguably the one human being who did more than any other to befoul the South Vietnamese struggle against Communism. Diem was not an American creation by any means, but he was an American installation who began almost immediately to slash at the strings of the puppet master. He began in the minds of his U.S. handlers as a brilliant idea—a leader who would turn South Vietnam into a fortress of non-Communism similar to those that existed in the Federal Republic of Germany, the Republic of Korea, and Nationalist China—and ended as an American migraine headache. Like Ho Chi Minh, Diem was a lifelong bachelor, a fluent speaker of numerous languages, a patriot who spent formative decades outside his native land, a man who understood (and rejected) Western systems of governance, and in most matters of temperament a tyrant. Unlike Ho Chi Minh, however, Diem was unloved, unwanted, and ultimately rejected by his own people; the day the man died, there were spontaneous parades. How and why this (in the words of the historian James Olson) "brilliant incompetent who beat the odds longer than anyone thought possible" came to be the linchpin of American aspiration in Vietnam is itself a story of incompetence.

The Geneva Conference of 1954 commenced the day after the Viet Minh finished overrunning the French at Dien Bien Phu. Although the timing was sheer coincidence, many Viet Minh read this as a cosmic endorsement of their victory. The conference was chaired by Great Britain and the Soviet Union and attended by delegates from China, France, the United States (who only "observed" the proceedings), Laos, Cambodia, and the various Communist and royalist representatives of Vietnam. (One of the American intelligence analysts sent to Geneva had this mission: "My first assignment at Geneva was to find out if there really was such a person as Ho Chi Minh.") Ultimately, the Geneva Conference divided Vietnam into two temporary entities: the Democratic Republic of Vietnam in the north and the Republic of Vietnam in the south. Their dividing line was the Seventeenth Parallel, which, according to the eventual language of the Geneva Agreements, was "only provisional and in no way constitutes a political or territorial boundary"—a significant victory for what became South Vietnam, given that in Bao Dai it had a leader uninterested in leading. In fact, Bao Dai did not even bother to attend Geneva and instead followed the conference from his

Cannes villa. Most of South Vietnam's other luminaries had either taken no side in the war against the French or aided the colonialists outright.

Despite the South's tenuous position, the Geneva Conference's major concessions were made by the North, most at the blunt-instrument urging of its allies China and the Soviet Union. For instance, the North agreed to the temporary partitioning along the Seventeenth Parallel even though it had sought a much lower division. The North agreed to elections that would unite the country under a government of popular choosing two years later even though it had initially demanded elections within six months of the conference. The North agreed to support a cease-fire in the South even though the Viet Minh controlled a significant amount of the South's territory. These concessions, which effectively nullified much of what the Viet Minh had won on the battlefield, were not the product of high-mindedness. Zhou Enlai, the Chinese delegate to the Geneva Conference and the first conference participant to suggest that the two Vietnams suffer division, privately assured the North's delegates that with "the final withdrawal of the French, all of Vietnam will be yours." Nonetheless, North Vietnam's Pham Van Dong would leave Geneva muttering that China had "double-crossed us."

Many people viewed the promised 1956 elections as the death knell of a salvageable non-Communist Vietnam. The CIA projected a landslide for Ho Chi Minh, as did President Eisenhower, who later wrote that "possibly 80 percent of the population" would have voted for Ho. Even if Ho Chi Minh had not won—it appears he might not have, as Pham Van Dong later admitted that the North had certain "control" of only 30 percent of South Vietnam's people at the time the elections were to have taken place—the Communists would almost certainly have ensured his victory through other means.

Enter the forbidding Vietnamese nationalist and Catholic Ngo Dinh Diem. This strange and fascinating man, once said by one of his own family members to have come "from another planet," had served Bao Dai as his minister of the interior several years before but had resigned when it became clear that Bao Dai's government had been granted no operational independence by the French. For much of the 1940s and half of the 1950s, Diem wandered the world from one island of Catholicism to another, ultimately winding up in the luxurious waiting room of Francis Cardinal Spellman, a leading member of a crypto-Catholic lobbying group known as the American Friends of Vietnam. Cardinal Spellman had been one of France's most vocal stateside supporters during its war in Indochina. Diem instantly became a favorite of Spellman, who was not unknown for leaving the mistaken impression upon his fellow Americans that Vietnam was a predominantly Catholic nation, just like the Philippines. (In 1979, the Vatican conducted routine background checks to determine the deceased Spellman's suitability for sainthood and learned that Spellman had been something troublingly close to a CIA agent.) Spellman introduced the socially awkward Diem to many other Friends of Vietnam, among them Senator John F. Kennedy.

Historians are at odds as to how Diem came to be offered the prime ministership of South Vietnam by Bao Dai (who cared not for Diem) in June 1954, when the Geneva Conference was still ongoing and Diem himself was in France. But whether Diem was selected by the CIA, President Eisenhower, or Bao Dai working with a relative amount of freedom, it is clear that Colonel Edward Lansdale had been the man to urge Diem forward. Colonel Lansdale was famous chiefly for helping to end a powerful Communist insurgency in the 1950s in the Philippines and serving as a partial model for Alden Pyle in Graham Greene's *The Quiet American* and as the total model for Colonel Edwin Hillandale in William Lederer and Eugene Burdick's *The Ugly American*. In 1954, there were many people with considerable knowledge of mainland Asia within the U.S. government, but most of them were China experts. When it came to Southeast Asia, Robert McNamara has written, there were "no senior officials" in U.S. government with significant knowledge of the region until at least the mid-1960s. Colonel Lansdale, in 1954 the senior official with the deepest knowledge of Southeast Asia, had been sent to Vietnam with this message from CIA Director Allen Dulles: "Save South Vietnam. God bless you."

To Lansdale's mind, Diem was perfect: a patriot who had not collaborated with the French and, as a bonus, hated Communists. Ominously, the French warned the United States about Diem, saying he had no base of support. The fact that Diem was Catholic—while far from a viscerally hated minority in Vietnam, nevertheless a minority viewed with considerable suspicion—did not, apparently, stagger the enthusiasm of Diem's American backers. To Lansdale's credit, he argued that such mindless support for Diem would result in a personality cult rather than a constitutional, democratic framework that would offer the people of South Vietnam something real and measurable. This plea was disregarded, as was his later augury that Communism in South Vietnam "will not die by being ignored, bombed, or smothered by us."

The first important thing Diem did was refuse to sign the Geneva Agreement, which he called "catastrophic and immoral." The United States also refused to sign, saying only that it "took note" of the agreement's signature. (Ultimately only France and North Vietnam signed.) Washington pledged not to upset Geneva's implementation but warned that it would view any "renewal of aggression" on the part of the North with sobriety and concern. The second important thing Diem did was name himself Bao Dai's replacement as head of state, after which Diem's regime was given diplomatic recognition by the United States. The third important thing Diem did was cancel the 1956 elections, which were supposed to unite Vietnam. It is worth pointing out that the Communists had never expected the elections to take place. Twenty-five years after the fact, former Secretary of State Dean Rusk not unreasonably pointed out that "at the same time, the Soviets were utterly opposed to free elections in Korea. So the question must have arisen why should we accommodate them in one spot if they wouldn't accommodate us in these places." Diem did hold an election, though. Diem's U.S. advisers had suggested he give himself, say, 60 percent of the vote. Diem demurred and allowed himself 98.2 percent of the vote—more than Ho Chi Minh gave himself in North Vietnam's equally rigged election. An unpromising start for our ally in nascent Vietnamese democracy.

Diem surrounded himself with largely Catholic generals. According to William J. Duiker, Diem "found southerners too easygoing to resist effectively the Communists" and consequently stocked his government with northerners living in exile and central Vietnamese. Most of these men had fought against the legendary Viet Minh. Few Vietnamese peasants knew much about a German economist who had lived most of his life in London or the young Russian lawyer who had refined this economist's views, but they knew the Viet Minh had defeated the French, whom they hated. Diem, the peasants slowly realized, was not of the Viet Minh. How, Diem's worried handlers wondered, does one distance those Viet Minh from heroism? One renames them *Viet Cong*.

After Geneva, North Vietnam's Politburo had ordered 10,000 Communist "stay-behinds" to remain in the South and stop all activities but "legal struggle." They were not ordered to start a war—not yet, at least—but Diem brought war to them. By 1957, Diem's brutal counterrevolutionary tactics had reduced the Communists' numbers in the South to 2,000, and in 1958 one American adviser said that Vietnam "can be classed as about as stable and peaceful a country in all of Asia." The South's Communists saw their darkest hour in 1959, by which time it was a "miracle," in one historian's words, that any of them were still alive. The late 1950s also saw the Diem regime go after South Vietnam's powerful religious sects, the Hoa Hao and Cao Dai, both of which were anti-Communist (the Viet Minh had stupidly assassinated the Hoa Hao's prophet) but secretly supported by Diem's malingering French adversaries. The resistance by these groups, too, was pulverized at the cost of alienating huge swaths of South Vietnam's people. How was Diem so initially successful at crushing dissent? As Neil Sheehan writes, a captain in the U.S. Army named Richard Ziegler personally witnessed Diem's soldiers engage in forms of torture and execution that ranged from the guillotine to skinning people alive to shooting them through the ear to dislocating people's shoulders to electroshocking genitalia with a crank-operated battery-powered field telephone—each method apparently sanctioned by Diem, who was not only a *Time* magazine cover subject but once proclaimed by Vice President Lyndon Johnson during a 1961 visit to South Vietnam to be "the Churchill of Asia" and judged by Robert McNamara to "rank with the two or three greatest" men he had ever met.

Soon the South's Communists began to fight back with increasing effectiveness, agitating among the peasants who were (at best) ignored and (at worst) mangled by the regime of Ngo Dinh Diem. In late 1960, the Communists founded the NLF, and in 1961 they created the People's Revolutionary Party. The 2,000 hunted and desperate Communists of 1958 had grown to 10,000 by 1960. By 1961, there were as many as 30,000, with a passive following perhaps ten times that number. This growth, spearheaded by the southern-born Communist Le Duan, occurred at a time when the North was trying to avoid war. This did not mean that the North was waiting peaceably. Resolution 15, a document released thirty years after it was approved in the late 1950s, establishes that Ho and his government's many public statements about not wanting war were merely a ruse. Resolution 15 said that the "fundamental path of development in South Vietnam is that of violent struggle." The approval of Resolution 15 meant that the Party had made reunification with the South its single greatest priority. The only question was when. Le Duan helped force the matter when he launched a brutal assassination campaign against South Vietnamese politicians and ARVN officers. More U.S. weapons poured into South Vietnam. For reasons typical to corruption, many of these weapons wound up in the hands of the NLF. The leaders of North Vietnam soon realized they had much to lose by sitting out the intensifying conflict between Diem and the NLF and with Le Duan's complicity began to direct the struggle. Of this bonfire one can say that Diem supplied the wood, the United States provided the tinder, Le Duan lit the match, and North Vietnam's Politburo fanned the flames.

President Diem began to lose hold, and a 1960 coup attempt left him floundering in paranoia. He had no wish to go the way of South Korea's dictatorial Syngman Rhee, recently dumped by his U.S. backers. Diem fired generals whom the Americans put forward for commendation because he worried that anyone the Americans admired could be used in another coup attempt against him. He also urged his generals to keep casualties down. Meanwhile, an ARVN Special Forces unit that the CIA had trained at great effort and expense was used by Diem not to kill Communists but as his personal bodyguards. Diem also raised taxes, not to provide for his people but to remove himself further from them. He lived in opulent barricaded fear in a way the leaders of North Vietnam, who were at least Diem's equals in brutality, did not. Many of North Vietnam's leaders walked freely through the streets of Hanoi, the police officers of which did not (and still do not) carry firearms. Soon Diem's taxes matched those of the old and hated French regime. (The NLF's impromptu "road taxes" were proportionately as high as Diem's— though unlike Diem, the NLF gave the peasants a receipt.)

As Diem turned further inward, he began to trust only his immediate family, especially his brother Nhu and Nhu's wife, Madame Nhu, who served as the chaste Diem's "Platonic wife." Diem on one occasion told an American diplomat that, when it came to his family, he viewed himself as the father of a holy trinity. His brother Nhu was the director of South Vietnam's thirteen separate intelligence agencies, a steady recipient of CIA aid, a reputed heroin and opium addict, a totalitarianism buff, and quite possibly a psychopath. Nhu's wife, Madame Nhu, the holy spirit of the trinity, also formed a private army, in her case an all-woman commando unit. Called by Robert McNamara a "true sorceress," Madame Nhu had an assortment of her own troubling peccadilloes and forced through South Vietnam's rubber-stamping legislature a series of bizarre laws that banned "sentimental songs," dancing "anywhere at all," divorce, boxing, cockfighting, condoms, beauty contests, padded bras, "spiritualism," and gambling—in short, everything Vietnamese people liked. During the crisis that saw Buddhists burning themselves alive in protest, criticism of the Ngos turned white hot in the American press. Madame Nhu said publicly that *The New York Times* reporter David Halberstam should be burned alive, and Nhu himself scribbled the names of Halberstam and his colleague Neil Sheehan onto an assassination list.

Even when Diem acted in accord with American advice, he bestowed upon the results his own poisonous spin. His Strategic Hamlets Program, while more effective than its detractors usually admit, essentially herded peasants into ad hoc villages surrounded by barbed wire to keep them separated from NLF agitprop. Many in these enclosed hamlets, despite being guilty of nothing, were forced to engage in government labor. At the United States' insistence Diem also initiated land reform. While it was not the bacchanal of violence that Communist land reform had been, Diem's land reform actually made the inequality of land distribution in South Vietnam worse. The man who headed this program to take land away from the Vietnamese landlords was a Diem appointee. His other job? Landlord.

Many U.S. officials consoled themselves with the thought that the government of North Vietnam was worse. That North Vietnam's Communists were finally more repressive is undoubtedly true, but winning a less-awful contest against Communist dictators was not the sort of victory for which so many people had already died or would die. By 1963, with the war against the Communists rushing toward the point of no recouping, the United States was at last forced to look very carefully at the Ngos and their government of "bayonets at every street corner," in the disgusted words of one U.S. official. What prompted deeper U.S. thought about the Ngos was not that they were publicly applauding their own people burning themselves to death in protest of their government, nor that the Ngos' supposed base, Vietnamese Catholics, had turned against them, nor that the Ngos were planning to murder American journalists. What was so agitating was news that Nhu was seeking rapprochement with the Communists.

In April 1963, Nhu told Australian diplomats that the United States should leave South Vietnam, as its way of life was not compatible with Vietnam's. Madame Nhu said that the Americans were acting like "little soldiers of fortune" in her country. The forces of autonomy the United States claimed to be protecting in South Vietnam were dangerously close to acting autonomously, and throughout the summer Nhu often hinted to foreign journalists that he was negotiating with NLF and even North Vietnamese representatives. Some argue that these were all stalling tactics to force the United States to give the Ngos more aid. While this view is probably accurate, it is also somewhat beside the point, since Nhu was in fact meeting with NLF representatives, though not, apparently, with North Vietnamese contacts. Nevertheless, by September 13, the CIA's director told the White House he was concerned that a deal between Hanoi and the Ngos was close to being fulfilled.

There have been few satisfying attempts to explain what exactly occurred during the long lead-up to the coup against Ngo Dinh Diem and his brother in November 1963. (A. J. Langguth's account in *Our*

Vietnam is the best I have read.) The coup has always had about it a heavy fog of mystery. It particularly fascinated Richard Nixon, who instructed one of his Watergate felons to fabricate cables that directly implicated Kennedy in Diem's downfall. Studied closely, it seems an affair of strictly unglamorous barbarian logic. Half of Kennedy's administration supported getting rid of Diem, half opposed it. Kennedy himself, who apparently viewed Diem, as a fellow Catholic, with some sympathy, vacillated. The initial agreement to back a group of skittish, coup-plotting generals was called by Robert McNamara "one of the truly pivotal decisions" of the United States' involvement in Vietnam. The coup's green light was given during a confusing weekend that found most of Kennedy's administration out of town, yet the coup itself did not occur for two more months. During that time Diem and Nhu sometimes appeared to be preparing for a literal war with the United States, reportedly adding U.S. Ambassador Henry Cabot Lodge to the death list. (They intended to blame Lodge's murder, and many others, on the NLF.) President Kennedy tried to back out of the coup at the last minute, but Ambassador Lodge, who was running things in Saigon, and who likely would have been fired had the coup not succeeded, blithely cabled back, "Do not think we have the power to delay or discourage a coup." The mood in the White House turned from that of puppet masters to frightened children. "If the coup fails," Robert Kennedy said a few days before it finally took place, "Diem throws us out." No doubt many in the Kennedy administration no longer knew whether they even wanted the coup to succeed.

The last message Diem communicated to Kennedy affirmed, per Lodge's later summary, that "I am a good and frank ally. . . . Tell President Kennedy that I take all his suggestions very seriously." Diem was not a good ally, or a frank one. He was a mystical bore and the cruel messiah of a religion of three. Diem's last known words in English, made to Lodge over the telephone, were "I am trying to reestablish order." Despite President Kennedy's personal request that Diem and Nhu not be harmed, the brothers were bound, deposited into an American-made armored personnel carrier, and shot in the back of the head, after which the hated Nhu was gruesomely disfigured with a bayonet. Their bodies were then driven out to Tan Son Nhut airport and pushed into unmarked graves.

At the time of Diem's death only seventy-eight Americans had been killed in South Vietnam. In the coming weeks, NLF attacks would increase by 250 percent, and a few months later it was clear to the CIA that the "statistics received over the past year or more from the [South Vietnamese] and reported by the U.S. mission on which we gauged the trends of the war were grossly in error." Two months after the coup, the CIA wrote with its typical concern, "There is no organized government in South Vietnam at this time." A coup against the generals who had deposed Diem became necessary after it was claimed that they, too, were at least notionally interested in trying to negotiate an end to the war. The womanizing Francophile General Nguyen Khanh took charge in 1964. But as his fortunes quickly soured, General Khanh, too, began to explore the possibility of negotiation with the NLF, with which his brother-in-law was aligned. As one historian writes, what was so concerning to U.S. officials "was not so much those forces that might get the United States into a war but those that might keep it out of one." (General Maxwell Taylor actually argued that the more representative the South Vietnamese government became, the "more susceptible to an accommodation with the Liberation Front" it would be.) When Khanh proved an utter wash, Ambassador Lodge cabled Washington that "the US should be prepared to run the country, possibly from Cam Ranh Bay."

By the fall of 1964, General Khanh was replaced by Phan Khac Suu, an agricultural engineer. Suu also indicated some interest in negotiating with the NLF. Khanh tried and failed to retake the government in December 1964 and openly called for revolt against the Americans. A concomitant NLF bomb that destroyed Saigon's Brink Hotel—the home of unmarried U.S. officers, named for General Francis G. Brink, the first U.S. commander in Vietnam and a suicide—was initially mistaken for a South Vietnamese attack on the United States. South Vietnam seemed, in Robert McNamara's words, on the edge "of total collapse." By now South Vietnam's central government had no direct access to many of its provincial offices, and in a few cities the only way in was by helicopter. Even General Westmoreland would later write that "few in the world would have faulted us at that point" had the United States withdrawn. Two years after Diem's overthrow, the situation had gone, in the words of a British official in Saigon, "from bad to worse . . . nothing is to be seen but drift, back-biting, corruption—and worse."

Why did the people of South Vietnam not care more about defending themselves? Why the constant plots and overthrows? Why the corruption? It is likely that the plots and overthrows came because, for the majority of the war, the only solution to South Vietnam's problems the United States could accept was military. The catch was that the only lasting solution to South Vietnam's problems was political. This is not hindsight-aided or even really arguable. Dozens of analysts and U.S. officials at varying levels of prominence made this very point as early as 1962. But the decision was to fight, even though by all evidence the South Vietnamese did not want to. So plots and overthrows were the rule until those who wanted to fight were found. But often those who claimed to want to fight did not actually want to fight either. Some were cowards, certainly, but a good number were simply sick of fighting. Unlike the United States and North Vietnam, South Vietnam saw the vivid horror of ground war uproot its fields and reduce its cities to rubble.

As for the corruption of South Vietnam, consider its trash. For several extended periods during the war, Saigon's sanitation services basically stopped and the garbage fragrantly piled up. A modest city job such as trash collector did not pay nearly as much as the U.S. military paid Vietnamese to mop the floors of its commissaries. Fewer and fewer Vietnamese were willing to do work that benefited solely Vietnamese. The United States tried to help by sending a fleet of garbage trucks to Saigon free of charge, but they were intercepted by corrupt ARVN generals, plundered, and sold for parts. The U.S. Army was ultimately charged with picking up Saigon's trash. Similarly, thousands of tons of cement sent to the South Vietnamese for use in building schools was stolen by the regime and replaced with sand.

But what of civic virtue? Many South Vietnamese simply took their cues from an oblivious occupying power. Because the Americans who occupied Vietnam had, in the aggregate, so little respect for or curiosity about the culture of their hosts, civic virtue and pride vanished into the ratholes of prostitution, graft, and corruption. One U.S. analyst said during the war, "We have corrupted the cities. Now, perhaps we can corrupt the countryside as well." Amazingly, this was meant as a serious statement of strategy. While fighting Communism, the United States bankrupted South Vietnam's families with record-breaking inflation and prolonged for years a war most wanted only to end. One wonders if this is what President Thieu meant when in 1979 he maintained from exile that "without the American presence we could have beaten the Communists." While Thieu was probably wrong, it seems certain that without the American presence South Vietnam would not have lost to the Communists quite so tragically, so completely, at such length, or with such losses.

Yes, South Vietnam's leaders were in the main corrupt, spineless, and endlessly inept. But it was the Americans who believed in them. Even when the Americans stopped believing in them, the abetment of motley crews of corrupt false democrats continued at the eventual cost of millions of lives. To have mistaken ineptitude for helplessness for so long was an American mistake that required considerable self-deception. But to be inept is not to be helpless; it is to be inept.

III

We drove for several hours, down the coast, along surprisingly well-maintained roads, through what felt like lush green tunnels of Vietnamese countryside. My father made satisfied little mouth noises as he pored over a copy of *Viet Nam News,* "The National English Language Daily" he had picked up at the airport upon our arrival in Ho Chi Minh City. Wherever he traveled, my father always made it a point to read the local newspapers. It was What He Did.

Viet Nam News suggested nothing so much as how crafty authoritarianism had become over the last twenty years. The paper contained two species of story. The first was about what a good job the government was doing. It was always merely a good job. Things were never ludicrously overstated. This had been the biggest problem of the Soviet propaganda found within *Pravda,* which apparently could not be read without appalled laughter. The second was about some difficult structural or social problem. "Education Needs More Reform," for example. Guess who was expected to reform it? Another fascinating thing was the numb linearity created by a few days' worth of *Viet Nam News* front pages: Monday: "South African President to Visit Viet Nam." Tuesday: "South African President Meets with Viet Nam Prime Minister." Wednesday: "South Africa, Viet Nam Pledge to Bolster Bilateral Ties." Thursday: "Viet Nam, South Africa Bolster Bilateral Ties." Friday: "Viet Nam Prime Minister Sees Bright Future for Ties with South Africa." The article my father was now reading was titled "Singapore Tightens Internet Laws."

"Interesting article?" I asked.

His head lifted with birdlike alertness, and he looked over at me. "I'm just enjoying this cultural exchange." Once he had finished memorizing the contents of *Viet Nam News,* he peppered Hien with questions such as "Is that a pigeon?" "Are those tea farmers?" "Is that sugarcane?" "When was this road built?" "Do the Vietnamese use much solar power?"

We were now growing closer to my father's area of Marine Corps operations. After Hien had finished debriefing him on the overall impact of rice exports upon the Vietnamese economy, I noticed him snapping and unsnapping the latch of his blocky black camera case. He was as fidgety as a carsick boy.

"So how do you feel?" I asked.

"Marvelous. Super. I'm having a ball."

"You're sure you're up for seeing some of your old stomping grounds?"

He waved this off. "It was a long time ago. I'll be fine."

We passed through the rural sprawl of several villages. I saw women wearing conical peasant hats, huge vase-shaped wicker baskets full of rice, all the stage-dressing clichés of the Vietnam War. Yet these were not NLF women, no GI would be along to bayonet the rice baskets in search of hidden ordnance, and the sky was absent of any steel dragonflies whooping overhead. The clichés meant nothing. They were not even clichés but rather staples of Vietnamese life. I had discerned already that the war informed much here but defined little, and it suddenly seemed very strange that we referred to the Vietnam War, a phrase whose adjectivelessness grew more bizarre as I pondered it. It managed to take an entire nation and plunge it into perpetual conflict.

In nearly every village and town we passed through, men sat roadside upon plastic chairs, on the lookout for backseat palefaces in well-appointed cars much like ours. Once they spotted us, these scouts launched up and suicidally ran out into traffic in an attempt to flag us down so we could stop and have a bowl of *pho bo* at their cafés. When we passed by a gated-off regional Communist Party headquarters I learned that in Vietnam Soviet-style hammer-and-sickle flags were still earnestly flown. (A few days later I would almost fall out of the car when we drifted by a funeral procession whose coffin was embossed with a swastika. The dark visceral charge of those eight right angles had temporarily rendered me an amnesiac: in Vietnam the swastika retained its original Buddhist, not Nazi, heritage.) Rural Vietnam's omnipresent roadside shops were draped with advertisements for Honda (often rendered as "Hon Da"), Coca-Cola, Happydent gum, even Kotex. Rainbow-colored incense cones were sold beneath green-and-white Fujifilm sun umbrellas or awnings branded with the La Vie water logo. Billboards advertised Sting, an Asian-market soft drink made by Pepsi, the taste of which was well captured by its name. Ancient thin Vietnamese women with raisiny skin sold cans of Red Bull. Poorer old Vietnamese women sold the local Red Bull knockoff, Super Horse. Even poorer old Vietnamese women sold the Super Horse knockoff, Commando Bear.

On the highway around us the scooters weaved and slowed. While in the bigger cities younger women on scooters wore long operagoing gloves and bank-robber-style masks to prevent getting tan (dark skin was not prized here, and "We have enough sun" was all Hien would say of the matter), the younger women in these villages were mostly uncovered. The scooters moved in thick tadpole clusters, and they had so many names. The Future, the Viva, the Dream, the Maxi, the Custom, the Sirius, the Magma, the Atilla, the Maestro, the Warrant, the Zebra, the Wave, the Wizard New Cooler Trend, the Dynamic, the Dylan, the Spacey. Learning these names was an exercise in naked hierarchy, as everyone in Vietnam knew exactly—it was practically occult—how much each type of scooter cost. Vietnamese scooters carried and hauled all manner of cargo. A duffel-sized wire cage filled with squirming puppies, for instance. A chest of drawers. A stack of four computer monitors. A sofa. Two live hogs. A stand-up bass guitar. A family of five. Another scooter. Meanwhile Truong was beeping his horn. My father pointed out the thumb-sized pad of wear on Truong's steering wheel, where he had literally beeped the wheel's covering down to its greenish underleather. Truong's horn-per-minute usage: 14.5. In New York City I had come to believe that car horns were one of the more overrated tools of behavior modification—but that, I now knew, was because they were used without any imagination. In Vietnam there was a very real language of horns. A short beep meant: *I'm behind you.* Two short beeps: *I'm passing.* One long beep: *Fuck you!*

"Look at these hills," my father said, pointing at the slopes and rises all around us. "How we fought and scratched for them."

Some brief, terrible recognition in his voice and eyes—some distance closed too quickly, some unexpectedly recovered past—spooked me deeply. My father was softly shaking his head. "Where are we?" I asked, if only to break the mood.

"We are nearing the Hai Van Pass," Hien said, pointing ahead to where the bus-clogged road corkscrewed up into the foothills of the Truong Son range. To our left a wall of thick, long-needled pine trees suddenly broke to reveal a steep drop. Beyond the cliff's edge was the blue universe of the South China Sea, a whitecapped chaos so astonishingly choppy I half expected to see the face of Yahweh moving across it.

"Very high, very beautiful pass," Hien said.

"The Hoi Vun Pass?" my father asked.

"Hai Van."

"Hey Vong?"

"Hai Van."

"Well," my father said, sitting back defeatedly, "it's certainly a beautiful pass."

I had sympathy for my father. Learning to speak Vietnamese, I would eventually learn, was rather like learning to sing using sounds you had never known existed. (Hearteningly, the Vietnamese had just as much trouble with English and its tricky "finishing" sounds: while many Vietnamee speak Engli very well in the grammatical sense, they can still be difficult to understand.) Every Vietnamese vowel—there are twelve different vowels—has six tonal possibilities. Depending on its tone, the word *chua,* for instance, could mean "sour," "pagoda," "Jesus," or "not yet." Vietnamese also had many diphthongs and triphthongs, and at first these were as baffling as any aspect of Vietnamese. For instance, while Hien was saying "Hai Van" it sounded like "Hai Vang," but with a crispness to the *ng* sound. There were at least a dozen more unexpected and (to an English speaker) counterintuitive diph- or triphthongs. Sonic muskegs, tonal jungles. . . . There was a famous story of how Robert McNamara once tried to say "Long live South Vietnam" at a government rally but fumbled the tones. To the listening Vietnamese it sounded as though McNamara said, "The southern duck wants to lie down." As we ascended the road, I whipped out my recently purchased Vietnamese-English dictionary and said that I felt I was operating at an extreme disadvantage among the local women when my name translated into Vietnamese as "shrimp." A thin, annoyed smile from Hien. Truong beeped at a cow. And my father merely shook his head.

We climbed. Numerous cranes were dredging up the mountain's rich, shockingly red soil. These holes, Hien explained, were vents for the tunnel currently being dug through this mountain at the cost of hundreds of billions of dong. (The early twenty-first century had found the Vietnamese in a spending mood. I would later learn of a billion-dong government program intended somehow to increase the average height of Vietnamese people.) The expensive tunnel, which was being built with U.S., Japanese, and South Korean aid, would be completed in 2005.

The road did not continuously climb a lone mountain but gradually wound upward around the faces of several. We could look across the gaps between these mountains and see small, toylike trucks that only minutes later were huge and honking and charging toward us. Several of these toys transformed into Russian-made Kamaz trucks, thick charcoal smoke chugging out of their tailpipes, which were a remnant of the decade and a half when Vietnam had served as one of the few places outside the USSR's captive market into which the Soviets could dump their shoddy equipment. The mountains themselves were covered in deep green layers of eucalyptus as thick as shag. No matter how hard the wind blew, the vegetation had a toupee stillness. In 1975, Hien told us, these mountains had been as bright red and empty as Martian hills. During the Vietnamese War the defoliant Agents Orange and White had been sprayed endlessly over this entire area.

Finally, at the top of the pass, we were stopped in a mild traffic jam, and my father got out of the car to take pictures. I followed him. It felt cold enough up here to snow, the clouds soppingly low and foggy. An open-air market was run atop the pass, and friendly merchants selling everything from coconuts to soft drinks to trinkets instantly set upon us. All of them made a uniquely convincing case for themselves: I was learning that the Vietnamese could sell water to hydrophobes, corpses to the morgue. I purchased some rubber balls of noteworthy uselessness from a beautiful, dirty-faced young Vietnamese woman while my father snapped pictures. When he wanted some photos of himself, he handed me his camera.

I stared at this relic, called a Yashica FX-7. "What is this?"

"That's my camera."

"Was it forged in the Third Age of the Elves or something?"

"I had that camera with me," my father announced proudly, "the first time I came to Vietnam."

"*This* is the camera you took all those slides with?" The John C. Bissell Vietnam Slide Show was a staple of my Michigan childhood and was always a standing-room-only occasion. I had a sudden recollection of those evenings, sitting in anticipatory wonder in our darkened living room, feeling the warmth of the bodies all around me, transfixed by the changing blasts of light, the harsh clack of the slide machine's carousel. Once I made the mistake of asking my father how many of the men in one group photo had died. He did not answer. The entire room went silent, in fact. I have no memory of any slide shows after that. I looked back to my father and held out toward him his Yashica FX-7. "Dad, this camera is thirty-eight years old!"

He looked back at me. "No, it isn't." His hand lifted and batted about frivolously. "It's . . . what? Thirty-*two* years old."

"It's thirty-eight years old, Dad. Almost *forty*."

"No, it's not, because 1960 plus forty years is 2000. I arrived in 1965, so—"

"So 2005 minus two is today."

My father was silent. Then all at once his color went. "Oh my God. Holy shit."

"Kinda incredible, isn't it?"

"I didn't know I was that old until just now."

He was touching his face as I lined him up in the viewfinder. "So if someone had told you thirty-eight years ago that you'd be having your photograph taken atop the Hai Van Pass, what would you have said?"

His hand dropped militarily to his side. "I would have expected to be here."

"You would have expected to be here? Say 'cheese,' by the way."

"As a conquering general. Cheese."

I walked up a small hill to an old stone gate, built by the French, that resembled a brick farmhouse. Beneath this gate's low stone arch, which was wide enough to allow the passage of only one vehicle at a time, all traffic had been monitored and checked. A grassed-over little road—the remains of the old Highway 1, which, then and now, reached from one tip of Vietnam to the other—was all that was left of this old colonial hourglass, while below and around the hill swept the wide blacktop carpet of the new Highway 1, which was being rebuilt and upgraded throughout the country thanks to a massive World Bank loan. The First Indochina War's greatest chronicler, Bernard Fall, had nicknamed Highway 1 the "Street without Joy," usage of which had carried over into my father's war.

Fall was one of the war's most fascinating noncombatants. Born in Austria, educated in the United States, active in the French Underground during World War II, an investigator during the Nuremberg Trials, and eventually seen as the foremost Western analyst of Southeast Asia, Fall was a thermometer of American fortunes during the war's earlier years. In 1965, Fall had some confidence that the United States would prevail, stressing the "determinative weight" of American intervention. But he also foresaw the dangers. "The Vietnamese," he wrote in 1965, "fall into two categories; the Viet Cong (also known as VC, Victor Charlie, Charlie, or 'the Congs'), and 'our' Vietnamese, for whom there are no particular nicknames, except perhaps 'our allies' or 'the friendlies'; both terms followed by a guffaw." But however strong a case the United States made for itself militarily in Vietnam, "a prostrate South Vietnam, plowed under by bombers and artillery and still in the hands of a politically irrelevant regime, may become the victim of aroused social and political forces for which no aircraft carrier and eight-jet bomber can provide a ready answer in the long run." Later he argued, "There must be negotiation and settlement sooner or later, unless the Johnson administration wishes to leave the Vietnamese War in what has been called the shadowland between unattainable victory and unacceptable surrender."

Fall understood North Vietnam—he conducted fascinating early interviews with Ho Chi Minh and Pham Van Dong—and knew there were monsters in the Politburo as well as men of relative honor. He also believed that the American, and French, way of life was probably preferable to that which the Communists wished to inflict on the South: "[W]hat America is seeking is not total victory over the Viet Cong. We are going for *total defeat* of the VC. The semantics are important, because what America should want to prove in Viet-Nam is that the Free World is 'better,' *not* that it can kill people more efficiently. If we could induce 100,000 Viet Cong to surrender to our side because our offers of social reform are better than those of the other side's, *that* would be victory." He would come to hold these articles of faith less strongly and ultimately came to regard the war as "a local conflict with outside support which has gotten out of hand." One must content oneself with wondering what Fall would have believed later. On February 21, 1967, during an operation in which he had been horrified to see the Marines he was traveling with open fire on some innocent peasant's water buffalo, Fall stepped on a land mine on the Street without Joy and finally traveled to his own shadowland.

On the other side of the Hai Van Pass, Vietnam grew more tropical, a great rotting chromatic extravagance of jungle and rice paddies. "*This* is my Vietnam," my father said with satisfied recognition. The jungle. When hit by the sun it looked golden and hot and desiccated, but when darkened by shade it looked green and cool and secret. The rice paddies seemed as massive as ten plantations after a deluge. One hectare of growing rice needed ten thousand tons of water. A thick mist hovered above these calm, endless reaches of standing water, the shoots of rice straw seven feet tall. Water buffaloes the size of small dinosaurs were sunk to their flanks in the mud, while rice farmers wearing condomlike body bags waded through chest-deep water holding bundled nets above their heads. The majority of the houses around these rice fields were tin-roofed concrete-block houses, the porches of which were stilted up by rough, unfinished lumber. Muddy, partially flooded yards were strewn with mangled tires, wooden Coca-Cola crates, and old gasoline cans. Perched dryly atop occasional mounds of gravel were wheelbarrows and bicycles. The inhabitants of all these homes were rice farmers. Thomas Jefferson planted Vietnamese rice at Monticello, I recalled reading. Just as suddenly I thought of Ho Chi Minh. "Rice fields," Ho once said, "are battlefields."

"Independence," my father muttered, as though reading my mind. The edges of his mouth pulled down, and his unsentimental face had gone slack. But our car was fast, and soon the rice paddies were behind us.

On the approach to Danang houses were bundled together along the road even more tightly than usual. In many cases one could take three steps from the highway's edge and be standing in the middle of some Vietnamese family's living room. Then we stopped at a shop: Truong needed cigarettes. I got out of the car and followed him inside, finding for sale on a discreetly low shelf various Vietnamese nostrums: deer-horn wine, stomach of porcupine wine, bird wine. Floating within each bottle was as advertised. Also available was something called Cobratox, or "ointment with snake venom." Asian herbalism had a dark side one rarely heard about from its grinning, vitamin-packed Western champions.

As we got closer to Danang, the architecture began to change. Now beside the low gray houses common to rural Vietnam were unusually tall and strikingly slender homes painted hot pink, mint green, lilac, and lavender. Some have called this style Lego Deco. The buildings looked like the kind of home one might find in seaside Miami if seaside Miami were filled with Vietnamese who had won the lottery and discovered the aesthetics of a certain kind of homosexuality. When I asked about the color of these homes, Hien explained that the Vietnamese "enjoy color-ful things." One of the sadder things about developing economies is the grim middle period during which people figure out that just because something *can* be bought does not necessarily mean it *should* be.

We passed a disused airport runway, one of many reminders in these vicinities that Danang once headquartered the United States Marines. All around us were areas the Marines had renamed: the Arizona Ter-ritory, China Beach, Marble Mountain, Elephant Valley. Another reminder was the city's Amerasians, the epithet given to the children of Vietnamese mothers and American fathers. Danang was said to have the largest number of Amerasians in all of Vietnam. Hien pointed out an Amerasian beggar alongside the road. The man looked at least thirty-five years old and had obviously been sired by a black father. One of the most depressing aspects of this altogether depressing phenomenon was how much harder life was for Amerasians of partially black descent, probably because of the fact that many Vietnamese identify black skin with Cambodians, with whom they have a long antipathetic history. A good number of Vietnam's Amerasians had over the last fifteen years or so been allowed into the United States to seek their fortunes.

"I never much liked Danang," my father said.

I looked over at him. "Weren't all your higher-ups here?"

"You got it."

"Your father-in-law was here, too, though. Colonel T."

"I didn't know him then."

"What did you think of Colonel T.?"

"My father-in-law? Good pilot. Experienced man. Honorable man. Steeped in the Marine Corps tradition. A wonderful guy. I loved him. And he and I pretty much saw eye to eye when I decided to leave the Marine Corps."

"But I read a letter from Colonel T. saying he thought you were mak-ing a mistake."

"At first he thought I was making a mistake, but he realized there was nobody to take care of my brother and sister. He was mad at me for about an hour. When I got out, Colonel T. and I became very close. We exchanged secrets. We knew a lot of things about each other. And I admired and respected him deeply."

"When he died, how did you feel?"

"How do you think I felt? Horrible. He and I were partners in business, you know."

"I didn't know that." Why did I not know that? "What business were you partners in?"

"We bought some property in northern Michigan. I told him about it, he said, 'All right, here's the seed money,' which I didn't have. But he and I were equal partners. I sold it two years after he died for about two thousand percent profit."

"Jesus."

"That's what I said at the time, as a matter of fact. It allowed your mom and me some momentary prosperity."

I waited. "Do you think Vietnam is the reason you and Mom divorced?"

My father looked out the window at a long stretch of empty beach. The ocean was on our right, and on our left was quite possibly the settled world's least utilized stretch of gorgeous beachfront. Nothing here but public housing slums—dim, beaten buildings whose laundry lines were full and whose doorways and windows were dark.

"We became incompatible," my father said finally.

I did not know what to say to that. Scars deadened the skin but were also easily torn. My father did not know why they had divorced. It seemed amazing, our inability to understand our own lives. The tires thunked along the road. Streaking beside us was part of the beachfront where both the French and United States had begun their invasions of Vietnam, 118 years apart. The weather was so rough during the U.S. invasion that the first landing had to be postponed. The waves looked truly splendid today—huge and blue and rolling beneath frothy crowns of white foam. But there was no one out here. These slum-town beaches were completely empty. It appeared that Charlie really did not surf.

My father cleared his throat. "Divorce is like a cancer that never goes away."

I looked at him. "It's painful."

"Not anymore."

"To think about, I mean."

"Those were sad days. Be glad you're too young to remember them."

"You didn't want to go back to Escanaba after the Marines."

"Not especially, no."

Again, we had never talked about this. How was it possible that we had never talked about this? "Are you glad you went back to Escanaba today?"

"Yeah," he said—though again, it took him a moment. "But I'm glad only because I don't know what would have happened otherwise. I'm quite happy with the way things turned out." His mouth puckered. "Actually, I don't know if I'm happy or not."

"You don't?"

A brisk shake of his head. "No, I'm happy. I've had a great life. I raised a wonderful son, and also you."

My overall impression of Danang was that of a city being augmented, enhanced, piled on, attached to. The Vietnamese government was said to be trying to avoid what economists have called "the dumbbell effect": the enrichment and development of Hanoi and Saigon while neglect rode herd upon Vietnam's slender middle. If the dumbbell effect was not foiled, it would not be for lack of trying: dusty air, metal scaffoldings, and shirtless construction workers were to Danang what orange-robed Buddhists and stately pagodas were to Hue.

Across many of Danang's streets stretched a high green canopy of thick tree foliage through which only pieces of sunlight were able to fall, giving many scooterists a flickering, film-stock aura as they drove along. Once our car had passed through the central part of Danang, we came upon an open riverside area where the city's famous Museum of Cham Sculpture sat across from the glass cube that was the state television station's new building. Like most of Vietnam's French-built administrative buildings, the museum was a Cheez Whiz orange-yellow and had grotty growths of moss and mold over much of its facing.

The Chams are a people of Indian descent who had the great misfortune to migrate to—and, for a while, flourish within—one of the most contested areas on earth. The Chams' kingdom, called Champa, endured in varying sizes from the second century to the 1800s, when the Vietnamese, after working at it for six centuries, drove the last of the landholding Chams from their final hectares of ancestral territory. Yet throughout the upheaval the Chams developed an elaborate, sophisticated, and extremely violent culture: one scholar calls them "the Norsemen of the South China Sea" due to their fondness for conducting raiding parties. Inside the Cham Museum itself was a good deal of phallic and mammillate sculpture. The real Cham treasures were found outdoors, all along central Vietnam's coast. These were the ancient towers of Champa—rutilant stone temples that from a distance often looked like spaceships perched atop a hill. A curiously large number of U.S. military bunkers were built on hilltops near Cham towers, probably due to very similar security fears, and to climb a hill on which either stood was to gaze from one structure to the other and marvel at the sad iterations of history.

My father had raced up and down coastal Vietnam, which was the hub of the Champa kingdom until the fifteenth century, and though he had noticed the towers he had given them no thought. "While here I wasn't really looking for artifacts from the Cham Dynasty," he explained as we walked through the museum. "I think we probably stood in the towers to get out of the rain a few times, but that's about it." While most of the sites of Cham architecture are now under UNESCO protection, and although there remain about 100,000 people of Cham descent in Vietnam, the ways of the Chams were imperiled. We learned this while looking upon some defiantly basic-looking Cham pottery that was being sold in the museum. The Chams made their pottery with no kiln and no potting wheel. Today only four women on the planet were said to know this almost literally prehistoric method of potting. All were Chams and in their eighties. Meanwhile, their vases were selling here for $10 apiece.

We drove out of Danang, past Monkey Mountain, past Marble Mountain (in which NLF guerrillas often hid, spying on U.S. soldiers swimming at nearby China Beach), while my father told Hien the story of how he had saved the life of my godfather during Vietnam. This had happened at the village of Tam Ky, a few hours south of where we now were. Suddenly Hien informed us that Tam Ky was where he had grown up.

"Really?" my father asked. "Because I was in Tam Ky a hell of a lot."

"I used to stand beside the road," Hien said, looking back at us, "and wave and say, 'Hello, GIs!' And they would throw me candy and cigarettes and C-rats."

My father stared at Hien. Something watery and bottomless in his gaze suddenly began to harden. "Hien, I used to toss C-rats to kids around here all the time."

Hien laughed. "I know!" he told my father. "I remember you!"

This was clearly intended as a joke, but my father did not laugh. Instead he looked even more deeply into Hien's eyes and took Hien by the forearm. "Maybe it was you," my father said. "Maybe it was."

Hien gave my father's arm a game return shake but quickly looked away. Within him some bright nerve of memory had obviously been touched. For all that had been written about the suffering of American soldiers and their families, during and after the Vietnamese War, people such as Hien had suffered far more thoroughly. My father crossed over into the inferno. Hien had woken up one morning to find the inferno consuming his bed, his bedroom, his entire home. The Vietnamese War was not only (in the words of various historians) "the end of America's absolute confidence in its moral exclusivity" or the "berserk American dream" or "perhaps the worst miscalculation in our history" but the final and most excruciating chapter in a deeply Vietnamese story in which the Vietnamese were the most meaningful actors and absorbed the most lasting damage.

While my father and Hien discussed their qualitatively different memories of Tam Ky, I looked out onto the ocean. The waves tumbled up to the shore and detonated in carbonated sprays of white. I could scarcely discern the waterline from the sky. The endless hazy blue miles simply devoured one's gaze. Much of interest had occurred off these coasts, and a good deal of it had come to light only fairly recently. Somewhere out there, for instance, was Cu Lao Cham Island, otherwise known as Paradise Island. Defenseless fishermen from North Vietnam were kidnapped by Vietnamese in the employ of U.S. intelligence, blind-folded, and taken to Paradise Island, which the kidnapped fishermen were told was a part of "liberated" North Vietnam. The kidnapped fishermen were then informed of a group of North Vietnamese dissidents called the Sacred Sword of the Patriots League. (The "sacred sword" referred to the story of the fifteenth-century Vietnamese patriot Le Loi, who was awarded by a divine tortoise a sword that Le Loi used to defeat Vietnam's Chinese invaders. After his triumph he returned the sword to Hoan Kiem Lake in Hanoi, where the sword is said to remain today.) The kidnapped North Vietnamese fishermen were then told that Paradise Island was a secret SSPL training camp. All the personnel working and living on the island either faked a northern accent or were themselves northerners who had come South in 1956. The fishermen were finally told that the SSPL was going to liberate North Vietnam from the Chinese Communists, who controlled the men of the Politburo. The fishermen were given SSPL literature, a few gifts, and some marginal training, then released back into North Vietnam.

No one on Paradise Island actually cared whether these fishermen worked toward the goals of the SSPL or immediately reported their ordeal to the authorities. As it turned out, there was no Sacred Sword of the Patriots League. The entire story was a creation of the Pentagon's Special Operations Group (SOG). The hope was that the story would create panic among the leaders of North Vietnam. Needless to say, as Richard H. Shultz, Jr., relates in *The Secret War Against Hanoi*, North Vietnam's intelligence apparatus saw through the charade more or less instantly.

Indeed, with the exception of an amazing 1970 U.S. raid on a North Vietnamese prison camp twenty-three miles away from Hanoi (though the American prisoners had been moved by the time the camp was stormed), the story of U.S. covert operations during the Vietnamese War is largely one of consistent failure. In response to the Bay of Pigs disaster, President Kennedy took the responsibility for covert operations in Vietnam away from the CIA and gave it to the Pentagon. The possibilities of the SOG's "unconditional warfare" were enthusiastically entertained by many in the Kennedy administration, Dean Rusk being a notable exception. Robert McNamara's early belief, crushed by reality within two years, was that covert operations could break the back of North Vietnam's Politburo, despite the CIA's predictions that such work had no chance in North Vietnam's "kind of society"—that is, tightly knit, xenophobic, and oppressive. General William Westmoreland believed that the "professors" in Kennedy's government were a bit too credulous when it came to unconditional warfare. What they did not understand, Westmoreland held, was that special operations tended to hog the most highly trained personnel and often got them killed.

The doubters were on to something. It was true that many of the SOG's operations were conceptually brilliant, such as the scheme of dropping into North Vietnam hundreds of parachutes with ice blocks in their harnesses, so that when patrols found the empty chutes they would believe North Vietnam had been infiltrated by a small guerrilla army. But many other operations resulted in the deaths of hundreds of local agents, most of whom were ethnic Nung, a group used by the United States, since the ARVN did not consider the Nung draftable. Thus the SOG sent five hundred "long-term agents" into North Vietnam. Not one was "exfiltrated." In other words, they were all killed or captured. Weirdly, the SOG's goal during these deadly shenanigans was never the toppling of Ho Chi Minh's government, only steady harassment. As the U.S. ambassador to South Vietnam Henry Cabot Lodge explained, if Ho Chi Minh fell, "his successor would undoubtedly be worse."

The SOG settled upon a program of dirty tricks. A chemical contaminant called Bitrex was used to poison the North's rice supplies. It did not kill but merely made rice inedibly bitter. The State Department initially failed to see the difference, regarding Bitrex as an illegal form of chemical warfare (though napalm was fine). The SOG also papered North Vietnam with pamphlets emblazoned with "I saw you" in Vietnamese above a picture of a North Vietnamese soldier within a rifle sight. Below that: "Next time *you die.*" It also dumped into North Vietnam AK-47s designed to explode when the trigger was pulled. In some areas SOG agents slapped up posters of Ho Chi Minh buggering children that triggered an explosive when torn down. According to Shultz, "highly authentic replicas" of North Vietnamese money were also printed. Agents were preparing to flood North Vietnam with the counterfeit money and destroy its economy until it was pointed out that this was actually unbelievably illegal.

This secret war was mostly shut down in 1968, when President Johnson announced a halt to the post–Tet Offensive bombing. When North Vietnam returned its 591 prisoners of war to the United States in 1973, there were no SOG or covert operators among them, despite the fact that some are known to have been taken alive. The final fates of these dozen or so secret warriors are the only actual POW/MIAs whose whereabouts the United States has any real call to question.

The coast was gone now. We were inland, amid the jungle, and soon a Vietnamese wedding procession began to pass us in the opposite direction, the lead car wrapped in yellow ribbons. Hien explained that, as with all things in Vietnam, there was a rigid hierarchy at work here. Rich families drove buses during their wedding processions; middle-class families drove cars; poor families drove scooters; really poor families walked. As the ribboned cars passed by, my father declaimed something about how, in America, people usually waited until the weekend to get married, so they did not miss work. Today was Wednesday. Most likely the day's date was regarded as some kind of "lucky" day: Vietnamese, by and large, tend toward numerological consultation and astral divination in most life matters.

"That is true?" Hien asked.

"Yes," my father said.

"I don't understand," Hien said.

"It's important to Americans that they don't miss work."

Despite a polite nod, Hien was obviously unconvinced. What was work when compared with the celebration of one's family?

I looked at my father. "It's really uncanny."

He returned my attention. "What's uncanny?"

"You're a complete and utter square."

"Cut it."

"No, really. Do you have corners?"

"Enough."

Query: *Why did officials at all levels of the U.S. military and
government lie so often during the war?*

A journalist named Murray Marder coined the term "credibility gap"
during the Vietnamese War's early years, and this shattering of the public trust is probably the war's most profound and seemingly irreversible
bequest. But any serious discussion of the war must consider the argument, made by some revisionists, that the lies told by those waging the
war were, in many cases, understandable. After all, the appropriateness
of "telling the truth" is always mutable in the face of higher imperatives.
During times of conflict, one can hardly expect governments to behave
with complete transparency, since a major component of every war is
secrecy of action and misdirection of intent.

Especially in a war that saw the United States constantly playing
catch-up. However one regards Vietnam's Communists, it is hard to
deny that they were on the verge of winning power in 1945 when a
multilateral fiat blew out that verge from beneath them. Or that the
Communists were again on the verge of winning power in 1954 when
another multilateral fiat blew out that verge from beneath them. Or that
the Communists were on the verge of winning power a third time in
1964 when the United States slammed down its foot to roadblock the
verge once and for all. For the U.S. officials responsible for widening the
Vietnamese War, anti-Communism as a practice had become synony-
mous with freedom as an ideal, and if one had to lie to ensure that freedom, so be it. Lying often and enthusiastically became not only desirable
but absolutely crucial to keep hidden the various miscalculations of U.S.
policy.

According to the historian Fredrik Logevall, Paul Kattenburg, the
State Department's leading expert on Vietnam, announced in 1963 that
the war was hopeless, that the South could never win, and that the only
option left for the United States was withdrawal. Within a year the State
Department's resident Vietnam expert had been excluded from all policy decisions involving Vietnam. Years later, with the oral historian
Christian G. Appy, Kattenburg would have words for the men who had
pushed him out: "[W]hat struck me more than anything else was just

the abysmal ignorance around the table of the particular facts of Vietnam, their ignorance of the actual place. They didn't know what they were talking about. It was robot thinking about Communism and no distinctions were being made." The meeting in which he voiced his career-ending objections ended with Kattenburg thinking to himself, "We're walking into a major disaster."

The fact remains that the type and quality of U.S. lies during the war varied greatly. There were, for example, institutional lies told by the military (inflated enemy body counts, exaggerations that turned indecisive skirmishes into victories and victories into Waterloo-grade routs); self-delusional lies told by government officials (hiding or eliding evidence that suggested the war was going badly, using the gag of patriotism to pressure pessimistic lower-ranking officials into silence); and finally the bigger-picture executive lies told by the likes of Richard Nixon (announcing in 1969 that the first withdrawal of American soldiers had been President Thieu's idea when in fact Thieu had fiercely opposed it) and Lyndon Johnson (who campaigned in 1964 as the "peace candidate" while fully intending to expand the war as soon as he was elected). Some lies, in other words, differed little from those told by all governments during wartime, while others were the sulfuric stuff of human malevolence itself. Robert McNamara has suggested that what in many cases looks like lying today was at the time more akin to a willful deafness and blindness. What they were often doing, McNamara argues, was not lying but reacting without bothering to examine the reasoning behind those reactions. McNamara's view finds some concurrence among scholars, one of whom has described U.S. policy during the period of 1961 to 1968 as "whatever looked like a good idea at the time."

The men of Lyndon Johnson's cabinet were contemptuous of the liberals who wanted to negotiate an end to the Vietnamese War and frightened of the conservatives who sought to widen the conflict at the risk of including China. (McNamara claims they were more worried about the latter group.) Lyndon Johnson and his advisers rejected both options early on, settling instead upon a radicalized middle course that became known as "flexible response" or "graduated pressure." This proved an easy doctrine to practice but an extremely difficult one to justify without a framework of lies. Intended to prevent peripheral struggles such as the war in Vietnam from escalating into a nuclear exchange, graduated pressure, it was thought, would compel North Vietnam's leadership toward recognizing that the more support South Vietnam's insurgency received, the more retaliatory U.S. action North Vietnam could expect. The many ways in which this approach was grossly inappropriate for the war in Vietnam are now obvious: the United States had little contact with the North Vietnamese, few conduits through which to transmit its subtler intentions, and virtually no understanding of Hanoi's mind-set. At the time, however, graduated pressure seemed a wise and even prudent path. President Johnson was especially taken with it, as it allowed him political leverage and the illusion of logical cause-and-effect. The Joint Chiefs of Staff, however, loathed graduated pressure and its clear suggestion that traditional military thinking was obsolete. Many military men loathed Robert McNamara, graduated pressure's most enthusiastic early supporter, as well.

In some ways McNamara earned the military's dislike, as he did not often have much use for standard military solutions. But the "almost cavalier" manner (McNamara's words) in which the generals discussed the use of nuclear weapons in Southeast Asia led McNamara to view much traditional military thinking with horror. As the generals began to sense their lack of access to McNamara, their disgust for him and his "whiz kids" in the Defense Department grew exponentially. (In 1967, the literary critic Dwight Macdonald noted sagely that McNamara "must be a great trial to the Joint Chiefs of Staff, as if the College of Cardinals found themselves with an atheist pope.") One of these whiz kids opined in a memo that, while planning military operations, actual military experience "can be a disadvantage because it discourages seeing the larger picture." A paternalistic, arrogant view—though can one really claim it is altogether false? Consider Curtis LeMay, the Air Force general who guaranteed President Kennedy that the Soviets would do nothing during the Cuban Missile Crisis if the United States invaded Cuba. As is now clear, the Soviets would have responded to an invasion of Cuba by rendering roughly a dozen stars on the U.S. flag unnecessary. Nevertheless, LeMay and the Joint Chiefs, who believed that Saigon was as militarily significant as Berlin, argued during the war's early years that using nuclear weapons in Vietnam might well lead to "confrontation" with the USSR or China, but on the plus side "atomic weapons should result in a considerable reduction in friendly casualties and in more rapid cessation of hostilities." (In 1961, the Joint Chiefs had also alluded to the advisability of nuking Laos.) McNamara, "appalled" by such thinking, began to suspect that these medaled, can-do men were utterly mad. Of course, the Joint Chiefs were not mad. They were trying to win a war, which in their analysis was a purely military exploit. Reluctant to question its own means, though quick to take issue with everyone else's, the U.S. military invariably sought to pursue the most effective—which is to say, the most extreme—path available to it in Vietnam. Nonmilitary concerns, such as South Vietnam's political problems and the sanctity of its civilians' lives, were often viewed as falling outside the parameters of military planning. Which suggests that McNamara's arrogant whiz-kid deputy was, in fact, on to something.

It also suggests why so many U.S. officials felt they needed to lie. One less well known aspect of the war's early years is, in one historian's words, the "pronounced pessimism at the center of American strategy on Vietnam," which appears as early as 1961. It is a myth that the U.S. public supported the war in Vietnam prior to its official beginning. There was, in fact, a widespread *lack* of support for the prospect of war before the Marines splashed ashore near Danang in 1965. In September 1963, *The New Republic* presciently argued that if the United States truly wanted to frustrate China's ambitions in Southeast Asia, support of Ho Chi Minh's government was a good bet to do so. Even the heartland's *Milwaukee Journal* came out for withdrawal in 1963. One 1964 poll gave an 81 percent approval rating to a negotiated "peace arrangement" in Vietnam (though another poll from the same year found that a quarter of the American people were unaware that China was a Communist country). Lyndon Johnson himself saw the danger of war in Vietnam, even as he lied to escalate it, which is what makes the war a Shakespearean, rather than a Greek, tragedy. This is Johnson from May 1964: "[Vietnam] just worries the hell out of me. I don't see what we can ever hope to get out of this. . . . It's damn easy to get into a war, but . . . it's going to be harder to ever extricate yourself if you get in."

Johnson was forced to dispatch deputies on so many "fact-finding" missions to South Vietnam because the information coming out of the embassy was not always trustworthy. Higher-level officials in the Johnson administration often kept vital strategic information from lower-level ones. The information the CIA station in Saigon sent through the embassy was occasionally altered. The information the CIA in Washington was sending the secretary of defense was being redacted as well. At one point the commander of the U.S. advisory mission in Vietnam and the U.S. ambassador to South Vietnam were not speaking. The Joint Chiefs squabbled among themselves for plums for their respective branches of service. McNamara routinely closed the Joint Chiefs out of discussions. Johnson himself was so personally averse to disagreement, and so astonishingly commanding a physical presence, that he actually made people frightened of the prospect of giving him bad news. A war game the Pentagon devised and carried out in 1964 basically predicted the war's final outcome. Unfortunately, no one passed these results on to Johnson.

Like another U.S. president, Johnson was a shrewd judge of people and the pressure points at which they could be influenced; he counted on this supernatural skill to get things done. Like another U.S. president, Johnson viewed "getting things done," the mere activity of it, as a virtue. Like another U.S. president, Johnson dodged dangerous duty during his military service. Like another U.S. president, Johnson overextended the military he unwisely deployed and attempted to fight an "easy" war on the cheap. (Johnson's gutting of the military before the war in Vietnam began is not widely known. U.S. forces were frightfully undermanned during the war's first two years. Lieutenant General Harold G. Moore wrote that at the time of the battle of Ia Drang in 1965, "Alpha Company had 115 men, 49 fewer than authorized. Bravo Company, at 114 men, was 50 short. Charlie Company had 106 men, down by 58. And the weapons company, Delta, had only 76 men, 42 fewer than authorized.") Like another U.S. president, Johnson dismissed as cowardice all neutral opinion. Like another U.S. president, Johnson's powers of persuasion, so overwhelming when one was face-to-face with him, had little effect on those thousands of miles away.

Nowhere is Lyndon Johnson's penchant for deceitfulness more notoriously evident than during the Gulf of Tonkin incident. In the three days before August 2, 1964, a South Vietnamese spy had been air-dropped into North Vietnamese territory and instantly captured, the North Vietnamese coast had been shelled by South Vietnamese gun-boats, and two inland areas had been bombed on succeeding days. In the midst of all this, a U.S. destroyer called the *Maddox* was ordered to travel along North Vietnam's coast at no closer than eight miles, then pro-ceed into Chinese waters to see what kind of cooperation commenced between China and North Vietnam. Hanoi had never declared what it viewed as its naval borders, but the U.S. assumed it was three miles, or perhaps twelve. (In fact, it was twelve.) The *Maddox* was also "showing the flag," which is to say floating around in enemy waters largely because it could. This was in itself not particularly bellicose behavior, as Edwin Moïse, the world's foremost Tonkin scholar, points out. Throughout the Cold War the Soviets ran their submarines mere yards beyond accepted U.S. territorial boundaries for the same purposes of mild intimidation. One of the men aboard the *Maddox*, Moïse writes, assumed it was going to be a "leisure cruise," while another crewman later reported a distinct feeling of being used as bait. The August 2 attack on the *Maddox* by North Vietnamese torpedo boats, whose orders are still debated, is today widely accepted by scholars and historians. The North Vietnamese launched three torpedoes, two of which missed and one of which hit. It was a Soviet torpedo, which is to say, it was a dud. One of the *Maddox*'s stacks was also hit by a shell apparently shot from a 14.5 mm machine gun, a piece of which Robert McNamara later personally requested to see.

The lies concerning the first attack on a U.S. Navy vessel since World War II instantly began to congeal. U.S. officials maintained that the *Maddox* had been thirty miles away from North Vietnam's coast, that it had been on a routine patrol, and that the North Vietnamese had fired first. (The *Maddox* fired first, though the manner in which the North Vietnamese approached left the *Maddox*'s commanding officer with no other option.) It was also claimed that U.S. fighters did not attempt to pursue and sink the aggressive torpedo boats after the skirmish, even though they did.

The following day, North Vietnam's coast was again attacked in a South Vietnamese raid, after which the North Vietnamese reported finding 125 mm shell fragments—the type a destroyer such as the *Maddox* would fire. The North Vietnamese probably lied about the shell size (the raid that carried out the attack in question had no weapon large enough to fire such a shell), which illustrates the bellicose suspicion that characterized these few significant days. By August 4, the *Maddox*'s rattled commander was sending messages to his superiors that, based on the intercepted messages he was seeing, it "is apparent that [North Vietnam] . . . now considers itself at war with us." The *Maddox*, having been ordered back out on patrol, was soon joined by the *Turner Joy.*

Many of those aboard the *Turner Joy* maintain to this day that they were attacked on August 4, despite the voluminous mass of evidence to have surfaced in the interim that all but proves otherwise. The most interesting argument against the attack's veracity is hinged upon the so-called Tonkin Gulf Ghost. There does seem to be an actual phenomenon—personally verified with a Vietnamese sailor who has spent his life in the South China Sea—that generates radar irregularities due to reasons of weather, humidity, flying fish, seabirds, or some combination thereof. Although Vietnamese sailors were well aware of the Tonkin Gulf Ghost phenomenon, U.S. sailors in 1964 were not. Why, then, do many of the *Turner Joy*'s sailors still believe they were attacked? It seems that yet another South Vietnamese raid was planned for August 5. North Vietnam learned of the raid and instructed its torpedo boats to sink any incoming ships. These instructions were intercepted by the *Turner Joy* and, combined with the strange atmospherics native to the Tonkin Gulf, created an understandably besieged impression in the minds of those on board the *Turner Joy.*

Moïse notes that the North Vietnamese did not make much of the first attack until after the United States did. Following the second incident, the Party paper in Hanoi ran a farcical account of the first incident, in which it was revealed that "patrol boats" (rather than aggressive torpedo boats) had driven the *Maddox* out of North Vietnamese waters. The second attack the North Vietnamese always denied. Soon after the second incident, Johnson came to suspect that it had not occurred—

information he shared only with select members of his cabinet. The reason for why he went ahead anyway is tragically uncomplicated: retaliatory bombing in the name of Pierce Arrow had already been decided upon, and the airtime announcing the bombing had been booked. Johnson's decision to announce the bombing, combined with unforeseen delays upon a U.S. aircraft carrier, inadvertently warned the North Vietnamese of the attack, and they were able to shoot two of the attacking U.S. planes from the sky. The targets in North Vietnam were arrived at so quickly because they had been drawn up and planned for almost six months prior to the incident.

In light of that fact in particular, the common belief, from Noam Chomsky to Vo Nguyen Giap, is that the United States deliberately set out to fashion a casus belli that would bring it to war with North Vietnam. Moïse rejects this interpretation, concluding that the decisions made in the aftermath of the two incidents—one real, the other false— were made less from a desire to deceive than from a desire not to affirm. The story was "too good to check," in journalistic terms. Moïse does believe that given the raids and the questionable orders of the *Maddox* and *Turner Joy,* a consensus existed among the Johnson administration "to avoid candid discussion of the subject." In August 1964, neither Johnson nor his men were looking for war in the Gulf of Tonkin. War was looking for them, and it found them. The Southeast Asia Resolution, quickly dubbed the Gulf of Tonkin Resolution, which claimed that the North Vietnamese had "repeatedly" attacked U.S. vessels, passed 416 to 0 in the House of Representatives and 88 to 2 in the Senate, despite what has been described as its "unusually vague and open-ended scope." Few understood that this resolution would increase U.S. forces in South Vietnam from 16,000 to 550,000 in only a few years. One who did understand the danger was Senator Wayne Morse of Oregon. "War cannot be declared," he said, "to meet hypothetical situations yet to arise on the horizons of the world."

The most profound result of the second phantom attack was Vietnamese, not American. In short, the North Vietnamese were accused of, and punished for, an attack they knew they had not committed. This, above all else, convinced Hanoi that the United States was seeking to conquer and exploit Vietnam and strengthened Hanoi's resistance to any terms of negotiation, save its own.

Johnson was well aware of war's disconnects and implausibilities. It in fact tortured him, and some of his less guarded statements regarding the war today have a Lear-like intensity. "We fight for values and we fight for principles," he said in April 1965, "rather than territories or colonies." Yet, privately, he referred to Vietnam—a "raggedy-ass, little fourth-rate country"—in both overly personal and reflexively possessive terms. "What the hell is Vietnam worth to me?" he asked his cabinet in 1964. "What is Laos worth to me? What is it worth to this country?" Of protestors, Johnson once said, "I don't blame them. They don't want to be killed in a war, and that's easy to understand." (A Secret Service agent remembers Johnson peering avidly out the window of his limousine while driving past some protestors: "The president was highly interested in what a hippie looked like, their dress, age groups, and items they carried.") "Light at the end of the tunnel?" Johnson once scoffed. "Hell, we don't even have a tunnel. We don't even know where the tunnel is." Alongside Johnson's seemingly honest torment, however, existed his cruelty, his brutishness, his dishonesty, his love of loyalty that too often became crass nepotism. Indeed, Johnson's administration sometimes bore more than a little resemblance to that of Ngo Dinh Diem, whose overthrow Johnson always rued.

As Tom Wicker, in his study of how the personalities of Kennedy and Johnson influenced events, has pointed out, Johnson "would look around him and see in Bob McNamara that it was technologically feasible, in McGeorge Bundy that it was intellectually respectable, and in Dean Rusk that it was historically necessary." One gets a sense of the pinched grandeur with which many of these men, almost all of them veterans in one way or another of World War II, regarded the world from what they titled their inevitable memoirs: *As I Saw It* (Dean Rusk), *The Past Has Another Pattern* (George Ball), *The Storm Has Many Eyes* (Henry Cabot Lodge), *A Tangled Web* (William Bundy), *Swords and Plowshares* (Maxwell Taylor), *In Retrospect* (Robert McNamara). Only National Security Adviser Walt Rostow—by all accounts an intelligent man, despite the unseemly pride he has taken in his refusal to refine the positions he defended during the war—failed to indulge in this arms race of titular pomposity, weighing in with titles such as *The United States and the Regional Organization of Asia and the Pacific, 1965–1985.* These intelligent, dedicated, and even wise men: how they betrayed their best selves; how they lied.

General Maxwell Taylor (who before coming aboard the Kennedy administration was president of the Lincoln Center for the Performing Arts) voiced early opposition to the introduction of U.S. troops into Vietnam if the intention was to use them as counterguerrillas. "The white-faced soldier," Taylor argued in a 1965 memo, "armed, equipped, and trained as he is, is not a suitable guerrilla fighter for Asian forests and jungles. The French tried to adapt their forces to this mission and failed. I doubt that U.S. forces could do much better." In 1964, Taylor's view of South Vietnam was that "only the emergence of an exceptional leader could improve the situation and no George Washington is in sight." (Actually, the Vietnamese George Washington, like it or not, was in Hanoi.) But even Taylor, a member of the so-called Never Again Club—a group of U.S. military minds so scarred by the nightmare of the Korean conflict that they had vowed never to engage in Asian land war again (at least, not without nuclear weapons)—was privately writing memos that contradicted every public and semipublic reservation he voiced: "I do not believe," he wrote President Johnson in a top secret cable, "that our program to save [South Vietnam] will succeed without [the introduction of] U.S. troops." He even suggested introducing U.S. troops under humanitarian camouflage by sending them to deal with South Vietnam's incessant flooding.

McGeorge Bundy, Kennedy and Johnson's special assistant for national security affairs, wrote to McNamara an agonized, conflicted memo in 1965: "I see no reason to suppose that the Viet Cong will accommodate us by fighting the kind of war we desire. . . . [D]o we want to invest 200,000 men to cover an eventual retreat? Can we not do that just as well where we are?" Yet despite his own analysis he, too, consistently advised staying the course. In fact, he opted for the war's escalation in order "to pull the South Vietnamese together," when he should have been able to conclude from the war's established narrative that the more the United States involved itself in South Vietnam the more South Vietnam disintegrated. "[Our] immediate targets," Bundy believed, accurately, "are in the South—in the minds of the South Vietnamese and in the minds of the Viet Cong cadres." Yet Bundy had a savantlike inability to understand the implications of what he himself argued. He supported the war but never sounded as though he did. Johnson eventually fired him for this seeming inconsistency of mind.

One sees similar sagaciousness, though more inclination to heed it, in Undersecretary of State George Ball, the house peacenik of the Johnson administration. Ball, who believed Europe was where the United States' struggle against Communism would live or die, wrote of the war in Vietnam more devastatingly, and far earlier, than any member of the Johnson administration. "Either everybody else is crazy," he once said in frustration, "or I am." When Ball began to realize Johnson's constant reassurance that he "listened hard" to Ball was completely false, he resigned in 1966, but not before composing a memo containing this memorable warning: "Once on the tiger's back we cannot be sure of picking the place to dismount." In 1946, Ho Chi Minh used a similar analogy for war in Indochina: "[T]he tiger does not stand still. He lurks in the jungle by day and emerges by night. He will leap upon the back of the elephant, tearing huge chunks from his hide, and then he will leap back into the dark jungle. And slowly the elephant will bleed to death." Ball, who was right about so much, was wrong about this. The United States was not on the tiger's back in Vietnam; it was on the elephant's.

Secretary of State Dean Rusk was socially removed from Kennedy and Johnson's inner circle; Kennedy did not even call him by his first name. Despite his rough looks (one of his colleagues' wives claimed he resembled nothing so much as a bartender), Rusk was the most priestly and imposing of the war's architects, and quite possibly the most intelligent. What truly strikes one when reading about the war's political history is the extent to which Rusk, America's chief diplomat, dismissed and belittled the devices of diplomacy when it came to Vietnam. It may have been McNamara's War, but in serious ways it was Rusk's Fault. (One promising early overture for negotiation, floated by North Vietnam's

Pham Van Dong through an intermediary in 1965, did not earn as much as a response from the American secretary of state. After another fumbled overture, Rusk explained that "there is a difference between rejecting a proposal and not accepting it.") Rusk is the man who turned the war from an attempt to save South Vietnam from Communism to an endeavor to save American credibility from itself. His unblinking hostility toward Communism, though admirably clear-sighted, led him to envision donnybrooks where there were none and to compare the feared "loss" of Vietnam with the "loss" of China, which had traumatized him politically. Rusk's claim that "the integrity of the U.S. commitment is the principal pillar of peace throughout the world," and that withdrawal or defeat in Vietnam would embolden the Communist bloc and higgledy-piggledy "lead to our ruin and almost certainly to catastrophic war," was worse than inaccurate; it was crazy. Rusk was also capable of spellbound cluelessness: "I don't believe," he said in 1965, "the VC have made large advances among the Vietnamese people." He refused to acknowledge that the NLF and North Vietnamese might have had differing goals. He also believed the antiwar movement was controlled by Communists. Rusk could apparently not bring himself to understand that "global conspiracy" is a contradiction in terms and that the same amount of debate concerning Vietnam he saw every day in the White House also gripped the administrative bodies of Moscow and Beijing. In Rusk's mind, Moscow dictated North Vietnam's policy: "I smell vodka and caviar in this proposal," he said of a North Vietnamese negotiation offer in 1968. On his way out of office, he told Richard Nixon that the war had been lost in "the editorial rooms of this country."

In *Dereliction of Duty,* H. R. McMaster writes that Robert Strange McNamara "viewed the war as another business management problem that, he assumed, would ultimately succumb to his reasoned judgment and others' rational calculation." In his memoir, McNamara himself writes, "I had always been confident that every problem could be solved, but now I found myself confronting one—involving national pride and human life—that could not." It is difficult to understand the depth of hatred many have for Robert McNamara—the journalist Mickey Kaus once argued that McNamara had harmed America more than any other figure during the twentieth century, and David Halberstam called him, simply, "a fool"—when, alone among the war's founding fathers, McNamara tried to explain why it occurred and the lessons that should be drawn from it. McNamara was not above assuring a browbeaten President Johnson that *The New York Times,* whose editorial page often went after him, was "influenced by Zionists"; or of having reports detailing the findings of fact-finding trips to South Vietnam written before he actually left Washington, D.C.; or of asking his assistant to write "six alternative lies for him" after a diplomatically embarrassing incident. Although he opposed the introduction of combat troops into Vietnam, McNamara lied about the effectiveness of the bombing early in the war and of the improving state of the ARVN. But once he realized the bombing was not effective and that the ARVN's performance was not getting notably better, McNamara, to his immense credit, stopped lying and then stopped supporting the war altogether. When very few in the U.S. government saw the war's futility, McNamara did. As he said to Johnson in 1967, "the war cannot be won by killing North Vietnamese. It can only be won by protecting the South Vietnamese." No doubt this is why he became, as Johnson once whispered to his press secretary, "an emotional basket case." (Both of McNamara's children were involved in the fringes of the antiwar movement, and his beloved wife Margy openly questioned the war's logic.) In May 1967, as he was turning against the war, McNamara wrote Johnson an extraordinary memo: "There may be a limit beyond which many Americans and much of the world will not permit the United States to go. The picture of the world's greatest superpower killing or seriously injuring 1000 noncombatants a week, while trying to pound a tiny backward nation into submission on an issue whose merits are hotly disputed, is not a pretty one."

The contempt people have for Robert McNamara, or even Dean Rusk, would be far better directed at a man such as Walt Whitman Rostow, Johnson's national security adviser. McNamara apologized for his behavior. Rusk's son apologized for the behavior of his father, who died a broken and depressed man. Rostow, though, has never apologized, despite some vaultingly ugly behavior during the war. Believing that war in Indochina was part of a large and inevitable U.S. battle against Asian

Communism as a whole (a view Communist China's leadership largely shared), Rostow had urged military action in Laos in 1961. When he realized he could not get war in Laos, he turned his attention to Vietnam, where the United States would show "that the Communist technique of guerrilla warfare can be dealt with." (He even wrote memos warning of "neutralist thought in Thailand." Send in the Marines.) This is from Edwin Moïse: "[James Thomson, of the National Security Council] was very startled to hear Walt Rostow at this luncheon say that it seemed unlikely that there had actually been an attack on the two U.S. destroyers on August 4. This was the first Thomson had heard that there was doubt about the reality of the incident. Rostow was openly gleeful about the fact that the U.S. armed forces had been turned loose to bomb North Vietnam in response to an attack that might not even have happened." After Tonkin, Rostow predicted that Ho Chi Minh would buckle under U.S. bombing since he was no longer "a guerrilla fighter with nothing to lose." In 1965, he told Daniel Ellsberg, "Dan, it looks very good. What we hear is that the Vietcong are already coming apart. . . . They're going to collapse within weeks. Not months, weeks." Living proof that anti-Communism can become as blindly dogmatic as Communism, Rostow was the valedictorian of the bombs-away school, maintaining that annihilating the gasoline tanks and other storage facilities in North Vietnam would cripple the insurgency in South Vietnam. So the storage facilities were bombed; the North Vietnamese, however, had fuel in other places. At several points during the war, bombing runs were ordered during times when the Johnson administration was attempting to open negotiations with North Vietnam. Not surprisingly, these bombings soured the North's willingness to talk. "I do not see any connection," Rostow calmly maintained, "between bombing and negotiation." Perhaps this is because North Vietnam was not bombing Maryland. "In the end," Rostow wrote recently, "Johnson left his successor a good post-Tet situation in the field, both military and political; but a difficult political position at home." The American people lost the war, then, because they were hippies. Rostow still defends the war. The linchpin of his argument is that the war in Vietnam gave Asia time to establish confidence against Communism, even though the United States was forced to bribe nations supposedly imperiled by the Communist threat to send allied soldiers to Vietnam. But let us get this straight: Walt Rostow believes that a war that killed nearly 60,000 of his countrymen and hundreds of thousands of innocent civilians, made refugees of 10 million more, damaged the image of the United States, and *did not even succeed in its most primary objective* was worthwhile? (Viva freedom: One confident Asian country, Ferdinand Marcos's Republic of the Philippines, declared itself a dictatorship in 1972.) Men such as Rostow lied to begin the war because the people would not understand why the United States needed to fight it so badly. They lied while the war was being fought because many could not understand why the United States was fighting it. Men such as Rostow are still lying, this time about what people do not understand . . . but we are no longer in the presence of argument but pathology.

Of course, a compilation of the lies North Vietnam told during the war would have Tolstoyan heft. Its Party paper, for instance, routinely claimed that its guns had shot down eight enemy planes, when actually it had shot down one, or none. But a crucial area in which the Communists did not lie was to themselves. As a PAVN major general once told an American journalist, "We knew that it would not be enough just to make propaganda saying that we were winning. We had to study how to fight the Americans." Among themselves, the Communists drew a line between propaganda and reality, and it was in no NLF insurgent or North Vietnamese soldier's interest to lie about the challenges they faced on the battlefield, where PAVN and NLF commanders were allowed far greater independence in their decision making than were their U.S. counterparts. "We should," a piece of captured NLF samizdat from the early 1960s read, "teach them [NLF inductees] to win without arrogance and to lose without discouragement."

This was not the case, unfortunately, for the U.S. military. To read the letters of the average U.S. soldier on the ground in Vietnam is to be shocked by the anger with which many of them responded to the common practice of inflating enemy battlefield casualties. It went like this: After a skirmish, if one man said he had seen two bodies and another said he had seen five, the number of enemy dead would be calculated as seven, even if there was a reasonable amount of certainty that the men had seen the same bodies. Or if one arm was found, and one leg, and nothing else, the number of enemy casualties would be counted as two. The numbers of enemy dead were more greatly exaggerated the higher they wended up the chain of command, so that when a captain claimed, say, ten more enemy dead than was accurate, a lieutenant colonel claimed thirty and a brigadier general claimed sixty. "There is no way to really figure out exact body count," one U.S. soldier later admitted. "I generally knew that if I lost a troop, I'd better come back with a body count of ten." The speaker was Lieutenant William Calley, the lead perpetrator of the My Lai massacre.

A famous story, retold in Neil Sheehan's *A Bright Shining Lie,* finds North Vietnam's prime minister Pham Van Dong running into a Polish diplomat in Hanoi. Pham Van Dong had something he wanted to discuss: "The American generals are always boasting of how they are winning the war in the South. Do they believe it?" The Polish diplomat said, Yes, it appeared they did. "You're joking," Dong said in exasperation. "Perhaps they boast for propaganda, but the CIA must tell them the truth in its secret reports." The Polish diplomat said, No, they really seem to believe they are winning. "Well," Dong replied, "I find it hard to believe what you say. Surely the American generals cannot be that naive?"

It is curious, though, that the U.S. belief system that encouraged such lying during the war eventually recalibrated in order to tell the truth about what really happened, while the Communist belief system that encouraged such frank honesty during the war eventually recalibrated in order to lie about what really happened. That the United States in defeat, Rostow notwithstanding, has proved less evasive than the victorious heirs of Pham Van Dong is, surely, a kind of victory.

IV

On our way to Chu Lai, the former site of a U.S. military base, the road was full of everything but traffic. Truong, consequently, was driving much faster than usual. This was not actually all that fast, since the Vietnamese do not seem to be much compelled by the theoretical ideal of speed. All the same, the road's chickens, dogs, cats, children, and rice farmers took several decisive steps away from the road moments before our car whizzed by. Even a few large, burdened cattle looked over, saw us coming, and plowed slowly head down toward the safety of the berm. It was early yet, the sun still turning from orange to white, the sky from pink to blue.

Soon enough we passed a martyrs' cemetery, where NLF and PAVN dead were interred in endless white rows of small square tombstones. Hien translated the words emblazoned upon the cemetery's arched front gate: "The Fatherland Will Never Forget Their Sacrifice." In many martyrs' cemeteries a number of the dead had tombstones that read CHUA BIET TEN: "Not yet known." During the war it had been fairly common for U.S. forces to bury enemy dead in large unmarked graves after relieving bodies of their diaries and letters, which sometimes contained useful intelligence. The particular cultural trauma of this practice was significant, for it effectively erased these fallen soldiers' identities. In the Vietnamese belief system a body was needed to secure safe passage into the afterlife. Those Vietnamese whose bodies were never found or identified—a considerable number, given the soldiers vaporized by napalm alone—were referred to as "those for whom no incense was burned"; their ghosts wandered the earth, in the words of the Vietnamese writer Bao Ninh, "whispering as they floated around like pale vapors, shredded with bullet-holes." I thought of the grief of the American families whose loved ones' bodies were similarly never found. As in so many instances when it came to the war, the shared grief of those Americans and Vietnamese whose sons, husbands, fathers, and brothers had never been recovered was similar but not quite analogous. Not that this mattered. War italicized the differences between people just as it made the differences ultimately futile to consider.

I studied my father as we passed by the cemetery. "How did you feel about seeing that?" I asked him.

"I'm excited. I want to see it."

"Not Chu Lai. The cemetery."

He cast a quick backward glance through the rear window. "Oh. That.

I don't know. It's just a cemetery." He lowered his voice and leaned in close to me. "You know, this morning at breakfast Hien astounded me. I said I wanted to try to find one particular place at the base and he said, 'We'll have to ask the old people.' I thought, 'You little twerp. You have to ask the *old* people?' I then realized that seventy percent of the population of Vietnam is under twenty-eight years of age. And Hien's . . . what, in his fifties? He was a kid during the war. He doesn't remember. Hardly anyone here does."

"It must feel like you never came here sometimes."

He regarded me pityingly. "I sure wouldn't say it ever feels like *that*."

"No, I guess you wouldn't. So how much time did you spend at Chu Lai?"

"I was stationed in Chu Lai. I lived there for five or six months." Suddenly he put on his sunglasses, and in a moment the man I knew as my father transformed into a tan, obliquely confident CIA field agent.

"What's with the shades?"

"The base is right on the ocean. The sun was always a killer here. You'll need yours, so put 'em on."

"Sir, I don't have any sunglasses, sir."

"Why have you not come prepared, corporal?"

"Sir, I suppose because I'm a fuckup, sir."

He let this charade drop gently. Then: "It's raining again."

"Did it ever actually *stop* raining? It's always a little raining here."

He tapped on his window. "In case you ever wondered why the jungle looks like the jungle—don't." Indeed, the well-watered vegetation beside this road was so preposterously dense you could walk five steps into it and be completely lost. Much of the tangled foliage grew right out into the road, all of it bright in so many different shades of green. Wherever your eyes fell was a chlorophyll contest. Tapioca plants grew in stunning emerald layers. Rubber trees were tall and slender and had a little green pompom on top. Coffee plants' big chunky leaves were as glossy green as poison ivy. Light green pepper vines grew around tree trunks as though strangling them. Then there were Vietnam's many varieties of palm tree: plain old palm trees, their trunks ringed white and black; banana palm trees, which had the most massive leaves; coconut palms, which had testicular bundles of fruit growing beneath green crowns that sat atop fat trunks; betel nut palms, which were towering and skinny and had dangerous-looking rostrate leaves. Occasionally, just off the road, a water buffalo stood out against the endless green backdrop, a huge breathing slab of flesh furred with hair the color of stale chocolate.

Everywhere here something was growing. This was Vietnam's great strength, as Ho Chi Minh understood. He once spoke of how, after "the American invaders have been defeated, we will rebuild our land ten times more beautiful," and in his will he requested that a crypt not be constructed for him, as the land would be better used for growing. He instead asked to be cremated. His ashes, he hoped, would be scattered in northern, central, and southern Vietnam. Then, Ho wrote, he would meet Marx and Lenin in the scarlet afterlife. Naturally, all mention of Ho's wish to be cremated and scattered was elided from the version of the will that was published in the Party paper. Shortly after he died on September 2, 1969—the Party even lied about the date of Ho's death, placing it a day later so as not to befoul the twenty-fourth anniversary of Vietnam's declared national independence from France—Soviet mummyologists were brought into Hanoi to do for Ho what they had done for Lenin.

As we neared the coast and the site of the former U.S. base, the jungle gave way to duney reaches of intensely yellow sand and spotty growths of evergreen trees and low shrubs. Hien explained that the sudden landscape switch was due to something he called "selective irrigation."

"Selective irrigation?" my father asked.

"Everything near the American Road is selectively irrigated."

I piped in. "This is called the American Road?"

"I sure hope so," my father said. "We built it."

"Marines built this road?"

"Not Marines, no. American engineers. Civilian contractors, I guess. I remember them well. Those guys were civilians, but they were tough. They carried weapons. And used 'em sometimes, too, as I recall. This road was all dirt when I first got here, and after a few weeks they'd paved the whole thing."

Truong swerved to avoid a pothole. I said, "It doesn't seem to have held up very well."

My father shrugged. "I doubt that anyone's much touched it for the last forty years."

"When was the base itself built?"

"I guess 1964 or so. But it was ongoing. They were always adding stuff. Keep in mind, it took at least two years before we had any solid logistical grounding beneath us anywhere in Vietnam." A humorless smile. "Do you know who owned controlling interest in the construction company that built these roads? Or the runways on the airstrip?"

"Uh. Dick Cheney?"

"No, but you're close. Lady Bird Johnson."

"Is that true?"

"I think it is. That was our understanding back then."

We passed a long roadside strip of huts and food shacks, the proprietors and customers of which regarded us impassively. Military men with assault rifles slung over their shoulders smoked while standing near low blue plastic tables, where older Vietnamese men played some checkerslike game. Beyond the shacks a little boy using a thin wooden switch tried to propel forward a fairly large herd of calves. He was failing spectacularly. The calves, with their devilish horns and enormous black eyes, had amassed alongside the road and were chewing on the nearby vegetation. In the distance, beyond the barren cactus and shrubby fields of sand, loomed some shadowy, haze-embraced mountains.

At this point a man walked out toward the middle of the road holding a snake. Truong shot a dismissive wave at this individual and gently maneuvered around him. While I was attempting to open the door, dive out of the car, and sprint to lower Manhattan, my father's large hand found its way to my shoulder. While he reassuringly gripped my deltoid, I fell back against my seat, swearing with quiet, steady thoroughness.

"What's wrong?" Hien asked, laughing.

"My son," my father explained, "is afraid of snakes." He nudged me. "Isn't that right, Guts?"

We stopped in a lonely parking area. From here a number of grownover paths led off to the former base. After Hien gave the area a thorough sweeping for snakes, I followed my father out of the car. Running around us were any number of small, brown, bat-eared, runty dogs. Dogs in Vietnam, I had noticed, tended to wear vaguely worried expressions. Before I came here I was told to make sure that, whenever I ordered something in a restaurant, I knew what it was before I ate it. Now that I was here I realized that this was needless. *Thit cho,* or "dog meat," was listed straightforwardly by the establishments that served it. More popular in the north than in the south (or so southerners always claimed to their American friends), dog was a delicacy usually eaten by men, as it was said to assist one's sexual appetite. (They ate cats—"little tiger"—in Vietnam, too, to less certain copulative ends.) I stopped to pet a few of these unhappy-looking little dogs, but not before Hien made a joke about eating them.

Truong elected to smoke cigarettes and wait with the car while we surveyed Chu Lai. Hien and my father and I started off down one of the trails. I took up the rear and while watching my father saunter confidently through the scrub—his large feet lifting high with each step, his head up and alert, his shoulders squared—had a vividly aggregate memory of all the times I had gone bird hunting with him as a boy. He hunted birds exclusively because, after Vietnam, my father found he could no longer hunt "mammals." The starkness of this morally Linnaean line had often troubled me as a boy. I was not a particularly able hunter. I tripped over every stump and branch, surrendered pints of blood to mosquitoes no matter how fragrantly I stank of repellent, could never spot birds even after they had been repeatedly pointed out to me, and once nearly perforated the chest of one of my father's hunting friends with an errant blast of my four-ten shotgun. This last near disaster earned me the nickname Accident Happening. Yet, wanting only to please my father, I went with him into the woods again and again.

He was different in the forest: more patient, but also more humorless; more fatherly, but also less friendly. He had a ranger's silent confidence even in areas I knew he had never hunted before. My father was good in the forest. He knew every answer and did everything so well, from the delicacy with which he loaded a shell to the mechanical ease with which he raised his gun and fired. When he knocked a bird from the air, he did so without emotion. He would crouch beside his downed pheasant, looking at it neutrally, then lift the carcass up by its legs and gently lower it into his game bag. Our black Lab Zorro would be in some feral ecstasy after a shotgun blast and often pranced droolingly around the heap of lifeless brown feathers, but my father would coax Zorro's brain back to domestication by working his fingers into the slack folds of black skin beneath his neck and softly, methodically scratching. I had always loved my father a little more while we were hunting, and now I wondered why I had ever stopped going with him. Then I remembered. I had shot a mallard, blown its beautiful Christmas-ornament green head right off, and in the car cried all the way back home. My father said nothing to comfort me but also nothing to chastise me. He was silent while I shivered and wept. The erasure of a life—its totality—was something my father understood. *Mammals.* I was a mammal. So was he. I loved him so much that day. I loved him so much. He never took me hunting again.

After a while the trail widened and the scrub dwindled from waist-to-knee-high. Somewhere ahead I could hear waves rolling ashore and the faint foamy hiss with which they died upon the sand. Within that sound larger waves were atomizing upon unseen shoreline rocks, a terrific sound not unlike huge watery cymbals crashing together. The breeze underwent a wind-tunnel hardening, the flesh on my forearms turning pocked and prickly. Sunglasses were not needed here. Along the ocean, the morning sky had become a low leaky ceiling of slushy grays and whites.

"I know Chu Lai was a Marine base," I called ahead, "but were there any other U.S. personnel here?"

My father neither slowed nor turned around. "It was about ninety-five percent Marines, I'd say. Some Coast Guard. Some Army intelligence. But mostly Marines. You know how Chu Lai got its name?"

I did. In early 1965, the Marine Corps's Lieutenant General Victor "Brute" Krulak first arrived at these windblown, grown-over wilds and deemed them suitable for a U.S. base. But a subaltern pointed out that this area was not indicated on any maps. Krulak said that was nonsense—this area was known as Chu Lai. But "Chu Lai" was merely Krulak's name in Mandarin Chinese transliteration. By the time someone figured that out, Krulak had gotten his base.

Despite Krulak's fearsome nickname—and his early confidence that the methods of conventional warfare would succeed in Vietnam—he ultimately came to believe that "pacification" was the key to defeating the NLF. Pacification changed conceptually throughout the war's early years. It went from a 1965 plan to "Find the enemy. . . . Fix the enemy in place so that he can be engaged successfully. . . . Fight and finish the enemy" to the MACV's later, more nuanced view of pacification as "the military, political, economic, and social process of establishing or reestablishing local government responsibility." Pacification was supposed to have worked hand in hand with the simultaneous war of attrition being waged by General William Westmoreland and his advisers. The thinking was that while the enemy was being hunted, areas of former enemy activity would be pacified, fortified, and safeguarded. Pacification ultimately fell under Marine Corps jurisdiction. Krulak, like many Marines, grew skeptical that one could defeat an enemy army that enjoyed a bottomless pool from which to recruit replacement soldiers. Rejecting the Pentagon's stated belief that the war had to be won "militarily" first, Krulak said, "You cannot win militarily. You have to win totally, or you are not winning at all." He also viewed body-count strategies as "a dubious index of success since, if killing is accompanied by devastation of friendly areas, we may end up having done more harm than good."

Krulak and others worked to establish a basic Marine strategy whereby the three Marine bases at Hue, Danang, and Chu Lai would expand in their areas of control, like peaceably growing blobs, until they all met— a strategy popularly known as "clear and hold"—causing the NLF to gradually lose the food and support of the Vietnamese people. Other Marine pacification projects included building medical clinics staffed by volunteer Navy doctors and a moderately successful (though little-used) program that joined a dozen Marines to small, select South Vietnamese militia units living among Vietnam's villagers. These were called Combined Action Platoons, or CAPs, and were invented by Lieutenant Colonel William Corson. Essentially, Corson's was an attempt to out-NLF the NLF. "Counterguerrilla forces," one State Department official responsible for urging forward the CAPs initiative wrote, "must adopt the tactics of the guerrilla himself." Indeed, there were reports of some

CAPs Marines exchanging their uniforms for black pajamas. One successful aspect of the CAPs program was that it prevented the NLF from collecting taxes, as even villagers emotionally committed to the insurgency resented the ever-increasing and ever more spontaneous nature of NLF tax collection as the war went on.

Despite this, General Westmoreland did not have much faith in Marine-led pacification and maintained that only ARVN soldiers should be charged with pacification duty—not realizing or caring that many ARVN soldiers were far more likely to harass the Vietnamese population than pacify it. (He also worried, perhaps presciently, that prolonged contact between the U.S. military and Vietnamese civilians would lead to "unfortunate incidents.") Westmoreland so frowned on the CAPs program in particular that he did not allow Marines to mark their time spent living with the Vietnamese as "days in the field." "Pacification," one of Westmoreland's aides later explained, "bored him."

The most crucial component of Westmoreland's preferred war of attrition was the search-and-destroy patrol—a term Westmoreland hated, preferring "offensive sweep." Amazingly, less than one percent of all search-and-destroy patrols actually encountered the enemy, and 90 percent of those encounters were enemy-initiated. Search-and-destroy patrols were not, as some have argued, a "corpse-exchange" program with the NLF. The idea was to initiate enemy contact and then quickly broadcast the enemy's position to nearby artillery or bombers. The NLF did not always allow U.S. forces effective use of artillery or bombing, either by sticking so close to Americans troops that to call in artillery fire became suicidal or by swiftly breaking away after an ambush. U.S. Army Major General William DePuy, in a moment of frustration, once said that NLF ambushes were "kind of a coward's way of fighting the war." But blasting men from artillery placements seven miles away was hair-shirt gallantry itself.

As the Army's search-and-destroy patrols floundered, the NLF and PAVN lured Marines from the populous coast toward Vietnam's center, where the Communists believed the geography was more in their favor. This was a conscious attempt to stall the pacification effort, the ultimate efficacy of which is still debated by scholars and historians. Some believe it more or less worked in harmony with the war of attrition, others believe it only appeared to work (none of the pacification efforts survived the United States' departure), and revisionists believe it worked so well that it triggered the desperate Tet Offensive. My father and I discussed the pacification effort, and I learned that in his opinion the Marines pretty much had everything under control at all times. It seemed pointless to argue. Instead I asked him, "What's with you Marines and your nicknames, anyway?"

"What do you mean?"

" 'Brute' Krulak. Lieutenant General Lewis 'Chesty' Puller. General Lewis 'Silent Lew' Walt. Whenever I come across the name of some prominent Marine, there's always this nom de guerre sandwich. So how about you? Did you have a nickname?"

My father stopped walking and looked back at me. By this point even Hien was listening to our conversation. "Actually, I did have a nickname: Captain John 'Nice Guy' Bissell."

I studied what I could see of the eyes floating behind his sunglasses' county-sheriff tint. "You're serious."

A shrug. "That's what they called me."

"Was it ironical?"

"I don't think so."

" 'Nice Guy' was your Marine Corps nickname?"

"One of them."

"Why did they call you 'Nice Guy'?"

"Once," my father said, "we were rolling down a highway probably not too far from here, and I had more problems than you can imagine. We were taking sporadic fire all along the road. And this general up there in a helicopter monitoring the situation is telling us to move out, which, for Christ's sake, we were already doing. Well, in moving out we plowed over and killed a water buffalo, which I had to explain to the general. 'I don't give a fuck,' the general said. I said to him, 'Hold it, this is Charlie six. We've both heard the orders about destroying the local people's animals: "If it happens, you *will* recompense them." General, I intend to obey those orders.' So what I did was take every dime from our recreation fund to recompense this poor, frightened peasant. I knew that the water buffalo was his tractor, his jeep, his engine, his car. So I paid him off, saying, 'I'm so sorry, I'm so terribly sorry.' And the general, who's still following me in the air, is shouting down, 'You get your ass out of there! That's an order, Lieutenant!' I finally grabbed the radio and said, 'Please fuck off, General.' I almost got a court-martial."

"Nice Guy was almost court-martialed?"

"For a while there it seemed to be almost a weekly deal for me. I was not rebellious. I just tried to do the right thing."

We came to the center of Chu Lai. All that remained of this storied military city—where for almost a decade tens of thousands of Americans had worked and eaten and defecated and slept—were bundled infestations of fist-sized green-gray cacti, several stands of breeze-blown pine trees, an occasional strip of buckled sidewalk, and the paved remnants of the odd runway. Beyond that: nothing. The writer Tim O'Brien once made a pilgrimage to his site of wartime deployment with the U.S. Army. "You'd think," O'Brien wrote, "there would be *something* left, some faint imprint." But everything from the landing zone to the medical tents to the post exchange was "utterly and forever razed from the earth." Indeed, at Chu Lai it was as though some great hand had swept this place clean of all that was man-made, leaving everything else fibrous and drab beneath an overcast sky.

"So," my father said, "this is where I lived all those horrible months."

"There's nothing left," I said.

He looked at me. "You expected there to be?"

"A Communist indoctrination center, at least, or some crappy museum showcasing the glories of the resistance. *Something.*" This was not an unreasonable expectation, given what had happened around Chu Lai. Operation Starlite, for instance. Initially called Operation Satellite but garbled by an overworked Marine clerk, Starlite was hatched when rumors of large-scale NLF massing around Chu Lai reached the ears of General Lewis Walt, commander of the Third Marine Amphibious Force, in the summer of 1965, shortly after my father arrived. The Marines' quickly arranged surprise attack was a dyad assault by air and sea. Despite the offshore hammering the NLF took from two destroyers and a heavy cruiser, the first Marines to alight upon the nearby battle-field's landing zone found themselves in a wasp's nest of bullets and flak. According to Edward F. Murphy, the fire was so intense that, in the words of one Marine helicopter pilot, "You just had to close your eyes and drop down to the deck." My father served as part of a "blocking force" during Starlite and now claimed to remember little of the battle other than running around and prodigiously discharging his weapon. The first two Medals of Honor bestowed upon Marines in Vietnam, one of them posthumously, were awarded after Starlite, and the battle's final tally was more than 600 slain NLF and 45 dead Marines (though the NLF claimed in its propaganda to have killed 900). American analysts maintained that if the United States could lose one soldier for every twelve lost by the NLF, as in Starlite, the war would be handily won. The NLF and North Vietnamese believed that if they could control how long battles lasted and limited their losses, the Americans would weary and go home.

My father walked alone twenty feet from where we stood, stopped suddenly, and turned back to us, nodding. "I remember some of this. Right here there were roads honeycombed every which way. And over there was the air base; we had a ton of jets and choppers there. I think the runways were something like eighty-five hundred feet long. Over in this direction was the mess tent, and over here was the bank."

"The first quality of a soldier," according to Napoléon, "is constancy in enduring fatigue and hardship. Courage is only the second. Poverty, privation and want are the school of good soldiers." How would Napoleon have felt about the forty ice-cream factories built for U.S. soldiers in Vietnam? The 340 pounds of supplies every soldier used up each day? The 10 million field rations eaten and 80,000 tons of ammunition used a month? The mountains of Coca-Cola and Pepsi on ice at every U.S. base? The fact that doughnuts and pastries were available if one woke up early enough? The shrimp cocktails and fresh strawberries?

To contrast this excess with the Napoleonic privation faced by the NLF and PAVN was revealing. The average NLF insurgent found himself at the begging end of a supply line that took porters two full months to travel. In lean times, NLF guerrillas received, if they were lucky, one can of corn. Per squad. PAVN soldiers typically received one or two khaki shirts, a pair of trousers, sandals made of tire treads, and a sewing kit. Those receiving this equipment were informed that it had to last for half a decade.

I thought of O'Brien again while looking upon the weedy remnants of Chu Lai, in particular his great story "The Things They Carried." After finding a "VC corpse, a boy of fifteen or sixteen," O'Brien's American soldiers note that when the boy died "he had been carrying a pouch of rice, a rifle, and three magazines of ammunition." One character says, "You want my opinion, there's a definite moral here." Was the moral that the NLF and PAVN, in the words of the left-leaning historian James P. Harrison, "vanquished perhaps the greatest odds in the history of warfare"? Or was the moral how unseemly it was for Americans to complain about the result of a war in which the United States enjoyed every imaginable technological advantage? These advantages ranged from armored personnel carriers to the availability of artillery fire to napalm bombs to quick-loading grenade launchers to helicopters loaded with Gatling guns capable of firing 100 rounds per second. The United States had access to so much in Vietnam, it did not even know how to use what it had. A surface-to-air missile defense system was installed in South Vietnam, for instance, at the order of Lyndon Johnson, even though for most of the war the North had no offensive air force to speak of.

What I said next to my father I felt I had to say: "Dad, forgive me, but how the hell did you guys manage to lose? You had every imaginable advantage."

"Funny," my father said, looking away. "I was just thinking about that myself. What can I tell you? When I was here I was always under the impression we were winning. In the end, I just don't know what happened. There was a lot of death, a lot of disillusionment. I think half a million Marines in total came through Vietnam. Thirteen thousand of them were killed, and ninety thousand, I believe, were wounded. That's one in five—a higher casualty rate than what the Marines suffered during World War II. Think about that. We had a lot of advantages—that's certainly true. But this wasn't our country. We were all a long way from home."

With these words—perhaps the most human sentiment I had ever heard my father utter about the war—pinned and wiggling upon my mind, we walked over to the cliff along which part of Chu Lai had been arranged and gazed down at the shoreline's anthracite black rocks and then out onto the ocean itself. No bobbing junks, no swift and wave-slicing boats, not a single hardy swimmer. The rough, sparkleless water heaved about in the farther reaches of our sight, and closer in gathered itself for whitened shoreward rushes. The spume flew up and covered us: when I licked my lips, my tongue took away a deposit of salt. My father had spent his first months in Vietnam contemplating these same waves, this same dreadfully vast sky. Somewhere behind us, hidden in the jungly pines, a water buffalo mooed. The same water buffaloes were mooing when my father walked amid Chu Lai's billions of dollars of weapons and equipment. Chu Lai could not have been a pleasant place under the best of circumstances. One combat memoirist noted that "Chu Lai was a free-fire zone. I was instructed to shoot at everything not American, ROK [Republic of Korea], or ARVN," and a U.S. Army major operating out of Chu Lai said, "We are at war with ten-year-old children. It may not be humanitarian, but that's what it's like." I wondered how significantly life had really changed for the poorest people in and around Chu Lai. Earlier Hien had mentioned that Chu Lai was currently designated an "economic revival zone" for which the government was "seeking for investors." Swords had become plowshares here, but only because all the swords had been shattered.

My father asked if there was a way to walk down to the rocks, but Hien told him it was forbidden. My father removed his sunglasses to reveal tired eyes. "Yeah," he said under his breath, "what the fuck isn't?" Suddenly he was pointing. "I think we used to go swimming down there, near those rocks. Sometimes we'd tie ropes around our waists and go diving for lobster."

Hien nodded. "Lobster is very good with beer." This was quite possibly as philosophical a statement as Hien's growingly evident politics could allow him.

My father wanted, finally, to find the site of the old Marine post exchange, which took us back through the thick and pointy scrub. Shortly we stumbled upon two ancient women sitting along the path.

They wore conical hats badly stained by salt water and were picking berries. When they smiled, they unleashed twin red crescents of betel nut–stained teeth. (Betel nuts are not nuts but seeds of the betel palm tree. Betel nut, when wrapped in leaves and cut with lime and chewed, provides a mildly mouth-numbing effect—that is, if you do not projectile vomit.) We smiled back at the old women and a few moments later found what my father believed had been the location of the PX. If it was possible, this area seemed even more neglected. The brush here had a dry, tindery feeling, and it was difficult to step anywhere without taking a wooden stiletto in the ankle or shin.

"Home sweet home," I said. "So. Were you a chronic mail checker like I am?"

My father shook his head and kicked at a tree stump. "I barely ever came to the PX. We were out in the field most days. We'd come back here at night to defend our base, then be gone again the next morning. Day after day after day. It became very tedious." He paused, and up floated a professorially clarifying index finger. "Until, one night, the VC or Revolutionary Force or whatever you'd care to call them broke through our lines. Now, these were brave men. They took dynamite packs, got 'em under three aircraft, and then blew the planes and themselves up. They did a lot of damage and scared the bejesus out of all of us, believe me. Very, very brave men."

The extent to which the insurgents relied upon "suicide squads" in battling the Americans was truly startling. One NLF directive from 1967 spoke of how its members needed to seek out every "opportunity to avenge evil done to our families. . . . All Party members and cadres must be willing to sacrifice their lives for the survival of the Fatherland. . . . To conduct an uprising, you must have a roster of all the tyrants and spies and be familiar with the way they live and where they live. Then use suicide cells to annihilate them by any means." By 1964, in one historian's estimation, these zealous insurgents had "destroyed or damaged" half the bombers the United States had dispatched to South Vietnam. The tactical advantages of using suicide bombers were obvious: if the Marines invaded an enemy base, they needed a division; the Vietnamese needed three men.

"What was that like," I asked, "to see these suicide attacks?"

"Frightening. And it made you angry, because you couldn't stop them. We had missile launchers placed all around us here. They were all over. We used to shoot them off for nothing sometimes, for practice. But what good are missiles against small groups of men willing to destroy themselves? I mean, that's war. It's horrible. You can't do a thing about it." He put his sunglasses back on. For the first time during this trip, I could hear anger in my father's voice. His head swung back and forth. "I remember some things so vividly. There was a Huey, I guess right over there. Someone out in the bush needed help—Christ, I can't remember. But we couldn't use it. 'We need that chopper here!' Care to guess why? It was for the news media. There were so many fuckups, all due to personal perverseness. False pride, not caring about people's men, not caring about the war effort overall. But most of our problems had to do with unit integrity."

Many authorities agreed: the lack of unit integrity was cardinally disjunctive to U.S. morale during the war. Personnel rotation in Vietnam worked in many ways, most of them unprecedented in the history of warfare. Officers above second lieutenant, for instance, were rotated out of combat assignments every six months. While this policy came from the sensible recognition that men under fire could not function indefinitely, it nevertheless meant that officers "still pissing stateside water," in Lieutenant General Harold G. Moore's memorable words, often replaced experienced officers in the middle of complicated combat maneuvers. The Marines rotated everyone out after a thirteen-month tour—one month longer than any other U.S. branch of service—thereby rendering useless, once again, whatever battlefield knowledge individual Marines had gleaned about various NLF tactics. The NLF, significantly, did not follow such procedures. In most cases an NLF insurgent fought until he died (or deserted). Thus the NLF learned how to counter seemingly insurmountable disadvantages while American soldiers had to keep figuring out how to fight the NLF.

"In the Second World War," my father went on, "when our fathers and grandfathers went off to war, they had six hundred percent replacement. That means one hundred men went into battle and if any one of them died they were replaced six times. But they always had the same unit, same flag unit, same name, same everything. Each man was replaced six times until the war stopped. Those that survived gutted out their time. It was horrible—it was horrific—but the unit remained intact. Well, our uppers decided, 'America can't stand that. So what we'll do is snap off a platoon here, a squad here, a company here, a battalion here, and we'll integrate them all with other units.' What that did was break down the entire communication structure, the average soldier's basic understanding of his duty. You couldn't really train anyone, or talk to anyone, because it was all in and out. No one had any method that everyone else could learn from. So we're not able to communicate, we have no real trust in one another, I don't know how you operate tactically, you don't know how I do things. We had so little connection. We didn't come here alongside the men we'd trained with, and we went home alone. And new guys always arrived alone."

"I read about that somewhere. No one would want to go out on patrol with a new guy because new guys smelled too clean. A lot of soldiers were convinced the Revolutionary Force could smell the soap on their skin."

"And we could smell the *nuoc mam* on theirs. Yeah, it's true. And it all hurt us, all of it—it hurt us badly."

"Why did the Americans decide to fight like that?" This was Hien, who sounded genuinely curious.

"Because the Army and the Marine Corps listened to our Congress and the president. If we'd held our unit integrity and told ourselves, 'We're here to fight until this thing is done,' everything would have turned out very differently."

Hien's presence beside me felt quietly prevailing. My legs traded my body weight back and forth. Finally I asked my father, almost entirely for Hien's sake, "Do you really believe that?"

He stared at me. "I know that."

"So in your view the war was lost because of poor leadership. Intelligent people making poor decisions."

"No. It has very little to do with intelligence, per se. It has to do with understanding. They would send over colonels and generals every six months to get them trained or retrained or get them 'active' in things. . . . None of these men had any idea of what we, especially the enlisted men, were going through. People were getting shot all the time. We may have had a lot here at Chu Lai, but it was a different story out in the field. Marines were always starved and scrounging for resources. Half the time we were living in holes in the ground or scraping around to find enough plywood to put a floor underneath our people so they wouldn't get leeches in their feet or in their boots. And my father-in-law, Colonel T., who I loved very much, was sitting up there in Danang having lobster and steak every night, formulating grand thoughts on how the war could be won. True. Do you know how many colonels died in combat in World War Two? Hundreds. *Hundreds.* Do you know how many died in combat in Vietnam? Hardly any."

His sudden, growled tone startled me, and I lowered the tape recorder from his mouth. "Hey, Dad—you okay? We can stop."

But he went on: "The one thing we were taught, and the one thing we taught: initiative, initiative, initiative. Mission. Find your mission. You find your mission, make your battle plan, and accomplish the mission no matter what it takes. The mission is paramount. Every case of human waste, or casualties, or suffering—that is beside the point. Do you understand what that means? You will accomplish your mission. And this is okay—this is expected—as long as the mission makes sense. As long as you can accomplish the mission with *reasonableness.* But when you have to destroy a company of men, or a battalion of men, or kill civilians, or keep choppers parked for the fucking news media, most men with a conscience, with a heart and soul, most men will say, 'I have to do this another way.' The final analysis is we fragmented, in my opinion. Our high command was playing with sandlots, moving tanks around, and never being on the ground, with us. I never saw a general go out on any patrol—not in a truck, not on foot. They deemed it *unnecessary.* And that's where they and their South Vietnamese counterparts, in my view, failed us. Rank is basically bullshit. In combat, respect is paramount. And when a general does not respect a lieutenant and orders him about summarily, with no idea of the tactical situation, no idea, just giving orders, because he thinks that's the right thing to do—well, quite frankly, we began to ignore them."

"Dad, I'm going to be honest and say you're freaking me out a little."

"Well, what do you want to talk about? The rights and wrongs of war? I don't know much about that. I don't even know that much about war. Except that I was in one, apparently."

We made our way back to the car, but soon all three of us stopped to pee. While voiding at our distant back-turned coordinates it began raining again, harder than the misty satin aerosol that often lingered in the air throughout a Vietnamese morning and early afternoon. My father had not freaked me out moments before. What he had done was irritate me. I was irritated by how certain he was of having been failed here in Vietnam. Irritated too by how he had apparently never paused to wonder if he had been failed because the mission—the initiative—he and his fellows had all been so determined to implement was in fact wrong and immoral. He had no idea how much of him I knew: the many kindnesses he had done for people back home and never discussed, the time he had dived over three pews to come to the aid of a boy who had fainted during mass, that on every trash day he still insisted on emptying the garbage cans of his Jurassically aged neighbors even though they had habitually threatened to shoot my father's dogs for running around in their yard. Here is the recording that greets those who telephone John "Nice Guy" Bissell at work: "This is John Bissell. Thank you very much for calling. I'm sorry I missed your call. Your call is very important to me. I will return your call as soon as possible. Again, thank you very much for your call." But how does one reconcile love when the object of one's love cannot, in one crucial moral arena, see the obvious? My decent father had killed men in this place. He had seen men killed. For him this whole country was a campus of death and loss. What on earth was I expecting of him? I looked down to see my dying arc of urine splash upon some shamrocky plants that, like tiny green fists, instantly folded in upon themselves. A brainless organism responding to stimulus from without. How practical a self-defense mechanism it suddenly seemed.

"Beware of snakes," Hien said as we all zipped up.

"Did you see one?" This statement left my mouth at a decibel level somewhere between shout and scream. Unfortunately none of the nearest trees looked climbable.

Hien smiled. "Maybe I heard one over there."

"Are you winding me up? Tell me you're kidding."

"Most snakes are not dangerous," Hien said. "You know this, yes?"

"Cobras," my father said.

Hien, nodding acceptingly: "Of course cobras are very dangerous."

"Are there fucking *cobras* here?"

My father and Hien: "Yeah."

I was now standing behind my father. "For Chri—why, then, are we walking here?"

Hien was still smiling. "Have you had the snake wine? You know the snake wine."

"Snake wine?" my father asked as I gauged his willingness to allow me to ride piggyback upon his shoulders back to the car. "No, what is it?"

"It means we have the snake blood with wine. Very strong."

"Let me guess," I said. "It makes your cock hard, right?"

"If," my father said, "it doesn't fall off after you drink it."

"Sometime we can go to the snake restaurant."

"No thank you, Hien. That dead snake we saw earlier was almost enough to cause me to poo."

We were walking again, my eyes peeled down to their rods and cones as I scanned the underbrush. My father said, "You know, cobras rearing up out of the bush around here used to scare the heck out of me. Cobras and our little friends who eat them."

"Which friends are those? They sound terrific."

"Mongooses," my father said. "Mongoose-cobra battle breaks down to about sixty-forty in favor of the mongoose, as I understand it."

"I thought that was just a legend."

"Absolutely not. The mongoose wins about sixty percent of the time. They never quit."

Hien: "I have never seen this."

My father: "If I were a betting man, I'd bet on the mongoose. I'd bet on the Marine—that's a mongoose."

"A Marine is a mongoose," I said.

"That's correct."

"You're a very strange man."

We passed the berry-picking women again, still as willing as ever to smile. While my father walked ahead, I told Hien that I wondered, sometimes, what it was like for older Vietnamese to watch people like my father and me traipse around their country. Despite its growing economy (which I dutifully recognized), I understood, I told Hien, that the average Vietnamese citizen's life was still filled with doubt and want. Might not the sight of our cameras, clean clothes, and sunny faces cause some resentment? How sincere, I tried to ask, were those smiles?

Hien explained that Vietnam had basically been on its own from 1975 to 1985, a time most remember as far more terrible than that of the American War. "The saddest years," as Hien called them, found Vietnam embroiled in two more conflicts a mere half decade after Saigon's fall. The first was against Cambodia, in 1978. The Vietnamese Communists' former client, Pol Pot, after killing, working to death, or starving one in every eight Cambodians, exacerbated the historic tensions, temporarily hidden by Communism, between Vietnam and Cambodia by unwisely launching some cross-border raids into Vietnam. Vietnam's Le Duan (who was not innocent of antagonizing Cambodia) finally had enough of this and ordered 100,000 Vietnamese troops into Cambodia to overthrow the Khmer Rouge.

For the heroic action of ending what the Vietnamese Communists themselves called "the most monstrous genocide ever," the Socialist Republic of Vietnam was rewarded with the status of International Pariah. In what is perhaps the most disturbing moment ever in U.S. foreign relations, the Carter administration refused to recognize Cambodia's Vietnamese-installed government in favor of the Khmer Rouge. Vietnam wound up occupying Cambodia for eleven years and in doing so lost thousands of soldiers: Vietnam's Vietnam. China, long irritated by Vietnam's intransigence, decided to avenge its deposed allies in Phnom Penh and ordered several hundred thousand invading troops into northern Vietnam. This invasion, China's eleventh of Vietnam, did not stir one peep of protest from the United States. China's Communism had always been too extreme for the Vietnamese, and the invasion rallied the Vietnamese people behind their government to an extent not seen during even the American War. (From California, Nguyen Cao Ky volunteered to fight for the Vietnamese Communists.) Chinese troops, who had not known a battlefield since the Korean conflict, managed to move roughly twenty miles into Vietnamese territory and lost a thousand men for every mile. After seventeen days, China withdrew— making Vietnam the only nation on earth that can claim to have militar- ily defeated three of the five permanent members of the United Nations Security Council. The ten years following Vietnam's Vietnam and its Chinese invasion left what was already one of the poorest countries on the planet in straits so economically dire that many Soviet advisers reportedly preferred to be dispatched to Africa than suffer placement in the world's newest socialist republic.

"And so," Hien told me, "you and your father do not bother the old women at all. You mean something to them. Do you know?"

"Tell me."

"Vietnam is no longer alone."

We soon headed for a place my father had no wish to see. This was the Son My Memorial, found six miles outside the provincial capital of Quang Ngai. Once upon a time Son My was a subdistrict village divided into several hamlets: Truong Dinh, Tu Cung, Co Luy, and My Lai. The most famous of these hamlets was Tu Cung, though it was and contin- ues to be popularly misidentified as My Lai due to errors of designation made by the U.S. military. It was in Tu Cung/My Lai where, in 1968, the most notorious U.S. war crimes against Vietnamese villagers took place.

My tape recorder, yet again, was pulled from my backpack, and I turned to my father. "Let's put this on the record: You did not want to come see the Son My Memorial."

My father sighed. "It wasn't my first choice."

"Why not?"

"Well, it's sort of a . . . it's just such a sad thing, that's all. But I guess we're going to do it, and that's fine with me."

There were various reasons why my father did not want to visit Son My, some easily grasped, others less so. One of the "less so" reasons was my father's unaccountable friendliness with Captain Ernest Medina, who commanded Charlie Company, the unit within the 11th Brigade, 23rd Light Infantry Division responsible for many of the My Lai killings. Medina, a Mexican American whose promising military career was garroted by My Lai, eventually wound up settling in northern Wisconsin, and occasionally my father would see him. My father had always maintained that Medina was a "great guy" who claimed to have given no order for what happened and had no explanation for it.

On the way to Son My, we passed bean fields and schoolkids in their white shirts and red kerchiefs. The road, already narrow, was tightened further by lingering floodwater courtesy of last night's torrent. In each standing pool the reflection of the tall palms seemed like a mirrored gateway into another, darker dimension. Quang Ngai was a poor province, and parts of it looked locust-scoured. Despite its proximity to the ocean and its rough beauty, Quang Ngai had always been poor and was largely known for its bricklayers. During the war it had also been one of the most revolutionary provinces in South Vietnam.

Over the last three and a half decades many commentators have attempted to minimize the ethical catastrophe of the massacre by pointing out, accurately, that Quang Ngai was largely sympathetic to the NLF. In their day Quang Ngai's people ferociously resisted Vietnam's Chinese, Japanese, and French occupiers. North Vietnam's prime minister Pham Van Dong was from Quang Ngai. In 1948, Ho Chi Minh lauded the people of Quang Ngai for becoming one of the first southerly provinces to rid itself of the French. The village of Son My was itself built by the Viet Minh. During the American War it was said that more NLF recruits came out of Quang Ngai than any other province. In his memoir *If I Die in a Combat Zone*, Tim O'Brien, who patrolled Quang Ngai, refers to the "patently hostile" faces of the area's inhabitants. Between 1965 and 1968, 70 percent of the province's villages were destroyed by Korean, U.S., and South Vietnamese forces; Quang Ngai's civilian casualties ran as high as 50,000 a year.

Amid the unpaved side roads, the shabby and closely arranged homes, the chicken coops and pigpens, and the kicked-up miasmas of dust, an occasional bit of floating-past visual incongruity caught one's eye: a shop with a gleamingly white wedding dress displayed behind its dirty front window, a Vietnamese blacksmith peppered in hot flecks of orange spark as he lowered a piece of metal onto a blurrily spinning wheel, bandanna-wearing teenagers holding children they looked far too young to have given birth to, and, finally, a health clinic built in part with funds donated by U.S. Army veterans of the Vietnamese War. My Lai had a new elementary school as well, also built with funds partially supplied by American veterans.

"How hard was it," I asked my father, "to deal with people who may have liked Americans, or at least were nice to you, and yet know that they often turned around and gave shelter to NLF guerrillas?"

"They had no choice."

"Are you sure about that?"

"Yeah."

"Really?"

"Yeah. Why?"

Yet again I decided I would not challenge him. While one can investigate the war's history and find anecdotal evidence of numerous South Vietnamese supporting the insurgency—such as the villager who told American surveyors in 1967 that the NLF knew "how to please the people; they behave politely so people feel like they are more favored. . . . [T]hey do not thunder at the people like government soldiers"—it has also been estimated that as much as 30 percent of the NLF's guerrillas were forcibly recruited. It was confusing. Of course it was confusing. Le Ly Hayslip, a Vietnamese with an extremely sympathetic view of the United States, addresses American war veterans directly in her memoir when she writes, "almost everyone in the country you tried to help resented, feared, and misunderstood you." When discussing the war in Vietnam, which in many cases meant attempting to chart the infinity of human nature, there were few categorical statements that could not be obviated by another, equally truthful categorical statement. Thus I said, both to my father and myself, "It's frustrating."

"It was. It was horrible. Terrible."

"Do you think that's part of the reason why American morale got so bad?"

He shook his head. "*We* didn't have bad morale. That happened later. That process took a few years."

"What's your worst memory?"

"Losing people. Seeing people get killed. Packing 'em up, shipping 'em home, writing letters."

"Like your and Phil's friend Walt Levy?"

"A good friend. A great man."

"So how does one go on? After losing a friend, I mean."

"You just do. You put it behind you. That's called discipline."

"Did you ever have any thoughts while you were here about getting out, about leaving?"

"Hell no."

"Not you personally—the United States. Did you ever, in a low moment, think, 'This is insane. What are we doing here?'"

"I never did. What I thought was, 'We have to do better.' That proved to be impossible."

"Because of things like the My Lai massacre."

For the first time since we had begun speaking—my father typically communicated his dislike of certain topics by engaging in laconism or staring fixedly away—he looked over at me. "What you don't understand is that things like My Lai happened all the time, only on a much smaller scale. All the time."

The night before the massacre, my father's friend Captain Medina spoke to Charlie Company. Medina was well liked by his troops, who regarded him as grumpy, garrulous, short-tempered, and essentially fair. But Medina had also ignored many instances of Charlie Company getting out of control. The retribution murder of an innocent Vietnamese girl riding her bicycle in the days after a soldier's death was hushed up by Medina, as were literally dozens of random beatings. Medina himself routinely smacked prisoners around and cautioned soldiers that if they captured anyone alive they would have to share their food with the captive. One month and a half after arriving in Vietnam, one member of Charlie Company later recalled, "we stopped taking prisoners."

Many individual soldiers within Charlie Company differed on what Medina's instructions for the following day's assault had amounted to. Most agree that revenge was implicitly in the air, as the company had recently lost a popular sergeant to a booby trap. Some soldiers maintained that Medina would have never ordered civilians killed (though all agree that Medina did not have much use for the Vietnamese), others claimed that his implication had been clear, and many testified that Medina had ordered the men to "kill everything." Even if the orders were not to kill civilians, the orders that all acknowledge were given by Medina (as well as Lieutenant Colonel Frank Barker, who also briefed the men) were themselves illegal. These included burning houses (which required official permission), poisoning wells with animal carcasses, and slaughtering livestock. Generally, the men who took part in the massacre remembered that Medina ordered everything killed while those who refused to take part did not. A minimal student of human nature can deduce some attempt on the part of murderers to assoil their sense of guilt. Most tellingly, a journal entry written by one member of Charlie Company immediately after the briefing does not mention the singularly striking order to "kill everything," only that "we are going to really hit something tomorrow going to hit 4 places its a hot place."

On March 16, 1968, Task Force Barker, a 500-man assault unit broken into three companies (Alpha, Bravo, and Charlie), set out to do what no previous group of soldiers—not U.S. Marines, not Korean Marines, and not the South Vietnamese Army—had so far managed: to pacify the area of Quang Ngai in which the Son My hamlets lay. Medina's Charlie Company had been in Vietnam for only three months and because of dire troop needs had left Hawaii before completing their training, which included one whole hour of nudge-nudge instruction regarding the Geneva Convention. In its twelve weeks in Vietnam, Charlie Company had taken twenty-eight casualties, five of them fatal, all from snipers or booby traps. Beyond this sniper fire, Charlie Company had not experienced any protracted fighting. The assault on Son My—known to the soldiers as "Pinkville," due not to its putative Communist infestation, as is commonly supposed, but because that was its color on military maps—was Charlie Company's first combat assault. In the words of Michael Bilton and Kevin Sim, authors of an exemplary book on the massacre, "They had never seen or encountered the enemy in any strength. There had been no heavy contact. They were battle-scarred without being battle-hardened."

In its assault on Son My, Task Force Barker was operating under several assumptions floated to it by inexperienced CIA officers: that the NLF's hated and elusive 48th Local Force Battalion would be in the area, that there were at least four hundred NLF insurgents in and around My Son's hamlets, that everyone in these hamlets was an active NLF supporter, and that all noncombatants would be at the market on the morning in question. Later evidence would suggest that the village had only ten active supporters of the NLF, though many, perhaps even most, of Son My's villagers had family members in the insurgency. In addition, the NLF's 48th Battalion was dozens of miles away from Son My at the time Task Force Barker arrived.

"Things like My Lai happened *all* the time?" I asked my father now.

"All the time, yes. Just not so severe."

"They did. All the time."

"Unfortunately, yes. That's the reality."

I looked at him, astonished. I knew what he meant, and he knew that I knew what he meant, but to hear him say these words—their buried tolerance for murder—was very nearly too much. I could have asked, and almost did: *Did you ever do anything like that?* But I did not ask, because no father should be lightly posed such a question by his son. Because no father should think, even for a moment, that his son believes him capable of such a thing. Because I knew my father was not capable of such a thing. So I was telling myself as we pulled up to Son My.

As we climbed out of the car, I caught a whiff of my father. At our last stop for the night, he had realized he had misplaced his Right Guard and purchased a new stick from the hotel. This was Glacier Mist Secret. It may have been strong enough for a man, but its gentle, pistilly bouquet was definitely intended for a woman. "Nice smell," I said.

"Goddamn it, you little creep. I told you—it was the only deodorant that last hotel had!"

Two tour buses were already parked here, both decorated with a splashy porpoise motif. As usual I asked Truong if he wanted to join us, and as usual he shook his head and lit a cigarette. I walked up to a large wooden sign that listed "The Regulations of Son My Vestige Area": "Everyone should be responsible to preserve this place as well as to look after the garden or bonsai trees. Visitors are not allowed to bring explosive powder, flaming, reating substances, poison or weapons into the museum. Also you should inform and stop any anti-attitudes toward this historical relic." I snatched up a brochure from the tourist booth. Opening it, I read, "*Dot sach! Giet sach! Pha sach!*" Translated it meant, "Burn all! Kill all! Destroy all!" These words—as words, at least—had nothing to do with My Lai. "Burn all! Kill all! Destroy all!" was instead the self-described policy of Japanese General Okamura Yasuji in China in the summer of 1941—now widely ventriloquized in Asian Communists' schoolbooks.

I walked around. The grounds were marked by a series of tall, wind-hissing palm trees, cobbled paths, cubically sheared evergreen hedges, and statuary, harrowing statuary: staggering gut-shot peasant women, beseeching children, defiant raised fists. These were the first examples of Communist sculpture I had ever seen that did not produce an initial impulse to have at them with a jackhammer. Meanwhile, my father was studying a headstone that listed the names and ages of some Son My victims.

"What don't you see?" he asked as I joined him.

I had a long look. One column of victims' ages worked out like this: 12, 10, 8, 6, 5, 46, 14, 45. Most were women. "I don't see any young men."

"That's because none of the young men were around. This was a VC village."

"Dad. *Dad.*"

"It's just an observation. This whole thing was probably a revenge mission. Actually, I know it was. They probably said, 'We're gonna teach 'em a lesson,' so they massacred everyone. Which is a slight violation of every rule and regulation both moral, written, military, and civilian."

I left him there and walked across an esplanade of long grass, momentarily cooled by the javelins of shade thrown down by the palm trees. This was such a beautiful place. Its green fields and bright red dirt and determined little roads made me somehow hopeful. Was it perverse to find hope and beauty in a place with so many poor, rasorial lives? But poverty was not the sum total of a place or a people. Around me women wearing sun masks worked at trimming Son My's hedges. All of them took the time to bow politely as I passed by. I did not trust the fulsomeness with which I returned their bows. Behind me, across the road, behind the porpoise buses, were a few businesses selling the bottled water Vietnam's perspiring tourists consumed by the gallon. I had a thought to go purchase a bottle but then came across a marker commemorating the death site of more than a dozen Son My victims. Almost all were children. I sat down, the hope and beauty I had just been contemplating as distant and transitory as a satellite.

The danger of events such as the My Lai massacre is that the iconic placement they assume in human consciousness overrides the horror of what actually took place. "My Lai" rarely meant a specific massacre anymore. It was instead a hyponym of human savagery and almost always an object of comparison, something that other instances of brutality either failed to equal or surpassed. Certainly "My Lai" connoted horror even to those who knew little about it. And who would not acknowledge that what had happened here was horrible? (Many people, in fact, argued that it had not been notably horrible. Many.) But My Lai's reflexive connotation of horror was the problem. Its generic horror no longer suggested the specific horror of American soldiers chasing down and bayoneting children among these trees and hedgerows.

On the morning of the massacre, an older Vietnamese man in a rice paddy near the landing zone watched Charlie Company disembark from their choppers. As Herbert Carter, the tunnel rat of the 1st Platoon, later told U.S. Army investigators, the old man "said some kind of greeting in Vietnamese and waved his arms at us. Someone—either Medina or Calley—said to kill him." The elderly man was the day's first victim. Then, in Carter's words, "a woman came out of the village and someone knocked her down and Medina shot her with his M-16 rifle. I was 50 or 60 feet from him and saw this. There was no reason to shoot this girl." Indeed, Charlie Company had taken no incoming fire. They would receive no fire all day. Michael Bernhardt, who did not take part in the massacre, later said that after these first two victims he knew, somehow, that they would not stop. After murdering the girl, Medina killed another boy, moved on to slaughtering some water buffalo, then asked Herbert Carter to help him throw an old man into a well. Carter refused.

Charlie Company broke into its platoons and moved through the village. Lieutenant William Laws Calley, Jr.—five feet four inches tall in his boots, a dropout from Palm Beach Junior College, known as "Rusty" to his few friends and as "Lieutenant Shithead" to Captain Medina— commanded the 1st Platoon. The U.S. Army's dearth of suitable officer material by 1968, caused in no small part by the draft deferments university students were given in order to avoid alienating their middle-class voter parents, helped lead to the human nadir that was Calley. Lieutenant Shithead graduated from Officer Candidates School not knowing how to read a map. Compasses baffled him. In one assessment, Calley displayed "absolutely zero leadership ability," and before and after My Lai his mistakes in the field led to the death and injury of several of his men. (The 1st Platoon would eventually put a bounty on Calley's head.)

Calley was always open, before and after the massacre, about his antipathy toward all Vietnamese, civilian or soldier, northern or southern. The Tet Offensive in particular had strengthened his resolve to "fix the problem" (the existence of Vietnamese people) and accomplish his "mission" (killing them). A later psychiatric evaluation done on Lieutenant Calley indicated that he considered Vietnamese "animals with whom one could not speak or reason." According to Vietnamese survivors of the massacre, here is what these animals were saying as Calley and his men murdered them: "I haven't done anything!" "Oh, my God!" "Have pity!" "We're shot!" "Have pity!" Reading Calley's court-martial testimony, one gets the impression that in his mediocrity, in his lack of imagination, in his deadened morality and thoughtlessness, he willingly blurred the already blurry line Medina had established for Charlie Company.

There were other contributors. During World War II, the U.S. military determined that 98 percent of soldiers who experience sixty days of continuous combat become "psychiatric casualties." The 2 percent who do not are those with "psychopathic personalities." Certain things can delay this process of emotional disintegration. One of them is leadership. If poorly led, soldiers at war rapidly lose their self-respect, their sense of mission, and their higher motives. Poorly led soldiers move to a midbrain place of strictly animal logic, and while they might not become psychopaths in the clinical sense, they can certainly become acquainted with psychopathia's temptations. Of Medina's contested orders the night before the massacre, Calley said, "The way I interpreted it was, if they were in the way, kill them." When asked at his court-martial if he knew the difference between an illegal order and a legal order, Calley responded, "I was never told that I had a choice, sir." When asked if he understood he had been killing innocent women and children, Calley responded, "I never sat down to analyze if they were men, women, and children." One gets a glimpse into Calley's primeval, two-percenter psychology during one moment in his testimony, when he explained that "the only time I denoted sex was when I stopped Conti from molesting a girl." Dennis Conti was not "molesting a girl." Conti was holding a .45 to the woman's baby's head while she tearfully fellated him. And why did Calley stop him? As he later wrote in his memoir, the unbelievably titled *Body Count*, "if a GI is getting a blow job, he isn't doing his job, he isn't destroying communism." Calley, who also raped Vietnamese women, led his men into a bestial cavern, and they became beasts. But Calley did not. Calley remained Calley. There was no place for him to descend to, nothing for him to change into. Calley's lawyer, for his part, maintained that his client had been a "good boy until he got into that Oriental situation."

The "good boy" and my father's "great guy" thus marched into combat. Here are some snapshots from the slaughter, as provided by Bilton and Sim:

Then Wood saw the pitiful sight of an elderly woman who had been wounded, staggering toward them. She had been shot with an M-79 grenade which had failed to explode and was still lodged in her stomach. An old man wearing a straw coolie hat and no shirt was with a water buffalo in a paddy 50 meters away. He put his hands in the air. Several members of the platoon opened fire as Calley watched.

Just then a child, aged about 2 years and parted from its mother, managed to crawl up to the top of the ditch. Dursi watched horrified as Calley picked the child up, shoved it back down the slope, and shot it before returning to question the monk. . . . Immediately Calley grabbed the monk, pulled him round, hurled him into the paddy, and opened fire with Meadlo's M-16. As the elderly *mama-san* tried to get up, she too was killed.

Dennis Conti, the aforementioned rapist and a minesweeper with the 1st Platoon, later described for Army investigators how he and Paul Meadlo had

rounded [some Vietnamese villagers] up. . . . Lieutenant Calley came back, and said: "Take care of them." So we said: "Okay." And we sat there and watched them like we usually do. And he came back again, and he said: "I thought you were going to take care of them." I said: "We're taking care of them." And he said: "I mean kill them." So I looked at Meadlo, and he looked at me, and I didn't want to do it. And he didn't want to do it. So we just kept looking at the people, and Calley calls over and says: "Come here, come here . . . we'll line them up here, we'll kill them. . . ." Then they opened up, and started firing. Meadlo fired a while. I don't know how much he fired, a clip, I think. It might have been more. He started to cry, and he gave me his weapon, and he told me to kill them. And I said I wasn't going to kill them. At the time, when we were talking, the only thing left was children. I told Meadlo, I said: "I'm not going to kill them. He [Calley] looks like he's enjoying it. I'm going to let him do it." So, like I said, the only thing left was children. He [Calley] started killing the children. I swore at him. It didn't go any good. And that was it. They were all dead. He turned around, and said: "Okay, let's go."

Paul Meadlo, a young man often teased by his fellow soldiers for being a "farm boy," was soon (as revealed by later testimony) "crouched, head in his hands, sobbing like a bewildered child." Meadlo's torment would lead, fourteen months later, to his blurting out a confession to Army investigators at a crucial early stage of the first official inquiry into the massacre.

The moral chaos was such that the 1st Platoon's medic went insane, too, and butchered several cows before regaining his senses. Men such as Fred Widmer, a radio operator who, only weeks before, had been photographed playing with Vietnamese children, now began to mow them down. (All the men loved Vietnamese children, Calley complained to Army investigators. "Not me. I hated them.") Varnardo Simpson would try to explain to Bilton and Sim how he had been able to kill children: "I just went. My mind just went. . . . I just killed. . . . And once you start, it's very easy to keep on. Once you start. The hardest—the part that's hard is to kill, but once you kill, that becomes easier, to kill the next person and the next one and the next one." The firing grew to be such that Captain Medina worried that his men were going to run out of ammunition, and others worried about being caught in the friendly cross fire.

Then the rapes began. Later investigations revealed that among Charlie Company the rape of civilian women was common. "It was predictable," Michael Bernhardt, one of the few soldiers in Charlie Company who had been well trained, later said. "In other words, if I saw a woman, I'd say, 'Well, it won't be too long.' That's how widespread it was." During the massacre there were approximately twenty separate rapes, most of the victims under the age of twenty and some of them as young as ten; almost all were murdered after the rapes were over. These were among the most unspeakable crimes committed by Charlie Company, and virtually none of the grisly details came out during the soldiers' various trials. Women were scalped, violated with rifle barrels, and then shot. Some victims' tongues were cut out, while others had their vaginas ripped open by bayonets. A few were decapitated. While all of this was going on, an "equally vicious massacre" (in the later words of the Army's investigation) was being enacted in the nearby hamlet of My Khe. The perpetrators were the men of Bravo Company, commanded by Stephen Brooks. Bravo Company killed dozens of children and wiped out cowering families by throwing fragmentation grenades into their grass huts. They were also responsible for many rapes. According to Bilton and

Sim, the actions of Bravo Company were never fully investigated or widely revealed, for one simple reason: unlike the men of Charlie Company, the perpetrators of Bravo Company's atrocities never talked.

Throughout the morning these gusts of horror were intercut with the stray kindness: the 2nd Platoon's medic, George Garza, bandaged several wounded children while around him their mothers were being raped and shot. A few in the 1st Platoon also refused to kill unarmed villagers—the most stirring suggestion that the "madness of war" cannot fully account for what happened. When Robert Maples, a machine gunner who disobeyed Calley's orders, was later asked by U.S. Army investigators after his questioning if he had anything to add, he said that he did: "Only that I expected something to happen about that incident and I did not expect that it would wait this long."

I returned to my father's side. He had not moved. I touched him on the shoulder, and with a kind of steadfast emotionlessness he nodded. As we walked over to the museum, I noticed that the palm trees were marked with little plaques to indicate the still visible bullet holes the soldiers had fired into them during the massacre. ("Kill some trees!" was, among American soldiers in Vietnam, the equivalent of "Fire at will!") I stopped at one tree. In addition to noting the bullet hole, the plaque named the murdered man whose property this tree had grown on. "Good Christ," my father said quietly, stopping to finger the tree's spiderwebbed bullet hole. His face was suddenly spectral. "Five hundred people."

"Five hundred and four," I said. "According to this pamphlet, at least. I don't think anyone knows how many were killed. Between four and five hundred. Over a hundred of them were under the age of five."

His head had not stopped shaking. "Good Christ."

The museum's three rooms were spacious and floored with dark wood. Around each room milled the porpoise buses' tourists, most of them older Europeans, all of whom were looking at the exhibits with something like cosmic dread splashed across their faces. I looked at a photo of the man Medina had thrown into a well, his shiny brain visible through the hole in his skull, and felt that same dread take up residence upon my own face. Another photo showed a little boy shielding his even littler brother, with this caption: "Truong Bon protecting his younger brother, Truong Nam, both were murdered by the GIs." More photos: a skinny man cut in two by machine-gun fire, a woman with her brains neatly piled beside her. These photos of the massacre were taken in medias res by the U.S. Army photographer Ronald Haeberle. All of them were astonishing, in their way. I lingered before a photo that showed a number of grunts relaxing along a ridge near a ditch. They looked as though they were having a break, perhaps preparing for lunch. None appeared particularly traumatized—with the exception of one ARVN soldier accompanying Charlie Company, whose face was a small epic of barely contained emotion. Just out of frame, several wounded villagers were calling out for help. In the words of the historians James S. Olson and Randy Roberts, "two members of Charlie Company put down their plates, picked up their rifles, killed the wounded Vietnamese villagers, and then returned to their meals." Some of Charlie Company's murderers—but, amazingly, only some—became reticent when Haeberle showed up with his camera. Shortly after the killing began, Haeberle told Bilton and Sim, "I asked some soldiers: 'Why?' They more or less shrugged their shoulders and kept on with the killing." And Haeberle kept taking pictures. Despite one photo's caption that enshrines Haeberle's claim that he took the pictures to prevent something like My Lai from ever happening again, the only thing Haeberle did while documenting one of the worst atrocities ever committed by American soldiers was switch from a black-and-white to a color camera.

My father drifted by. "Hey, Dad."

"Hey, yourself."

"How are you?"

"I'm . . . okay."

"What do you think?"

"What I thought before."

I paused. "I hope you don't feel like I dragged you here."

He shook his head. "No, no. I'm glad we're here now."

"Okay." Again I paused. "You're sure?"

"Not really, no."

I followed him into the adjacent room. Hien was also here. A rogues' gallery of My Lai perpetrators—huge blowups of badly Xeroxed photocopies, the pixels as big as dimes—stared back at us. Let their last names stand: Calley, Hodges, Reid, Widmer, Simpson, and Medina, at his court-martial in 1971, at which he was acquitted after fifty-seven minutes of deliberation. He soon resigned from duty and shortly thereafter admitted he had lied during his trial. Because he was no longer in uniform—the arm of military justice is particularly short—he was never tried for perjury, just as most of the murderers of Charlie Company, already having been discharged when the story broke, were never tried for their crimes.

There were also photos of Lawrence Colburn, Hugh Thompson, and Herbert Carter. Thompson, a helicopter pilot, was twenty-five years old at the time of the massacre, which he watched from his bubble-domed H-23 observation chopper. Lawrence Colburn was Thompson's eighteen-year-old door gunner. During the massacre Thompson marked with smoke a wounded villager writhing on the ground. As he was radioing for help for the woman, he watched Medina approach and execute her. An outraged Thompson then landed his chopper between a group of wounded villagers and Lieutenant Calley. Thompson had words with Calley, who, true to gutless form, stood down. As soon as Thompson lifted off, however, the villagers were murdered. Thompson found another batch of villagers and, once again, landed between them and their pursuers, Lieutenant Stephen Brooks of the 2nd Platoon among them. Before leaving the chopper to confront Brooks, Thompson told Colburn—in an order that went out over a frequency monitored by Thompson's superiors back at base—that if the Americans fired on the villagers, "Open up on 'em—blow 'em away." Once again Thompson confronted a monster, and, once again, the monster backed off. Another chopper was radioed, quickly landed, and ferried the ten imperiled Vietnamese, including six children, to safety.

Colburn flew back to the ditch where Calley had overseen one of the day's mass executions, landed, and with his crew chief, Glenn Andreotta (who would be killed three weeks later), waded into the bodies and rescued a miraculously unhurt eight-year-old boy. Thompson flew the boy to an ARVN hospital in Quang Ngai, weeping the entire way. Andreotta, Colburn, and Thompson would receive medals for their actions (Thompson would throw his away), which cited their bravery in risking "enemy fire" while rescuing the villagers. Herbert Carter was less heroic. Although he refused to take part in the massacre, he accidentally shot himself in the foot with his pistol moments after Fred Widmer had used it to shoot "fifteen or so" villagers. It was the operation's only casualty. Carter, greatly scarred by My Lai, would testify before the massacre's investigatory committee stoned out of his gourd on heroin. Nearby, in a building adjacent to the main museum, Colburn and Thompson's Soldier's Medals for Heroism, awarded decades after the real nature of their actions came to light, were on display, though not very conspicuously.

I saw my father ducking outside with Hien, both of them gray and punched-looking, and began to follow after them when behind me I heard a heavily accented German voice declaim, "I have been to Auschwitz, and it is moving, but this is so much *more* moving, *ja?*" I turned. The people this German woman was speaking to were Canadian, and visibly discomfited.

"Excuse me?" I less said than heard myself say.

She looked at me unapologetically. She was wearing a chunky jade necklace I had seen being sold on the streets. "More moving. Because of the life. The life around this place." She waved her hands, which were long, thin skeleton hands, while the Canadians stealthily took their leave.

"Are you," I asked her, "honestly comparing this place to Auschwitz?" My voice italicized each word differently. *Auschwitz? This* place? **You?**

With one step she halved the space between us. "No, it is just more *moving.*"

An ant farm spontaneously developed in my stomach. "Because of the life."

She jumped on this assumed bit of concord. "*Ja, ja.* The life."

Although I was fairly sure this constituted some form of "anti-attitude," I did not report her. I did not say anything and stalked off to an adjacent building. Some little goblin of anger jumped around inside me and then, unopposed, possessed me. I felt anger toward my country, those men. This anger had nowhere to go. It sat within me, stagnating. Anger toward the all-pervading taint of this place. Anger toward my anger. Anger toward the doorway, this floor, the Son My Memorial visitors' guest book. I flipped through its wide-ruled pages, muttering. Unsurprisingly, it had scarcely any American entries. It was, however, filled with German entries. My college German had left me with enough ability to translate one entry, headed "*Barbarei,*" as something along the lines of "this establishes for me my anti-American feeling for the politics of the USA." Someone from Holland had written, in English, "The madness of war. . . . Let's keep the words of the Vietnamese in mind. Do not forget the past but look to the future." From Australia: "I feel the pain." From Spain, something about "Vietnam" and "Irak." From Italy: "I have always thought that Americans are the biggest terrorist country in the world." From England: "It's so sad to see what human beings are capable of. Hope it never happens again!" And this: "War is terrible and cruel. I remember counting 57 pieces of what appeared to be meat hanging on a wire. As a ranger during the war in 1969 I saw <u>many</u> cruel things. About 25 miles from <u>this memorial</u> is the abandoned site where I counted what turned out to be <u>57 tongues</u> of children the <u>Viet Cong</u> cut out during a night raid. Their memorial is written only in my memory but will never fade with time." Signed: "An American." I scribbled my name in the book with full intention of writing something, but the pen grew heavy and my mind went weightless, emptied of the stern, pretty sentiment of which, only a few seconds before, I had felt capable. Soon the pen was quietly set down, the page empty but for my name.

Was this massacre, I wondered, so affecting—so terrible—merely because it was carried out by Americans? Was it so terrible because of how few Americans were willing to condemn those responsible? A poll taken shortly after the story broke revealed that 65 percent of Americans were "not upset" by My Lai. Why was it that those who maintained the fiercest faith in American greatness were the first to resort to nihilistic relativism when American ideals were sullied and spat upon? Was My Lai terrible because of how thoroughly it was covered up, which involved the machinations of at least fifty American officers? Or was it terrible because virtually every man guilty of taking part in it was never brought to justice? Was it really so surprising? As Jonathan Shay, in his fascinating book *Achilles in Vietnam* points out, the central poem of Western civilization, *The Iliad,* begins with the word "Rage." *The Iliad* is about a soldier going mad and desecrating the body of an honorable enemy. In this way it can be seen as a poem about the difference between war and atrocity. And there is a difference. Homer knew it. Somewhere within them, so did the men of Charlie Company.

The Battle of Pinkville's Combat Action Report, written by Colonel Frank Barker, read, "This operation was well planned, well executed and successful. Friendly casualties were light and the enemy suffered heavily. On this operation this civilian population supporting the VC in the area numbered approximately 200. This created a problem in population control and medical care of those civilians caught in fire of the opposing forces." The Army's press release was equally chipper: "For the third time in recent weeks, the American Division's 11th Brigade infantrymen from Task Force Barker raided a Viet Cong stronghold known as 'Pinkville' six miles northeast of Quang Ngai, killing 128 enemy in a running battle. . . . They recovered two M1 rifles, a carbine, a short-wave radio and enemy documents." The author of this dispatch was an Army journalist named Jay Roberts, who, like Ronald Haeberle, had witnessed everything. And although the helicopter pilot Hugh Thompson reported the massacre to three people (his chaplain, a captain, and the commander of the 11th Infantry Brigade), nothing was done and no investigation began, despite rampant assumptions that a massacre had taken place and widespread talk of Thompson's order to shoot his countrymen. Three weeks later, Task Force Barker was disbanded, perhaps to separate the men responsible for the slaughter and stifle further talk. Charlie Company staggered on, and soon many men beneath Medina began to fall apart emotionally while others continued to commit acts of atrocity. One newcomer to Charlie Company almost shot one rape-happy grunt, amazed that such lawlessness could exist among American servicemen.

Were it not for Ronald Ridenhour's chance beer while in Vietnam with a fellow veteran of the 11th Brigade, the story of the My Lai massacre would likely have never reached the public. Ridenhour, a highly trained quasi–Special Forces Army operative during the war, had been repeatedly dispatched on dangerous missions in Vietnam but always managed to maintain a moral understanding of the rules of engagement. (It probably helped that while in Vietnam he had read all of Bernard Fall's books and understood the war's complications.) Over the fateful beer, Ridenhour learned of a "village called 'Pinkville' " and of the horrible things that had happened there. After being discharged and while studying American literature at an Arizona university, he talked to more 11th Brigade veterans, pieced together the story, and finally decided to write about what he had heard to his Democratic congressman, which he copied to thirty others, including President Nixon and Senators Edward Kennedy, Barry Goldwater, and Eugene McCarthy. Ridenhour's extremely detailed letter described how one Lieutenant "Kally" (more like Kali) had been the prime mover of the unit's atrocities.

To William Westmoreland's immense credit, he ordered an investigation of the twenty-five men implicated in the massacre as soon as word of it reached him, but he was frustrated, as were many others, that "since they had already been discharged from the Army, they were beyond the Army's jurisdiction." Westmoreland was equally frustrated by the initially phlegmatic response from the Nixon administration: "When I learned that some members of President Nixon's administration wanted to white-wash any possible negligence within the chain of command, I threatened . . . to exercise my prerogative as a member of the Joint Chiefs of Staff to go personally to the President and object. That squelched any further pressure for whitewash." As Bilton and Sim write, White House transcripts reveal Nixon's belief that "dirty rotten Jews" were behind the massacre's exposure.

Defenders of William Calley—who quickly became the locus of the investigation, charged as he was with killing 109 "Oriental human beings"—were legion. He received so much fan mail he had to hire a secretary. *Esquire* serialized his memoirs ("And babies. On babies everybody's really hung up. 'But babies! The little innocent babies!' Of course, we've been in Vietnam for ten years now. If we're in Vietnam in another ten, if your son is killed by those babies you'll cry at me, 'Why didn't you kill those babies that day?' ") for $150,000. Lieutenant Shithead was also besieged by pretty young admirers who wanted a glimpse of the man who had murdered an entire village and called it his duty. The *National*

Review editorialized in a piece called "The Great Atrocity Hunt" that whether "atrocities were committed at Songmy [*sic*] we do not as yet know; but more than enough atrocities against human reason have been committed in response by the American media. . . . [T]here is something dark and sick about much of the reaction from the liberal Left." As Bilton and Sim note, a Georgia minister proclaimed during Calley's trial, "There was a crucifixion 2,000 years ago of a man named Jesus Christ. I don't think we need another crucifixion of a man named Rusty Calley."

After a closed military trial that left even Calley's defenders speechless, the calm young psychopath was sentenced to life in prison at hard labor. As Nixon tells it in his memoir, Calley's conviction triggered more than five thousand telegrams to the White House, which ran "100 to 1 in favor of clemency." Many prominent Republicans recommended that Nixon intervene in the Calley case. Although Nixon did order Calley removed from the stockade and put up in more accommodating confinement, executive intervention never went beyond that. Nor did it need to. The message had been sent: on appeal, Calley's sentence was reduced from life to ten years, with the chance for parole after one year. "Three months after I resigned," Nixon wrote, "the Secretary of the Army decided to parole Calley." The rest of the My Lai murderers tried for their crimes were acquitted, while those who covered up the massacre received nothing worse than censure.

I saw Hien and my father standing by the ditch from which Hugh Thompson pulled the unhurt, gore-slathered eight-year-old Vietnamese boy. Nearby was a long *Guernica*-style mural with death-spraying choppers and wicked-faced American soldiers looming over defenseless Vietnamese women and children. As I closed in, I saw that the American soldiers' helmets were fashioned in the steel glans style reminiscent of Nazi helmets. I walked toward the ditch, less sad than emotionally excavated. The ditch itself was not very deep, long, or wide, and was largely grown over with scrub. The little water in the ditch was filthy, though two short-legged jackal-like dogs were lapping it up between wary looks over at me.

"Why would one man," I arrived to find Hien saying, "like Calley, kill, while another man, like Colburn, try to prevent it? What is the difference?"

My father was staring into the ditch. "It's just . . . war," he told Hien. Hien nodded, but I knew he was not satisfied by this. I was not satisfied by this. Neither, it seemed, was my father. "I guess what it comes down to," he went on, searchingly, "is discipline." (Michael Bernhardt said something similar to the historian Christian G. Appy: "A lot of people think My Lai happened because there was too much military discipline, too much indoctrination. Not so. It was the exact opposite. There was way too little in that company.") After Hien left, my father rubbed his chest through his shirt and said, "My heart hurts."

I nodded. "Yeah."

"I've seen American Marines take revenge, but they just killed men, not women and children. It's horrible. When I came here we were . . . we were like crusaders! We were going to help people. We were going to make their lives better, give them democracy. And the way we did it was so morally . . ." He sighed, rubbed his mouth, shook his head, all the willful gestures of sense-making and significance assembly. But there were none. My Lai occurred two years after my father left Vietnam. The Vietnamese War of 1966 was not the Vietnamese War of 1968, which had by then scythed down whole fields of men and goodwill, including that of the war's own planners and originators. Kennedy, McNamara, Johnson: by 1968 all had fallen. I thought about the story my father had told me a day or two ago about how he been asked to transport an NLF prisoner by helicopter to the village of Tam Ky. He had described this prisoner as "a little guy who's terrified, frightened to death, tied up, but still bucking and heaving. And he fought and he fought and he fought for forty-five minutes. He knew he was going to be thrown out of the helicopter. He *knew* that. So we arrived in Tam Ky, and they asked me, 'What'd you learn?' I said, 'I learned that this little guy wants to kill me because he thought I was going to pitch him out of the helicopter!' And goddamnit, at one point I was about to." We had both laughed, grimly. War stories. My father would not have been capable of throwing a bound man from a helicopter, under any circumstances. But I imagined him—I imagined myself—here in Son My during those first moments that saw the day's terrible momentum gather, the evil freedom of the trigger availing itself upon the minds of friends and comrades, the various ecstasies of murder, and I did not like the range of possibilities that I saw.

"Do you feel sympathy for the Vietnamese who were killed here?" I asked my father.

He looked at me as though I had gone mad. "What's the matter with you? Of course I do."

"How about the soldiers who killed them?"

Now he realized why I had asked and what I was actually asking. He looked away. "Yeah, I do. And probably more than I should."

"I don't. I don't have any sympathy for them. I just realized that. I wish they'd all hanged. Medina especially."

"You weren't here. You'll never understand."

"I'm sick of that argument. Being present during a war doesn't automatically trump all other moralities. What war does is distort normal feelings, not validate abnormal ones. War may be a reason, but it's no excuse."

"You could be right."

"So what do we do?"

"You do what I've been trying to do for the past ten minutes, which is stand here and quietly pay my respects."

The heat seemed to gain a drowsy, atmospheric weight. As we stood there, the day went on obliviously, just as it had thirty-five years before. A dragonfly used my shoulder as a landing pad, then took off. The filthy water burped up a small black frog, which investigated the tip of my father's Hush Puppy and hopped away. The emboldened dogs had edged closer to us, and my father lowered for a moment to pet one of them. I wanted to tell him that what those who attempted to rationalize atrocities such as My Lai did not understand was that atrocities helped lose wars. As Michael Bernhardt put it during the investigation, "[My Lai] didn't have strategic value to it at all. . . . When you go out and do something like this, I believe what you are doing is breeding more Viet Cong." Bernhardt was right. Shortly after the massacre the Vietnamese countryside was papered in NLF propaganda publicizing the massacre:

"In the operation of 15 March [*sic*] 1968 in Son Tinh District the American enemies went crazy. They used machine guns and every other kind of weapon to kill 500 people who had empty hands." When the National Liberation Front Committee of Quang Ngai province wrote up its official denunciation of the massacre, the propaganda was far more overt: "This was by far the most barbaric killing in human history. . . . The Heavens will not tolerate this! The blue ocean waters will not wash away the hatred. These murders are even more savage than Hitler." The NLF of Quang Ngai put the number killed at 2,060, quadrupling the actual number killed. When the U.S. military claimed 128 "enemy" dead, it was of course guilty of the same fourfold distortion.

Before I could share any of this, my father looked up across this miserable ditch into a verdant neighboring pasture. "I wish Hien were here," he said. Did he have, finally, a better answer for him as to why some men only kill while others, amid the same killing, think to save? No, actually. He wanted to know if that was corn or wheat growing over there or what.

Query: *Could the United States have won the war in Vietnam?*

Because of the lack of agreement, both during the war and among historians and scholars today, about what "winning" the war would have entailed, or meant, or cost, this question is more problematic than any other that lingers around the Vietnamese War. Townsend Hoopes, for instance, the undersecretary of the Air Force, said in 1968 that "Anything resembling a clear-cut military victory in Vietnam appears possible only at the price of literally destroying [South Vietnam]."

The major problem confronting U.S. war planners was the hydralike nature of Vietnam's unrest. It was a political struggle, a proxy fight, a revolution, a civil war, a conflict thick with colonial residues, and the attempted hostile takeover of one nation by another all in one. This was difficult enough for the Vietnamese themselves to parse, much less a foreign force with a dewdrop of historical experience in the region. The only lasting solution to such a war would have been a careful alchemy of approach that attempted to address all of these issues, but North Vietnam's ceaseless destabilization disallowed any such potion from developing. Doing nothing would have led to South Vietnam's collapse. Doing too much, it was feared, might cause World War III—for which the Joint Chiefs of Staff had a winning strategy that envisioned killing 325 million Soviets and Chinese, absorbing tens of millions of U.S. casualties, and, with fallout factored in, causing the incidental deaths of 500 million to 600 million other people, many of them in allied European countries. (These were the Joint Chiefs' own estimates!)

Did winning mean an independent South Vietnam free of insurgents or a South Vietnam weighed down by a heavy U.S. troop presence for decades? Did it mean democracy or autocracy? Did it mean the downfall or eradication of Ho Chi Minh's government? What would "victory" in Vietnam have looked like, and would the common people of Vietnam have recognized their country afterward? There are no answers to these questions. What can be addressed is what the United States could have done differently in Vietnam, both diplomatically and militarily.

Many have argued that the war could have ended far earlier had negotiations with North Vietnam been conducted properly, yet Hanoi never wavered from its one most important position: the United States had absolutely no right to dictate its policy to either North or South Vietnam. Thus most of its attempts to negotiate with the United States were as rigged as a basket toss, including its "Four Points" peace proposal from 1965. The first three points—no foreign soldiers in either Vietnam, recognition of the Vietnamese people's basic rights, and that Vietnam's two "zones" refuse any foreign alignment and third-party military assistance until formal reunification—were acceptable to most in the U.S. government. The fourth—that South Vietnam's government, along with the NLF, work out its shared political future according to the NLF platform—was not, even though it was essentially the same deal Kissinger and Nixon would cut with North Vietnam in 1973. It is hard to argue, however, that the United States was any less intransigent during the war's numerous halfhearted negotiation attempts. In *The Pentagon Papers*, one finds the directive that the United States should define its negotiation position "in a way which makes Communist acceptance unlikely."

Rarely, then, did either North Vietnam *or* the United States negotiate in good faith. (Ho Chi Minh and Lyndon Johnson's scant epistolary exchanges suggest something of this: Johnson told Ho he would halt the U.S. bombing of North Vietnam if North Vietnam stopped sending its troops into the South. But Ho was seeking the bombing halt precisely because it would allow North Vietnam greater mobility in moving its troops south. Johnson could not stop the bombing, since one of its major purposes was to frustrate North Vietnam's incursions. Hanoi did, however, offer a reciprocal pledge not to invade or bomb the United States.) North Vietnam in particular was a talented violator of any number of accords, and one of its favorite tricks was to wage massive offensives after coming to a gentleman's agreement with the United States that both nations' forces would stand down during negotiation attempts. What this suggests, among other things, is a severe disparity of purpose. The fate of Vietnam was worth only a limited war to the United States, while the men of Hanoi were willing to fight until the end for their country—which, rightly or wrongly, for them included South Vietnam.

Many have pointed out that North Vietnam's leaders were less willing to fight until the end than to send millions of North Vietnamese to certain death, which is indisputably true. But every member of North Vietnam's Politburo knew Hanoi could have been wiped out in an afternoon if the United States chose to do so. For all the talk of the "limitations" placed on the U.S. military during the Vietnamese War, it is important to recognize that the North Vietnamese had little idea of these limitations and believed they were getting the worst the United States had to offer. ("Hanoi, Haiphong, and other cities may be destroyed," Ho Chi Minh warned his people in one postbombing address, "but the Vietnamese people will not be intimidated.") They prepared for the U.S. invasion of North Vietnam on at least two occasions and greatly worried about the possibility of an invasion throughout the war. Despite General Giap's reported postwar statement that the war "would not have evolved in our favor" had the United States invaded North Vietnam, most North Vietnamese were willing to die, if it came to that, in the "unlimited" war that many argue to this day should have been fought against a determined and xenophobic enemy in the enemy's own country. As Daniel

Ellsberg writes, "In South Vietnam we were not fighting all the population; even so, we were thoroughly stalemated with five hundred thousand U.S. troops. In North Vietnam we would have been fighting every man, woman, and child."

A former peace activist, long after the war, once asked Colonel Bui Tin, who accepted South Vietnam's surrender in 1975, if there was anything the United States could have done to win the war. The peace activist was clearly expecting Tin to say there was not. But Tin admitted that if the Ho Chi Minh Trail had been severed, Hanoi could not have forced South Vietnam's surrender. Later Tin would argue that if "the American forces had not begun to withdraw under Nixon in 1969, they could have punished us severely." Such comments have given ammunition to a group of largely American revisionist scholars and historians who might best be known as the We Almost Won School. By the time Tin offered these thoughts, he had already turned against Vietnam's Communist regime and been chased into exile in Paris. Tin believes that while the war was "unwinnable" in the sense that South Vietnam was unlikely to have ever become a viable nation without massive U.S. aid, he persuasively argues that a different military strategy could have resulted in "a seesaw situation, one in which there could be no (clear) winners or losers, and perhaps have forced a compromise resulting in a fairer settlement." The way to have done that, as he told the peace activist, was to strangle off the aid South Vietnam's insurgents received from the North.

In December 1963, North Vietnam's Politburo dispatched Bui Tin to South Vietnam to learn if the war could be won solely by the NLF. Tin returned to inform the Politburo that the only way to win was to send PAVN divisions south and "move from the guerrilla phase into conventional war." Shortly thereafter the Ho Chi Minh Trail (known to the Vietnamese as the Truong Son Strategic Supply Route) began to be developed. The decision to augment the trail, which had existed in aboriginal form and been used by insurgents since the late 1950s, was so secret that there are no records—at least, none that have been released—attesting to when it was first approved or, indeed, who approved it. The Ho Chi Minh Trail was not one trail but a network of paths and switchbacks and roads and highways that began in North Vietnam, wended through Laos and Cambodia, and emptied into South Vietnam. Ultimately the trail covered 10,000 miles, and many important storage and destination sites had more than ten separate feeder roads. By 1968, the trail was blessed with "bungalows" for visitors, rest stops, a fuel pipeline, telecommunications, garages, bunkers, mechanics' shops, and truck parts facilities. Between 1959 and 1975, millions braved the trail, upon which, in one Vietnamese's estimation, there were twenty-four different ways you could die. Causes of death ranged from tiger attack to snakebite to bombs to road accidents to tumbling off cliffs to an arrow in the back courtesy of the local indigenous peoples to the trail's primary cause of death, which was plain old febrile sickness.

One revisionist historian argues that cutting the Ho Chi Minh Trail should have been "the primary combat mission of US ground forces in Indochina," a position with which it is difficult to take issue. The trail was the very doom of Westmoreland's war of attrition, as it allowed the North Vietnamese and South Vietnam's insurgents to endlessly replace lost weapons and personnel. Yet decisively "cutting" the trail—a possibility that terrified North Vietnam—meant to many U.S. strategists invading the notionally neutral nations of Laos and Cambodia. Laos was not aligned with North Vietnam but was too weak to do much of anything about its neighbor's illegal appropriation of Lao territory. Cambodia's Prince Sihanouk had a secret 1964 agreement with the North Vietnamese that allowed troops to operate in his nation "so long as they respected its inhabitants," according to the historian David P. Chandler.

The first U.S. bombs landed on Cambodia's Communist sanctuaries, of which there numbered at least fourteen, in 1969. This was called Operation Menu and kept hidden from the American people. Prince Sihanouk, wary of the Vietnamese Communists, allowed the bombing as long as Cambodian civilians were not affected. When news of the illegal bombing got out, President Nixon defended his decision by using, of all things, the Hague Convention of 1907: "A neutral country has the obligation not to allow its territory to be used by a belligerent. If the neutral country is unwilling or unable to prevent this, the other belligerent has the right to take appropriate counteraction." As one historian writes, "The whole matter had a surrealistic cast to it. The Cambodians pretended that the North Vietnamese had not taken over the border areas of their country, the Americans pretended that they were not bombing those enemy sanctuaries, the Cambodians pretended not to notice the bombing, and the North Vietnamese pretended they weren't there in the first place."

When it became clear that the bombing was not fatally effective, 80,000 U.S. and South Vietnamese troops invaded Cambodia in 1970. This short-lived and limited "incursion," as Nixon pointedly called it, saw the NLF and PAVN abandon their Cambodian sanctuaries and draw deeper into the jungle, just beyond the approved reach (thirty kilometers) of the U.S. invasion. The raid netted six months' worth of NLF supplies and ammunition. As one lieutenant general said at the time, "Why didn't we do this years ago? Why don't the American people understand why we're doing this?" While these sanctuaries were attacked by ground troops in force, the trails they fed were not. Bui Tin writes, "It defies imagination to think that the American side was willing to send U.S. troops into Cambodia in May 1970 yet never dared to touch this strategic link [the Ho Chi Minh Trail] to the southern theater." As Tin notes, such a move would not have generated anywhere near the moral outrage as did the Cambodian invasion. While the occupation of important trail exit points (which, as Tin notes, could have been "carried out by as few as three thousand GIs") does seem a ruinously lost opportunity, to have delved deeper into Cambodia does not. It was known that Vietnamese and Cambodian Communists in Cambodia were engaging in much of the same agitation they employed in South Vietnam: establishing cadres, forming political structures, luring villagers into their web, and working to subvert all government institutions. If the United States had chased the Communists deeper into Cambodia or been allowed to operate there on a long-term basis, many of the problems the U.S. military faced in South Vietnam would have been replicated.

The invasion of Laos came in 1971 (though the country had been secretly and devastatingly bombed by the United States since 1964), shortly after the passage of the Cooper-Church Amendment to the defense appropriations bill that forbade the United States to finance any ground war in Laos or Cambodia. The United States could only accompany ARVN forces to the borders of those countries and support them by air. By the time Laos was finally invaded, North Vietnamese soldiers had been operating there for more than a decade, as had an indigenous army of Lao tribesmen funded and controlled by the Central Intelligence Agency. (A 1962 diplomatic agreement among the United States, the USSR, North Vietnam, and Laos forbade the military use of Lao territory by third-party nations. Every party mostly obeyed this agreement, with the exception of North Vietnam, which did not obey it at all.) According to the North Vietnamese, a permanent PAVN deployment numbering 7,000 soldiers was kept in Laos at all times, though few were battle-hardened. The ARVN incursion into Laos to destroy these illegal stay-behinds resulted in a 1971 battle known as Lam Son 719. Lam Son, named for the birthplace of the fifteenth-century Vietnamese patriot Le Loi, was a disaster for several reasons, some (inclement weather) beyond U.S. and ARVN control, others (ARVN's military ineptitude) less so. After a promising start, 150 ARVN tanks were abandoned—many of them still running—by retreating and terrified South Vietnamese soldiers. During the operation the ARVN took more than 8,000 casualties, thereby wiping out some of its most elite units, and the final outcome was "successful" only because of U.S. air support. These bombings punished the massed North Vietnamese forces greatly, resulting in around 17,000 dead. Despite Nixon's claim that Lam Son 719 was a great victory for the ARVN, the battle suggested how difficult eliminating North Vietnam's sanctuaries in Laos would be.

What could and could not get down the Ho Chi Minh Trail is still fiercely debated. Lewis Sorley, one of the war's most thoughtful revisionist historians, writes that after the Tet Offensive, "in order to get one ton of material down the Ho Chi Minh Trail, the enemy had to put approximately ten tons into the pipeline, since interdiction would destroy or block 90 percent of what he tried to move." By July 1968, "the enemy had been moving more than 1,100 trucks a day, the most traffic ever observed on the trail. One week into the new interdiction campaign, that had been cut in half, and less than a week later by half again." But the North Vietnamese had shifted tactics. As the former CIA analyst Frank Snepp writes, in 1970 the U.S. Embassy in Saigon learned that "nearly eighty percent" of the weapons recently injected into South Vietnam had been "shipped in by boat from North Vietnam and unloaded at the Cambodian port of Sihanoukville," a revelation Snepp calls "a shock to everyone." Although use of the trail was hindered, thousands of tons of arms were still reaching South Vietnam from Cambodian sanctuaries—this at the point when the United States and ARVN believed they were intercepting and destroying more incoming matériel than ever before. The North Vietnamese were going to keep figuring out how to evade aerial countermeasures. The more the trail was bombed, the more its "carrying capacity" was enhanced by desperately inventive engineers.

The trail was born of necessity, developed out of necessity, and partially abandoned by necessity. Its occupation was certainly possible and probably advisable, but the trail itself is one of the most profound arguments against the long-term success of "cutting" it. Apart from thousands of U.S. and ARVN soldiers along the South Vietnamese side of the Lao and Cambodian borders, flotillas of ceaselessly patrolling swift boats along every adjoining river, Marines in the mountains, and flocks of surveillance planes, the North Vietnamese were always going to be able to send arms and soldiers south. What they sent might not have been able to win the war, but they did not need to win the war, only lengthen it.

Kennedy, Johnson, and Nixon all forbade the use of nuclear weapons in Vietnam, though with Kissinger Nixon occasionally toyed with the idea: "The nuclear bomb, does that bother you? . . . I just want you to think big, Henry, for Christsakes." Johnson and Nixon also rejected the slightly less monstrous Joint Chiefs' idée fixe of bombing North Vietnam's irrigation dikes on the Red River, which would have inflicted hundreds of thousands of incidental starvation and flood casualties on North Vietnamese noncombatants. Nixon toyed with that idea, too, though: "I still think we ought to take out the dikes now." In lieu of the imposition of an apocalypse in miniature, it was decided that North Vietnam had to be conventionally bombed until its leaders saw the error of their ways.

The received wisdom about the U.S. bombing of North Vietnam holds that it was as brutal as the campaigns that had annihilated Germany and Japan during World War II, but in fact only 7 percent of the total bombing conducted during the war was against North Vietnam. The truth is that, despite the unprecedented number of bombs dropped upon North and South Vietnam during the war (16 million tons of explosives—the equivalent of seven hundred Hiroshimas—not to mention 19 million gallons of herbicide), Lyndon Johnson, in deference to the accepted logic of graduated pressure, mainly stayed his hand when it came to bombing civilian areas in North Vietnam. The bombing of South Vietnam, which with Laos received the dreadful brunt of the U.S. air war, caused far more civilian casualties. It was also self-defeating in a conflict in which broad success was dependent upon knowing exactly whom one was killing. ("Hearts and minds, after all," the American war correspondent Martha Gellhorn wrote, "live in bodies.") As Daniel Ellsberg notes, the language the U.S. government used in describing the bombings ("one more turn of the screw," "pain in the North," "would be even more painful to the population of the North," "It is important not to 'kill the hostage' ") is, in fact, the language of torturers.

Although Richard Nixon once claimed in a televised address that the bombing of Vietnam had been conducted with a "degree of restraint unprecedented in the annals of war," he was less concerned with civilian casualties than Johnson had been. As Nixon said to Henry Kissinger, "You're so goddamned concerned about the civilians and I don't give a damn. I don't care." The two major air operations ordered by Nixon were known as Linebacker I and Linebacker II. The first Linebacker operation was a response to North Vietnam's treacherous Easter Offensive of 1972. Forty-one thousand sorties were unleashed upon North Vietnam over an eight-month period, during which six of its power plants were blown up, every one of its oil storage facilities was annihilated, and tens of thousands of PAVN soldiers were killed. Said one U.S. lieutenant general, "Linebacker was not [Lyndon Johnson's campaign of] Rolling Thunder—it was war." After Linebacker I, North Vietnam was crippled for more than two years.

Many revisionists have cited the effectiveness of the devastation to argue that similar butchery should have been the order of the day far earlier in the war. But the growing U.S. withdrawal from South Vietnam had been one of the Easter Offensive's triggers, and Linebacker I was a response to unambiguous and in many ways unprecedented enemy aggression. A Linebacker I–style bombing earlier in the war, in response to less definitive belligerence, might well have been too much for most Americans to stomach. Even the gentle caress of President Johnson's Rolling Thunder, during which all but 5.8 percent of the Joint Chiefs' requested targets were allowed to be bombed, gave many Americans pause. Preserving the freedom of the imperiled people of South Vietnam was not the same thing as annihilating the people of North Vietnam, although many were prepared to make such an argument.

More complicated is Linebacker II, an eleven-day bombing campaign said to have been ordered in December 1972 to compel the North Vietnamese leadership back to the peace table in Paris, though the North Vietnamese themselves claimed only to have asked for a suspension of the talks while the Politburo consulted. Popularly vilified as the Christmas Bombing, Linebacker II had a much-debated effect upon the North Vietnamese. In the analyst Douglas Pike's words, during Linebacker II "Hanoi officials experienced true, all-out strategic air war for the first time. It had a profound effect, causing them to reverse virtually overnight their bargaining position at the Paris talks." Henry Kissinger called Linebacker II "jugular diplomacy" but was later cowed and humiliated by Le Duc Tho when the Paris talks resumed for "bombing North Vietnam, just at the moment I reached home." The North Vietnamese have thus always denied the neatly beribboned explanation that the bombing forced them to reevaluate their willingness to settle matters with the United States in Paris. Given the ghastly results of Linebacker II's "all-out" war, this is hard to believe, even if one grants that the North Vietnamese were bombed unfairly.

Twenty thousand tons of bombs were dropped on North Vietnam during Linebacker II. Anything even remotely industrial (rail yards, oil facilities, warehouses, missile storage areas) was destroyed. Linebacker II also wiped out a poor Hanoi neighborhood, Hanoi's Bach Mai Hospital, the Indian Embassy, the French Consulate, a water filtration plant, a noodle factory, and a hundred schools. Although the mayor of Hanoi claimed 10,000 civilian victims of U.S. "carpet bombing," news of which was quickly seized upon by antiwar activists, the actual civilian deaths were (a not inconsiderable) 2,000, with thousands more injured. These numbers would have been far more severe had not Hanoi and Haiphong been largely evacuated earlier in the war. Yet it is important to note that North Vietnam was not helpless during the bombings and in many cases welcomed civilian deaths by placing its antiaircraft guns in the middle of populated areas. (Though, from the North Vietnamese perspective, what was the alternative? Putting their guns in places where they could be easily bombed?) During the operation, the North's extremely sophisticated batteries of Soviet-installed surface-to-air missile launchers knocked from the sky more than two dozen U.S. aircraft, leading to the death or capture of nearly a hundred American pilots. The only reason the North Vietnamese stopped firing on the planes was that they ran out of missiles. But Hanoi was not leveled, as can be attested to today by a nighttime stroll through its surviving old quarters. Other parts of North Vietnam, particularly the cities of Nam Dinh and Vinh, the latter an entrance point to the Ho Chi Minh Trail, were not so fortunate. Sixty percent of Nam Dinh was flattened, and the Vinh that exists today is an entirely new (and famously unlovely) city built from the ground up by Soviet and Vietnamese architects after the war.

Did winning the war really require, as some revisionists today claim, that Hanoi share Vinh's fate? In 1967, Robert McNamara told a closed-door session of the Senate Armed Services Committee that bombing could not win the war—"short, that is, of the virtual annihilation of North Vietnam and its people." Senator Strom Thurmond said he was "terribly disappointed" by McNamara's reluctance to wipe North Vietnam from the face of the earth, as this was clearly a strategy of "appeasing the Communists." Perhaps the revisionists are right, then, as this surely would have been the most straightforward way to measure the cost of the war. By destroying the place entirely, we finally would have known if Vietnam was worth Vietnam.

Here is Lewis Sorley: "There came a time when the war was won. The fighting wasn't over, but the war was won. This achievement can probably best be dated in late 1970. . . . By then the South Vietnamese coun-tryside had been widely pacified, so much so that the term 'pacification' was no longer even used." (Sorley does not note that the process by which parcels of countryside were upgraded to "pacified" was often wishfully subjective.) The war would have kept being won, Sorley writes, if the United States had maintained its support for the South and con-tinued to provide the sort of air strikes it would later unleash during the Easter Offensive. It did not, and so, "unsurprisingly, the war was no longer won." It does not take a logician to see the problem with this summation. Sorley is on firmer ground when he argues for the improved tactical situation after the Tet Offensive in 1968, when, it is largely agreed, the war in Vietnam went from an insurgency with conventional components to a conventional war with insurgency components. (At least 80 percent of the fighting after 1970 involved PAVN regular forces rather than NLF guerrillas.) The war's new vectors did not always favor the North Vietnamese or the NLF. In the early 1980s, one former NLF guerrilla said of those days that there "was nothing to eat. We were dis-couraged, very discouraged. We seriously considered surrender. But each time we were tempted we talked about our traditions, about our country, and we kept on fighting." Does a starved and desperate enemy truly mean the United States was on the verge of winning the war, even though by 1970 "winning" only meant ensuring that the South Viet-namese could defend themselves? As Ambassador Ellsworth Bunker put it at the time, "[W]hen we talk of winning the war, we mean it in the sense of an acceptable political settlement which gives the Vietnamese people the opportunity to choose freely their own government." Even Henry Kissinger admitted that much of the post-Tet fighting was "for negotiating objectives," not victory, and Nixon recognized that "total military victory was no longer possible."

The limited success of the post-Tet years was largely to the credit of Westmoreland's replacement, General Creighton Abrams, a short and pugnacious World War II tank commander. The signature feature of Abrams's tenure was his "one-war strategy," which integrated pacifica-tion, combat operations, and advising the South Vietnamese into a cohesive battle plan. Abrams also provided badly needed moral leadership when he maintained that the most hitherto neglected area of the war was "human relations . . . a respect for the Vietnamese. It's sensitivity, a sensitivity to humans." Things did improve. The arming of and reliance upon South Vietnam's Regional and Popular Forces (essentially, village militias) increased under Abrams—there were 1.3 million armed Vietnamese fighting for the South by 1971—and these soldiers proved ferocious enemies of the NLF and PAVN, as the South Vietnamese could always be relied upon to fight well when their own families were in danger. In addition, the ranks of the NLF, which were routed after Tet, were increasingly filled by North Vietnamese who did not hesitate to use terrorism against South Vietnam's people. The percentage of South Vietnamese living in what the U.S. military charitably described as "relatively secure" areas increased to 90 percent immediately after Tet, and at one point (in November 1969) U.S. public support for the war reached 77 percent, which somewhat belies the common revisionist supposition that dour media reporting poisoned Americans on the war. Everyone from Daniel Ellsberg to *The New Yorker*'s Robert Shaplen (who famously said that Abrams was so good, it was a shame he did not have a better war to fight in) to Vo Nguyen Giap noticed these improvements.

Unfortunately, they were most keenly felt and most often highlighted by men near the top of the U.S. and ARVN commands. Many American and South Vietnamese infantrymen felt numb and defeatist, which is to say, realistic. To this state of affairs there were many contributors, such as General Westmoreland's outgoing order as the U.S. drawdown gathered momentum to rotate stateside the most experienced American soldiers. Westmoreland's rotation decision was, in the words of one general, "a disaster." Incoming units brought with them everything (racism, drug abuse, disillusionment) that was plaguing the United States from Portland to Portland. American soldiers' deaths creditable to drug overdose went from 16 in 1969 to 700 in 1970. A later study indicated that by the early 1970s at least 34 percent of U.S. troops in Vietnam regularly used heroin. Worldwide desertions from the U.S. military increased sharply from 1968 to 1970, while instances of "fragging" (men killing their commanding officers) more than doubled during the same period.

Many U.S. veterans who served in the early 1970s have described going on "search-and-avoid" patrols rather than search-and-destroy patrols, or "sandbagging" their missions and calling in fictitious reports. In 1970, one U.S. Army division had thirty-five cases of "combat refusal." ("Is this a goddamned army or a mental hospital?" General Abrams complained. "Officers are afraid to lead their men into battle, and the men won't follow. Jesus Christ!") None of this suggests a U.S. force confident of its post-Tet mission.

The common American grunt had some reason to withdraw into an individual nepenthe. An enemy document known as Resolution 9, written in response to the failed second Tet Offensive of 1969, was captured by the South Vietnamese three months after its issue. Resolution 9 did not admit that the war had been won by the South Vietnamese and the United States. What it did was admit that current tactics were not working, urge an increase in terrorism and other counterpacification efforts, and finally suggest outlasting the United States as a winning strategy, which, in fact, it was. Contra Sorley, the Vietnamese War being fought in the early 1970s was at best a stalemate, and around the following facts there is no easy way: The Soviets were not bombing South Vietnam as the United States was bombing North Vietnam. No Soviet soldiers were fighting for North Vietnam. Nor were any Chinese. North Vietnam had access to a far smaller war chest than did South Vietnam, yet South Vietnam, even with American help, could not decisively end the war or, for that matter, protect itself. Had the offensive of 1975 failed, as the offensive of 1972 failed, as the offensive of 1969 failed, as the offensive of 1968 failed, there would have been an offensive of 1977, and 1979, and 1981. As Pham Van Dong once said to an American reporter, "How long do you Americans want to fight? One year? Five years? Twenty years? We will accommodate you."

This brings us to the scholar C. Dale Walton's *The Myth of Inevitable U.S. Defeat in Vietnam*. Called by no less than Walt Rostow "a breath of fresh air" in the literature of the Vietnamese War, Walton's is among the more interesting and well-argued revisionist takes on the war. It is also hopping mad. Walton: "[T]he United States was an immensely wealthy superpower, while its major opponent was a small, impoverished country with little industry and less-than-reliable great power allies. There was no fundamental reason why—compared to most weighty military-political tasks undertaken by great powers throughout history—the odds for US success in Vietnam should not have been very high." The "fatal error," according to Walton, was that "the United States enjoyed a robust military advantage in Vietnam, but the American home front was vulnerable. The strategic military efforts of the United States were not, as themselves, fatal for the war effort, but, in misjudging the patience of the American people and the tenacity of the enemy, US leaders provided a key strategic opportunity to Hanoi."

But—and this is essential—it was not that the American people considered the war unwinnable after 1968. It was that it was clear that winning the war was going to require more time and lives than seemed appropriate or reasonable. For this Walton has some potential solutions: "At no point did the US government pledge to take specific actions that would grievously damage North Vietnam, topple its government, or even prevent it from conducting an expeditionary war by, for example, striving to curtail imports to and disrupt road traffic within that country. This vague and irresolute position put steel in the negotiating posture of the North Vietnamese, and confused the American public about the nature of the war."

Undeniably, there were peculiarities of decision that hampered the U.S. war effort in numerous ways. For instance, the command structure of the U.S. effort in Vietnam was formidably bizarre. Generals Westmoreland and Abrams were in charge of ground forces in Vietnam but not of the air war against the North. Air-attack targets in North Vietnam were scrupulously reviewed and approved by civilian policy makers and even by the president himself. The reason for this, as noted, was because the civilian war planners had no faith that the U.S. military would not drag China into the war. And here Walton's book enters the seventh dimension.

Of the possibility of war with China, Walton notes that Mao Zedong "was apparently inclined to avoid unnecessary confrontation with the United States." That is a big "unnecessary" and a gargantuan "apparently." The degree to which China was willing to enter the war will remain, at least until Chinese archives are completely opened, controversial. For what it is worth, former South Vietnamese Vice President Nguyen Cao Ky told me in Saigon in 2005 that, in his opinion, the North Vietnamese would have "never asked the Chinese" to help defend them from a U.S. invasion. Complicating matters is Bui Tin's assertion that the North Vietnamese had dolefully accepted by the mid-1960s the reality that China would not come to their aid. Yet many scholars maintain that China would have intervened the moment U.S. forces crossed the Seventeenth Parallel trip wire and moved into North Vietnam. Walton admits that throughout the 1960s, "the Chinese government hinted that it would intervene militarily in Vietnam if the United States invaded [North Vietnam]. After US air attacks on [North Vietnam], Premier Zhou Enlai warned the United States that the PRC [People's Republic of China] might not idly stand by while the United States committed 'aggression.' " Other Chinese leaders claimed that "the Vietnamese people are intimate brothers of the Chinese people" and that China "will absolutely not stand idly by without lending a helping hand. The debt of blood incurred by the United States to the Vietnamese people must be repaid." Walton claims that China "tended to qualify" its more combative rhetoric. China also tended to complicate its rhetoric: in 1965, Mao told the Soviets that "as long as China itself was not attacked" he would not intervene in Vietnam, but months later he told Ho that he would intervene if North Vietnam was invaded.

Arguing that the caution with which U.S. policy makers regarded China's possible entry into the war was "self-defeating," Walton writes that "[e]ven very energetic action against North Vietnam might not have brought China into the war, although there certainly would have been a substantial possibility of this outcome." But that does not matter, Walton claims, because we could have whipped 'em: "Chinese intervention most likely would not have prevented a positive outcome of the Vietnam situation for the United States. . . . When Chinese capabilities and disadvantages are weighed dispassionately, it is even imaginable that, if the United States had invaded North Vietnam and been met with PLA [China's People's Liberation Army] resistance, the resulting US casualties would have been fewer than occurred in the drawn-out war that actually did take place in Vietnam." That this is precisely the type of thinking the United States had going into its struggle against Vietnam's Communists and insurgents is utterly lost on Walton, who is not stupid—though he can be astonishingly obtuse: "In American war reporting and anti-Saigon propaganda there was considerable comment about the allegedly disastrous effects of the US presence on traditional Vietnamese culture and morality." His parenthetical admission that foreign troops "inevitably disrupt a small society" is akin to kicking down someone's door, blasting his living room with a flamethrower, and then lamenting the inevitability of fire burning things.

However, it is true that China was not in its best shape during the Vietnamese War. Mao's Great Leap Forward of the 1950s devastated Chinese society for a generation (anywhere between 30 to 60 million Chinese starved to death), and the more directly murderous Cultural Revolution of the mid-1960s, with its "cudgels roaming the land," ushered in a largely hermetic phase in Chinese international relations. The Chinese military had its own problems, with anti-Maoist "professional" soldiers greatly resenting the ideological, and illogical, war strategies insisted upon by the military's growingly consolidated Maoists. It does not take much to imagine what might have united China and temporarily stanched many of its internal wounds: war with a foreign power every Chinese citizen had been indoctrinated to believe wanted to overtake and destroy it. Only when the final links in the Sino-Vietnamese relationship were broken in 1972 with Richard Nixon's cunning visit to the People's Republic did China finally trust that the United States had no wish to attack it. But this trust was possible only because China, and the United States, knew the war in Vietnam had effectively been lost.

Walton's major argument is that "conducting the war with a less constrained approach would have had a salutary effect on public opinion." The United States did fight a constrained war—that is clear and inarguable. Here are some of the realities of this constrained war: 14,592 American soldiers dead in one year (1968) alone. Mental breakdowns accounting for 50 percent of all U.S. medical evacuations from Vietnam in 1971. Massively criminal operations such as Cedar Falls, in which sixty square miles of South Vietnamese territory saw their inhabitants forcibly removed, their homes bulldozed (the U.S. military boasted of having created "a military desert"), and the entire area pounded by air strikes while the majority of the NLF guerrillas operating there, tipped off to the operation, went underground or simply moved on to another quadrant. The growing use of "free-fire zones" (known officially as Specified Strike Zones), which allowed the military to fire on anyone or anything it desired in a given area, despite the fact that the general who had come up with the original and far more limited idea behind the free-fire zone said, as more and more of South Vietnam was designated a slaughterhouse, "If we wish to serve the interests of the Communists, this is the step to take." The fact that one in every twenty adult males in South Vietnam had been killed or wounded by 1970. That more than 25 percent of South Vietnam's people had to leave their homes, at some point during the war, to avoid being killed. The journalist Jonathan Schell, who rode on many U.S. helicopters during the war, told the historian Christian G. Appy: "The idea that the U.S. military was operating under constraints in South Vietnam is ridiculous. We pulverized villages from the air if we merely imagined that we received hostile fire. I witnessed it with my own eyes.... U.S. planes were actually bombing churches. They would see the church, target it, and blow it up. I saw that happen."

"If," C. Dale Walton writes, "there had been no Watergate scandal ... the Republic of Vietnam would today be a functioning state." Nonetheless, one must wonder whether functioning, unnaturally divided states were truly the most preferable outcome of the Vietnamese War. South Korea today is independent, after all—home of the world's largest Starbucks, its twelfth largest economy, and the popular song "Fucking USA." North Korea, on the other hand, is currently the single largest source of potential global destabilization. That is the war America "won." Vietnam, home to the war America "lost," is today independent, unified, a member of the global community, and a threat to no one. All available evidence indicates that the Vietnam that will exist even a decade from now will be a better and, most likely, freer Vietnam than the one that exists today. Vietnamese people will be the reason for this. That is why young South Koreans sing "Fucking USA" in the cafés of Seoul while in the cafés of Hanoi any attempt to plumb the depths of anti-Americanism among young Vietnamese is met with quizzical stares. This is not good enough for Walton, who still wonders why the United States did not win without ever asking himself if the United States *should* have won. After all, he writes, "the expansion of Mongol power under Genghis Khan and his successors presented far more difficult challenges than the ones the United States faced in Vietnam."

Walton fails to note one of the world's few nations that managed to resist and then defeat all three of its Mongol invasions: Vietnam.

V

By the time we reached the edge of Qui Nhon, the capital of Binh Dinh province and home to some beautiful beaches (and a leper colony), the taller trees and two-story buildings stood in etched black silhouette against an orange, dusk-streaked sky. The steeple of a ramshackle Catholic church thrust up from the foliage on a forested sunlit slope outside the city proper. The steeple's moss-fuzzy cross appeared majestically misplaced among the surrounding palm leaves and coconut bundles: Jungle Christ.

In provincial Vietnam one saw little of the frantic pace common to Saigon, Danang, and Hue, and as we came into town I noted the easy manner with which Qui Nhonese bicycled. Every rider looked to be a mirror of every other rider. They sat weightlessly, straight-backed, their heads held as high as their ratcheted-up seats, their legs working as steadily and gently as clock gears. Our car coasted along an oceanside road while on our right city structures flowed by: a government building, a park, a café selling dog meat. While we were stopped at a red light, I looked over to see a little coffin shop. Outside, the caskets were piled like cordwood. Some were plain and unvarnished, others stained a rich gold; some were stamped with a lotus, others with Buddhist swastikas, others yet with crosses. The shop's proprietor, an old man with a Ho Chi

Minh beard, sat outside beside the caskets, as peaceful as death, smoking a long curved wooden pipe.

By the time we got to the hotel, the lowering darkness was colored with sudden scribbles of nighttime neon, though the ocean beyond our hotel's rear veranda was nebular. We asked Hien if, tonight, we could bypass the tourist traps and have dinner someplace that catered to a more exclusively Vietnamese clientele. We also insisted that he and Truong join us. Hien shortly squired us to a seafood restaurant packed with more Germans than the Reichstag. We sat down at a table that appeared hewn from tin. Almost immediately a squirrel-sized rat ran between my legs, then somehow reduced its body mass by 70 percent and squeezed into a wall nook at the dining room's opposite end, just below a Buddhist shrine. A strike force of pretty twenty-year-old Vietnamese women abruptly surrounded our table. All were employed by Vietnamese beer distribution companies and wore T-shirts indicating the beer of their particular allegiance: Tiger, Saigon, Heineken, Carlsberg. The more orders each woman racked up (measured by the number of empty bottles beneath one's chair at night's end), the more money she took home. I chose Carlsberg, whose T-shirt the least attractive of these young women was wearing. My father ordered a Tiger, as did Hien and Truong. I could see why: the Tiger woman was stunning, and, most fetchingly, wore camouflage pants. As our beers were poured, an older woman came along and with plastic tongs dropped small icebergs into our glasses.

My father asked Hien to order for us "a real Vietnamese meal," and Hien quickly devolved into a rice-paddy dictator, ordering around everyone within sight. A couple of the young women, including the Tiger girl, still hovered around the table, sometimes speaking to Hien and Truong and sometimes marshaling their bravery to chat a little with us: Why were we in Vietnam? How long were we staying? Was it our first time here? Their dégagé reaction to the news that my father was a veteran of the war was no longer surprising. He might as well have told them he had been Colonel George Washington's boot polisher during the Indian Wars.

A few tables away, some young, doughy-faced German men in soccer jerseys scowled. We had stolen their beer girls. There was some barbed thrill to this, and I could not deny that being peppered with questions by a trio of lovely young women filled the air with voltage. The lightning of attraction struck one all over Vietnam, all the time, every day. But this was not wartime, they were not prostitutes, I had already learned that the Tiger girl was married, my father was absolutely not interested, and neither, really, was I. But even among all these contingencies of forbid-dance the charge remained.

The charge was not merely a by-product of travel, which has the ten-dency to eroticize even the boldly unerotic: body odor, bus travel, rats. It was, rather, my first fully felt sense of the mutual fascination that often existed between Vietnamese women and American men. One side of this fascination was relatively straightforward. Vietnamese women, with their sylphlike bodies and apparent invulnerability to dumpiness, were, quite simply, heartslayers. A goatish observation, yes, but when thinking or writing about Vietnam the question of Vietnamese women always managed to rear its head. On my first reading of Graham Greene's *The Quiet American*, I flinched when Fowler describes Vietnamese women to Pyle (this is around the time when Pyle admits that his most pro-found sexual experience had been having a "chink and a negress" in bed together). "It's a cliché," Fowler admits, "to call them children— but there's one thing which is childish. They love you in return for kindness, security, the presents you give them." Of course, Fowler and his Vietnamese lover Phuong's relationship is basically founded upon her feeding him opium nightly. I had snorted at these Greenelandian mores—until I found myself involved in something that instanta-neously escalated into a relationship with a Vietnamese woman, for whom I bought a present, after which she told me she loved me.

During the war, the first lecture many U.S. soldiers were given con-cerned the hazards of sex with Vietnamese women. Prostitution in Viet-nam was such an overriding fact of life that the military actually monitored whores to make sure they were not overcharging GIs. U.S. Ambassador Ellsworth Bunker once said, "There's a lot of plain and fancy screwing going on around here, but I suppose it's all in the interest of the war effort." Needless to say, Vietnamese women's sleeping with

Americans (to say nothing of the French) has always been a sensitive matter to Vietnamese men. For the Communists and insurgents it had been a thrown gauntlet. One piece of NLF propaganda read, "In Saigon there are some Americans that put their penis outside of their pants and put a dollar on it to pay the girls who sell themselves. The Americans get laid in every public place. This beast in the street is not afraid of the presence of the people." It also had its comical aspects: one historian writes of an establishment known as the Million Fingers Massage Parlor, Laundry and Tank Wash, which sprang up in the Central Highlands near a U.S. Army base. When a number of his soldiers had been venereally struck down, the U.S. division commander demanded that the place be closed. The establishment's owner changed tack and put up this sign: "No More Whorehouse, Only Laundry." For years after the war, there were numerous sightings of unimprisoned white men lingering around Vietnam's villages—even a few in Hanoi. There was only one plausible explanation for these haunted laggards: Vietnamese women.

The attraction between American men and Vietnamese women had many headwaters, not all of them ignoble. Many times the American man and Vietnamese woman become partners in a secret exchange that could offend and enrage not a few around them. No doubt a large part of the desire drew its energy from this disapproval, and sometimes even from mutual suspicion. Was the Vietnamese woman simply fixating upon escape? Was the American man merely anticipating the docile, uncomplaining nature of his partner? But once one comes to know them, most Vietnamese women are not very docile at all, and many American men had no intention of marrying their Vietnamese lovers, as these women well knew. The crude and commonly accepted causes of the attraction were, then, something of an evasion.

So was it some misguided attempt to make amends? Some baser form of apology? These women! They giggled, they teased, they left, they came back, they pulled you down a path the end of which they had no intention of letting you reach without a proper courtship—and you were dazed, dazed by all this broken-English coquetry and decorousness. It was what courting must have felt like for a nineteenth-century English country gentleman. But such cogitation did not allow for the dislocated intimacy an American man and a Vietnamese woman could create together. Lying in bed, the woman complaining about her boy-friends who wanted to control her, keep her home; the American man telling her no, that is wrong, it should not be like that; the woman, per-haps touching his face, saying in the darkness, "You are so different, so different," and the man knowing he is not, not really, because what was he offering her but a different, less obvious form of control? At this attraction's lambent core was something both manipulative and caring.

One heard some strange, alarming, and possibly even true things from those who had thoroughly caverned into this attraction: that when you had sex with a Vietnamese woman it often pained her, that Viet-namese women were notoriously lousy kissers, that after love had been established they could transform into shrieking harpies. These poor women. What could they do in a culture with folk sayings as troubling as "One boy, that's something; ten girls, that's nothing" or "A hundred girls aren't worth a single testicle." What could they do? Among other things, they could stare into your eyes with so much longing you wished to take them into your arms but then look away the moment you asked them about their husbands.

The following morning, as my father and I made our way down a devas-tatingly bright beach, which felt like nothing so much as having been swallowed by a postcard, I found myself comparing my constitution with his. My father imbibed a fraction as much as he used to, but he still possessed the cast-iron disposition every alcoholic needs if he or she is looking to make a life of it. I looked and smelled as though I had spent the night in a halfway house urinal, whereas he looked and smelled as though he had just slept fifteen hours in some enchanted flower bed. I was reminded of the various times I had, while growing up, seen my father triumphantly insensate after a bottle of Johnnie Walker Red, wearing only underwear and a winter jacket, off to do some 3 a.m. snow shoveling. Mere hours later he would be healthfully pink and whis-tling as he knotted his tie before work. Constitutionally, I was not this man's spawn. Two shots of vodka gave me a protuberant headache, four beers annihilated the proceeding twenty-four hours, and five glasses of red wine landed me in intensive care. I pictured my father's alcohol-processing unit as some deafening, barn-sized combine. My own alcohol-processing unit, which was evidently powered by a gerbil, could not keep up with it, or him, and here on the beach he patted my back as I dry heaved into some bushes.

We were looking for the exact spot where my father had come ashore with a thousand other Marines in April 1965, one month after the deployment, in Danang, of the first U.S. Marines sent to Vietnam explicitly as combat troops. Men such as my father took the Corps's principle of being the first into combat quite solemnly. At this impulse the Army, Navy, and Air Force often rolled their collective eyes. Indeed, during the war the Army's chief of staff chastised the Marines for the "heads down and charge" manner in which they fought.

The Marines who landed at Danang a month before my father were greeted by cheering Vietnamese, and several young women stepped forth to hang wreaths of flowers around their sunburned necks. By this point the war was universally viewed as being lost, governmental chaos reigned in Saigon, and General Westmoreland no longer had any trust that the ARVN could defeat the insurgency. (One of the ARVN's most elite and expensively trained units had been ambushed and nearly wiped out at Bien Gia by NLF guerrillas on the eve of 1965.) Marines would no longer stand impotent guard beside airports and radio towers and hospitals but would hunt down and kill insurgents. Many expected a quick victory, as it was assumed that NLF and PAVN troops could not withstand America's superior firepower. "We are going to stomp them to death," one U.S. major general said at the time. A Gallup Poll conducted shortly after the Marines landed revealed that the percentage of Americans who believed that the war would end with a Communist victory or the United States pulling out was precisely zero.

Yet despite the long-standing expectation of many in the Pentagon that an American ground war in Vietnam was inevitable, very little work had been done to prepare for the Marines' arrival. Equipment shortages and logistical snafus would plague the Marines for months. Part of the problem was the deceit that shrouded the Marines' arrival. President Johnson, worried that most Americans would see the offensive use of

Marines as a reckless escalation of the conflict, instructed Robert McNamara to downplay the deployment with the press, going so far as to suggest that McNamara claim that the Marines had been dispatched at the
"request" of the South Vietnamese government—an overt lie. Secretary
of State Dean Rusk assured reporters that the troops would only be
guarding Danang's air base and some missile batteries. After a three-
week moratorium on combat operations, that promise went out the
window. Until a low-level bureaucrat accidentally spilled the beans a few
weeks later that U.S. forces in Vietnam were taking part in "offensive
killing operations," few were aware of the Marines' real purpose in Vietnam. General Westmoreland had been certain that an injection of U.S.
troops would reverse South Vietnam's fortunes: "Introducing three U.S.
divisions [about 60,000 men] onto the mainland of Southeast Asia," he
believed, "would so change the balance of power on the peninsula that
the Communist choice would be limited to (1) whether they should sue
for peace as quickly as possible to prevent the eventual loss of their present control over North Vietnam and northern Laos, or (2) take on the
U.S. and its allies [sic] in a major war." Many in the U.S. military failed to
share this view, arguing that driving the NLF out of South Vietnam
would require decades and as many as a million men. Johnson's decision
to go ahead with the limited deployment that many believed would fail
caused one member of the Joint Chiefs, General Harold Johnson, to
nearly resign. General Johnson later called his decision not to resign "the
worst, most immoral decision I've ever made." It would not be until
June 1965, four months after the Marines arrived, that anyone in the
Johnson administration would admit to the American people that a
major war had indeed begun.

It took us fifteen minutes' worth of beachcombing to find the site of my
father's landing: a thin stand of coastline palm trees, miraculously unaltered since 1965, hardened his memory into place. We stood looking out
on the sea in a black grid of shadows cast by the cranes and scaffolds of
the resort being built a few dozen yards away. I began asking him questions, but very gently he asked if I might not give him a moment.
Instantly I realized my error. He could not talk right now, and he stared

out at the ocean in both confusion and recognition. This was where the man I knew as my father was born. It was as though he were looking upon himself through a bloody veil of memory.

"They told us this was going to be a combat landing," he said after a while, "to expect the very worst. The ships we were in flooded themselves, and the landing craft and amphibious vehicles swam off. We came ashore, heavily armed, locked, cocked, ready to go to war. We had tanks and trucks and Ontos."

"Ontos?"

"Lightly armored vehicles mounted with six recoilless rifles. They shot all kinds of ammunition. Armor-piercing. Antipersonnel ammunition. Willy Peter, which is white phosphorous, one of the most deadly things you could ever get hit with. When the shell explodes, it sprays white phosphorous, and if you put water on it, it flares right up. It's oxygen-fed, and you have to take mud and smother it. Lovely weapon."

I had read a description of white phosphorous once, how it exploded "with a fulsome elegance, wreathing its target in intense and billowing white smoke, throwing out glowing red comets trailing brilliant white fumes." It burned through skin, through bone, though anything. I asked, "Didn't the Geneva Convention forbid the use of white phosphorous against troops? It was only supposed to be used against equipment, right?"

He did not even look at me. "Uh-huh. Right."

"How old were you with all this at your disposal?"

He hesitated. "I was twenty-three years old. A platoon leader. Later I became a company commander, and I had all of the infantry and supply people under me. I was probably one of the youngest company commanders in Vietnam—if not the youngest." Of this, I could tell, he was still proud. "So we hit the beach and we're peering over the gunwales of the landing craft, and all of a sudden I hear people swearing at me—in English." He shook his head. "We had landed smack in the middle of a swimming hole for the United States Army. 'Goddamn Marines, what the fuck are you doing here?' "

"Quite an arrival."

"It gets worse. On we went down the beach road"—he turned—

"I guess over there, which I was told to do, and we went into the city of Qui Nhon and promptly came to a dead end. I missed the turn. Or the map was out of date. The whole Second Marine Battalion could have been destroyed—but there was no hostility. Everyone was cheering us. It was glorious. That's my biggest frustration when I talk to people who weren't here. They'll say, 'Nobody really wanted us to come to Vietnam.' Well, they sure as hell welcomed us with open arms."

"When did it start to go bad?"

He pointed to the hills beyond Qui Nhon—an arcadia of rough, beautiful triangles of fuzzy jade and sharp spurs of exposed white rock, a few sparkling white waterfalls pouring down the hills' faces. "Those look beautiful, but they're meaner than a son of a bitch to walk up and down. The VC was there, as we found out. It only took two days before we were fired on. The first six people we killed were all women—armed and shooting at us, mind you."

He had never told me this before. "Dad. My God. What was that . . . how did you . . . ?"

"What was it like? It was like about what you'd expect it to be like. I threw up. No one joins the Marines to shoot women."

Internally, the North Vietnamese and the NLF referred to their Kalashnikov-wielding women as "long-haired troops." One can quibble, to little probable value, about the ethics of using women in guerrilla war, but women warriors were not unknown in Vietnam. Not a few of its most storied military victories were at least partially led by women, and one Vietnamese adage holds, "When pirates come into the house, even women must take up arms." Despite Vietnamese Communists' egalitarian view of warfare, however, the Politburo did not have a single woman member until 1996.

"But," my father went on, "those women killed a couple of us, too. We were so inexperienced, we were shooting ourselves at first. One guy, tragically, fell asleep on watch and turned himself around in his foxhole. He woke up, saw people, and opened fire. Killed the rest of his fire team."

"So what happened to him?"

"He went crazy. They shipped him off to Japan; that's the last we ever heard of him."

"Were the parents of the guys who got killed told what really happened?"

"I don't know. I doubt it. They were probably told their sons 'bravely died in combat.' Who would want to know their kid died asleep in a hole?" Colonel David Hackworth, the most decorated Vietnam veteran and also among the war's most vocal and eloquent critics, has estimated that as much as 20 percent of American deaths in Vietnam were caused by friendly fire.

I left my father's side and walked toward the incoming surf, stepping around a beached jellyfish pulsatingly expiring in the sand, and tried to imagine myself, at twenty-three years of age, having to deal with the reality of my friends massacring my friends. Having to face that struck me, both intellectually and emotionally, as an extraterrestrial impossibility. My first quasi-experience with war was a terrifying game of college paintball, during which, at my first glimpse of the opposing army cresting a nearby hill, I climbed out of my two-man foxhole and sprinted back toward the rear line as fast as I could—leaving behind my best friend, Mike, who has since reminded me, many times, that I shouted "Sorry!" over my shoulder as I ran. My second, more substantial encounter with war occurred while I attempted to cover the U.S. invasion of Afghanistan in December 2001. I was in Afghanistan for five days, and while almost nothing happened to me, the psychic vise that closed around my mind did not loosen when I stepped back across the Afghan-Uzbek border. Instead it grew worse. For months I talked endlessly of my five days of war. For months when I closed my eyes I saw the abandoned Soviet tanks and endless gray sands of northern Afghanistan's Dasht-i-Laili desert. But then the desert went away, and the only aspects of the experience I could any longer remember were the adumbrations of an expedient mind, which is to say, my imagination.

What, then, did *real* war do to a person? What had it done to my father, and what might it have done to me? Would I have been one of those dead American boys they found sometimes in Vietnam's jungles, whose M16 barrels were respectfully kicked out from beneath their chins so no one would know they had shot themselves in the middle of battle? Would I have been one of the "shitbirds" I had read about in so many combat memoirs? A coward, a fuckup? Had I been drafted, I might well have opted for a steady diet of poutine and Montreal croissants. Or would I have been an antiwar activist? Could I see myself among the young souls who tore down the Justice Department's American flag in 1969 and replaced it with the colors of the NLF? Or, would I, like Dick Cheney, have simply gone to my college classes and regarded with tepid annoyance the gallery of traitors between me and the Chemistry Building?

Many Americans still believe that antiwar activists were traitors. There is no doubt that those who protested the war were effective in frustrating the war's enactment. One U.S. admiral admitted after the war that the "reaction of the noisy radical groups was considered all the time. And it served to inhibit and restrain the decision makers." North Vietnam's Vo Nguyen Giap called antiwar activists "a valuable mark of sympathy." Some of North Vietnam's luminaries cabled antiwar movement leaders statements such as: "EARNESTLY CALL YOU MOBILIZE PEACE FORCES IN YOUR COUNTRY. CHECK U.S. DANGEROUS VENTURES IN INDOCHINA," and Bui Tin once described how every morning "our leadership would listen to world news over the radio . . . to follow the growth of the American antiwar movement." The postmaster general of the United States announced in 1969 that antiwar protestors were in effect "killing American boys." What is wartime dissent, and is it still dissent when it is demonstrably bolstering enemy spirits? (The NLF used to caution its members from referring to Ho Chi Minh or North Vietnam directly, lest the American peace movement figure out that victory for one would be victory for the other. This was in retrospect a rather charitable assumption for the NLF to have entertained of many antiwar activists' loyalties.) I did not think it fair to cover antiwar activity with a blanket of treason (even Tom Hayden, who once declared, "We are all Viet Cong now," clearly believed he was acting in his nation's best interest), but the matter was surely more complicated than most wanted to admit—though not so complicated as to allow literally or figuratively spitting on American soldiers to achieve the status of coherent political expression. Today one often hears that one can oppose a given war but still support the troops. "Support," it will be explained, means getting the troops home as quickly as possible. But the nature of soldiering creates men and women who expect, and in some ways even want, to fight and kill. How, then, does one oppose a war but support those fighting it? I was not sure one could. To oppose a war that soldiers were fighting meant that one opposed the soldiers. It had to.

It was also beside the point. War is its own country, and creates its own citizens. Many soldiers, when interviewed by military psychologists, have admitted that the bond that formed between themselves and their fellow soldiers during combat was the most intense they had ever felt: more vivid than the bond between them and their parents, siblings, children, even their spouses. As Philip Caputo writes in *A Rumor of War*, camaraderie in combat "does not demand for its sustenance the reciprocity, the pledge of affection, the endless reassurances required by the love of men and women. It is, unlike marriage, a bond that cannot be broken by a word, by boredom or divorce, or by anything other than death."

These men: Who were they, really? Sometimes it seemed as though there were almost as many myths and countermyths about the men who fought in Vietnam as there were men who fought in Vietnam. The so-called Vietnam Generation numbered about 27 million men. Of them, 3.1 million (about 12 percent) served in Vietnam, and roughly 800,000 (about 3 percent) saw combat while there. Was Vietnam, in Frances FitzGerald's withering words, truly "a white man's war being fought by blacks, a rich man's war being fought by the poor, an old man's war being fought by the young"? The average soldier's age in Vietnam was nineteen, but FitzGerald's other assertions are belied by the facts. Black soldiers, for instance, made up 12.5 percent of combat deaths during the war, a full percentage point less than their share of the U.S. population at the time. (Early in the war, however, blacks' deaths were massively out of proportion: 25 percent in 1965 and 1966, almost twice their general population.) Seventy-three percent of those killed in Vietnam were volunteers; 30 percent were Catholic, despite Catholics' accounting for 23 percent of the U.S. population; and contrary to popular belief there was no great disparity of death by income level (though, again, the war's earlier years saw stark economic disparity among those killed). My father and Phil Caputo could surely speak to that: their friend Walter Levy hailed from a privileged New York City family.

The devastating aftereffects of the war upon its veterans were also routinely cited. But unemployment rates for veterans after the war were actually lower than those of nonveterans, and their rate of suicide was no different from that of the rest of the American populace. However, studies done on veterans that take into account the amount and intensity of experienced combat have suggested that those who saw an unusual amount of action have extremely high percentages of divorce, joblessness, alcoholism, and health problems. In all these discrepancies two things seem clear. The first is that the view that Vietnam veterans are subject to endless suffering is too indulgent. The second is that the view that Vietnam veterans are, by and large, well adjusted is too selective. A survey is not a mind, and a statistic is not reality. It seems clear that more highly educated officers and servicemen who saw service in Vietnam have coped well, psychologically speaking, whereas the less educated boys from the ghettos and farms of America—teenagers who believed that God was good, just, and American—were far less mentally prepared to deal with the confusions and ethical bonfires of guerrilla war in a country they knew nothing about. The trauma for them was far stranger, the questions unanswerable. Where did that leave my father? Here on the beach that had chopped his life in two, with a son who loved him but could not understand him, and whom he could not understand.

As we drove on to the village of Tuy Phuoc, I asked my father about the severance between the kind of fighting he had been trained to do and the kind of fighting the NLF forced him to engage in. During Vietnam, and especially throughout the war's opening innings, American soldiers experienced fighting unlike any they had ever seen before. General Giap instructed his cadres to "apply guerrilla warfare, which consists in being secret, rapid, active, now in the east, now in the west, arriving unexpectedly and leaving unnoticed." Thus there was no land to take, no front to hold, and few opportunities to glory in the routing of the enemy. All-out battles were few and far between, and enemy combatants perpetually melted away into the forest only to reappear, in the minds of increasingly (and understandably) jittery American soldiers, in the form of putatively innocent villagers.

"The VC," my father said, "would not close with us. They didn't have the firepower. And we knew that if they made a stand against us, they would lose ass, hat, and fixtures. So they would pick on our patrols, ambush us." He was agitated now and stared with cool determination out his window. Tuy Phuoc, the village we were headed to, was where my father was wounded.

"And you were mostly in charge of running convoys, so . . ."

"We were the prime targets. I'd get called to provide transportation and logistics for missions. It was boring, boring, boring, and then it was terrifying. And you never knew what was going to happen, if the operation was going to be totally uneventful, which many of them were, or if it was going to turn into a nightmare, as a few became."

"So you were fired on . . . a lot?"

"Mm-hmm. Hien, what's this up here? Is this construction?"

"Dad. Come on."

He was silent for a while. "Mortars," he said finally. "They loved to mortar us. And they'd bracket a road. So we'd change routes all the time, take different roads."

"Bracketing."

"They'd shoot until they knew exactly where the shells would go, then they would click their mortar launchers up or down, left or right. That's called bracketing. 'Bracketed' means you're in deep shit." He pointed out the window at the railroad track that ran contiguous to the road, on an elevated mound of packed sod perhaps eight feet high. "See that? That's what we used to hide behind, as a fortified position." At this he enjoyed a small chuckle.

"How many firefights were you in?"

"A dozen, twenty. They would last anywhere from ten seconds to two hours. Then the VC would break off and run. We lost a tremendous amount of people trying to save our wounded and retrieve our bodies. And they knew it. They knew we would. That's how Walt Levy died, you know: trying to haul someone out of a rice paddy who was wounded."

"I'm sensing some anxiety here. You're sweating."

"Really?" He touched his temple, a lagoon of perspiration. He quickly wiped his fingers on his shirt. "Well, maybe a little."

"How do you feel about the old Revolutionary Force now?"

I was joking, not really expecting an answer, but he looked at his camera as he turned it over in his hands. "We were all soldiers. They suffered terribly, you know, compared to us. Brave people. Committed. To their country. We sort of . . . lost that."

"I'm sorry," I said, surprising myself.

"Yeah," he said. "Me too."

"One of the books I read says that World War Two taught its generation that the world is dark but essentially just. Vietnam taught its generation that the world is absurd."

"That's horseshit. Forgive me, but that's just not true. What Vietnam taught me was the seven Ps: 'Proper prior planning prevents piss-poor performance.' "

"Okay. But it should be the six Ps, shouldn't it? Since one is a compound adjective."

My father leaned forward to address Hien and Truong. "Would you stop the car? I'd like your help beating my son."

Tuy Phuoc was less a village than a series of islands spread across a large plain now completely flooded by the seasonal rains. We rode among these islands along a long straight path that cleared the greedy waterline by only a few inches. Each island was a little node of Swiss Family Robinson–type existence: a modest house, a collapsing wooden fence, a damp sandy yard, a small dock, a wooden boat tied up to it. Plastic bags and limp old bicycle-tire linings hung with obscure meaning from the branches of several trees. Within the thick jungle, pink and yellow flowers, as bright as seashells, popped out at the eye from their dark green backdrops. Everywhere people were fishing; a few laughing children rode their bicycles through knee-deep water. My father mentioned that, forty years ago, all of these houses had been thatched huts. Hien jumped in to say, with some pride, that the government had been building and modernizing all of Vietnam's villages since 1975.

The narrow road was crammed with pedestrians. Water buffaloes farted and snorted beside us, while above the sky was a spacious gray cemetery of dead clouds. The surrounding floodwater was tea-colored where it was deep and green where it was shallow. As we moved toward the center of Tuy Phuoc, the severity of the area's recent flooding appeared quite serious. I watched men take off their sport coats, fold them over their shoulder, and with a snowshoeing gait wade through deep puddles to their front doors. Cars submerged up to their windshields were parked beside the road. People sat on the edges of their porches, pants rolled up to their knees, their dangling legs idly kicking at the water. Truong plowed through flooded-out sections of the road, vigorously splashing those walking beside us, none of whom even looked up. Flooding, the cultural marinade of rural Vietnam, was of little matter to these people.

"Viet Cong villages," my father said suddenly, looking around at Tuy Phuoc's islands. "All of these."

I imagined that coming down this road, even in a heavily armed convoy, must have been nerve-flaying. One slender path through a tropic of hostility, and nowhere to go but forward or back. We finally parked when the road was too flooded out to continue and stood next to the car. My father was wounded, he guessed, perhaps a hundred yards ahead of where we were forced to stop, just beyond a stand of trees as thick as green toothbrush bristles. He was visibly jittery and lit a cigarette to distract himself. On either side of the flooded-out road lingered a crowd of Vietnamese. They called to one another across the water, waving and laughing. Every few minutes some brave soul mounted a scooter charge through the floodwaters, the water parting before his tires with Mosaic instantaneity. The few who did not go fast enough saw their scooters conk out in the middle of their journey, and to cheerful catcalls they sheepishly pushed their scooters across the remainder of the submerged road.

Tuy Phuoc, I gathered, was not much of a tourist town, and for the most part we were left alone. But nearly everyone was looking at us. The people of Tuy Phuoc were short and damp and suntanned in a vaguely unhealthy way. The women smiled, the men nodded civilly, and the children rushed at us before thinking better of it and retreating behind their mothers' legs. One old woman sitting in the jamb of her tiny pink house spat black betel-nut juice into the soil.

"So," I said to my father, "this is it, right?"

He looked around, smoke leaking from his nostrils. "This is the place."

My tape recorder was activated yet again. "You want to tell me what happened?" This was mostly a courtesy, since I knew what happened. My father was shot—in the back, buttock, arm, and shoulder—at the beginning of a roadside melee and was dragged to safety by a black Marine. One of the things I had long admired about my father was his absence of racial animosity, a fairly uncommon trait among the men of rural Michigan. I had always attributed this to the black Marine who had saved his life. I identically credited my own youthful stridency on racial matters—I was forever jumping down the throats of my parents' dinner guests or high school friends whenever the word "nigger" made its unlovely entrance from stage right—to this same mysterious savior.

"We were on a search-and-destroy mission," my father explained. "We entered Tuy Phuoc in a convoy. After twenty minutes of driving we found the road was cut by a huge earthen mound. The VC obviously knew we were coming, so we were all very suspicious. We fanned out. I was at the head of the convoy and called up the engineers. They were going to blow up the mound and rebuild the road so we could continue. About fifteen men came up and I turned around to talk to the gunnery sergeant from the lead infantry platoon, and the mound exploded. Inside the dirt they'd packed a bunch of steel and shrapnel. The only reason I'm here is that I turned around to speak to the gunnery sergeant. I remember saying, 'Gunny, I'll go back and get some more equipment.' You know, shovels, stuff like that. The bomb caught Gunny in the face, and I went flying through the air. Then I tried to get up. Couldn't. There were people lying all over the place. I think fifteen were wounded. Gunny was the only guy killed. My platoon sergeant hauled me into a ditch, and they field-dressed me and jammed me full of morphine and then flew in the choppers. I was very fucked up, in total shock. I had two hundred separate wounds. They counted 'em. My left arm caught the brunt of the blast. I thought they were going to have to take it off. I thought I was going to die. I *knew* I was going to die. I said to myself, 'It's all done.' I took my pistol out with my one good hand. I took it out and I gave it to Scotty. I said, 'You're in charge. You've got the platoon. Lead them well. Good-bye.' I remember that everyone was crying. So that ended my war for a while."

"Wait a minute," I said, the tape recorder whirring. "I thought you were shot."

"No, I never got shot. Which is fine by me."

"But that's not the story you told me."

He looked at me. "I don't think I ever told you that story."

"Then why do I remember you being shot, and a black Marine dragging you to safety?"

"I have no idea."

"Was the sergeant who pulled you into the ditch black?"

"I don't think so. I honestly don't remember."

My father's sleeve was rolled up, and I was now looking at his left arm. Incredibly, I had never before noticed the scoring of crosshatched scar tissue running up and down his forearm or how thin his left arm seemed compared with his right. I had, however, many times, noticed the bright pink nickel-sized scars on his bicep and his shoulder blade, the small keloidal lightning bolt on his neck. When I was young I used to stare at these obvious wounds and, sometimes, even touch them, my tiny fingers freshly alive to their rubbery difference in texture. For me they were little talismans, the faded proofs of an unimaginable past. But I had to admit, now, that I did not actually remember my father ever telling me he was shot, or that a black man had saved his life. I remembered telling that story myself but did not remember being told that story. At some point the story simply appeared in my mind. Why did I create this story? Because it made my father heroic? In the emergency of growing up we all need heroes. But the father I grew up with was no hero to me, not then. He was too wounded in the head, too endlessly and terribly sad. Too funny, too explosive, too confusing. Heroes are uncomplicated. *This* makes them do *that*. The active heroism of my imaginary black Marine made a passive hero of my father; they huddled together, alongside a road in the Vietnam of my mind, shrouded in nitroglycerin, the cordite of bravery. The story made sense of the senseless. But war does not make sense. War senselessly wounded everyone right down the line. A body bag fitted more than just its intended corpse. Take the 58,000 American soldiers lost in Vietnam and multiply by four, five, six—and only then does one begin to realize the damage this war had done. (Project outward from the millions of slain Vietnamese and see, for the first time, an entire continent of loss.) War, when necessary, was unspeakable. When unnecessary, it was unforgivable. It was not an occasion for heroism. It was an occasion only for survival and death. To regard war in any other way only guaranteed its reappearance.

I studied my father, who was still smoking and peering around. Suddenly he appeared very old. He did not look bad. He was in fact in better physical shape than I—a topic of persistent agony for me and ceaseless delight for him—but he was older-looking than I had ever seen him before. His neck had begun to give up and sag, his eyes were bigger and more yellowy, the long wolfish hair at the base of his throat was gray. Age was squeezing him, shrinking him, bleeding him of color; age was doing what age does. I was twenty-nine, six years older than my father was when he was wounded. Could I really know the young man who had gone flying through the air, ripped apart by a booby trap? Could I even know this man, still flying, and in some ways still ripped apart? Ultimately our lives are only partially ours. Crucial pieces of our personal mythologies are shed at every turn. The parts of our lives that change most are those that intrude with mythic vividness into the lives of those we love: our parents, our children, our brothers and sisters. As these stories overlap they change, but we have no voice as to how or why. One by one our stories are dragged away from us, pulled into the ditches of shared human memory. They are saved, but they are changed. One day my father will be gone but for the parts of him I remember and the stories he has told me. That man, and those stories, will be different from what my brother will remember, or what my stepmother or mother will remember. What else did I not know? How much else about him had I gotten wrong? What have I not asked? And looking at him I wanted him never to go. Why did I have to lose him? I want him always to be here. There was too much left for us to talk about.

A lone Vietnamese man shoelessly wandered over to greet us. His chewed-up T-shirt looked to have been on the receiving end of a moth offensive, and the legs of his dirty blue trousers terminated just above his calves. His hairless legs and arms were so thin and brown they looked made of teak. As he and my father shook hands and (with Hien's assistance) chatted, I realized that this man was around my father's age. It was in fact not at all beyond possibility that this man had personally wired the booby trap that nearly killed my father. But his solar friendliness was not feigned, and beneath its insistent emotional heat I could see my father's discomfort soften and wilt. He leaned in, ear first, to listen to Hien's translation, and within moments the man and my father were laughing over something together.

I listened to my father and his new Vietnamese friend talk respectfully around the small matter of having taken up arms against each other as young men: yes, my father *had* been to Vietnam before; no, the Vietnamese man had not always lived in Tuy Phuoc. Their conversation slid into a respectful silence, and they nodded and looked each other over. With a smile, the man suddenly asked my father what had brought him to Tuy Phuoc, since it was so far away from anything of note. For a long time my father thought about how to answer, looking up at the low gray clouds, a few small trapezoids of blue showing through. To Hien he finally said, "Tell him . . . tell him that, a very long time ago, I got hurt here."

When we reached Nha Trang we opted to split up for the day: not a difficult decision. My father had spent five weeks in Nha Trang recuperating from his wounds, and I was beginning to sense that the more I questioned him the less he was able to contemplate his experience here. Contemplation is not an archaeology of explanation but the quiet solitary assembly of questions. After we had agreed to meet at 7 p.m. at something called the Nha Trang Sailing Club, my father and Hien went off to find the hospital in which he had physically recovered. I stuffed Duiker's Ho biography under my arm—I was marooned in the low 500s—and elected to wander the beaches and streets of Nha Trang.

Called by one writer "Nice in beggar's clothing," Nha Trang still retained some of its French heritage, but these days the beggar was living on velvet. Its saltine beaches, the bright gray ocean, the dandelion yellows and laundered whites of the seaside resorts and shops, the haze along the horizon that shadowed the distant green hills with a soft shade of lavender—the city was a scrum of color. A wide and well-paved four-lane street separated the beach from most of Nha Trang's better hotels, some of them quite tall, which resulted in a Maui-like aura of tropical urbanity.

I headed for the beach, passing a billboard that said VIETNAM: THE DESTINATION FOR A NEW MILLENNIUM. There were few people here but many seashells, pieces of trash, and shredded old tires. (Tires, along with a dozen tied-together flip-flop sandals, are often used in coastal Vietnam as buoys.) A few miles off the coast I could make out through the haze some of Nha Trang's small slug-shaped outlying islands. Among them floated several fishing boats. Nha Trang's surf was so loud I had been able to hear it on the thirteenth story of our hotel; standing beside the ocean now was like having one's thoughts turn hydraulic. I abandoned the beach for a stroll through the city center and saw countless scuba-diving advertisements, massage parlors, and karaoke bars. Every settled part of Vietnam had at least a few karaoke bars. I was beginning to suspect that Vietnamese molecules had tiny karaoke bars inside of them. Deeper into the city the newer buildings were of the Lego Deco mold and surrounded by pointy iron gates. Tucked away between these fortresses were worn little shingle-roofed buildings, obvious vestiges of the French colonial presence. Here and there hung a few NHA BAN signs: House for Sale.

I sat down in a burgers-and-fries restaurant, the menu of which read, "We are happy to sever you." On the menu's opposite side was a long jeremiad against pedophilia, which even in this "paradise," it seemed, had "reared its ugly head." As a word of warning it recounted one dismal Australian man's recent conviction in Sydney of molesting a nine-year-old Vietnamese girl in a Nha Trang swimming pool. Allowing those guilty of abusing Vietnamese children to face criminal charges back home was the result of a new international law whose mechanisms were being enthusiastically activated throughout Southeast Asia and in the nations of its most frequent tourists. I had read in *Viet Nam News* of at least three recent similar convictions. My wicker chair was planted right off the sidewalk, and before long a Vietnamese boy selling postcards and wearing a T-shirt with a large @ sign on it pestered me until I gave him 20,000 dong. After the boy left, a legless older man riding a bike he maneuvered by pumping a long red handle moved in. He handed me his card: "I am a Viet Nam veteran (ARVN) who lost both legs in a fight against the Charlies." I gave him some money, too.

Nha Trang was the first city I had seen here where the streets appeared traveled more by Westerners than by Vietnamese. I was no travel bully or tourist hater, but finding oneself almost exclusively surrounded by other tourists (said the tourist eating a hamburger in Vietnam) had a way of frustrating one's interaction with a place. Overhearing a French couple attempting to talk down a cyclo driver from his two-dollar asking price; observing an American couple brush away some poor but friendly children; monitoring the progress of a Korean couple out to videographize every square inch of Nha Trang with their wallet-sized Sony Handycam; or watching the tour buses discharge their human cargo at some place of significance, the passengers milling about like fanny-packed cattle, asking few questions before taking their obligatory photo. All had come chasing the same butterflies of beauty and fascination, yet no one had anything to say to anyone else. I missed my father already, and after finishing the Duiker book, I walked back to the hotel, napped to the sound of faraway surf until 6:45, and made my way over to the Nha Trang Sailing Club.

To enter, one passed through a tall wooden archway next to a scuba lessons shop and walked down a long breezeway to the restaurant proper. This open area was inconsistently covered by a fake thatched roof, from which a number of glowing orange lamps hung. The tables were low and onyx black. Several palm and coconut trees had been left standing around the restaurant's edges. A pool table shone like a hard green pool beneath a suspended rectangular light. Beyond was the club's porch, edged with low adobe walls and scattered with huge earthen pots sprouting cacti. The bar itself, where my father sat with his back to me, was the club's most expensively swaggering touch. It looked like a candlelit glen of wood and metal. A massive Foster's beer tap was prominently centered upon the bar like a bright blue idol. Behind the bar a trio of actor/model barkeeps glided before a backdrop of bourbons and vodkas and gins. I stood there looking at my father in his pressed green shirt and khaki pants, his ears gone burgundy from the wine he had already put away this evening. I was hesitant to approach him. He seemed so contentedly alone.

When I touched his back he turned, and suddenly his arms went around me. As he squeezed, his loose fists softly pounded my scapulae. "This is so wonderful," he said upon release. "Thank you for bringing me here. What a magnificent country."

"What a magnificent glass of wine, it sounds like."

"No, the country. It's . . . just wonderful."

"I'm really glad you're having a good time."

"It's not just Vietnam. I like all of Asia."

I sat next to him. "What do you like about it?"

His mouth screwed over. "Gosh. I have to think about that. I guess I like the people. Of course I like the food. The scenery. Asians are just indomitable. They don't feel sorry for themselves. They're not whiners; they do what has to be done. Always trying to succeed—like America used to be."

"Oh, boy."

He waved this off. "I'm starving. Let's eat next to the beach."

We were escorted to our table. The late-supping expat crowd had not yet descended, and we had the porch almost entirely to ourselves. The unseen sun, not yet set, filled the sky to the west with diffuse auburn light. To the east, above the sea, the moon was set into the sky like a smooth pale marble. We looked at each other, my father smiling. Before us were two plastic sleeves that contained premoistened towelettes, which every Vietnamese establishment provided its customers. I opened mine Vietnamese-style, gripping one end of the packet to rush the trapped air to the other, and then popping the thin plastic bubble against my palm. My father peeled his open.

"I swear," I said, "this entire country's economy runs on scooters and premoistened towelettes."

"This country's economy doesn't run," my father, or rather my father's wine, said grimly. "There's so much pointless waste here. It's depressing."

"Cease-fire, Captain. I thought this was a 'magnificent country'?"

He peacefully contemplated the ocean. "It is. It could be."

I decided to throw out to him a conversational life preserver. "Did something happen to you today?"

He examined his thumbnail, checked his watch, scratched his nose. His stare, when it finally fell on me, had an odd ferocity. "The god-damned hospital, the Ninth Army hospital I got better in—Hien and I went to find it. I knew it's near the airfield because I remember being flown in and then immediately being placed on a gurney and taken to the hospital—all of which took two minutes. So we went to the airport. Of course a policeman was there. We asked him, a very affable guy, where it was, and he said, 'Oh yeah, it's right down there.' We pulled up to the hospital, and I asked Hien if he would take a picture of me in front of it. And he said no, it's not allowed. I asked why, and he didn't answer. Then he went in and talked to some local people, and they said absolutely not, no pictures. No, no, no, no, no, no, no. I said, 'Well, why not? Tell the guards that I used to be a patient here, during the American War.' And Hien said, 'It does not work that way in my country.' That made me sad: 'It does not work that way in my country.' "

"Dad, look at it from their side. How much hospitality do you expect these people to show you?"

"It's not that. I can live with that. It's this aura of . . . *secrecy* about going to a *hospital*."

I shrugged. "It's very Communist."

"It's not an antiaircraft battery, or a nuclear zone." He shook his head. "When we were driving back, I asked Hien, 'Why? Why is it like this?' And he said, 'I know, I know—but it is my government.' So I don't even have a picture to show Carolyn."

"What's the building look like?"

"Like it always did."

"Then it's not a big deal. It's just a hospital."

"But it's not just the hospital. It's this whole fuckin' place. You remember the restaurant we stopped at, between Chu Lai and Qui Nhon?"

"The beachside place, with the toilets that drained right into the river?"

Once again, up floated his long, thick index finger. "That right there: Communism."

"Communism?"

"This lovely little restaurant, and there's the water closet right next to you, and some young lady ducks into it, and I'm watching this with Truong, and pretty soon I see a big brown dragon fall through the floor and into the stream. I thought, 'I'm glad I'm not downstream washing my clothes.' "

"Dad, what can you do?"

"What I think is that there's no incentive for anyone to work at doing something like building a better sewage system. The State will take care of it."

"Incentive has nothing to do with it. There's no *money*. Rural Vietnam struggles along on whatever pennies the government manages to throw its way."

"What I'm saying is that private enterprise would not allow that to happen."

"That's . . . forgive me, but that's nutty."

"Just hear me out. After the hospital I went to the bar in our hotel. I said to the bartender, 'I would like a bottle of wine.' And this wonderfully nice man said, 'Oh, good, which one do you want?' I asked him for a wine list. He brought it to me and I said, 'Oh yes, this is the bottle I want,' and he said, 'Sauvignon?' and I said, 'No, chardonnay.' I pointed it out again. Twenty minutes—no, twenty-five minutes later, because now I was keeping track—the man arrived with five bottles of wine. Four red, one white."

"Not sure I see your point here."

"You need to listen. So he picked up the phone, he made a call. He said, 'Lac, chardonnay, please.' Twenty minutes later, another man, this Mr. Lac, arrives. Then a woman came in, and they brought the bottle of sauvignon. Now we have three people involved."

"Okay. I hear you. Now, if I—may I say something?"

"The people themselves are marvelously wonderful. Don't misunderstand me. I mean, they're just down-to-earth, doing everything they can to succeed. But these rules that none of them—it takes so many to—"

"Dad, there's stuff that socialism or capitalism or whatever ism you want to bring up does not and cannot—"

"I'm not done yet, philosopher. So they bring the wrong bottle of wine. I say, 'No,' but I say this very gently. And we're conversing in pidgin English and Vietnamese. I had my dictionary out. And he said, basically, 'This is not the right bottle of wine.' He was talking about the one I ordered! It took me over an hour, because of the strictures they have, to finally get me the bottle of wine I ordered."

"You're exaggerating. I know you when you're exaggerating and you're exaggerating right now."

His face darkened. "Let me retrace things."

"Look, I know what you're saying."

"I was horrified! Horrified for the people. There's just no continuity, efficiency, productivity, or good service."

"The service since we've been here has been tremendous. What the fuck are you talking about?"

Again he looked away. "Only you, my son . . ."

"I know you think I'm a Communist, but the fact is—"

"So then, when I asked for ice, it took another person. It took one more person. It took another person to get a glass. And it took three people to get the right bottle of wine. What I'm saying is that they're about as efficient as a snail trying to make pancakes. They're marvelous, they're friendly, but they have no initiative to do anything better."

"You're being completely unreasonable. For one, Vietnamese operate under an utterly different set of cultural assumptions than you and me."

"I knew you were a Communist!"

By now we really did have the porch to ourselves. The middle-aged couple sitting a few tables away had moved into the bar with much theatrically appalled shaking of head.

"Now listen to me," my father said quietly, "because I actually know a little. I know a little bit more than you think." He went thoughtfully silent. Then: "What is the basis of culture?"

"Art. Art is the basis of culture."

"I think economics is the basis of culture. Economics. If you are well off, well fed, well clothed, well housed, and comfortable in your political situation, then—"

"What about poets or painters who don't care about being well fed or well off?"

"They won't be able to write their poetry or paint their portraits until somebody comes along and is able to support them. Which is why I keep telling you to find some nice young lawyer."

"A lot of artists have died in poverty just to be able to do their work."

"Fine, but they had a chance to do their work because they weren't digging up rice paddies, because somebody gave them the latitude to be able to develop their artistic talents."

"You're dodging the question."

"All right, I'll start over. Economics, to my mind, is the basis of all development of all civilization."

"I can agree with that. The development part. But art sustains civilization."

"If I'm forced to defend my fort, there is no art. If I'm starving, there is no art. Art needs benefactors. People need to *buy* it, right? This art of yours needs an audience, however small. What is that, then? What provides this audience? Economics, solid economics. Only with a solid economic picture can your art develop."

I tossed my towelette between us: truce. "Okay. I just resent the fact that you make me into a Communist sympathizer with your harebrained theorizing."

"And I resent that you just called me a harebrained theorizer."

"But it took four people to get your bottle of wine."

"No, it took five, because you forgot about the guy who brought me my ice."

Our slender, androgynous waiter approached, somewhat cautiously, and asked if we were ready to order. My father told him, "We're going to sit tight for a while. But we'd like another bottle of wine." The waiter stood there looking at us, puzzled, then walked away.

As my father dumped the dregs of his wine into his mouth, I said, "You know, you shouldn't use so many idioms when speaking to Vietnamese."

"What do you mean?"

"Idioms are usually the last and most difficult part of a language to master. And every English-speaking culture has different idioms. I don't think he had any idea what you meant by 'sit tight.' I'm just saying."

"Well," he said, "they should know them. It's his job to know idioms."

I listened to the waves and watched the growing number of Nha Trang's prostitutes troll up and down the beach. Soon my father was biting his nails and smoking one cigarette after another. I knew I was sitting across from a different man now. Drinking emboldened him, made him sit up straighter, his voice louder, his stories longer, the ultimate point of these stories more opaque. The wine had colored all the cartilaged parts of his face bright pink. He was talking now, but I was only half listening. Instead I stared at the little red light of my tape recorder.

I finally interrupted him: "Tell me about Nha Trang. Tell me about what you remember."

He fell back against his chair. "Gosh. There's a lot. I remember recuperating and I was on crutches and I was sort of a mess. I didn't have a lot of strength and I couldn't go to the beach, so I'd hire a taxi and the nurse at the desk would give me a chit, good for three hours, or four hours. I would come down here in a taxi, and get dropped off. All these hotels you see now? They weren't here, of course. But I'd go have dinner. And there was one place I looked for earlier today, but I couldn't find it. It's gone."

"What was it?"

"A little restaurant. Now, this woman had the best abalone; she knew seafood. The fishermen here all brought all their best catch to her. And if you came in alone she fixed you up with a woman."

"So you were getting laid a lot in your recuperation?"

"Uh, no. But I was feeling well enough to think about it. But I got involved with this woman, and we were having dinner there. We had abalone and lobster and this little thing would go, 'Ooooooooh!' She spoke English. She said to me, 'You are badly hurt.' I said, 'Yes, I am, but I'm getting better.' "

"Can you remember her name?"

"I don't think I ever knew her name."

Our waiter came back, and finally we ordered. Once he was gone, I said, "So you have fond memories of Nha Trang."

"I made one friend here—this guy had been an engineer in Vietnam in the 1950s. Now he was back. He was very well known in Nha Trang— what you'd call a noncombatant. He knew all the local contractors, cement and et cetera. He knew it all. Sand. Brick. He said to me, 'You wanna have some fun downtown?' And I said, 'Christ, yes. Get me the fuck out of here.' So, we got passes and came downtown."

"You were better by this point?"

"No. He was in the same ward that I was."

"He was a fellow patient."

"Yeah, and he liked me. I think his name was Bill or something. I'm John and he's Bill. We went out for two rollicking days. Ate in the best restaurants."

"How was he wounded? Do you remember?"

"Yes. He had a very difficult disease called 'not taking care of your dick.' Well, one day, he's better, and I'm feeling great, and then that great leader of ours, General Westmoreland, came through our ward. This is the truth, and you may print it if you'd like. If you don't care to write about it, that's fine. But Westmoreland comes to the first guy he sees, a guy in an oxygen tent, and says, 'Our country is honored by your sacrifice.' He then proceeds to pin this great big medal—the Purple Heart— to the poor guy's oxygen tent, and the air starts escaping. Now the medics are running around trying to patch the thing."

"William Westmoreland pinned a Purple Heart to an oxygen tent? Is that true?"

"It's absolutely true. General Westmoreland also gave me my Purple Heart."

"Here? In Nha Trang?"

"Right here. Just a few blocks away. He said to me, 'Congratulations, Lieutenant.' "

"Wow. Did he kick you in the nuts while he presented it to you or something?"

"No. But I didn't finish my story. After puncturing the guy's oxygen tent, Westmoreland sees all the guys with swollen dicks and goes crazy. 'What are you guys doing here? You're dishonoring your country!' "

"Swollen dicks."

"They were recovering from a severe form of enlarged penis, I guess you'd call it."

" 'Enlarged penis.' Meet my father, the doctor."

"I don't know what the hell it was; their dicks were as big as your fist. But Westmoreland gave them bloody hell, and these guys were embarrassed. These were Army chopper pilots who had been out in the bush for probably a year. And for him to denigrate them. . . . I was in my bed, listening. Not able to move very much, but I'm listening. And I'm getting angry. Nha Trang was a peaceful area, and these guys were the ones who'd made it that way."

"It was calm here?"

"Oh yeah, we had it controlled."

"When you got off your crutches, did you ever come down here and sit on the beach?"

"Yeah. Sit on the beach. Think."

"Sit and watch stuff go by?"

"Sure. Lovely people would walk over and say, 'Hi. How you?' "

"You mean whores?"

"No, no. Get your mind out of the crapper. Just people—marvelous people." He stopped for a moment, gazed over at the ocean, and started to talk again, but I stopped listening.

What does your father do? A question young men are asked all the time. Women in particular ask it of young men, I suppose in the spirit of a kind of secular astrology. Who will you be in ten years, and do I want to be involved? The common belief is that every young man, like the weeping Jesus of Gethsemane, has two choices when it comes to his father: rejection or emulation. In some ways my father and I could not have been more different. While I had inherited his sense of humor, his sense of loyalty, and his lycanthropically hairy back, I was my mother's child in all matters of commerce and emotion. I am terrible with money, weep over nothing, and typically feel before I think. I could anticipate my mother because her heart was mine. My father remained more mysterious. What does my father do? I had always answered it thus: "My father is a Marine." This typically resulted in a pinch-faced look of sympathy. But the truth was, my father and I got along. We had not always gotten along—I maintained a solid D average in high school, he viewed my determination to be a writer (at least initially) as a dreamer's errand, and lurking in our history were various wrecked Chevys and uncovered marijuana caches—but we had always been close. As I grew older, I noticed the troubles many of my friends had with their fathers: the animosities and disappointments, held so long in the arrears of late adolescence, suddenly coming up due on both ends. But my father and I, if anything, had grown closer, even as I understood him less and less.

"So I got up there on crutches and they sat me down at this marvelous table, this beautiful lacquer table. Before I know it there's a woman alongside me. 'I love you. You Marine? You GI?' I said, 'I'm a Marine.' She said, 'I love Marines more than GIs.' So we began to order our food, and they did it right. They would bring out prawns, soup, a little plate of lobster. And we were on the beach. I remember walking across the road in my crutches, a couple of nights, and having this woman just talk to me. I wasn't so sure what she was saying all the time. But she was just . . . she made me feel good. She had this room, I think my major took care of it; I never paid a dime, I don't know. We did this for two nights. And I remember she'd say, 'Shower now, shower now.' So we'd go into this room and I can't even recollect if it was in our hotel room or in the commons, but I'd take a shower and she would wash me. It was one of the most marvelous things. She would lather me up, wash me head to toe. And she'd put me in bed, she'd look at the bandages and there was blood coming out and she'd say, 'Not good, you must go hospital.' The blood was coming out again, on my back, on my butt, on my arms and my legs and my feet. Let's just say I was a little too energetic in my recovery. God, it's coming back in floods now. I remember feeling this tremendous relief. No tension. Nothing to do, just be yourself. Recover."

My father was a Marine. But how poorly that captured him. He was not a tall man, but he was so thin he appeared tall. His head was perfectly egg-shaped, which accounted for my brother's and my nickname for him: Egghead. (Although nothing explained his nicknames for us: Ringworm and Remus.) His ducklike gait, a strange combination of the goofy and the determined, saw his big floppy feet inclined outward at forty-five-degree angles. (I used to make fun of him for this until a girlfriend pointed out to me that I walk precisely the same way.) My father, then, was no Great Santini, no Knight Templar of bruising manhood. During the neighborhood basketball games of my childhood, which were played in our driveway, my father, for instance, unforgivably shot granny-style free throws. "Hugs and kisses" is how he used to announce that he was putting me to bed. Hugs and kisses. I unself-consciously kissed my father until I was in high school, when some friends busted me for it: "You kiss your *dad*?" But we fought all the time. I do not mean argue. I mean we *fought*. I would often announce my presence by punching him hard on the shoulder, whereupon he would put me in a full nelson until I sang the following song, which for years I believed he had made up: "Why this feeling? / Why this joy? / Because you're near me, oh you fool. / Mister Wonderful, that's you." I have told people these stories expecting a great burst of laughter only to find a room of people staring silently back at me. And it got worse. Once, after a particularly inhuman game of Rock, Paper, Scissors (the loser of each round received the arm twist popularly known as a snakebite), I called a child abuse hotline on him. It took about a week to straighten out. The torment was not just physical. When I was very young, my father would tell me he had invented trees and fought in the Civil War, and would laugh until he had tears in his eyes when my teachers called home to upbraid him. In return my brother and I simply besieged the poor man, pouring liquid Ex-Lax into his coffee before work, loading his cigarettes with tiny slivers of treated pine that exploded after a few drags. One went off in a board meeting at his bank. Another while he was on his way to church, sending him up onto the curb. He always got us back. In high school I brought a date over and was showing off with my smart-aleckry, only to be knocked to the floor by my father and held down while he rubbed pizza all over my face and called our dogs over to lick it off. There was, needless to say, no second date.

"And I'm badly hurt, okay? And the Viet Cong were pounding the outskirts of Nha Trang. And this gunnery sergeant comes in and says, 'I need some good fuckin' Marines. We're gonna go fight those motherfuckers.' I'm saying, 'Well, that's great, but at the moment I'm quite unable to complement your platoon.' He says, 'What's wrong, Lieutenant, don't you have any balls?' I actually got out of bed, but I fell down. He says, 'Shit, you'll be of no use whatsoever.' I'd always admired gunnery sergeants, but I said, 'All of us here in this ward got banged up doing the real thing, and now you're gonna round up a patrol of cripples to go out and fight the enemy? What chance would we have?' He abruptly left. But you see—I admire the training, the instinct, the drive. I am full of total admiration. And I know you're sitting there thinking, 'How much of this is bullshit? Or brainwashing?' But there's no bullshit. The Marines change your mind-set. They change you from a civilian into a military person. Call it brainwashing? Okay. But they turn you into a person who can kill people, hold a unit together, look at the man next to you and say, 'You and I are brothers, and we will—we'll do it together,' and if you go down someone else comes up, and that's the marvelous part of the Marine Corps. The men who trained us . . . *nothing* prepares you for actually shooting at people, seeing people die. And the best advice I ever got was from a couple of master sergeants, men who never got any further in their . . . they were Marines. That was it. You have no idea. You would not have gotten along with them. They were not English majors, not writers, not poets. I'm not making any judgments. I'm just saying that's why I'm alive today. They taught me. We fought for our wounded. And the Vietnamese, the bad guys—they're all good guys now, yeah—but they'd pick us off. Red Cross, anyone with an arm patch, they'd shoot. None of us wore any insignia. Radio operator? We put him behind four other people, because he was Death. Anyone who had a radio could call down Death. We'd hide our radios, hide it on a guy's ass, so they couldn't see it. Most courageous people I've ever known."

My father is a Marine. He could be cruel. After a high school party that left his house demolished and our Christmas presents stolen, I sought him out to tell him I was sorry, that I loved him. "No," he said, not even looking at me as he swept up the glass from a broken picture frame. "I don't think you do." We owned a large stuffed diplodocus named Dino, which became a kind of makeshift couch we used to prop ourselves against while watching television, for my father was the kind of father who got down on the floor with his children. Once, resting against Dino while we watched *Sands of Iwo Jima,* I asked my father what it felt like to get wounded. He looked at me, grabbed the flesh of my forearm, and pinched me so hard sudden tears slickened my eyes. I returned fire by callously asking him if he had ever killed anyone. I was ten, eleven, and my cold, hurt little stare drilled into his, sheer will being one of the few human passions ungoverned by age. He looked away first. But he is a Marine. To this I attributed much of the insanity of growing up with him. One Fourth of July he and my uncle destroyed a neighbor's garbage cans by filling them with fireworks and a splash of gasoline, my uncle igniting the concoction by tossing in a cigarette smoked down to its filter. Another neighbor deposited half a dozen garter snakes into our bathtub; my father responded by taking the snakes over to the neighbor's house and calmly stuffing them under his bedspread. Once, at dinner, Phil Caputo recounted a story that saw my father drunkenly commandeering a tour bus in Key West, Florida, and flooring it across a crowded parking lot while his passengers, about seventy touring seniors, screamed. Only later did I realize that Caputo had not lived in Key West until the early 1980s—which would have made my father a forty-year-old bus thief.

"I went out to California once on a special trip; I took your mother there. And I tried to go see a lot of my officer friends at the officers' club. But with me were a bunch of enlisted men, so we could not enter the officers' club. I told the guy at the door, the staff sergeant or whatever he was, 'This is a travesty on their honor. Two years ago they fought for their nation, for the whole world! I was with them! And today, because they're enlisted, they can't enter. Do you really mean to tell me that after all the shit we've been through, we cannot, together as a group, come into this officers' club?' He said, 'I cannot let you in. I know what you're saying, sir, but no, I can't.' I said, 'It's sick, isn't it?' And he said, 'Yes, sir, it certainly is fuckin' sick.' You see, and you won't understand this, to be a good combat leader you have to love and respect your men. You have to *love* them. And you also have to be able to sacrifice them—for a piece of land, for a hill, sometimes for nothing but position. You have to make that decision. You have to be able to. . . . Goddamnit, Tommy, quit looking at that thing. Turn the fuckin' thing off. I can't talk with that fuckin' thing on."

Because, perhaps, my father is a Marine, I joined the Peace Corps after college. When I washed out and returned home, the mansion of his disappointment had many rooms, and even years later I could not much stand to reread the letters he sent me as I was preparing to come home. They are loving, they are cruel, they are the letters of a man who fiercely loves his son, and whose own past is so painful he forgets, sometimes, that suffering is a misfortune some of us are forced to experience rather than a human requirement. But what had I done with my life? I had become a writer greatly interested in sites of human suffering. And lately it had occurred to me that this might have been my attempt to approximate something of what my father went through.

"So anyway, I leave my troops down there, and *Christ*—we had a convoy of two thousand Marines. A big operation. I'm part of the operation and the South Vietnamese rangers led first. And these were good troops, we thought. It was a wood line—the wood line was a thousand yards away. Well, these ARVN rangers shot off all of their ammunition doing reconnaissance fire. Didn't have any ammo left. And they said, 'Good, now the American Marines can go investigate.' So I went out ahead on foot. Everywhere I turn I'm looking for spider holes, tunnels, trenches. They almost always put themselves in villages, thinking we wouldn't attack. And for many—we didn't always attack, a lot of times. And we'd get slaughtered because of it. So anyway, we advance, and I'm on foot because we had to find out where the trucks and the tanks could go. So I'm through the water, with the radio, thank God, I had communications with the airplanes and with the helicopters, and halfway there I said, 'Start hitting the tree line, please, now.' Just about after I said that, those fuckers began to fire. And it was devastating. They began to kill us. It was a full regimental assault. And guess where the Vietnamese were? They were fuckin' rearming. They always said, 'Let's let the Americans do this.' And we bled, we bled so much. But those Hueys came in, the best aircraft we had. God, they were good. We had Marine jets, you know: A-4s and F-4s. They'd cruise in and drop their bombs and ask us, 'How we doin'?' And I'd say, 'That's really neat, except you missed everything.' An F-4 Phantom was useless when it came to supporting ground troops. They came in too fast. They couldn't drop the ordnance in the right place. They couldn't see where we were. Once in a while they fired too short and that killed us. Other times they fired too far, did nothing, and that killed us in a different way. But those Hueys. They were wonderful. They'd stay, they'd be above us. I was the convoy commander, and I'd say, 'I need some help here,' and they'd say, 'Roger, we're comin' in.' They did the most marvelous job. God."

During the war in Afghanistan, I got stuck in Mazar-i-Sharif with dangerously low funds and one friend, Michael, a Danish journalist I had followed into the war. On our way out, despite our having all the proper credentials, the Uzbek border patrol turned us back three times in a row. We had brought only enough money for a few days, and at fifty dollars a cab ride from Mazar to the border, we were running out of options. After striking out with the American Embassy in Uzbekistan ("Well," the press officer I spoke to reasoned, "it *is* the Uzbeks' bridge"), I dialed my father on the borrowed satellite phone of an Associated Press journalist, a call that cost seven dollars a minute. It was Christmas Eve in Michigan, and he and my stepmother were alone, probably waiting for my brother or me to call. He had no idea I was in Afghanistan, since I had more or less promised I was going to stay in Uzbekistan. My father picked up after one ring. Where was I? How was it going? His voice was edged with joy. "Dad," I said, "please listen because I don't have much time. I'm stuck in Afghanistan. The Uzbeks won't let us back into the country. I don't have any money. I may need you to make some calls. Did you hear me?" The link was quiet but for a faint, cold static. While I waited for him to answer I felt, out of habit, the hidden money belt I wore against my skin. Normally it held a papery, reassuring bulge. It now felt as insubstantial as a garter. "Dad?" "I heard you," he said quietly. At this, at hearing *him*, my eyes went hot. "I'm in trouble, I think." "Have they hurt you?" In a moment I went from boyishly sniveling to nearly laughing. How could I tell him that the people of Afghanistan were extremely kind? That, at least in terms of safety, things actually could not have gone better? That I was not in any immediate danger at all? How could I *then* explain that I was so frightened I was nearly shaking? "No one's hurt me, Dad. I'm just worried." He asked, "Are you speaking code? Tell me where you are." His panic, preserved perfectly after its journey through cloud and space and the digital guts of some tiny metal moon, beamed down and hit me with all the force of an actual voice. "Dad, I'm not a *captive*, I'm—" But he was gone. The line was silent, the satellite having glided into some nebula of link-terminating interference. I chose not to ponder the state in which my father would spend the remainder of his Christmas, though I later learned he spent it falling apart. And for a short while, at least, the unimaginable had become my life, not his. I was him, and he was me.

"And then I told that fucker, 'We need to do better. We have to get better—' "

"Dad," I said. The food on our plates had barely been touched, and the Nha Trang Sailing Club was rapidly filling up: in the wind were a dozen different perfumes and colognes. I no longer had any wish to be the poor American boy being browbeaten by his father. "Let's go back to the hotel."

He turned sullen, but there was shame in his eyes. He looked at his food. "I don't want to go back to the fuckin' hotel."

"Dad, come on. Let's go." I walked around to his side of the table and lifted him out of his chair. Holding his arm I walked him out front, paid for our meal, and booked us a cab back to our hotel. Outside its lobby was a surreal nocturne. A Western woman walked her pit bull past several loitering Vietnamese men, scooters were parked at every angle, and a pair of young women wearing "Tommy Jean" T-shirts attempted to earn some form of attention. I hurried my father past all of them. In the elevator (which was equipped with something called "an emergency elevator landing device," about which the less I knew the better) we did not speak. In the quiet, vacuumed-smelling hallway outside our rooms we did not say good night. He staggered off toward his door as though seasick; the last I saw of him he was struggling with his room key.

I sat on the hard edge of my bed for a long time, soaking in the weak-light loneliness peculiar to hotel rooms. After twenty minutes I scouted the minibar for something with which to wash down my useless antimalarial pills (my father had insisted we bring them) and found a tall slim can that contained something called "Bird's Nest." Its apparent active ingredients were "white fungus" and "nature." I returned the can to the minibar and walked back to the Nha Trang Sailing Club. I was not sure why, but it felt good to be outside, and I tried to tell myself the tears in my eyes were from the wind, which was blowing quite hard.

Query: *What was the Soviet Union actually attempting to accomplish in Vietnam?*

One characteristic of proxy wars is their tendency to erase questions of motivation on one side while horrendously complicating the same questions on the opposing side. A U.S. soldier had to work through the logical calisthenics of fighting the Vietnamese because the Vietnamese were Communist, which was necessary because Soviets and Chinamen were Communist, trying to take over the world, and using Vietnam as a staging ground. The average Vietnamese—who in John Kenneth Galbraith's words "understood the intervention of a seeming colonial power much better than they understood the difference between Communism and democracy"—had a far shorter psychic path to travel before pulling the trigger. ("We Vietnamese have a long tradition of heroism," a PAVN soldier in Duong Thu Huong's *Novel Without a Name* exults. "And now, on top of it, we're armed with the dialectical materialism of Marxist thought. Who can beat us?") In short, the proxy war the United States believed it was fighting was not the same independence war many Vietnamese believed they were fighting, wherein Communism was a weapon, not an end. The U.S. war was substitutive and abstract; the Vietnamese war direct and historically familiar. One was hard to justify dying for, the other far less so. This leads to one of the war's focal paradoxes: while most Vietnamese would not have agreed, the conflict that tore their nation apart really *was,* in important ways, a proxy war.

The nature of the Soviet Union—its stated fraternity with revolutionary movements around the world, its steadfast opposition to capitalism—led the United States to see the clouds' red lining wherever storms of insurrection gathered. Yet for years the Soviet Union only fitfully aided such movements. Stalin was too fatally inward-looking, Khrushchev too addled and inconsistent. Regardless, it seemed to many observers, not all of whom were Red Scare hysterics, that the Soviets were puppet-mastering every Communist movement, whether Greek, German, Persian, Filipino, Cuban, or Vietnamese. But inspiration and support were different properties. One of the singular brilliances of Communism is its adaptability. Marxist Communism was not Soviet Communism, which was not Chinese Communism, which was not Cuban Communism (even Castro locked horns with his Soviet sponsors), which was not Vietnamese Communism. Many have argued, with varying degrees of plausibility, that Vietnam's Communism, given its unique qualities, might have gone down a different road had not the binary involvement of the planet's most powerful nations excessively polarized the Vietnamese themselves.

The Cold War had a system of checks and balances made possible by the fact that most U.S. and Soviet decision makers understood that a direct military confrontation could destroy half the world. The clashes between the United States and the Soviet Union could thus take only two forms. The first form was political, cultural, Olympic. The second form was military, but only in places so peripheral to either nation's main interests that there was no chance for direct military confrontation. These boundaries were always more sensed than actively charted out. The times when this tacit policy was nearly voided, such as during the Cuban Missile Crisis, the results were alarming. Leaders of both nations knew that if one wanted to plunge one's nation directly into a peripheral conflict upon the greater canvas of the Cold War, the intervention would have to be short, relatively cheap, and above all successful. Despite the warnings of men such as George Ball, who believed that Vietnam offered the likelihood of being costly and unsuccessful, and the predictions of men such as Pham Van Dong, who said that "Americans don't like long, inconclusive wars—and this is going to be a long, inconclusive war," the leaders of the United States believed they could snatch victory from the jaws of defeat and transform a peripheral victory in South Vietnam into a beacon for all nations that sought shelter beneath an American umbrella of liberty. In the midst of America's long, costly failure in Vietnam, one understanding was that the Soviets cheered and aided the United States down its disgraced and chosen path. "Soviet policy, it turned out," Ilya V. Gaiduk writes in *The Soviet Union and the Viet-*

nam War, one of the only English-language histories available on the subject, "was not as straightforward and one-dimensional as Communist propaganda had tried to suggest."

For the United States, the war in Vietnam had three stages. The first (1965–1967) was fighting. The second (1967–1970) was fighting while negotiating. The third (1970–1972) was negotiating while fighting. Between these stages Soviet mediators often offered the United States the necessary political lubrication to move forward to the next, sometimes hindering attempts to negotiate but more often sincerely attempting to help—though, of course, for their own benefit. One might ask why, if they were so interested in negotiations, were the Soviets so fulsomely arming the North Vietnamese? As in the United States, the Soviet Union had its own hard-liners and reactionaries to contend with. The Soviets engaged in differently intended wartime activities in an attempt to cover all possible peacetime contingencies and secure a place for the Soviet Union in the future of a reunified Vietnam. Gaiduk, into whose hands fell a significant amount of Soviet archival material concerning Vietnam, believes that the USSR, however divided, had three goals in Vietnam. The first was that it would—within certain, carefully calibrated limits—provide military and financial aid to North Vietnam. The second was that it would not do anything to endanger détente with the United States (and would reexamine its Vietnam policy as tremors dictated). The third was that it would encourage Hanoi to consider a negotiated settlement, as the Soviets themselves worried endlessly about being pulled directly into the war and moreover believed the North Vietnamese would never win.

With these goals came various wartime stages of Soviet ambition. During the Khrushchev years the prevailing Soviet mood was "overcautiousness," in Gaiduk's words. From 1965 to 1970, the Soviet Union was alternately a garrulous spendthrift happy to be outpacing its rival China but troubled by its fellow superpower's growing anger. From 1970 to 1972, the Soviets were primarily diplomats. Following 1972, when the war no longer posed any danger of direct confrontation with the United States, the Soviets revived their earliest Indochinese ambitions. Such ambition went back many decades. The platform of the Indochinese

Communist Party, which was written with Moscow's guidance in the 1930s, held that Laos, Cambodia, and Vietnam should be linked together, and, in one scholar's words, envisioned "an Indochinese federation under Vietnamese guidance that would be similar to the Union of Soviet Socialist Republics." When, decades later, the time had come to fulfill this ambition, the world dialectic was far more complicated than the Comintern had ever dreamed.

As the likelihood of an American war in Vietnam increased in the early 1960s, many Soviet diplomats were pushed to the verge of panic. Virtually no Soviet agreement existed on the Indochina issue. This sentence of Gaiduk's begins to suggest some strange U.S.-Soviet parallelisms: "Soviet leaders had not yet settled on a course of policy. For months to come, the Soviets would improvise a policy toward the war while trying to measure their involvement in the conflict." Another parallel was ultimate and disastrously determinative: a terror of the People's Republic of China that often obscured the real nature of the war.

Nikita Khrushchev's impatience with the Vietnamese Communists did little to help Soviet fortunes in Vietnam. Despite his claim to support all "liberation wars and popular uprisings," Khrushchev had publicly advocated Vietnam's peaceful reunification. During his first meeting with the North Vietnamese in the early 1960s, Khrushchev said that a prerequisite for continued Soviet support was that the North Vietnamese tone down their revolutionary rhetoric and maintain an open mind about a negotiated settlement with the United States. The North Vietnamese regarded Khrushchev's proposition as insufficiently revolutionary. At the recent Ninth Plenum in Hanoi, they had concluded that armed struggle was the only solution to the situation in South Vietnam. Nevertheless, *Pravda* continued to publish articles headlined with sentiment such as "It Is Impossible to Overcome South Vietnam Patriots," and the Soviets still sent aid, including bundles of the one thing Vietnam's Communists needed most: American dollars.

In 1962, as Mao determined to pursue a more radical and ideologically pure path than the Soviets', Chinese aid to North Vietnam began to vastly outweigh that of the Soviets. Chinese ideologues ridiculed

Khrushchev for his "revisionism" (that is, his denunciation of Stalin) and promised their Vietnamese brothers support against American adventurism. Khrushchev, in turn, tried to impress upon his Asian comrades that the American "paper tiger" Mao spoke of had nuclear fangs. Many Vietnamese Communists jumped on the anti-Soviet bandwagon. The more pro-Soviet Ho Chi Minh—he once complained to a comrade that Mao was too willing to "stand on the mountaintop while the tigers fight"—saw his reticence about a Chinese role in Vietnam's future justified in 1964, when Mao said to a North Vietnamese official, "Your business is my business and my business is your business." This was shortly before China's Cultural Revolution—the chaos and violence of which would be too much even for the Maoist Truong Chinh—and Mao's clear implication greatly alarmed the Vietnamese.

This recondite state of affairs was rudely shattered in 1964, when the Soviet Union's Central Committee replaced Khrushchev with Leonid Brezhnev as first secretary and Alexei Kosygin as premier (Khrushchev had held both titles) one day before China exploded its first atom bomb. Brezhnev had taken personally the criticism the Soviet Union had received for its hitherto shy involvement in the Vietnam morass. As Gaiduk writes, "Moscow's failure to defend [North Vietnam] might make suspect its ability to protect such regimes as East Germany, Czechoslovakia, and Poland in a similar encounter with the West." This was of course exactly analogous to the Joint Chiefs' fear of what would happen if the United States failed to defend South Vietnam. The Soviets also hoped, as Gaiduk notes, to use Communist Vietnam as a place to base their support of other insurgencies in Malaysia and Thailand. More sensible Soviet policy makers weighed these presumed advantages against the suddenly real danger of accidentally starting World War III, and began pressing North Vietnam to use its influence with the NLF to come to some sort of agreement that would allow the United States a face-saving withdrawal.

After Khrushchev's removal, and the greater Soviet abandonment of his strategy of "peaceful coexistence" with the United States (a strategy hinged upon Khrushchev's belief that the Soviet system would triumph economically), the nature of Soviet support for the North Vietnamese quickly changed from largely propagandistic to overtly military. Brezhnev even opened the first NLF office in Moscow. More important, the USSR pledged to intervene if the United States brought the war into North Vietnam proper (a guarantee China had already made), though there is no evidence that any kind of coordinated response was ever officially drawn up. Kosygin, while visiting Hanoi shortly before the war's 1965 escalation, promised North Vietnam "all necessary assistance if aggressors dare encroach upon [North Vietnam's] independence and sovereignty." The North Vietnamese pledged in return to behave more respectfully toward the USSR. Some new breeze of militancy seemed to drift from Brezhnev's Kremlin each week, and in one speech the Soviet leader spoke of the willingness of Soviet citizens to travel to Vietnam to fight U.S. imperialism. Although no Soviet "volunteers" were ever sent to Vietnam (other than standard military advisers), the NLF in the war's early years repeatedly asked for volunteers from Socialist countries to fight alongside them. Hanoi, worried of expanding the war any further, was always quick to deny that the NLF needed any volunteers.

By now the Soviets worried less about American advisers in South Vietnam than they did about Chinese advisers in North Vietnam. This was a double swing door. In 1964, China's Zhou Enlai had warned the North Vietnamese that the more the Soviet presence grew in North Vietnam, the more Sino-Vietnamese relations would be endangered. (When Chinese students protested the war in front of the American Embassy in Moscow in March 1965, Soviet policemen beat them.) This competitiveness would prevent the Soviets and Chinese from coming to any sort of agreement about the use of Chinese soil as a conduit for Soviet arms into North Vietnam until the spring of 1965. The first major Soviet war package—radar equipment, rockets, MiG fighter planes (many of them twenty years old)—arrived in North Vietnam at the beginning of 1965, and by summer of the same year the first air defense sites were being built with Soviet help around Hanoi and Haiphong. By 1967, North Vietnam had 7,000 antiaircraft artillery guns. The following year, almost 3,000 Vietnamese—many of them NLF cadre members—were trained in Soviet military institutions. Also in 1965, a Soviet "special group," which apparently escaped the notice of U.S. intelligence, began working in North Vietnam and, perhaps, South Vietnam. Their duty was to find, analyze, and send back to Moscow parts of downed and destroyed American aircraft and weapons. More than seven hundred such "items" were recovered and shipped back to Moscow. Despite this cooperation, not until 1968 did the USSR's aid to North Vietnam surpass that of China, by which time it was floating the North half a billion dollars a year. China remained the NLF's chief supplier, especially when it came to hard currency, again paid in U.S. dollars. (It is worth noting that the United States spent $150 billion on South Vietnam—seven times as much as China spent in total on North Vietnam and the NLF and three times the wartime Soviet outlay.)

In 1967, the North Vietnamese realized that total military victory over the United States was unlikely and approached Moscow to help them figure out the Americans' intentions, though not to negotiate for them. The Soviets, in turn, put themselves forward to the United States as a "third party" able to negotiate a "commonsense solution" to the war in Vietnam, even as the war, abetted by Soviet support, reached new levels of intensity. Alexei Kosygin urged the U.S. diplomat Averell Harriman to tell President Johnson to work through Hanoi directly and negotiate. "The question of Vietnam will never be settled by force," Kosygin said. "You will only have more bloodshed and, in the end[,] the Vietnamese will finally liberate themselves from dependence on the U.S., as [have] people elsewhere. It would be a blot on the U.S. and the responsibility would inescapably lie on the president who, by force of circumstances, is responsible for all American actions. It seems to me that this would not be in his interest or in the interest of the American people." A Soviet diplomat in 1968 would be far blunter. The Soviets, the diplomat told his American counterpart, did not wish to cause a complete U.S. withdrawal from the region, despite their aid to North Vietnam: "Don't forget, we face a common enemy in Asia."

By the late 1960s, the United States continually looked to the Soviets for insight into Hanoi's inner workings; the Soviets often made up opinions at odds with North Vietnamese reality and other times simply shrugged. One reason for this was the scrambled messages the North

Vietnamese themselves were sending. They had publicly adopted a somewhat more open tone toward negotiations, but scholars now recognize these gestures as twenty-four-karat propaganda. At the end of 1966, for instance, Le Duan told Zhou Enlai that North Vietnam intended to end the war with "maximal advantages to itself." A year later Pham Van Dong told the Soviets, "The talks will begin when the Americans have inflicted a defeat on us or when we have inflicted a defeat on them. Everything will be resolved on the battlefield." When the Soviets pressed upon Dong the desirability of negotiations, Dong only grunted. As the Soviets massaged the North Vietnamese, they also worked on assuaging the United States, with Kosygin telling his U.S. counterpart that the war "was actually helping the Chinese in achieving their very worst designs." Upon receiving this message President Johnson bucked up. The result was a meeting between Kosygin (speaking for the North Vietnamese) and President Johnson (speaking for a rapidly decreasing percentage of Americans) in Glassboro, New Jersey, in June 1967. (How they arrived at using Glassboro as a meeting point is practically a book in itself.) These talks came closer to forcing a negotiated settlement than ever before, but the results were scuttled by Nixon and Kissinger, working secretly with President Thieu, on the eve of the 1968 U.S. presidential election.

According to Gaiduk, the main reason for this Soviet push was the USSR's fear "of a possible alliance between Washington and Beijing. . . . Thus Moscow's strategy included, at first glance, contradictory goals: to enlist American aid in solving the domestic problems of the Soviet Union [in the form of economic cooperation], to gain advantages over the United States in international competition, and to prevent the Americans from utilizing Soviet weaknesses." The North Vietnamese behaved in a manner similar to the Soviets', which is to say in a manner simultaneously cunning and completely baffling. After they finally agreed among themselves that a negotiated settlement to the war was probably inevitable, they began to plan the Tet Offensive. When the Tet Offensive came to pass, much of America's anger was directed toward the Soviets. What of all the willingness to negotiate the Soviets had spoken of? What the Americans did not know, and what the Soviets did not want to admit, was that the North Vietnamese kept from the Soviets most of their war plans, including those for the Tet Offensive.

The extent to which the Soviets were ever able to influence the fiercely and, at times, counterproductively willful North Vietnamese has been revealed over the years. "Russian diplomats today," Robert Templer writes, "scoff at the suggestion that they ever had much ideological control in Vietnam." Other histories find Soviet Foreign Minister Andrei Gromyko admitting he had "given up" trying to influence Hanoi and one Soviet adviser calling the North Vietnamese "a bunch of stubborn bastards." Gaiduk himself writes, "The Vietnamese Communists turned out to be unreliable and selfish allies who often caused difficulties for their Soviet comrades." Just as the United States habitually blamed Moscow for not being able to control the North Vietnamese, the Soviets despaired over the Americans' inability to control the South Vietnamese, particularly as negotiations grew closer to being fulfilled in 1969 and 1970. As the Saigon regime demanded more and more from the Americans while providing less and less incentive to provide, the North Vietnamese constantly badgered Moscow to send more missiles and equipment, even after Soviet advisers warned them to take better care with what they were given. (The North Vietnamese typically disregarded Soviet advice as to how to store weaponry, and often it was ruined. Other times North Vietnamese soldiers fired antiaircraft missiles without bothering to lock on to their targets, driving more than one Soviet military adviser to the vodka bottle.) In addition, Soviet citizens living in North Vietnam were often poorly treated and lived under constant surveillance. A nasty Soviet humiliation came when it was revealed that Ho Chi Minh had exchanged letters with President Nixon; the Soviets learned of this significant epistolary meeting by reading the newspaper. (Ho's letter was dated seven days before he died. As the historian A. J. Langguth writes, "Kissinger had shrugged off Ho's letter. . . . Since U.S. intelligence could provide no accurate information about Ho's last months, Nixon concluded that he had controlled the Politburo up to the minute he died. . . . [Nixon] hoped Ho's successors would understand that he was assuming they were not bound by Ho's response to his letter. But it was those successors who had written it.")

Averell Harriman told the Soviets in 1969 that the United States was "quite willing" to allow North Vietnam to remain Communist. All the

United States wanted was to allow the people of South Vietnam to choose their own government. The Soviets had no problem with this. China did. When the talks began in Paris that would ultimately remove the United States from the war, China refused to participate in or even acknowledge them and meanwhile worked to frustrate all Soviet aims in North Vietnam. Incidents of "agitation" by Chinese soldiers against Soviet border patrols increased sharply. Most infuriating to the North Vietnamese, China increased its aid to the NLF and publicly proclaimed that a compromise between the United States and North Vietnam would be a "serious failure and a large loss for the Vietnamese people." The Soviets accurately believed that China opposed the growing mood of negotiation because the longer the war in Vietnam went on, the greater the chance the United States and the Soviet Union would come into direct confrontation.

Richard Nixon and Henry Kissinger's policy of détente—which enabled the United States to ensure its wholly separate cooperation with the Soviet Union and China—complicated every party's already byzantine understanding of the war. As Kissinger himself argued, détente would allow economic assistance between the United States and the Soviet Union, encourage arms reduction, and provide further impetus for Soviet efforts to encourage the North Vietnamese to allow an "honorable" American withdrawal from Vietnam. The war in Vietnam thus began as a bloody division between the USSR and the United States and gradually became a bandage. But again the Soviets were trapped by their own pretension as the leader of the world's revolutionary movements. Nixon once stunned the Soviet ambassador by saying that U.S.-Soviet relations depended on the Soviets' willingness "to do something in Vietnam." Nixon and Kissinger could not believe, and Nixon went to his grave refusing to believe, that the Soviets simply could not bend North Vietnam to their will. Kissinger: "On about ten occasions in 1969, in my monthly meetings with [Soviet Ambassador to the United States Anatoly] Dobrynin I tried to enlist Soviet cooperation to help end the war in Vietnam. Dobrynin was always evasive. He denied that the Soviet Union had any interest in continuing the war . . . [but] he never came up with a concrete proposal to end the war." There was little Dobrynin could propose, much less do. As one Soviet report summed up North Vietnam's position: "[D]o not spoil or aggravate relations with the Soviet Union, but do not draw closer to it with complete confidence." It is hard to believe that Nixon and Kissinger could not understand the limitations of Soviet influence as they repeatedly wandered in the same frustrating circles with South Vietnam's President Thieu.

As Nixon and Kissinger's triangulation policy of détente took shape in the early 1970s, all affected parties worked to spin its results to their advantage. The KGB attempted to create problems between the United States and China by simultaneously feeding damaging information to both nations' intelligence services. When the Chinese politely asked for approval to meet with Nixon in Beijing, the North Vietnamese refused to give it. China went forward anyway. The North Vietnamese, already ninjas in their own form of triangulation, responded to U.S. overtures to the Soviets and Chinese by launching the Easter Offensive of 1972, which occurred on the eve of the U.S.-Soviet summit and one month after the U.S.-China summit. North Vietnam's first hope was that the offensive would cause a break in the growing friendliness between the United States and its Communist adversaries. Its second hope was that the offensive would succeed in gaining North Vietnam a clear military advantage, since it was obvious that the closer the United States drew to the Soviets and the Chinese, the quicker North Vietnam would be forced to the negotiation table. They nearly succeeded in the first and failed badly in the second.

"From the outset," Gaiduk writes, "Washington blamed the Soviet Union for the North Vietnamese offensive. Moscow had provided Hanoi with the bulk of its military aid and knew of North Vietnamese plans without trying to dissuade its friends from such a move." The Soviets countered that many of the weapons the North Vietnamese used had been hoarded for two years, and in any case the North Vietnamese were so poorly trained in using them that much of the offensive had floundered. The Soviets also argued that the offensive had been encouraged by China in order to drive a wedge between the Soviets and the Americans. All of this was true, but Nixon and Kissinger were unmoved.

The 1972 U.S.-Soviet summit was denounced by the North Viet-

namese, as they were fully aware that the major purpose of the summit
was to force Hanoi to agree to the negotiations that for three years they
had disingenuously claimed they were willing to take part in. Hanoi still
resisted the Soviets' efforts—until its leaders finally realized, many years
too late, that if the Americans were allowed to withdraw, the final overthrow of the Saigon regime, and the reunification of their nation, would
be much easier. The United States left Vietnam on March 23, 1973, and
twenty-five months later, despite China's fretful advice that North Vietnam show patience in moving into South Vietnam, Saigon fell to the
North Vietnamese army.

The 7,000 Soviet advisers who moved into a reunified Vietnam after
1975 quickly became known to the Vietnamese as "Americans without
dollars." Despite this unkind sobriquet, the Soviets would spend more in
Vietnam in the latter half of the 1970s—$1.5 billion in 1979 alone—
than they spent during the entire war, earning Vietnam a complete severance of Chinese aid and an eventual Chinese war. The level of Soviet
expenditure is especially impressive when one considers that of all the
Soviet aid given to Communist countries from 1964 to 1974, 50 percent
went to North Vietnam. (By 1991, Vietnam would owe the Soviet Union
more than $15 billion.) After the war the Soviets did considerable
rebuilding in Vietnam. The virtual entirety of this effort was rejected by
all but the most hardened Vietnamese Communists, as a song sung
furtively after the war suggests: "With anger, I hate the Viet Cong. / You
brought the elephant home / To walk upon our graves. / You took our
pretty country, / And sold it to the Soviets."

"For Moscow," Gaiduk writes, "the end of the Vietnam War marked a
new stage of its foreign policy. . . . It meant the chance of a more aggressive Soviet policy in Southeast Asia and in the third world. . . . Instead of
seeing the U.S. defeat in Indochina as a warning against similar adven-
tures of their own, Soviet leaders, blinded by Marxist-Leninist philosophy and by the conviction that the revolutionary trend of history was on
their side, believed that where imperialism had failed they would certainly succeed." This conviction—and what came to be an incidental
achievement of Soviet policy in Vietnam—formed the basis of the

"Brezhnev Doctrine," which had been used earlier to justify the 1968 Soviet invasion of Czechoslovakia when its Communist regime was in danger of falling. (The North Vietnamese praised the Soviet decision to invade Czechoslovakia, saying it had been done "for a noble purpose.") The Brezhnev Doctrine would be used again to justify the 1979 Soviet invasion of Afghanistan, when its one-year-old Communist government began to crumble against popular revolt after its attempts to, among other things, abolish marriage customs and land ownership, allow more education for girls and equality for women, forbid the veil, strictly curtail religious observance, and crush all dissidents.

Kosygin saw little good in the Soviet invasion, believing that Afghanistan (in language that eerily echoes that of the United States in the early years of the war in Vietnam) was a "complex political and international issue." When Soviet troops came under fire from Afghan militias and Islamist groups, the Soviets quickly accused the CIA, along with Pakistan and Saudi Arabia, of funding the mujahedeen. In fact, it was not until the Soviets made this accusation that the CIA had any real idea to do so. The Islamist revolution in Iran in 1979 gave the CIA an inkling of the power of political Islam, and the Soviet invasion of Afghanistan allowed the CIA its first chance to harness political Islam's energy for putative American benefit.

Despite the CIA's eagerness, the U.S. leadership was not sure how to respond to the Soviet invasion. As Steve Coll notes, National Security Adviser Zbigniew Brzezinski wrote President Jimmy Carter a memo that said, "We should not be too sanguine about Afghanistan becoming a Soviet Vietnam. The guerrillas are badly organized and poorly led. They have no sanctuary, no organized army, and no central government—all of which North Vietnam had." Nonetheless: "We should encourage the Chinese[!] to help the rebels also. We should concert with Islamic countries both in a propaganda campaign and in a covert action campaign to help the rebels." Brzezinski later wrote, "Our ultimate goal is the withdrawal of Soviet troops from Afghanistan. Even if this is not attainable, we should make Soviet involvement as costly as possible."

By 1984, the CIA estimated that the mujahedeen had killed 17,000 Soviet troops and controlled more than half the Afghan countryside.

The Soviets had lost 400 aircraft, 2,700 tanks, and 8,000 other vehicles. The CIA's director, William Casey, a fundamentalist Christian, had apparently not blanched at the idea of funding Islamist holy warriors. Casey believed that the "primary battlefield" between the Soviets and the United States was "in the countryside of the Third World" and that "Afghan freedom fighters" were the frontline forces in this new proxy struggle. Thus spake Casey: "Just as there is a classic formula for communist subversion and takeover, there also is a proven method of overthrowing repressive government that can be applied successfully in the Third World. . . . Far fewer people and weapons are needed to put a government on the defensive than are needed to protect it." Vo Nguyen Giap could not have said it better.

The Soviet response to the growing insurgency was, in one writer's words, "one of the most vicious, scorched-earth counterguerrilla campaigns in history. They carpet-bombed villages, destroyed irrigation systems, and systematically sowed millions of mines across huge swaths of productive farmland." They even dropped brightly colored ordnance upon the countryside to attract Afghan children. The massacre of civilians by Soviet troops in Afghanistan "like the one at My Lai were the norm rather than the aberration," according to one analyst. Forty percent of Afghanistan's population became refugees, and perhaps a million civilians died.

The immediate result, however, was a Soviet experience in Afghanistan that resembled much of what had plagued the United States in Vietnam. Just as the Chinese and Soviets had competed to fund Vietnam's anti-American insurgency, Saudi Arabia matched American funding of Afghanistan's anti-Soviet insurgency dollar for dollar. Just as the United States tired of attacks launched out of Laos and Cambodia, the Soviets tired of attacks launched out of Pakistan and in the mid-1980s basically threatened to invade Pakistan if the attacks did not stop. ("Please don't start a third world war," a CIA field officer begged one of his mujahedeen contacts.) Just as South Vietnam's leaders repeatedly incensed their U.S. sponsors, Nur Mohammed Taraki, the thuggish boss of the Afghan Communist Party, exasperated the Soviets, as did his successors: the psychotic Hafizullah Amin, the relatively suave Babrak Karmal, and the hugely self-absorbed Najib Ahmadzai (who later renamed himself Najibullah, or "Najib of God").

Mikhail Gorbachev, who upon taking office had authorized any means of force necessary to defeat the mujahedeen, said shortly before the first Soviet withdrawals began, "A million of our soldiers went through Afghanistan. And we will not be able to explain to our people why we did not complete it. We suffered such heavy losses! And what for?" In 1987, the Soviet foreign minister Eduard Shevardnadze asked Secretary of State George Shultz for help in containing the spread of "Islamic fundamentalism." In Steve Coll's words, "no high-level Reagan administration officials ever gave much thought to the issue. . . . The CIA and others in Washington discounted warnings from Soviet leadership about Islamic radicalism. The warnings were just a way to deflect attention from Soviet failings, American hard-liners decided."

In Vietnam, the Soviets funded an insurgency inspired by its system of political governance. In Afghanistan, the United States funded an insurgency opposed in most ways to American democracy. The Soviets lost their proxy war, as did the United States. There the similarities end. The Soviet Union collapsed. After years of suffering, Vietnam is emerging as a growingly prosperous, if not yet politically open, nation. The United States maintained its power and prestige. Afghanistan remained—and remains—one of the poorest countries in the world, and within its borders metastasized a terrorist training ground begun not by the Taliban, as is often supposed, but by the very insurgents the United States encouraged and armed. In 1996, one Afghan insurgent leader funded by U.S., Saudi, and Pakistani money, Abdul Rasul Sayyaf, invited Osama bin Laden to come to Afghanistan.

Considering the brigands and terrorists it willingly funded in Afghanistan, what did the United States really have to fear from Vietnam's Communists, other than their political inclination? In some ways the men of North Vietnam's Politburo were not all that different from, say, Richard Nixon or Ronald Reagan. They hated crime, criminals, social frivolousness, and pornography. They approved of the death penalty and exalted their military. They were at least equals in social conservatism, if leagues apart in their tolerance of dissent. There is a great lesson here, surely: the Soviet Union, for all its meddling in the world, never aided an insurgency in direct opposition to its political goals or philosophical beliefs. The Vietnamese may never have learned to speak Russian very well or appreciate the efforts of Soviet civic engineers to rebuild their cities, but they never tried to kill them.

VI

We had come to discover the ways in which my father's Vietnam no longer existed—ruminants in search of lost times and past selves. By now it was clear that few tangible ligaments joined the place in which my father had fought to the landscape upon which we now looked with something less than fresh interest. My father seemed exhausted. Short of a flaming unicorn galloping alongside the car, the nap he was fighting off by occasionally widening his eyes was going to overtake him. I wondered if it was the travel itself or all the simple, impossible demands I had made that he remember himself for me. Our trip, whatever the precise nature of its exhaustions, had been hard on him. Provided one was not a member of its Politburo, Vietnam was no country for old men— but then what country is?

I tried to take some notes, found I had nothing to say, and softly folded shut my notebook. What was there to say? To travel is to become part of a larger story, to find oneself reduced to a comma in a book whose last page one will never live to read. In a story as epically tragic as Vietnam's, there was something crushing about this realization. Our trip was nearly over, we were once again passengers in Truong's car, and I felt a thorny despair sink into me. Vietnam Vietnam Vietnam: could we really have been there?

No one had managed a sound for many miles. The longer it lasted, the more curdled and awful the silence became. Finally I thrust into it a vocal stirring spoon: "So! Dad. Any thoughts?"

His mouth dropped open as though to speak, but instead he sighed. He blinked in a recalibrating way. "What do you want me to say?"

I showed him my empty hands. My tape recorder was off. My note-book was in my backpack. "I just want to know if you had any thoughts."

"One. Which is that I have to go to the bathroom really bad."

"I mean the trip. It's getting to the end."

"It's gone quickly. But I've been enjoying it. Especially this."

"What?"

"This nice comfortable silence. I was almost asleep. But I really liked going back to Nha Trang. I was just thinking about that. I'm still upset that I couldn't go to that hospital."

"We are all fully aware of the disappointment you felt after your foiled visit to Nha Trang's hospital."

"But I was glad to see that it's still in use because it was a very nice hospital. Did you know it's only had three owners in forty years?"

"Can we never talk about Nha Trang's hospital again?"

"Only the Vietnamese would consider a hospital top secret."

"I can't think of more fitting final words about Nha Trang's hospital."

More, equally intolerable silence followed.

"So! What's your general feeling?"

"I'm just sad that Carolyn won't get to see any pictures of—"

"Not the fucking hospital! The trip, I mean. How do you feel about the trip?"

"This trip?"

"No. Your trip to Nha Trang's hospital. *Yes,* this trip."

He looked out his window, his chin held high as the sun shined hard on his face. An indistinct green world hurtled past his profile. "Well, I think it's just been great. The two of us being together, getting to know each other in a new way. Arguing politics and philosophy and . . ." He leaned forward. "Tommy, look at this. I think that's all tea farming."

We were drifting through a southeastern corner of the Central High-lands, on our way to the city of Da Lat, and enjoying some of the first rolling, open country we had seen anywhere in Vietnam. Much of it looked like a green-and-brown quilt of tea and coffee farms. Beyond these farms were huge stony mountains, their bases edged with teak and mahogany forests and their tops as starkly empty as volcanic islands. After a while, the farms disappeared and were replaced with lichen green

valleys across which roamed several hundred sheep. Much of the Highlands had been long closed to foreigners due to the fact that many of the
Communist regime's reeducation camps had been located here. A good
deal of the unrest that continued to exist in contemporary Vietnam had
its home in the Central Highlands as well. As recently as the late 1980s,
the Highlands gave birth to a speedily crushed attempt to overthrow the
Vietnamese government. This putsch was sponsored by some former
South Vietnamese military officers and aided by some of the region's
minority-group guerrillas. Few discussed this today, and those Western
journalists who attempted to explore Highlands unrest were often told
to leave it alone or suffer deportation.

We began our way up a twisty series of roads to Da Lat, Truong occasionally swerving around a few bone white boulders that had apparently
tumbled down the mountainside. As we ascended it was getting cooler by
the foot, the tangles of jungle becoming more orderly rows of evergreen
forest, and many of the people we passed on the road where wearing
bright, blankety garments that amounted to the closest winter-clothing
equivalent the southern half of Vietnam had. From up here the shadowy
green valleys below looked even wilder and richer than they had as we
passed through them.

Hien was offering little tour-guidery. When my father asked Hien if
the Catholic churches we had passed by on the way here were founded
by those who had fled the North after the Geneva Accords, he said,
uncharacteristically, "Yeah." His cell phone rang. He spoke for a few
minutes and hung up.

"Good news or bad news?" my father wanted to know.

"Yeah," Hien said.

"Are those tea or mango plants down there?"

"Uh-huh."

My father turned to me. "What kind of trees are those, do you think?"

"I am sure I have no idea."

"God. Look at that."

I looked. Layers upon layers of pine trees growing above dense green
bushes blistered with tiny red fractals of poinsettia. In many places the
soil was exposed and rust-colored and as hard-looking as clay. "How
does anything grow out of that?" I wondered.

"Are you kidding? That's great soil. Everything grows in it. You could spread out a little patch on the moon and you'd have a palm tree sprouting out of it in a few hours. I'd love to have some of this soil back home."

My father had, since I moved away from Michigan a decade ago, developed an alarmingly consuming tree-planting fetish. Related to that was his ongoing Final Solution against the squirrel—in particular the squirrels that ransacked the bird feeders he hung from the boughs of his more successful trees. Occasionally, while we spoke on the phone, I would hear my father say, "Oh, hold on a second," put down the receiver, and, a few moments later, the crack of a .22, followed by his return to our conversation as though nothing had happened.

"How come you like planting trees so much?"

He smiled as though overcome by some near-erotic reverie concerning saplings and watering cans. "I love to watch them grow. It gives me a great deal of satisfaction. My wife thinks I'm slightly off my rocker, of course. I don't know. It's nice to grow things."

We were now on a level, straight road majestically colonnaded by some of the most massive pines I had ever seen. And there, fixed in the distant emerald lap of several surrounding mountains, was Da Lat. Nearly every leader of South Vietnam, from Bao Dai to Ngo Dinh Diem to Nguyen Khanh to Nguyen Van Thieu, had weekend villas in Da Lat (Bao Dai's was now a tourist attraction), and with its plenitude of nearby waterfalls and lakes—only in Da Lat could one drink from the tap in Vietnam—the city was today the most popular honeymoon spot in the country's southern half. During the war Da Lat was not touched until the final weeks, and on April 3, 1975, Da Lat's people made what has been described as "their own accommodations" with the Communists, who entered the city and instantly put an end to ARVN looting. (Hours before the Communists arrived, Da Lat's CIA station helped dismantle the city's small nuclear reactor, which had been built by the United States in the mid-1960s.) But to say Da Lat was largely unaffected by the war did not mean it knew nothing of the war. An ARVN military academy had been located here, as had an NLF villa for tired, vacation-needing guerrillas. Both sides were aware of the other, but there is no record that any of them ever exchanged anything but dark glances in the market.

Once known as Little Paris, Da Lat was Vietnam's most Gallic city, as its red-and-white Eiffel Tower replica alone suggested. Developed by French colonialists in the late nineteenth century and once intended to serve as the capital of French Cochin China, Da Lat was less a city than a postcard template. Across its gorgeous central lake floated a dozen pairs of lovers in swan-shaped boats. There were cable cars, massive private gardens in the middle of town, row upon layered row of orange and white and yellow villas, hilltop palaces perimetered by pine. Upon entering the city we saw our first Vietnamese joggers, and within the light (by Vietnamese standards) traffic weaved numerous Ford SUVs. Young Vietnamese men with long hair and tattoos walked beside Vietnamese girls with dyed-blond hair. (A large percentage of Vietnam's counterculture—poets, painters, musicians, and various quidnuncs—made its home in Da Lat.) The old moss- and stucco-covered French mansions looked dingy in the overcast light, but then the sun glowed against their shingled roofs and it was 1920 and I could almost see the mustached, pocket-watched Frenchmen on their way to the café and opium den. The horse-and-buggy Xing signs seemed absurd overkill upon an already too-magical veneer.

We had absolutely nothing to do in Da Lat. Read, eat, sleep, and, tomorrow, go back to Saigon. Then, the day after next, my father would leave for home, though I would remain in Vietnam for an additional ten days. While Truong pointed out to Hien a young woman's notably striking backside, I asked my father, "What's your single happiest, most vivid memory of Vietnam?"

His answer was instant. "Leaving."

"Really?"

"Going home, yeah. Of course."

"What was that like?"

He moved a flat hand past his eyes. "Relief. I was done."

"You'd lived. You made it."

"Yeah, and it was just . . . it was just *good*."

"Did you think you'd ever come back?"

He was quiet for a while. "Yeah, I think I probably did. Before getting on my plane home I probably said to someone, 'I'd like to come back here someday, revisit all the places.' I imagine whomever I said that to probably then knocked out my teeth. Though I never, in my wildest dreams, thought I'd be here with you, Tommy, my second son. And for once you have not been an asshole. I'm totally impressed, by the way."

"Thank you. So would you recommend coming back to all veterans of the war?"

His head shook sternly. "No. Absolutely not."

This surprised me. "Why?"

"Because many of them have no desire to ever see this place again. Before I came I told a few vets back home I was on my way to Vietnam, and almost all of them said, 'Why the hell do you want to see that place again?' "

"Really."

" 'I'll never go there again, not ever. I hated it. Why should I go back to something I hate?' "

My face twisted up. "Assholes. Small-town, ignorant, cow-raping assho—"

"Be kinder, my son. Keep in mind a number of them almost bought it here or had friends of theirs buy it here. Why do you think a guy who has nothing but hatred for what this place represents to him should come back? What good would it do?"

"Because they might see that it's a different place now. They might replace the place that exists in their minds with something better, something healthy. That's how you kill a ghost. You replace it with what's real."

"That's very easy to say when you're not the haunted one."

We were stopped at an intersection. No fewer than three wedding processions were either driving across the intersection or waiting to. "I like it here," my father said, watching one of the processions pass. "This is a really nice little town."

"The untouched jewel of Vietnam," I said mildly.

"No," he said. "The South Vietnamese had it at one point. They had their military academy here or something."

"I know. It was for ARVN rangers."

My father was quiet a moment. "Rangers, huh? Well. I imagine the difficult surroundings of Da Lat really drove into their hearts a hardness and a fury." Then he laughed.

"Why, Father. I think I hear some forgiveness in your voice."

"I've forgiven everyone. Including myself."

"What do you feel you need to forgive yourself for?"

He laughed again. He also never answered me.

The next day, back in Saigon, I walked alone through warm rain down Nam Ky Khoi Nghia Street. I was on my way to the War Remnants Museum, which I was unable to interest my father in visiting with me. The museum's previous name, the Museum of Chinese and American War Crimes, best suggests why. He had opted instead for a daylong nap in order to prepare his circadian machinery for its planet-spanning journey the following night. For me it had already been a long day. We had arrived from Da Lat early, and I had spent the morning's remainder wandering Saigon's Chinatown, where I had allowed myself to be swindled by a little boy I paid to be shown where Ngo Dinh Diem had been captured, even though he had no idea who Ngo Dinh Diem was. I then visited the Ho Chi Minh Museum, found my way to Ham Nghi Street (named for the thirteen-year-old king of Vietnam who abandoned his throne to fight the French as a guerrilla in the 1880s), turned onto Le Loi Street (named for the patriot who defeated the Chinese), and recalled the journalist who told Frances FitzGerald during the war, "I finally realized we'd never win this war when I noticed that all of the streets in Saigon were named after Vietnamese heroes who fought against foreign invaders."

At the park-hemmed dead-end intersection of Le Duan and Nam Ky Khoi Nghia I bought a coconut from a conical-hatted vendor, watched her lop off its crown with a small machete and then dunk into the hole a straw. I stood drinking the sweet, artery-befouling milk before the former Presidential Palace, currently Reunification Palace. Long, splendidly terraced, and mostly eggshell-colored, the palace stood about one hundred yards back from the gate. It had been built on the grounds of a mansion belonging to a former French governor-general of Indochina, which may be one reason why the Saigon regime had such difficulty convincing the Vietnamese of its nationalist legitimacy. The local legend held that everything inside the palace was left the way it had been when President Minh capitulated in 1975, but that seemed unlikely. However, the essential point stood. This was one of the grandest modern structures in all of Vietnam, and the Communists were wise to let it serve as an unused symbol of everything they were overthrowing. Compared with this palace, Ho Chi Minh's living quarters in Hanoi were far less ostentatious. In his biographer's words, Ho Chi Minh's residence amounted to "a small stilt house on the grounds of the presidential palace, just a few yards away from the gardener's cottage he had [formerly] occupied. Built at the Party's order in the simple style of the houses of the mountain minorities settled in the Viet Bac, it served as his main office and residence for the remainder of his life." How much time Ho actually spent in his stilt house is debated, but as one Vietnamese told the writer William Broyles, Jr., in the early 1980s, "The people could see how Ho lived, that pure simplicity, and they saw how Diem and Thieu lived. They saw how our officers bought their commands, how they sold off their military supplies on the black market, how they kept mistresses and Swiss bank accounts. The people weren't blind."

But what was their eyesight like today? Coming into town this morning, I had noticed on the edge of Saigon a large Ford Motor billboard: "The first automobile in the world." Before becoming secretary of defense, of course, Robert McNamara had been the president of Ford Motor—and now there was a Ford factory in Hanoi. Hoa Lo Prison, also known as the Hanoi Hilton, where U.S. pilots had been held and often tortured during the war, was today a deluxe office-and-apartment complex. Today Hanoi really *did* have a Hilton—called, naturally, the Hanoi Hilton. What was strange was how little comment such ironies elicited from the Vietnamese themselves. Hien, for instance, saw nothing even slightly funny about an actual Hanoi Hilton or a billboard advertising the company once helmed by a man who, in living memory, had ordered bombs dropped on Vietnam. This strange Vietnamese mixture of obliviousness and shamelessness was not new. At one point during the war, Saigon's Ministry of Tourism had sponsored a campaign that attempted to lure unarmed visitors to Vietnam. The slogan? "Vietnam—you've heard about it, now come see it."

After I crossed a few streets the War Remnants Museum came into view. Outside its large front gate tourists beat off the children selling pirated copies of Robert McNamara's *In Retrospect* and Stanley Karnow's *Vietnam* and ignored the whiskered and ball-capped cyclo drivers looking to pedal them to their next destination. Professional Vietnamese tour guides shooed away the freelancers attempting to shanghai their clients. As I approached to buy my ticket, at least five languages were being spoken around me. It felt like being on the jabbering floor of a stock market apportioning out shares of historical guilt that everyone was eager to sell and buy but no one seemed interested in examining too closely. Why do they come to this place? I wondered, handing over my ticket to the gatekeeper. I then caught the stupidity of the thought. Of course, *my* motives were different. It occurred to me that "*My* Motives Were Different" would not be an unfitting slogan for the War Remnants Museum.

The museum is housed in the former U.S. Information Services building. Before that, I had heard, it was a pagoda. Just inside the entrance, in the shade of a large bamboo tree, an older woman sold Happydent gum and cans of Coke and Lipton and water bottles across from a mural that read "Solidarity for a Better World" above an image of a fist smashing a bomb. On these grounds were six separate exhibit rooms, all differently themed. In the central courtyard, around which the rooms were angled, an assemblage of military hardware hulked impotently. Most of it was American. I started my tour by wandering around these relics. All had a small "No Climbing" sign affixed to them. The Huey helicopter, M48 tank, and 105 mm artillery gun had apparently been repainted a Soviet gray and had an old-news, rained-on veneer. Despite its sign, two children were hanging from the barrel of the 175 mm howitzer, and several Asian tourists were photographing, for some reason, the collection's military-grade bulldozer, known as a Rome plow. The most sinister-looking vehicle, as low to the ground and predation-minded as a manta ray, was the M132 A1 flamethrowing tank, which was forcefully denounced on an accompanying plaque. Despite how large and forbidding these vehicles and armaments were, up close they seemed somehow cheap and fragile. A waste of metal. The swinging children had the right idea: these death machines made a splendid playground. Finally I came to the CBU bomb. The plaque said: "In 1975 CBU's were dorpped [*sic*] for the last time in Vietnam." This was at Xuan Loc, as the war ended. The CBU was a tall, missilelike bomb, topped with a little—in fact, positively adorable—metal nipple. Gazing upon this fléchette-throwing cutie was somehow emotionally radioactive. Its plaque also indicated that Americans had "dorpped" the CBU, when, of course, it had been a Vietnamese-on-Vietnamese atrocity.

I started with room six, the theme of which was "The World Supports Vietnam in Its Resistance." Most of the illustrative photos were either a Xerox or a Xerox of a Xerox, and errors of spelling and fact were profligate. I walked past photos of the Kent State massacre, the My Lai heroes Hugh Thompson and Lance Colburn (how exactly they had supported Vietnam in its resistance was left unelucidated), and Michael Heck, a B-52 pilot who had refused to bomb North Vietnam. Under glass were photocopies of letters Ho had written to his American OSS handlers, as well as a prominent display that showed Sergeant William Brown's medals, among them the Purple Heart, the Bronze Star, and the Silver Star, which Brown himself had sent here in 1990, along with this dedication: "To the People of a United Vietnam. I was wrong. I am sorry."

I walked along, my Nikes producing some of the only silent footsteps in the room, most of its other occupants swishing along the gritty floor in their sandals. A newer-looking wall of photos highlighted the improved relations between Vietnam and the United States: Robert McNamara talking happily with General Giap, John Kerry standing beside Do Muoi (sometimes called the anti-Gorbachev of Vietnam). At the room's opposite end there was a photo of Fidel Castro holding up an NLF flag, and nearby were the placards of worldly support the room promised. From the USSR: RUKI PROCH OT VIETNAMA! From East Germany: SOLIDARITÄT MIT VIETNAM. Finland's progressive movement pitched in with a protest poster featuring laughing-shot photos of McNamara, Kennedy, Johnson, and Nixon above a Vietnamese woman holding her dead baby. Walking out of room six, I noticed a small photo of Martin Luther King, Jr., who had turned against the war because of the naphthenic and palmitic acid compound known as napalm.

King's was not an unreasonable reaction to napalm, surely one of modern warfare's most horrendous weapons. The most infamous use of napalm in Vietnam occurred on June 8, 1972, when the photographer Huynh Cong Ut snapped a shot of a Vietnamese girl as she ran down Highway One with gobs of napalm still sticking to her flesh. (Not many are aware that the napalm in question was dropped by the South Vietnamese Air Force, not the U.S. Air Force; or that the North Vietnamese and NLF possessed napalm themselves and notoriously employed it against 250 inadequately Communist villagers at Dak Son in 1967.) Napalm—basically bathtub-chemistry gasoline gelatin that, when ignited, burns at 2,000 degrees Fahrenheit—was first tested on the Germans in World War II, but was used most effectively against bunkered Japanese during that conflict's ferocious island fighting. Its major manufacturer during the war in Vietnam became Dow Chemical of Midland, Michigan. Dow did not invent napalm, but the company took a tremendous amount of criticism for continuing to provide it to the military. During the napalm debates, people actually took issue with the assertion that napalm melted flesh. After all, napalm's apologists said, cooked turkeys' flesh is not melted. But then turkeys are not typically prepared at 2,000 degrees. Even within Dow there was a movement to stop making napalm. "If we're found wrong after the war," Dow's then-president said, "we'll be glad to be hung for it." Napalm is still used by the United States, despite the now well-documented psychological trauma it wreaks upon those who drop it. One U.S. pilot described to the writer Jonathan Shay how he had gone for his 7.62 mm machine guns, which were capable of firing several thousand rounds per minute, when he wanted to be more merciful: "How could you say bullets are fucking humanized? But they were. To see what napalm does—napalm was for *revenge.*" In *The Quiet American* a French pilot tells Fowler that he drops napalm according to his "moods." Revenge, moods: napalm was a weapon for when the call of Thanatos was particularly clear.

Room five announced how "The War Destroyed the North Vietnam" (Vietnam, I reflected, needed a Ministry of Proofreading) and offered a spooky reconstruction of a South Vietnamese jail, or rather the "Imprisonment system under the Ngo Dinh Diem and Nguyen Van Thieu Government," complete with the notorious "tiger cages" that left so many prisoners paralyzed from the waist down. I felt for the family whose house was next door to the museum; their windows looked down into this ghastly simulacrum for a year-round view of barbed wire, gravel flooring, and a guillotine. I hurried through to room four, which was the "Vestige of War Crimes Building," as well as the most crowded yet. Visitors milled about it looking slapped and broken. Even the children who moments ago had been monkeying around on the howitzer were reduced to staring silently at their shoes before their parents came to their senses and rushed them out.

It began tamely enough: a few photos of U.S. soldiers torturing their captives, parading insurgents on leashes, or dragging corpses behind armored personnel carriers. Then came one's graduation to photos of U.S. soldiers pouring water into Vietnamese men's ears, a snapshot of four grinning Special Forces commandos squatting around the headless corpses of two dead Vietnamese. One of the commandos proprietarily holds the muddy, battered heads by their hair. Beneath the photo was this caption, taken from its source text, which was apparently a U.S. soldier's memoir: "The above picture shows exactly what the brass want you to do in the Nam. The reason for printing the picture is not to put down G.I.'s but rather to illustrate the fact that the Army can really fuck over your mind if you let it." Even more clearly destined for the bad-dream slide show was a large photo of a U.S. soldier holding up—a bit as though it were a lake-fished pike—the head, left shoulder, and one half of the left arm of a blown-apart Vietnamese. The museum's caption read, "The American soldier laughed satisfactorily while carrying a part of the body of a liberation soldier." The soldier was hardly laughing. He instead looked terribly awed. At what point, I wondered, does one think to photograph such a thing, much less offer oneself up as the photo's shared subject? But I had had my answer a moment before. This photographer and soldier had obviously let the Army fuck over their minds.

Believing the worst was over, I began to relax. Then I came to a series of color photos: a woman with a napalm-blackened hand, another woman with her jaw melted to her chest, a baby so warped and deformed it looked like a funhouse-mirror reflection of a baby, and another baby—still alive and lovingly held by his mother—who had a normal baby face and healthily fleshy arms but whose remaining body resembled that of a piglet. Someone beside me laughed in shock. I turned a corner to find a large glass jar filled with flaxen formaldehyde. Inside floated a two-headed baby with gray mutant skin, the features of both pickled faces mashed into a moue of identical agony. Seconds later I stepped outside into the still lightly falling rain and wished my father were here with me, not because I wanted him to have seen any of this, or to have wished this guilt upon him, but rather because I missed him, and loved him, and it felt good to have someone you loved beside you when abstractions such as war or conflict or struggle stood embodied as piglet babies and chopped-off heads.

I backtracked to room one, the "Historic Truths" exhibit, which was largely concerned with the war's military history. Right off the entrance was a hardcover copy of Robert McNamara's *In Retrospect* alongside its Vietnamese translation, *Nhin Lai Qua Khu* (literally, "Look again at the past"). The remainder of the room featured massive hand-painted murals that showed the distribution of U.S. forces around Vietnam, timetables of the war's development, and casualty enumerations. Many of the statistics and assertions here were flatly untrue, and I came across a young American man intent on sharing this fact with anyone who would listen. He was wearing a Chicago Cubs baseball hat, sunglasses, crisp new designer jeans. His T-shirt said DARTMOUTH RUGBY. He was my age, perhaps a little younger, solidly pudgy in a way that suggested recurrent encounters with weight lifting, and around him were his travel partners and several others, including a few Asians. He was patiently and knowledgeably describing the ways in which this museum distorted the truth of the war, how it failed to include the many "documented instances" of Communist atrocities. His face was calm, though his voice was quite loud. He had staked out a corner of room one and walked along the wall and pointed out to his audience the analytical inadequacy of many photos' captions. Most of the museumgoers were giving the man's little corner of historical veracity a wide berth, but I stood and listened to him. After a while it seemed he was talking directly to me. I then realized he *was* talking directly to me, because everyone else had left.

Finally, shaking his head, he told me, "It just makes me mad." A young Asian woman—his girlfriend—came over to fetch him, speaking in Vietnamese. He answered her in same, and they walked off, her hand unsalaciously finding his backside.

The final room I visited—narrower and as a consequence even more crowded than the others—was filled with a sweat-and-sawdust sauna smell. This was the room dedicated to the most derided, lionized, and argued-over army to descend upon Vietnam: its journalists. Near the end of the war, General Creighton Abrams said this of Vietnam's journalists: "They're all a bunch of shits." In the jingoistic film *Hamburger Hill*, an American soldier tells a journalist, "At least they [the North Vietnamese] take sides. You just take pictures." Contempt for journalists comes up repeatedly in the war's combat memoirs as well. "Not everybody fighting is in the newspapers," one such memoirist is told. "You'll never see a reporter up there. It's too rough for them." During a 1965 visit to South Vietnam, Senator Barry Goldwater referred to the "pansy press. . . . No guts, no guts. I wish they'd let me have my way out here. There wouldn't be a gook or a fucking reporter left in six months. . . . You're nothing but a bunch of yellow bastards."

The room's first displayed photo was perhaps the most haunting of the entire war: Larry Burrows's *Reaching Out, Battle for Hill 484, DMZ, 1966*. In it, a head-bandaged black soldier reaches out for his white friend, who is covered in mud and, despite his peacefulness, looks as though he is either dying or already dead. The black soldier is being held back from his lunge; it appears as though he was simply walking by when he noticed his wounded friend sitting in filth. Despite—or because of—its beauty, there is something painterly about Burrows's photo, almost staged. It has been described as a photo about one man attempting to stop another from joining death. It has been described as a photo about friendship. It has been described as a photo about how war can, sometimes, erase all that divides us as human beings, even though, far more commonly, it separates us along identical lines.

Turning away from *Reaching Out, Battle for Hill 484, DMZ, 1966*, I found a display commemorating all the journalists who were killed in 1970 alone, when the ground war spread into Cambodia: Gilles Caron,

Roger Coine, Sean Flynn (Errol's son), Dana Stone, Tomoharu Ishii. This theme, sadly, held strong throughout much of the room. Many of the featured photographers, like Larry Burrows, were dead. Here was Robert J. Ellison's astounding photo of Khe Sanh's shell-struck ammunition dump exploding the moment he snapped his shutter. Ellison would die at Khe Sanh. Here was a display of Bernard Fall, killed on Highway One, and here was Sam Castan, a Brooklyn-born journalist who crossed the line from documentarian to participant when he helped five Army troops fight their way out of a PAVN ambush. Castan killed several enemy soldiers, his caption read, before being felled by a bullet to his brain. Charlie Chellapah's last photo was of one soldier holding another after the latter stepped on a claymore. The photo is close-focus, dark and silty. The caregiving soldier looks calm, as though he is confident he can save his friend's life. Right after Chellapah took the photo, all three were killed by another claymore. I stepped away from this image, a fan blowing sour air over me, to find the last photo of Dickey Chapelle (née Georgette Louise Meyer), a gender-bending correspondent from Shorewood, Wisconsin. She survived Iwo Jima but not Vietnam. Her "last photo" differed in that it was taken of her, not by her. She lies facedown in the mud while a priest performs her last rites. There is blood coming out of her ear. The man who took this photo, Chapelle's friend Henri Huet, who was born in Da Lat, was later killed covering combat. Here was Robert Capa's last photo. Capa, the most famous war correspondent in America, who survived D-Day and the Spanish Civil War, snapped his final photo of some Saigon regime soldiers trudging along a dike. Capa climbed the dike he had just photographed, perhaps to get a better shot. The land mine buried in the dike killed him. It was 1954. He was the first U.S. journalist to die chronicling the war.

The room's most moving and impressive display was the final list of every journalist—Vietnamese, French, Japanese, American, Australian— who had been killed in Vietnam. An angled, waist-high ledge provided a photo and short description of every slain reporter. Above the display was a large blow-up photo of Taizo Ichinose's camera, which had been ripped open by a bullet, though Ichinose himself survived the war. I read through each journalist's description, then stared at their photos.

So many of them twenty-five and thirty years old, so many of them smiling, so many of them good-looking. Or perhaps, since so many of them were photographers themselves, they knew how to be photographed. My heart grew small as the accumulated waste of it all bore upon its chambers. Though these men and women may have been admirable, they were not romantic. "Why, Monsieur Sully," U.S. Ambassador to South Vietnam Frederick Nolting once asked the French journalist François Sully, "do you always see the hole in the doughnut?" Sully answered, "Because, Monsieur l'Ambassadeur, there is a hole in the doughnut." Sully, whom Ngo Dinh Diem once banned from South Vietnam, died covering the botched ARVN invasion of Laos for *Newsweek*. Was proving there was a hole in the doughnut worth dying for? The smiling faces of men or women long dead were not easily read, particularly if they died doing something for which they believed their lives were worth risking.

A journalist's death is not a soldier's; their ends are differently charged. A soldier dies for causes, for ideologies, for ground, and for other soldiers. A journalist dies for a story, for an image, and for the conviction that politics could shape but had difficulty truly controlling. The soldier dies for ideas, but the journalist dies for one idea. The faces of the dead seemed to me far stranger, then: smiling up from their underworld at this country few of them could have imagined, this country they neither loved nor hated nor killed for, this country that refused to spare them.

The next afternoon, one final excursion with Truong and Hien took us by car on a forty-five-minute journey outside Saigon to the village of Ben Duoc, part of the battleground known as Cu Chi. I slept most of the way, awakening only near the end to see miles of rubber trees planted in paranormally straight rows—the sort of forest in which a sorcerer or some flute-playing, goat-legged little demigod might live. As Truong slowed to turn onto a gravel road, gangly bare-chested Vietnamese boys ran alongside us, then waved as we drew away. My father was quiet; in eight hours he would be on a plane heading home. This morning, over breakfast, he had gently tried to talk Hien out of taking us here, preferring instead an excursion to one of Saigon's Buddhist temples or perhaps its zoo. Hien had been adamant that Cu Chi was worth seeing, and when I betrayed a desire to visit it as well, my father relented. "If it's more goddamned glorification of the revolution," he had nevertheless whispered as we got moving, "I'm going home to reenlist."

In a dusty, empty parking lot we exited the car to hear a number of loud, distant, sudden sounds not unlike a procession of slammed-shut storm windows. A few moments later, another procession. Hien went to procure tickets while my father and Truong enjoyed a cigarette and talked things over in their improvised but apparently mutually comprehensible imaginary language. Within sight of the parking lot was a post office, a tiny hotel, tennis courts (tennis was once a hated colonialist pastime), and a merry-go-round with paint-chipped green and yellow and white horses. The forest all around us had a thin, struggling look to it, which was one consequence of the area's long history of resistance. For much of the previous century the surrounding countryside had been a series of rubber plantations, including one run by Michelin, a French company famous for the savagery with which it treated its Vietnamese workers. (According to Larry Heinemann, the U.S. Army had to pay Michelin $1,000 for every rubber tree it destroyed in the area.) This legacy no doubt explained some of the Cu Chi district's revolutionary fervor.

During the American War, the majority of this area was designated a free-fire zone, which meant that anyone in it was considered an enemy combatant. (The "enemy" part of that pitiless designation may not have been far from the truth. A few months before the Marines first arrived in Vietnam, the NLF was brazenly holding parades in the middle of Cu Chi City.) Thus Cu Chi district was napalmed, gassed, Agent Oranged and Whited, B-52'd, bulldozed, and otherwise completely razed. In their history of the Cu Chi battleground, Tom Mangold and John Penycate write that on "military maps, over what had been villages and plantations, [the Americans] printed—repeatedly and brutally—the word 'destroyed.' " But Cu Chi's resistance remained stubborn and, it sometimes seemed, mystically immortal.

A few miles away, near the village of Dong Du, the U.S. 25th Infantry

Division had built its base camp in 1966. (When the 25th arrived, Cu Chi was being clobbered with 180,000 shells a month.) The base was visited by Robert McNamara, who also stopped in at Cu Chi City, then a "showcase village" for the results of pacification. The Dong Du base, which housed 4,500 American soldiers and staff, ranked among Vietnam's more luxurious. Within its wire were a radio station, a football field, a mini–golf course, several lifeguard-staffed swimming pools, officers' and enlisted men's clubs. The men of the 25th Infantry were also privy to an extensive basewide prostitution ring that naturally doubled as an NLF information-gathering service. Every Vietnamese barber employed by the 25th was also an NLF spy.

After the 25th had completed its base, no one could figure out why it kept suffering attack, especially given the Army's apparent success at pacifying the surrounding area. For months the 25th's helicopters were blown up, its food stolen, its men garroted in bed, yet there never seemed to be a traceable perimeter breach. (One horrific raid resulted in the destruction of fourteen CH-47 Chinooks and the deaths of thirty-eight U.S. soldiers—and the escape of every one of the thirteen attacking guerrillas.) Tobias Wolff, addressing the terror with which many U.S. soldiers regarded Vietnam's insurgents, writes of the legends that accumulated upon them, such as how "before battle they got stoned on some kind of special communist reefer that made them suicidally brave; that their tunnels were like cities and ran right under our bases; that they had tanks and helicopters; that American deserters were fighting on their side." Most of these legends were not true, or at least not often true. The insurgents did, however, use tunnels, and the 25th Infantry Division happened to have built its base right on top of one of the most extensive tunnel systems in Vietnam.

The laterite clay soil around the Cu Chi area made it perfect for tunnels, the digging of which was done by hand or with little basket scoops and spades. The soil was easy to grub into, eventually solidified into a surface as durable as concrete, yet still allowed for oxygen penetration. In addition, most of Cu Chi district was twenty meters above sea level, and the water table was far below what one normally encountered in soggy Vietnam. (This was part of what had made Dong Du so attractive to U.S. Army engineers.) The 25th, which came to jokingly call itself the Cu Chi National Guard, was among the only Army units to have been appropriately trained in guerrilla warfare tactics at the Special Asian Warfare Training and Oriental Center in Oahu, Hawaii, and their training covered nearly every NLF tactic—except tunnels. This was in spite of the fact that the Viet Minh had used tunnel warfare during Dien Bien Phu and that the ARVN, which had developed an efficient counter-tunnel strategy of pretending they did not exist, had warned the United States of the tunnels as early as 1963.

The first tunnel was discovered accidentally, when an American soldier sat upon a trapdoor's extruding nail. Believing the tunnel was merely a weapons cache or hidey-hole, the soldiers heaved into it a few red smoke grenades. Red smoke was shortly pouring out of every airhole and trapdoor for dozens of yards in every direction. The tunnels quickly became a plague upon U.S. forces. "We were just sittin' there," one soldier told Mangold and Penycate, "almost on top of [a trapdoor], when the friggin' thing pops open, out comes Charlie, throws two grenades, reaches down, grabs a carbine, sprays us, and before we can pick up our weapons, he's back in the ground and that goddamn trapdoor shuts over him." The trapdoors inside the 25th Infantry Division's base were eventually found and, at great pain, sealed off, and ultimately used as a training center for antitunnel tactics. The interconnected tunnels all over the base's perimeter, called by the NLF the "belt," continued to create havoc.

Today one surviving portion of the tunnel complex was home to a museum, and we entered one of its small schoolhouselike buildings to find a diorama that, in cutaway, illustrated an idealized tunnel system. Above ground, the dioramist had crafted crashed helicopters, burning tanks, scorched earth, and dying U.S. soldiers. Safely below ground, however, in an ant-farm gallery of winding tunnels and rooms, tiny plastic Vietnamese sat at desks, slept contentedly in hammocks, and crawled indefatigably through laterite clay passageways. The schoolhouse also contained a large situation map, said to be a replica of a U.S. military situation map. With differently colored blinking lights the map illustrated the tunnel system's astonishing breadth. In total the tunnels covered 150 miles. The tunnels could take one from the suburbs of Saigon to the border of Cambodia and back again, all without a glimpse of the sun.

"Holy shit," my father said, looking at the situation map with a drawn expression.

Hien's arms went proudly akimbo. He nodded. "Yes. It is very impressive."

"Holy shit," my father said again.

"You didn't know about the tunnels?" I asked him.

"No, I did. It's just that . . . holy shit."

I dragged a finger along one of the blinking-light rows. "I have to admit: it's sobering to me, and I didn't even fight here."

"It just goes to show you," my father said, as we walked outside.

"What's that?"

"The first law of war. If you can figure out a way to kill someone, they will figure out a way to avoid being killed. And they will probably do it quickly, in ways you cannot imagine."

We followed Hien along a packed-sand pathway to the jungle's entrance. Beside a tree-trunk-shaped garbage can, a smiling young Vietnamese man dressed in an NLF pith helmet and pocketed green fatigues waited for us. (The pith helmet—the revolutionary symbol of both the Viet Minh and the NLF—had originally been introduced to Vietnam by the French, and one could buy one here for a little over a dollar.) Coming toward us up the trail, a young Vietnamese woman led out of the jungle a small contingent of tourists. She too was wearing a pith helmet but black pajamas and a black-checked white scarf (the NLF's accouterment of choice). I looked back at my father to discern whether his emotional shock-support system could withstand being led around a former battleground by fit, attractive young Vietnamese dressed like the guerrillas who had once tried to kill him. Of course, he was smiling and saying "Hello! Hot day!" to the young woman and the tourists she led.

As we plunged into the forest, our young guerrilla guide described to us how the tunnels had been begun in French times. They were not a product of Communist Party directive but rather the result of a long process of trial and error. Their original inspiration was the Chinese,

who had used them in the resistance against the Japanese during World
War II. The extensive nature of Vietnam's tunnels, however, was unique.
The first tunnels were mostly family bomb shelters that, little by little,
were connected. Later, ingenious additions to tunnel methodology
included digging at zigzag angles to frustrate clear firing lines for any
intruders and sublevel trapdoors, sealed with wax or white rubber-tree
sap, that allowed for quick escape to other hidden tunnels and that also
largely foiled attempts to flood or gas the system. The tunnels contained
kitchens, primitive bathrooms, wells, surgical wards, schools, storage
rooms, map rooms, operations rooms, even factories for producing
homemade ordnance. Insurgents peddling rigged-up stationary bicycles
provided the tunnels with power, and thanks to a bamboo-pipe system
some had access to running water. Only a few Revolutionary Force
members knew the whole layout, and when visitors from the North
came to inspect the tunnels, they were flabbergasted. Finally our guide
described how the tunnels had been the staging area of the Tet Offensive—NLF guerrillas had even built a mock-up of the U.S. Embassy's
outer compound in Cu Chi's forest to prepare them for its assault—the
success of which drove "the enemy" (not, I noticed, the Americans) out
of Vietnam. My father's response to all this was to loose a long, quiet fart
as he listened.

We were taken to a clearing in the middle of Cu Chi's jungle, where a
thatch-roofed outdoor patio had been built. It was filled with rows of
empty foldout chairs. My father and I sat in the front row—Hien had
gone back to the car—while the guide moved to the weathered wooden
home entertainment center at the patio's front. I glanced around. From
one patio wall a portrait of Ho looked down on us, and above a silent
fan turned endlessly. Inside the home entertainment center were a JVC
television and a shiny silver Daewoo VCR. The guide hit "Play" and
gingerly stepped to the patio's wings. A documentary called *Cu Chi
Guerrillas* began. The film looked water-damaged, and the surf-king
electric-guitar soundtrack sounded like the outtakes of a particularly
LSD-damaged Brian Wilson recording session. I had to imagine that
much of the film's battlefield footage had been staged, for I could not
imagine that many NLF guerrillas had been laughing during combat.

The film's statements about the tunnels and the guerrillas who had used them ranged from true ("Bamboo traps used to hunt animals now were used to hunt U.S. enemy") to arguable ("No architect can design such a system") to interpretive ("But the merciless American bombs have wanted to kill this peaceful area so far away from America") to weird ("Like a crazy bunch of devils, the Americans fired into women, children, pots and pans, even Buddha statues") to demonstrably untrue ("The life of guerrillas in Cu Chi was wonderful"). It fairly unnerved one to watch a film that gloried in how a people "always found ways to kill Americans," but *Cu Chi Guerrillas* reached a height of tragically inadvertent comedy when it condemned the killing of Vietnamese women and children seconds before offering up a teenage girl who slaughtered sixteen Americans as an "American killer hero." Near the end of the film, a few Americans who had voiced grudging respect for the tunnels were greedily quoted. Here, I thought, was the colonial mind-set, served up in a steaming coconut shell: "We hate you! But are you impressed?" Meanwhile, another volley of slamming storm windows filled the air.

"Well," I said as the film ended, "it's not as if *Platoon* gives the roundest portrayal of the Vietnam side of things."

My father waved me off. "We make our movies, they do their thing. Who cares?"

As we stood we heard clapping and looked over at a group of Vietnamese men being led by their own tour guide. Many of these men were wearing military medals, and all were old enough to have been veterans of my father's war. They were clapping hard, clapping like Communists afraid to be the first to stop clapping. They were applauding, no doubt, their victory, their memories, their war. By 1971, only 6,000 of the 16,000 guerrillas operating out of the tunnels had survived. (Vo Van Kiet, Vietnam's prime minister until 1997, was one of them.) Cu Chi, the Iron Land, had done its part, and paid dearly for it. The district had been annihilated. "There were only about four guerrillas left in each village," one NLF fighter said, in describing to Mangold and Penycate life after the tunnels. "The guerrillas ate leaves to survive and washed their wounds in salted water." A war memorial not far from these tunnels contained a list of those who had been killed in the six-hundred-square-mile district of Cu Chi. It contained almost as many names as the Vietnam Veterans Memorial in Washington, D.C.

My father stood there observing the veterans, as did I. I believed the war was wrong. I believed it was badly fought. I even believed that PAVN's soldiers and the NLF's guerrillas were, in the main, more tenacious than the Americans they outfaced. But watching these applauding men caused my tar-pumping heart to crawl up into my throat. My toes dug into my shoes, and my palms tasted fingernail. One of the Vietnamese looked over at us, turned quickly away, and tugged on the shirtsleeve of the man nearest to him. That man also looked at us: two Americans, a father and his son, powerless guests in his land. The second man, too, stopped clapping. Both lowered their heads while all around them the clapping continued. My fists came undone, my ectopic heart slowly sank. My father, without a word, walked away while reaching into his pocket for his Chapstick. I waited for the men to look back at me—I wanted to somehow acknowledge their gesture—but they did not. When their group moved on, they kept their backs to me.

We left the patio and walked deeper into the sparse jungle. Once this had all been triple-canopy forest. Only in the last decade or so had the area's vegetation managed to bounce back from the biochemical caning it had absorbed during the war. Much of the district's water and soil was still considered damaged.

Followed by a pregnant dog with engorged black nipples hanging from her belly, we walked through the forest and attached ourselves to a larger tour group gathered around some of the scars of Cu Chi's destruction. These were B-52 craters, in which little grew but some crawling vegetation and a few twisty, double-trunked cashew trees. Most of the craters were twenty feet deep and a hundred feet in diameter and filled with muddy water. Some were big enough to hold a camper or a small house. The dog, I noticed, stayed away from them.

My father stared into one of the bigger holes, then let a whistle push through the greased blowhole formed by his pressed-together, freshly Chapsticked lips. "And that's what they do."

I looked at him. "Jesus, Dad. 'That's what they do'?"

He shrugged. "That's what they do."

I shook my head. "Sorry. Not good enough."

"What do you want me to say?"

"How about nothing."

As our group walked on, we passed air vents disguised as termite mounds, the ingeniousness of which was lavishly remarked upon. The talk was extinguished when we came to a mine-wrecked tank. Its cannon was sadly tilted toward the ground, its treads were gone, and its body was crumbling from rust. This tank's inhabitants, we learned, had all been killed. Vietnam's guerrillas were horrified by tanks and armored personnel carriers, and it was easy to understand why today the Vietnamese displayed the slain iron behemoths as trophies. (In 1966, the NLF actually managed to capture an American tank from the ARVN. They buried it near Cu Chi and used it as a command center. When the tank was discovered three years later, its batteries and radios were still working.) Thirty years on, however, it seemed slightly ghoulish.

We moved on down the path, wet composty leaves squishing beneath our feet. At one bend in the jungle a vortex of tiny birds swirled up from some bushes, strafing the path below with startled bombs of watery guano. After whistling for our attention, one of the Vietnamese guides removed his pith helmet and handed it to the other guide. With our curious eyes fastened upon him, the guide crouched, lifted from the jungle floor a tiny and completely hidden trapdoor, hopped inside, and after him slid shut the wooden slat, over which the other guide quickly scattered a few leaves with his foot. The whole demonstration lasted four or five seconds, and during it several in our group actually gasped. I pushed through the crowd and held over the trapdoor the spiral notebook in which I had been scribbling impressions. My notebook was slightly larger than the trapdoor. I stepped back as the tiny Vietnamese Morlock popped back out, smiling at the applause he had earned.

The guides quickly led us to tunnels we could enter for ourselves, all of which had been enlarged for plus-sized Westerners. Did I want to enter a tunnel? I did not. My father gamely ducked into one while I pondered what living in darkness, beneath the hard rain of ordnance, not only for days or weeks but *years,* must have been like. "The tunnels,"

William Broyles, Jr., remembered, "were a part of the special terror of Vietnam. In our minds the enemy wasn't another soldier, a man like us. He was mysterious and elusive—a vision from the unknown, a bogey-man with terrible powers rising up out of the earth. Vietnam was a nightmare war, the deepest childhood fears come true." But was the enemy in this nightmare war truly "everywhere all at once like spider cancer," in Michael Herr's typically lysergic words? "Phantoms, I thought," Philip Caputo wrote, "we're fighting phantoms." George Ball told President Johnson in 1965 that "I have grave doubts that any Western army can successfully fight Orientals in an Asian jungle," and during the war one Marine Corps colonel said, "The enemy always has the advantage of operating in the jungle."

This is actually extremely debatable. The Vietnamese were regarded by their American foes as being simultaneously sub- and superhuman; what they were not was equally human. But the Vietnamese as a people were hardly bioengineered for jungle war. Many NLF guerrillas were city kids as lost in the jungle as an American teenager from the Bronx. The guiding principle of the NLF was "Walk without a trace, talk without noise, cook without smoke," but these men and women were not ghosts. Many carried booklets that described which berries could be eaten, which leaves could be ground into medicine. The skin-burrowing chiggers in the tunnels alone were enough to drive many NLF guerrillas insane. When NFL guerrillas were captured, it was determined that fully 100 percent of them had some form of intestinal parasite. To become an NLF cadre, one had to take virtual oaths of poverty and chastity and promise to fight until one died. Yet despite this fanaticism they took boyishly mugging photos of one another and themselves, keepsakes that were often found on their bodies. They wrote poetry. Whenever they could they slept in villages, where they were most vulnerable, for the simple reason that villages were more comfortable. They sometimes held preemptive funerals for one another before going on dangerous missions.

The fact is that their supposedly superhuman powers were the product of endurance, intelligence, and adaptability. In many cases they were able to avoid being wiped out by aerial bombing due to the robotic sameness of U.S. operating procedure. NLF guerrillas calculated the number of minutes that typically passed between the overhead passage of an observation plane and the napalm-spilling monsters that followed it, and would hide underground while the jungle burned above them. They sent top secret messages north via bicycle-riding children. They entered contested areas in coffins during fake funerals or climbed into a coffin and rode with the corpse if the funeral was real. They shouted code to one another in cities by posing as singing drunks in the street. NLF village sentries—often little girls—wore one of three shirts while working in the field. If the shirt was brown, all was clear; white, U.S. or ARVN soldiers were about; black, clear out of the area. But they also made the same mistakes in combat as their putatively bungling American enemies: Johnnie Clark's combat memoir *Guns Up!* contains a mind-bending moment in which Clark realizes his squad is marching directly behind an enemy squad on night patrol, both having mistaken the other as friendlies. The NLF ran. They retreated. After its first encounter with a missile-spraying helicopter, an entire NLF company deserted. They were often commanded in such a rigid way that desertion was common. They accidentally shot one another. They ran out of rice. They were reduced to hunting apes for food or using ash as seasoning. They died of beriberi. They starved in jungles. An internal NLF memorandum captured by the CIA in 1967 listed seven reasons why the NLF was losing its footing. Reason one was that they were tired of the war. Yet so many of them kept on fighting.

When my father and his fellow tunnel rats resurfaced sweating and dirty and laughing (except for a woman who while underground had been hit in the face by a bat: she was crying, actually), we walked to something called the "Home-made Weapons Gallery." Set out on tables or crudely mounted, these awful, monstrous devices—made of wood and nail and vine and hook—seemed to beg one to believe they were not real. This was relatively easy, in that they looked like the fanciful props of some satanic dentist's office, a torture-chamber phantasmagoria. As weapons they ranged from crossbow traps (triggered by a tree-root tripwire; the arrows were often poisoned) to punji-stick-filled pit traps (feces were often smeared along the points to promote infection) to swinging traps (giant spiky balls that went sailing across a jungle path) to bamboo whips (taut-wire traps that snapped a huge fishhook across one's face) to balance traps (a boot-sized trapdoor above a bed of metal spikes) to crocodile-bite traps (the angled teeth of which were often poisoned) to door traps (a double trap that slapped two nail-covered wooden boards upon one's chest and thigh; you could stop one but not the other). A nearby hand-painted mural showed hapless U.S. soldiers falling into pits, being impaled on punji sticks, tripping grenade traps. I picked up a conical, three-pronged Bouncing Betty, perhaps the most feared of all NLF booby traps. It was usually set in the ground. Once it was tripped, a tiny explosion sent it no more than three feet into the air, whereupon the second, more terrible explosion occurred.

My father was standing next to me, looking at the Bouncing Betty as I turned it over in my troubled hands. "Were these things," I asked, "really as terrifying as—"

"Oh Jesus God yes," he said quickly. "I still sometimes have nightmares."

"Still?"

"Not often. But sometimes. I think booby traps were the most effective thing they used against us. Psychologically speaking, I mean." In World War II, 4 percent of U.S. casualties were caused by booby traps. In Vietnam that number was 28 percent. "But keep in mind," my father went on, "we used them against the VC too. We had a deadly little mine shaped like a leaf, as I recall. Our antipersonnel weapons were used very, very successfully sometimes."

" 'Antipersonnel.' All the terror is scrubbed right out, isn't it?"

"Yeah. Until one of them takes off your leg, your feet, your genitals. That's what so many guys worried about. Losing their nuts. That weapon you're holding right there was designed for that. It was designed to emasculate. And they filled them with whatever we dropped. Screws, scrap metal. Our own garbage was used against us. Coke-can grenades. The spoon in your mess kit could become a detonator."

"And parachute silk was used as hammocks or to store rice."

"Exactly. After a while—after way too long, I think—the order finally came down: Stop leaving your garbage around. Pick up after yourself. If someone lost a lighter, we'd spend half the morning crawling around looking for it."

That was not all. For the NLF, every U.S. bomb that was dropped but did not explode—a number thought to be between 1 and 5 percent—became a weapon. (U.S. ordnance also found other uses: in rural Vietnam one will often find that the village bell is an old hollowed-out artillery shell.) Howitzer shells were sometimes turned into pressure-activated traps and buried, or their explosives were salvaged for coconut-shell grenades and homemade mines. One NLF mine, the DH-5, detonated with the equivalent force of seventy twelve-gauge shotguns going off at once. The NLF also used more local materials. For instance, hornets. Actual hornets were trained to attack U.S. soldiers. In the tunnels, boxes of scorpions were rigged to pop open when the invader tripped a wire. Bamboo vipers were hung from tunnel ceilings or placed in shallow pits. In 1961, the counterinsurgency expert Colonel Edward Lansdale, fresh from a trip to Vietnam, stopped to see Robert McNamara in his office. After Lansdale dumped out onto McNamara's desk a collection of homemade NLF mines, booby-trap remnants, and captured insurgent clothing, McNamara asked what was the big idea. "Mister Secretary," Lansdale said, "I thought you ought to see how the enemies we're fighting in South Vietnam are armed. . . . They have old French weapons they've captured from our side; they make their own mortars and grenades and mines in the jungle. They wear black pajamas like these, and they make these rubber sandals they wear from truck tires. They're beating the shit out of us."

I put the Bouncing Betty down, filled with a vague impulse to wash my hands. "I read somewhere," I told my father, "that the NLF was so effective using booby traps because they knew which trails you'd take. They knew American soldiers would always take the easiest, driest-looking path."

"I am sorry to say," my father admitted, "that what you read is probably true."

"Well. That's kind of a problem, wouldn't you say?"

"I'm not arguing. But war is long and hard. At a certain point you begin to do the math. You divide how tired you are by your chances of hitting a booby trap, and you say, 'Fuck it,' and hump up a dangerous trail."

"But it seems to me the VC didn't do the same math. They seemed far more able to avoid your weapons than you did theirs."

My father fixed upon me a grinding-bicuspids stare. "Do you have any idea how many VC were killed? They lost half a million men in the war's first three years. You saw those craters back there. Every one of those holes is a mass grave."

For a moment I was quiet. Then: "I'm sorry about that, by the way."

"Sorry about what?"

"For being rude. At the crater."

"Squirt," he said. "I survived Vietnam. I think I can handle you."

For some reason, the Cu Chi Tunnels had a small zoo. While glumly looking at two caged and sore-covered mandrill baboons and thinking about how I could liberate them, I once again heard the curious slamming storm windows. It was far louder this time, the echoes were more saturated, and I collared my father and dragged him to the sounds' source. This was the "National Defense Sports Shooting Range"—located, somewhat ominously, directly across from the "Rice-Paper and Rice Wine House." Most of our heavily European group bypassed the shooting range, though many of the Asian tourists made a beeline for it. I followed them. Once I was inside the shooting range's perimeter, a scowling Vietnamese woman approached me. "What kind of gun you like?" she asked brusquely. It appeared that the National Defense Sports Shooting Range allowed its visitors to unload at several targets that, until recently, had been shaped like American-soldier silhouettes. "What kind of gun?" she asked again. Her complexion was nacreous, her nostrils flared.

"Tommy," my father said, coming up from behind me. "Let's go."

"No. I want to shoot."

"Tommy," my father said. "Come on. You're frankly the last person I want to be firing an automatic weapon if I'm anywhere within five miles of the target."

The storm windows slammed again, and I flinched. I looked over. At the range itself a Chinese girl in a coral blue shirt was shooting an M16, laughing between bursts, while her parents took pictures and her even younger siblings hopped about excitedly.

"What kind of guns can you shoot?" I asked the woman.

She rattled them off: AK-47, M16, M14, M3, M60, M1, Thompson, grease gun, sten gun. "One dollar, one bullet," she said. "Thirty dollars for magazine."

I looked back at my father.

"You're serious about this," he said. This was not a question.

"I just want to see what it's like."

"It's not like anything. It's what it is. You've fired shotguns. It's like that, except faster."

I handed the woman a fifty-dollar bill and walked after her to the weapons procurement counter.

"Tommy!" my father called after me.

I looked at the selection of weapons. Some were mounted on the wall, others simply propped against it. All were old and had a dim, ancient-chalkboard hue. The AK-47s looked strange and anonymous without their banana clips. The M14s were as long and unfussy as a hunting rifle. The M16's carrying handle gave it a vaguely briefcase air. Chests and buckets of ammunition were stacked behind the men and women sitting at the counter. Every tourist here, save for me, was Asian. As I deliberated, hundreds of dollars were being exchanged for handfuls of shiny, pointed bullets. My father was now beside me, still shaking his head. "So," I said to him, "what gun should I fire?"

He rubbed his face hard, revealing the split-second horror of skin pulled away from its facial musculature and his eye sockets' wet red ocular rims. When his hand fell away he stared at me. Suddenly he was a Marine. "What specifically are you looking to do?"

"I'm looking to shoot a cool gun. Did you carry an M16, or did you have a sidearm?"

"I carried a sidearm and a grease gun. And I usually rode with an M14 in the backseat. A very fine weapon. When we got to Chu Lai, they replaced our M14s with the M16, which I didn't like as much. So I managed to hold on to my M14."

"Why didn't you like the M16?"

"For rapid fire it was fine. The bullet was also very fast. But it wasn't real good for jungle fighting because the bullet was such a small caliber that if it hit anything—a leaf, anything—it would be deflected. The M14 round would go where you put it."

My father's rejection of the M16 (originally called the AR-15 and created by Colt) was not uncommon. Its surplus of plastic parts led many soldiers to call the weapon "my Mattel toy." In addition, the alpha generation of M16 was so "plagued by stoppages," one retired officer put it, that many units requested the reissue of the older, less defective M14. Broken, internally melted M16s were sometimes found upon the battlefields of Vietnam next to dead American grunts. The House Armed Services Subcommittee issued at least one devastating report attacking the military for widely issuing such a faulty, untested rifle. The malfunctions, it was determined, had their origin in the fact that the weapon had been tested with one kind of gunpowder and issued for battlefield usage with another.

"Is it true that some men threw their M16s away and replaced them with enemy AK-47s?"

"I never saw that, but I wouldn't doubt it. The AK doesn't break down, it's uncomplicated, it's very easy to maintain, you can get it as dirty as you want, and parts for it are pretty simple to manufacture. It's a good rifle. The bullet is large and light and doesn't go very fast, and it's not as accurate as you'd like, but the barrel is bored in such a way that the bullet tumbles. So when it hits a bone the bone usually shatters."

"Great. That settles it. I'm taking the AK."

"You're taking the AK," my father said. Again, this was not a question. "You know, all this time, I've been kidding—but this clinches it. I really do believe you're a Communist."

I was handed fifty dollars' worth of AK-47 ammunition and protective headphones. Once I put the headphones on, it became clear that they were not in the least insulated against sound. I then realized they were not protective headphones but rather headphones that had been liberated from a home stereo system. For all the insulation these headphones provided, they might as well have given me a bathrobe. I went back to the counter. "Don't you have better headphones?" The man to whom I put this question cupped a hand around his ear and asked that I repeat it, so apparently not.

Every one of the range's dozen firing stands was covered by a little thatched roof. Most of the weapons were attached to their firing stand; some were not. Down at the far end of the range a squat Japanese man with a gorilloid frame was going to town with an unattached sten gun, the French weapon of choice during the First Indochina War. He fired in quick, nasty little bursts, the muzzle flashing fire. All he had to do to create a serious international incident was turn forty-five degrees to his right. I was guided to the AK stand, where a pith-helmeted older Vietnamese man was waiting. I gave him my ammunition and in seconds he loaded the gun and savagely yanked back its bolt. "Single shot or rock and roll?" he asked.

"Excuse me?"

"Single fire or automatic," my father said. I turned. He was standing directly behind me, on the other side of a small fence.

I turned back to my guerrilla instructor. "Let's try rock and roll."

He flipped some tiny lever and, with trepidation, I approached the rifle. My earlier excitement was somewhat diluted by the fact that I had no conception of what to expect once I pulled the trigger. Firing a shotgun under my father's tutelage had been a long time ago. I leaned against the firing stand and felt the rifle comfortably fill my arms and hands. One did not hold a rifle, it dawned on me, so much as embrace it. The sight was a tiny black square with a little gouge cut into it. The targets: an elephant, a lion, and a tiger. I lined up the elephant only to be interrupted by my instructor. "Right eye," he said. "Not left eye. Right eye." I was aiming with the wrong eye. The fingers of my right hand were wrapped firmly around the stock. I extended my index and tried to wrap it around the trigger, which I somehow managed to miss. I was thus forced to crane my head around and sight-guide my finger into the iron ring that surrounded the trigger.

"You're doing great," my father said. "Can't find the trigger? No problem."

"Take up slack," my instructor said.

I turned to him and in the process managed to knock my protective headphones askew. "What?"

"Take up slack. With finger." Very gently he placed his finger over mine and pushed until my finger was flush against the trigger. "Okay. Good now."

I pulled. The multiple recoils slammed the rifle hard into my shoulder. The sound itself was monstrous eardrum vibrato, a long loud *brrrrrd*. My eyes had involuntarily slammed shut. When I opened them, the rifle, for some reason, was aimed at the sun. Smoke leaked out of the barrel and the chamber and daggered into my nostrils—an industrious firework smell. My guide hand was covered with sooty black flecks. "Holy shit," I said. "How many rounds was that?"

"Five," my instructor said.

"I have forty-five of those left?"

"Yes. Forty-five."

Jean-Luc Godard once wrote that the problem with war films was that, when experienced onscreen, war was inevitably invigorating, a sense-surround of exhilaration. Some tiny experiential sliver of that Godardian exhilaration had just passed through me. But I was also alarmed. I had felt the bullets' launch in every tendon and joint of my body. In this way many have linked firing a weapon to the male experience of orgasm. I could now say that I did not agree. What I had just done had not felt good. It had felt powerful, and dreadfully awakening, but not good. I suddenly could not think of an activity I would place farther from the sexual act than firing an automatic weapon. But then I was not a psychopath. At least, not after five bullets.

"Now imagine," my father piped up, "that twenty guys are firing back at you, and people everywhere are screaming."

I fired again and this time managed to keep my eyes open. I had been expecting to see a little puff of kicked-up dirt behind my targeted elephant (I had given up on the idea of actually hitting it), but my three bullets had struck the dirt with such force it resembled the detonation of a grenade. Then I fired again.

"Good!" my instructor said. "You hit elephant! Good! Lion now! Lion!"

I fired again, my ears and nerves still not adjusted to the sound. It felt as though, each time I fired, a newly overwhelmed segment of my brain quietly powered down. I suddenly understood the Vietnamese proverb: "Deaf people are not scared of guns." Next to me the Chinese girl was still firing. Her M16 made a completely different sort of sound from my AK-47: a *sshhhhtt* edged front and back with weird sonic suction.

"Good! Lion again!"

I fired again. Some quick hummingbird sensation darted around the periphery of my conscience, and I supposed this was shame.

"Lower!"

I fired again.

"Good! Now try tiger!"

It is thought that fifty thousand bullets were fired for every enemy soldier killed in Vietnam. Which meant I could have spent $50,000 here before reaching the equivalent of one enemy dead. During one particularly trigger-happy month, the U.S. military fired a *trillion* bullets in Vietnam.

"Good! Higher! Get tiger!"

I kept firing, more calmly now, taking my time and thinking about what was taking place inside this weapon: the ejection of shells, the gas collection, the tiny arrangements of force, the physics of death. When a bullet hits a human being (or an elephant, lion, or tiger), the kinetic-energy transfer is so intense that an "instantaneous internal steam explosion," according to one authority, kills all surrounding tissue. This is called cavitation. When a bullet hits bone or teeth, the resultant human "secondary fragments" can kill someone standing nearby. An AK-47 or M16 round that hits someone in the head can create a shock wave inside the skull so powerful that the brain is vomited out of the exit wound.

"Good!"

I stopped firing and turned around to look at my father. His shirt was blue, a silver pen peeking from his pocket. The buckle of his thick brown belt was miscentered. He shook his head at me. His eyes were bunchy, grim; his smile was both lenient and unforgiving. He seemed taller and thinner—long-limbed, like a cowboy—than I usually pictured him. His hair was grayer. The rest of the range's firing had stopped for a moment, and wind sailed through the jungle around us like an invisible convoy of sound. The breeze lifted the peninsular brown remnant of my father's hairline and flipped it; it hung there, off his forehead, like a fern. I looked at him and he at me. This gulf between us: Was it just the war? Could I ever close it? Certain kinds of experience were not transferable, and some belonged only to us. If there were such a thing as a soul, perhaps this gulf between all people—lovers, friends, foes, fathers, sons— was its airless residence. Something coldly interior swiped at my ribs: if we were ineffably both what we experienced and more than what we experienced, if there were mysteries, why, then, was I firing this gun? I asked my instructor, "How many rounds do I have left?"

He was smiling. "I think five."

I stepped back from the gun and took off my headphones. "I'm done," I said.

An hour before my father's taxi took him to Tan Son Nhut Airport, we were finishing our dinner in the outdoor garden of a District One restaurant that my father had been told was good for seafood. It was. We had devoured plates of squid and coconut-battered shrimp, and squirted each other with incidental citric fire while wringing out our lemons over our spiny brown-shelled lobsters, and now we sat quietly, drinking tiny cups of Vietnamese coffee. At a nearby table a rich young Saigonese couple sat turned away from each other, talking on their cell phones, while, next to us, a young Vietnamese woman occasionally leaned across a candlelit table and fork-fed her older Australian date. Next door to the restaurant was a basketball court. Its lights threw up into the sky a bright yellow borealis, and the steady thumping dribbles were as hypnotic as a metronome. We had discussed little during dinner. I was sad to see him leave, and I knew he was sad to go. Beyond that, there seemed little to talk about.

"Do you think," I finally said, setting down my coffee, "that this trip was cathartic for you?"

He rubbed his fingers together as he thought this over. "It's been pleasant, it's been wonderful. I don't know if it's been cathartic."

"Do you think it's going to help you with any of the lingering bad feelings you still have about the war?"

"I don't know if I have any lingering bad feelings. I told you that before we started."

"And I told you I didn't believe you."

"If I have them, I'm not aware of them. Honestly, Tommy. I'm not."

"When you drink, though—they come out. Surely you recognize that."

"Well, okay. Then now I'll just drink and not talk about the war."

I laughed. "You know what I mean."

He laughed too. We laughed together. My father's open mouth revealed a top row of large straight teeth and a bottom row that had the jagged dentition of a saw put to ill use. "Okay," he finally said.

We listened to a few swished jumpers and the low, giggling conversation next to us. My father blew into his coffee.

"When," I asked, "do you think the bad feelings started to go away?"

His free hand shot up and flicked back. "I think they just did. I couldn't tell you when."

"You've mellowed a ton since I was a kid. I know that. You used to scare the hell out of me."

"And I'm very sorry about that. It makes me feel terrible, knowing I put you through that."

"No, that's not what I mean. I understand why you were the way you were. What I'm interested in is the process of letting all those feelings go."

He shook his head. "It's just time. That's all it is. When you focus less on it and it's not on the news and you've got a family and you've got other interests, everything changes. It just sort of dissipates, goes away. I *will* tell you that sometimes I see those movies and read the books, and it brings back the pain. And that hurts. But I can deal with it now."

"Right. Okay. That's what I'm trying to get at. Is it really just time? It's not recognizing that the war was different from what you thought?"

"That's politics, and I have nothing to say about politics. At least not as they concern the war. I'm sorry. I know you want me to tell you I think the war was wrong. But I don't."

"I *don't* want you to tell me you think the war is—"

His glare silenced me. "However, in the end, I think, after twelve days here, I think, probably, in all likelihood, though I say this with some misgiving, I think, all in all, it's best that everything turned out the way it did."

"Really? You can say that?"

"I can now."

"So how does that make you feel?"

He looked away. "Eh. Sad that the whole thing occurred. But mostly understanding." He seemed to think about this word. His eyebrows lifted and stayed there.

"Understanding, you mean, that the war wasn't your story, or an American story, but a different story, a Vietnamese story, in which you only played a small and terrible part?"

"Let's not go crazy. Just understanding. You can't predict the future. What would we have done? Say we won everything here, took over all the country's provinces, crushed the Communists. What would we have done? The government was corrupt, and too many people hated the government. Who would we have appointed? When you hear the folks, like Hien, we've been talking to . . . you've seen how they talk about reunification. It means something to them. That's what I mean about understanding. I see their faces. This is such a happier place than it was when I was here."

"It's amazing to hear you say that, Dad. It really is. I know it's hard for you to—"

"No, it's not. Not now."

Before I could pursue this, the restaurant's manager came over to our table. He was a short, balding, turtlelike man wearing a silver dress shirt and a black tie. It appeared that one of his waitresses had mentioned to him that she had overheard us talking about the war, and he now informed my father that he was a former ARVN soldier and had worked in intelligence during the war. He wanted to thank us for eating here, pass along his good tidings, and wish my father a pleasant time in Vietnam. The manager was speaking perfect English, albeit with a strong Vietnamese inflection. Nevertheless, my father had out his Vietnamese phrasebook and quickly found the Vietnamese word for "veteran." Yes, the manager said, smiling, when my father showed him the word. My father stood and embraced his fellow veteran. The manager, clearly surprised, patted my father on the back. This man and my father, I noticed, were balding in the exact same pattern. After they pulled apart, my father's hands remained upon the man's shoulders, while the man held my father by his elbows. I looked at them, these two men who had fought for a cause no longer understood in the United States and officially disdained in Vietnam. Several of the waitresses were looking at them and whispering to one another.

"The war is over," my father said.

"Yes," the manager told him. "It's good to forget, to put it behind."

"I drank, and cried, and drank, and nothing worked. Now I'm here. In your wonderful country."

"It's good you're here. Very good."

"The bad memories—"

"Oh, many bad memories."

"The bad memories," my father said, "like this." He then pantomimed taking his brain out of his head, slipped the imaginary brain it into his shirt pocket, and slyly patted it.

The manager laughed, and then obliged my father with an identical pantomime. "Can't forget, though," he said suddenly. "Not really." If he had worked in ARVN intelligence, given what had happened to such people during reeducation, I imagined that his memories were indeed hard to forget. "But we're old men now."

My father cackled and stomped a foot. "Yes! Old men. We are. I can't believe it, but we are."

"It was a long time ago."

"And your country is unified."

"Yes. It's good to be unified. Sadness and danger are all over now. The bad times are good times now."

With a wave of his hand my father presented me to the man. "This is my son."

"Your father is a good man," the manager told me, smiling. "He loves you. I think he loves all people."

My father threw up his hands. "Put it behind!" He was, for some reason, speaking with a Vietnamese accent. "All bad memories! Put it behind!"

THREE

The Children of the War Speak

A person who has lived through a great war is different from someone who never lived through any war. They are two different species of human beings. They will never find a common language, because you cannot really describe the war, you cannot share it, you cannot tell someone: Here, take a little bit of my war.

—RYSZARD KAPUŚCIŃSKI, *THE SOCCER WAR*

Believe it or not, I once had a high school teacher who took us out in the woods for an afternoon in order to teach us about the war. It was . . . oh, God, what was it? I guess I'd say that it was completely crazy. My teacher was one of these vets that refuses to eat Chinese food, always sits facing the door in any room, always *announces* why he's sitting facing the door in any room, and maintained—in class—that the United States did not lose the Vietnam War. Remember Kevin Kline's character in *A Fish Called Wanda,* who says Vietnam was "a tie"? That was him. He taught history. This is the Midwest, right?

So he has us out there. He makes me and a few other kids Viet Cong. I think he made all the students he didn't like Viet Cong, but I was the only girl guerrilla. He sends us to one side of the woods to hide with some Ziplocs filled with rice—orange Rice-a-Roni rice that his wife made. The students he assigned as U.S. infantry he has doing some other idiotic thing. Formations or whatever. I honestly don't even remember what they were doing. But they had Spam to eat. While we're running around in the woods with our Spam and Rice-a-Roni, he begins his lecture about the disadvantages Americans faced in Southeast Asia. The guy did this with his history classes every year.

My dad was a medic in Vietnam, and when I told him about our field trip he got this very sad look in his eyes. He sat me down and talked to me, for the first time, about the war. What did he tell me? Well, he said that war, all war, was basically cruelty and anyone who sought to justify it, or explain it, or rationalize it, was not worth listening to. We had this huge talk. My father had never opened up about the war before. Vietnam had always been this black hole or forbidden zone. Later I told my mom about what he'd said. She was shocked. He'd never really talked to her about it, not once in twenty-five years of marriage. Of course, little things came up, but nothing like what he told me. Can you believe it took this moron at my high school to get my dad to talk about it? I think it offended his sense of honor or something. Maybe that was the only good thing about that war. For all the men it made like my high school teacher, it made men like my father too. He was the gentlest person I've ever known.

Do I hate Americans? I know why you ask. Because now I'm a little angry while I'm talking to you. You know, I'll be honest and tell you I do hate them a little. A little. Not all Americans, but many. I think you hate us a little too. Why do I hate them? I hate them because they think they have suffered. A lot of them come here and they cry, but they forget what they did. I've seen this many times. But have they really suffered? Okay, yes, that's true, but not like us. My brother suffered. My mother suffered. My other brother died. My uncle died. They never found my father's body. Do you know how many members of our Party lost wives, sons, and daughters to American bombs? In our government there are many such people, and now they must welcome your country's investments. Have you thought about that? Would you want to do that?

You said yesterday you were surprised by how little anger you have felt here, but there is anger within all Vietnamese who were alive then. Most of us can let it go, some of us can't. Often I can. Most often I am able to do my job and smile and be a good person. But if I think of my brother long enough I am not such a good person anymore. How? He was hit by a bomb. My uncle too. No, different bombs. I don't blame you. It's not your fault. Do I blame your father? Did he drop the bomb? He was a Marine? Well, no, probably he didn't drop the bomb. I don't blame your father. I guess there is no blame.

Today I don't have any work, so I drink beer and smoke cigarettes. My days are very long. What was my brother's name? Triet. Yes, Triet. Today my little brother would be thirty-four years old.

For some reason I was always sad when I was growing up. I wasn't a good student, either. I had trouble with other kids. I fought, stole, and did a lot of other bad shit. Something always seemed to just eat at me. Now that I'm older, I think a lot of this had to do with my dad.

When he wasn't drunk, he was getting drunk. There were some serious drug problems when I was a kid, actually; he may have spent a few nights in jail. My dad couldn't maintain human relationships, for one thing. He had so much *fury* in him. It's an odd word to use, but I think it's an accurate one. Fury. Hate. Distrust. It came out in all different ways, but it was always totally undirected, though he was absolutely racist against any and all Asians. When he didn't have anything to do, he would walk around with panic in his eyes. He could never be alone. But no one could really stand being around him for long either. That should suggest some of my father's ongoing problems. But I love the guy, despite it all.

Who really knows how much of this is attributable to Vietnam? I'm not even sure how much combat he even saw. But from what I've read, that wasn't a big consolation, considering that at certain points in the war you were as liable to get killed at your desk in Saigon as you were out in the jungle. He's gotten better in the last few years. Better, not good. I doubt he'll ever be good. Good is not really within my father's potentiality, if you know what I mean. I could blame Vietnam for that. Sometimes I do. But in the end I don't know.

Mostly I remember bombs falling, airplanes coming. I remember always moving. My father was political. He was a farmer, then he was VC. My mother was not political. My brother was not political. We were poor. We were chased out of our home many times. Sometimes by the VC when my father was gone, sometimes by the bombs.

I remember, as a little girl, not believing I would survive. I remember that: thinking, "Tomorrow, I will die." Can you imagine? Later when I went to the United States to study, many professors asked me, "Why do you want to come here? Don't you hate Americans?" I said, "Behind the soldiers, behind the governments, there are always hearts, families, memories, childhoods, pasts." I wanted to know more about the people behind those U.S. soldiers. I wanted to learn about American culture. So I told those professors that the United States was not just for Vietnamese refugees. Communists are people, too!

I started to read short stories about the war, stories by American authors. I don't really like them, no. I suppose because I never recognize the war in those stories. The war in those stories. . . . That was not my war. My war was my mother crying, my brother crying, always moving.

When I was in fourth or fifth grade, I found a section of the library that had a bunch of books about the war, and there was this one that had diagrams of booby traps and pictures of dead people and all that other bad stuff. I was very interested because I knew my dad had been there and I wanted to learn more about it.

My dad was a helicopter pilot for the Navy. I remember that this was something we all thought was very cool growing up, and my dad was proud of being a pilot. He loved to fly. In Vietnam he picked up wounded people and dropped off SEAL teams on covert operations, people going in at night, stuff like that. He had Purple Hearts—I think three or four. He crashed a couple of times. He was never seriously wounded, though. He was very dismissive of his Purple Hearts. He didn't show them off or anything; he didn't wear them around. I just found them in a box one day.

He didn't really talk to me about what happened to him, but there was one fantastic story—I say "fantastic" not in the positive sense—I remember hearing from my older brother, who my dad talked to more about the war because he was older. Anyway, one time, while he was flying in the middle of a firefight, the communications wire on my dad's helmet was cut by a bullet. The other guy could hear him, the next minute he couldn't. At the time, it sounded very exciting. When I was growing up, the way the war was talked about, or even not talked about . . . you internalize all that stuff. I don't think my dad, to this day, could bring himself to say that the war was a bad idea or that we were wrong to be there. No, I don't really know when I forged my own political ideas about it. There wasn't a whole lot of guidance from him.

I can sympathize, in some sense, with what it must have been like at the time, why we got involved. My dad's father fought in World War Two, and thus he grew up in a very patriotic household. He thought the United States could do no wrong. So when he volunteered he was just a kid who didn't understand what he was getting into. It's hard for me to point fingers about what part he must have played in the war. I'm not ready to do that.

A really weird thing happened a couple of years ago. I was visiting my grandparents, and they were giving away everything they had, and there was this little box of stuff my dad had sent them from Vietnam, and inside were some audiotapes he'd made while serving. I never knew these things existed, so I snatched them up and took them home. It was so bizarre. He recorded them at exactly the age that I was when I was listening to them. There he was sitting in this base and you could hear mortar shells, all these explosions, in the background. He had just come back from a mission, and I could hear the fatigue in his voice. He'd gone for two days without getting more than fifteen minutes of sleep. They were taking fire, and he was very blasé about it. For the first time I thought about all the suffering he must have seen. He just sounded so tired. Not at all like the person I would know later, the guy who would endlessly justify the war. He was instead this exhausted guy who sounded so incredibly confused and weary, so completely unsure.

When my father turned eighteen, he got drafted. He had no choice. He was in the South, he was drafted. I think at that time my father had no idea about the war: one day, suddenly, he was holding a rifle. He was married during the war. His first daughter was born in 1967. In 1969, another daughter. Then another in 1972. He got very nervous. What if he died tomorrow with no son? He got a desk job in Saigon to avoid getting killed, so then they had me—that's all he's ever said to me about it.

I think my father doesn't tell me much about the war because of all the difficulty he had after. The Communists were very bad to him. When I was ten, he beat me because of the stress. He even beat my mom. But you should know that I think Ho Chi Minh was a great man. So does my father. It's very complicated.

Finally I think the war made our lives better. That's the biggest point. My father had a lot of GI friends, and he learned many things from them. He learned how important education was. Even the lowest-ranking American soldiers had gone to high school. Do you know he learned to read English because that was the only way he could read the canned food that came from America? He would want chicken, but he opened beef, or pork. So he had to learn how to read. He always dreamed of settling down in America, but he failed the exam at the U.S. Embassy in Saigon. It was like the sky collapsed for my father. He had saved so much money for that.

He used to talk about things that were made in the U.S.A. That was enough for him: if it was made in the U.S.A., it was good. So I think he was very amazed by those soldiers who came here. They had nice food, good cigarettes, clean hair. They even waited in line for everything and never pushed. My father used to dream about America. He is still dreaming about going to America—but now he is so old.

I think when my dad heard he was going to Vietnam he bought into the whole thing about war: "It's exciting, it's different, it's valiant!" But he always told me that from the minute he got there the most important thing to him—aside from anything that we think was important now, like stopping Communism—was that his men didn't get hurt in any way. Even when it became clear that there was no sure reason why they were there, they still needed to get home, and it was his job to get them home.

Do I feel like less of a man because I didn't go through that? When I think I'm having a bad day, I realize that I've not had a bad day. There's not one single issue in my entire life that compares—and I've even had a gun pointed at me. (It was on a sales job. In Texas. A shotgun. Long story.) At some point I realized that I was alive because he had dealt with problems greater than I had ever dealt with or was going to deal with. I'll give you a quick story. After he had reconnected with his Marine buddies in the late 1980s, he had them all up to Connecticut, up to the house, and I think I was disagreeing with him about something while we were barbecuing—a "Will you go get the lemonade?" type of thing—and this guy B———, who was a New York City cop, pulled me aside and said, "Your father was a different man over there. Every single one of us has him to thank for being alive." I was like fourteen. And I was arguing with him. About lemonade.

My dad's situation in Vietnam sucked, on an exponential level, but he was able to deal with it. So in a way Vietnam was the only thing I really *knew* about him. It was the only past he had. He had no youth other than the Vietnam War. When he had a story to tell, it tended to be about the guys, the situation from Vietnam. Those were all his stories. That was all he had.

Do you see this river? It separated my country for twenty years. Yes, we can walk to the other side. You asked about my family. First you must know that it was illegal for family members on different sides of this river to talk. My father went North and my uncles joined the ARVN, so you can see that in my family there were difficulties. In this province, Quang Tri province, there were many families with these difficulties. I think Quang Tri province suffered more than any other in Vietnam. Most of the Agent Orange victims are here. There were so many dead bodies around Quang Tri that tigers used to eat them. Brothers and sisters fought against each other in these fields every night. Sometimes they killed each other. I read a story about that once: one man discovers he has killed his older brother, and then he kills himself. Then their mother kills herself when she learns she has lost both of her sons. A terrible story. Well, it's a Quang Tri story. The man who wrote it is from Quang Tri.

One night, long after the war ended, my father and my uncles talked and learned that they all fought in the same battle in 1974. They may have shot at each other. No, I don't think they thought that was funny. I think it made them frightened and sad. It took them many years to become friends again—at least ten years. One of my uncles was reeducated, and for a long time he refused to talk about anything related to the war. My other uncle became a drunken man. They will all talk about it now only when they're drunk, and only when they're alone. That's why I decided to study history, to learn about both sides of my country. But it's very difficult to learn about the southern side. I've had to ask my friends in France and America to bring me books about that.

The only thing I can remember being said about the war when I was a kid was when we saw the fireworks at the Mall in Washington, D.C., on the Fourth of July. My dad said there was a firework he liked because it reminded him of the sound of artillery. And once he told me that in Vietnam someone in his compound had a tame skunk as a pet. Literally those are the only things I remember him telling me when I was a kid. And this was in the 1980s, when all those movies started showing terribly traumatized vets. My dad wasn't at all like that. He was still an active-duty soldier at that point. My impression of him as a soldier was that he went to the office, carried a briefcase, occasionally traveled to Israel or Turkey, and brought me back stamps. Very different from my brothers. They know all about it.

It's not like it's a forbidden subject. It's just that I never had any curiosity about it when I was a kid, and I never thought to ask. I have to think this is because I'm a girl. My dad served two tours, both before I was born. First he was with the First Cav doing intelligence, usually enemy interrogation. The second tour was with MACV. Of course I think about the fact that my father may have done stuff that encroached upon the morally disturbing. I think about it a lot now. During all the Abu Ghraib stuff I thought, "Oh, yeah. My dad sort of knows something about that." His take on it was that it signified a failure in the chain of command, basically. He said, "There are always going to be some sadists in there, and my job was to weed those people out." He told my

husband—not me—that one of his strategies when interrogating people was to take out a big knife and threaten prisoners with it. He said
he had to come on very strong, right away, if he wanted information,
because the people he was interrogating figured out pretty quickly that
he wasn't going to use the knife. When my husband told me that, something clicked. The way he dealt with us growing up when we got in trouble was like: explosion! He'd just blow up, get totally furious, and then,
as soon as he'd made his point, he'd calm down. So it's like those tactics
carried over, which is kind of spooky. It was hard to reconcile that with
the impression I'd always gotten—and this may be very naive—that to
my dad Vietnam was this extended Boy Scout expedition. See, he's very
upright. He's that kind of guy. He loves nature, rules, proper procedure.

He did once admit to me, though—and it's amazing what's coming
back now that I'm talking to you—he did once admit, "We Americans
did terrible things, and the Vietnamese did terrible things." But no, Vietnam doesn't have much resonance to me—at all. Vietnam has not
loomed over me. I don't feel like there's something I have to settle there.
I don't know that much about it and don't feel any need to know much
about it. But you know what? I wonder if it's because I didn't ask my dad
about the war that I don't know anything, or because maybe there was a
part of him that liked having this one person in his family who had no
conception of him in that role.

We weren't lucky. My father was drafted into ARVN and told me he
never saw a Communist until the tanks came into Saigon. He tried to get
out, but he wasn't lucky. Maybe we could have gotten out, but my
mother didn't want to go. So we stayed. It's not that unusual. Why do
you want to talk to me? I have nothing to say. We were just unlucky.

My father was reeducated for one year. After, he never talked about
the war. He also never worked again, not a real job. My parents were very
poor after the war. They still are, and I have to help them. That's why I
do this work. No, they know what I do. It makes them very unhappy.
Sometimes I like it. Sometimes the men are kind.

For me, what I think—what I think is that the war was like a thing that happened to us, do you know? Like an animal that attacked, or a storm. It took my family and pushed it in another direction and made it different. Everyone in my family has always been very sad. But nothing terrible happened to us, not really. We're not special. The worst my father was ever hurt was when a jeep ran over his foot. And yet the war changed everything for him, and us. I think that is so strange to think about.

As far back as I can remember, the war was who my dad was. He was in the Army. I think he was an infantryman. First Cavalry. I think. I don't really know any specifics because he won't talk much about it. Well, he would tell stories. And I always wanted to know, because as his daughter I was obsessed with this aspect of who he was. I was also obsessed with war movies—any war movie. Totally obsessed. In sixth grade we all had to do reports on something: space, Columbus, George Washington. I did mine on Vietnam.

The stories he would tell me were always very innocuous human interest stories. Like how when he was eating in the field the flies were so big and so numerous that he always had to brush them off his food or how the Vietnamese cut up snakes and ate them. As for the details of what he did, all I had to work off were the newspaper articles. They told the story about how he got the Silver Star. Yeah, he got the Silver Star. He and his buddies were in a situation in which they were overrun and his commanding officer was shot down while running up a hill toward the enemy. When the commanding officer went down, everyone started retreating. But my dad didn't, even though he had the radio on his back, which made him a target. He went back, by himself, and took out multiple foxholes filled with Vietnamese and went up and grabbed his C.O. and dragged him back down. The guy died, eventually, but my dad tried to save him and while doing that single-handedly killed a bunch of people. The other newspaper story described how he was injured. He was actually pretty seriously injured. He was shot between the eyes, but the bullet exploded as it made contact with his face. Obviously if it hadn't he wouldn't be here and I wouldn't be here. His face was just blown apart.

His nose today is plastic. His whole face was reconstructed. Anyway, after he got shot in the face, a medic bandaged up his head and put him in a helicopter. That helicopter got shot down. So he was on the ground next to a guy who'd been shot in the spine or something and couldn't move. But he could see and speak. My father could move and hear but he couldn't speak or see. So he was holding a gun and the other guy was sprawled next to him—they were all alone at this point; the pilots were dead—and the other guy started giving my dad the time on the clock. "Nine o'clock fire! Eleven o'clock fire!" And the two of them stayed together that way and managed to hang in there until someone came for them.

I have these monumental stories of what he did. It's hard for me to reconcile the man he is today with these superhuman stories. I wish I knew the man in those stories. We don't have a relationship now. We're estranged. I told him I couldn't speak to him anymore. He's just got too much hostility and aggression. No one in his life is ever good enough. He's really fucked up. He blames it all on the war and says he has post-traumatic stress syndrome. Personally, I have a hard time understanding this. He was a much different person ten years ago, fifteen years ago. I don't know why there would be such a delayed reaction to what he experienced. But maybe that's the way war is. He's been such a huge influence on my life. He was the parent I was closest to when I was young. He's the one who's been the best to me and the worst to me, out of anyone in my life. I've always believed that if I can somehow understand who he was then—that wonderful and brave and shiny young man—and figure out what's different now, and how those two people connect . . . God, I don't know. I just want to know that person so badly.

I was born in Hanoi on the first night of the Christmas bombings in 1972, and my dad was a very traditional Communist. In the war he was a communications soldier, not a frontline soldier. He doesn't talk about the war with me, but he's the kind of person who would have done what the others did. I don't know if he really wanted to fight. He still thinks that Americans are very dangerous. He thinks we must be really careful around people like you. When I had a job with an NGO, he asked me, "Where is the headquarters?" I said, "New York." He said, "I don't want you to work for them. If you work with them, you must be really careful."

I can understand his feelings. We were so poor after the war. When I was a girl in Nam Dinh—that's a very Communist province and one of the poorest—the conditions were terrible. We had a one-room apartment in a dormitory. No bathrooms, no kitchen, just one room. We had to share restrooms with two dozen other families, and there was rationed water and meat. I don't know how much we earned every month, but like everyone we usually ate noodles and rice powder. And my father was a Party member!

My feelings about the war? What I really think is that the war was about two small groups. The group here in Vietnam is the people who called themselves Communists. They raised that flag and told the people, "Go, go—fight for freedom!" But what is freedom? I think "freedom" is just for their benefit. A lot of my friends are teachers, and now their students are asking them, "Why didn't we just let the Americans own the country? Why did we have to fight? After ten or twenty years, they would have had to give us everything back, and we'd have such better conditions!" So I don't like the war. I don't like the way many people here—in my opinion—take the war and say it was for everyone when it was just for some people.

Does my father know about all the Communist abuses? Sure, he knows. One day I brought home a banned book, and I showed it to him. I asked him if he wanted to read it. He read some pages and gave it back to me and told me, "I know. I know all of this. There's nothing new in this. Everyone knows. And no one cares. I don't care. You shouldn't read this—it's too dangerous." If you lived in the North and you didn't want to be a Communist and you didn't follow the Party, then what did you do? If you wanted to survive, then you needed your monthly Party ticket. Tickets for meat, for milk, for bicycle tires. Everything was in the Party's control. If you didn't go with them you had nothing. So you had no choice. There was no thinking. And they controlled the war. They still control it.

I have this very old friend in Hanoi. He's eighty now, and he has red blood, just like my father. He's *red*. Totally red. I asked him once about the Party, the war, and everything that happened afterwards, and he said, "From the bottom of my heart, we didn't want to do any bad things. We tried to be good. But it all became such a mess."

That's my father right there. No, I've been here before. The first time I was here was right after it was dedicated. I guess I was twenty-one or twenty-two. If you recall, there was a lot of debate about whether or not this was a fitting or suitable memorial to the men who died. The starkness of it freaked a lot of people out. I mean, look around here. Statues, huge towers, domes: *that's* heroism, *that's* sacrifice. This is just a big scary wall with a bunch of names written on it. That it was designed by an Asian woman did not, I suspect, help matters. Yeah, I think I was a little troubled by it the first time I saw it. Now I can't imagine any better monument. I mean, look at it. It's just beautiful. It's perfect. It's probably the best memorial in the country, in my opinion.

I think about what my father would have thought about it sometimes. I was ten when he died, so I can't really say I have much of a sense of him beyond what my mom has told me or the letters he wrote me. Since he was writing those letters to a little boy, I don't know what his politics were or what he truly felt about the war. My mom's pretty liberal—she actually spoke out against the war after he died, and I think he probably would have not objected to that. I don't know. When someone you love dies, so much of your memory of him becomes really wishful. I try to avoid thinking about his true feelings, actually. Sure, I still have all those letters, but I haven't read them in years. It's not painful anymore, no. It all feels like it was a long time ago.

But growing up without a father was definitely hard, and even today there are things that I experience that produce this strange impulse to call him and tell him about it. I can't explain that impulse. God, I even remember looking for him in the bleachers when I graduated from high school. Maybe a child is hardwired that way, or somehow psychologically determined to have parents. If he'd lived, he'd probably still be alive today. So that's kind of bittersweet.

How did he die? Of friendly fire, in an accident. He was hit by artillery. Seven other men died with him. I've become pretty close with the kids of some of those other guys. We send one another Christmas cards, birthday cards. You try—I try—to avoid thinking about the war, any war, in terms of the sheer human waste they create, but look at all these names. My dad's just one name, one tiny name on this wall. And looking at it at this moment all I can think is "What a fucking waste."

I always say to foreigners that my father was not VC. "Not VC! No, not VC! He was a good man. He was in the southern Army." The truth is that he was VC. My mother hardly saw him for five years. One day the VC came in and took him. After that we heard very little from him. Sometimes we saw him but never for long. The VC took many men from our village. Some of them didn't want to go with them, some of them did. My father did. He was religious, and I think he believed it was his fate to fight. I had a father, but I don't know my father. I never knew my father. Do you know what I mean? He died five years ago, and I wasn't that sad. Who was my father? He was just a man who lived in our house.

My mother always said to me he was not the same when he came back. I was one when he left, seven when we reunified. My mother told me that sometimes when she woke up he would be sitting on the edge of the bed, holding his head in his hands, crying. We lived in the country-side, and at night it was quite loud. He couldn't sleep because of the noise of the countryside—the grass, the river, the insects. It reminded him of too many bad memories. But he never talked about it. He never really talked about anything. I don't know why. Maybe no one really talked about it because that generation all suffered so much. But I think my father saw and did awful things. The war took too many fathers and made them strangers to their families.

My father dodged the draft and fled to Canada. My mother went with him, and I wound up being born in Montreal. Eventually he came back, was prosecuted, defended himself—and won. That decision became the basis of President Carter's pardon for everyone who dodged the draft. I think the Vietnam War really drove my father's generation crazy, in a way. My dad, when he was a kid, had his "I Like Ike" buttons, so he grew up with one image of America and then had that image crash against the whole experience of the Vietnam War. He didn't go and bomb things or anything like that—he became a totally different kind of radical—but he essentially came to believe that the society he grew up in is a complete lie.

As a little boy, at the playground, I'd hear kids say, "My father is a lawyer" or "My father is a fireman" or "My father owns a store," and I would say, "My father is an American traitor!" As if that were the most honorable thing you could be. I remember these times when I'd sit with my mother, looking through our family scrapbook. See, when his case was up, there was a television documentary made about him and *Time* and *Newsweek* did stories, so we had this huge scrapbook. My mom would say, "Now, here's your daddy being taken off to jail." This was our family heirloom. But she was proud of it, and my father was proud of it. And I'm proud of it. I think he did the right thing. But I also can't have conversations with him when it comes to international issues or foreign policy without being pulled inexorably back into the orbit of Vietnam. Everything is looked at through that lens. I guess what I'm saying is that I was so indoctrinated into my family's way of looking at the war that only later did I ever even come across the idea that there was any meaningful debate about it.

For too long Vietnam didn't mean anything to me. Vietnam for me was a symbol, a code word, the thing that had thrown our family into the footnotes of history. In a way I criticize my father a little bit for that. As much as he didn't want to be a part of the war, and as much as he felt that what was happening to the Vietnamese was immoral, he didn't want to deal with Vietnam too much. He never learned that much about the history, the politics. I know vastly more about Vietnamese history and politics than he does. All he knows is that it was bad and he didn't want any part of it. Now that I've been to Vietnam, I realize everything is so complicated. The last time I was there I met Nguyen Cao Ky, and I found myself having a lot of sympathy for him and what he was trying

to do as a Vietnamese patriot. I think Ky was deeply wrong and misguided about many things, but once you really wrestle with the war,
solid notions of right and wrong seem incapable of capturing it.

Understand that I make clear political and moral distinctions. I still
think it was wrong, but I have come to believe that maybe my dad recognized that in order to maintain the consistency of his opinions it was
better not to know too much about Vietnam. So many people, once the
war was over, once the choppers left Saigon, thought it was all done
with. They do not know what happened to Vietnam after, and they don't
care. I mean, they care. My father cares. But he doesn't care enough to
know. I think caring enough to know makes it difficult to have the
absolute moral high ground. Even Neil Sheehan. *A Bright Shining Lie* is
a great book; it really does illustrate the weird American delusions that
drove our foreign policy, but in his next book, which is about going back
to Vietnam years later, you really begin to see the failure of the 1960s
generation in dealing with this next step. They can only blame the way
Vietnam is fucked up on the lingering aftereffects of the war, as if there
is no agency among the Vietnamese themselves.

At a certain point I think my father's generation put the Vietnamese
into the role of pure victim in such a way that it became intellectually
stifling. So as a member of a very different generation, going to Vietnam
was personally important. I felt like I was completing a project. I felt
some need to both live up to the ideals of my father and the pathos of his
generation and at the same time overcome those ideals and that pathos.

I never really pushed my parents on it. It was their version of the war,
and I accepted it. You know, that the South would have won if the Americans hadn't pulled out. I should have asked them more about it. There's
a lot that I probably should talk to my parents about, but I still haven't.
How do they feel about my living in Vietnam today? I don't think they
can accept what Vietnam is now. They can't accept that anything good
can happen here. Vietnam has to be bad. When I was growing up, the
whole Vietnamese thing was just kind of there. I didn't have Vietnamese

friends. I liked Vietnamese food, but that was about it. My parents thought we were racist against Vietnamese! But my mom told me before I came over, "Don't trust anyone with a northern accent." Which is *unbelievable.*

What does the war mean? For me, the war is what made me into a Vietnamese person brought up with Vietnamese values in a culture with American values. But no, there's no war inside me. I don't think so, at least. When I came back, it felt like the right thing to do at the time. The third day I was back here, everything felt good. Two years later, I'm still here. That said, I usually don't tell people, unless they seem like they're honestly asking, that I grew up in the States. You get such a huge range of reactions. I usually tell people I'm Korean. But I was very lucky to get out. We got out the last day. But I have no memories of that. I was eleven months old. That was the defining moment of my life, but I don't even know what happened.

My dad was a doctor, a ranger. He wasn't the guy fighting; he was patching other people up. But he was always proud to be a ranger. Beyond his pride, I never heard much about what my dad did. Once—I had just turned twenty-one—a bunch of my dad's friends from his ranger days got together in Houston in a very Vietnamese restaurant. They were all talking, and I suddenly saw my dad drinking beer the way you see Vietnamese men drink all the time here, and for the first time I heard stories of how my dad was running around the battlefield, being covered by these drinking buddies, while he saved people's lives. You need to realize that these weren't guys my dad hung out with typically. Most of his friends were doctors. These were different men. It was weird. But no, I don't have any lingering anger for the Communists. I think they're fucked up for reasons that are beyond ideology. It's just incompetence and no different from any other place where a small group has power and wants to serve its own self-interest. This is not my personal resentment, understand—it's an extension of my father's resentment. But it's not something I walk around Saigon thinking about.

The really fucked-up thing is that my dad's older brother was an officer in the North Vietnamese Army, and he has a son in Saigon. I know them. I met them the first time I came back. My uncle had passed away right before. This is all so messed up. My dad had two older brothers who died fighting the French and a sister who died fighting the French. She was one of those girls pushing a fruit cart around launching grenades out of it. So my family came out of that very rare ARVN few who fought the French. Anyway, my father and uncle never reconciled. I barely even knew he existed until right before he died. And then all I ever heard was how evil my uncle was. When I came back, my uncle had just passed away and my aunt and cousin were sitting there talking to me, and it turned out that my uncle had written a letter to us—I never saw the letter—but it was very apologetic, saying this never should have happened, it should have never divided our family like this, and when the letter came around to my father he refused to read it. Keep in mind, my uncle was dead. My dad still refused. My uncle protected everyone on my mom's side that was still here, even though he wasn't related to them by blood. Without my uncle, so many in my mom's family would have gone through hell. My uncle was a good officer, and really cared about my mom's family—a really fine man, it turns out. I would never hear this from my father. It all came out later.

But I don't know. I don't know what all this is, or means. I need to fig-ure out Vietnam for myself. Do I have any reaction to Americans whose fathers fought here? No. I told you I don't think about the war. It's abstract to me. It's not even an issue.

My dad didn't talk about it very much when I was growing up. I always knew he was a Marine and was proud of that—that's part of what made me want to be a Marine—but his experiences over there weren't shared with the family. He's part of the reason I'm here in Iraq, sure. Not all of it. I used to work at a gas station in high school, and the Marine recruiter regularly filled up his government vehicle there. I talked to him a lot, just as a friend. He never approached me about being a Marine. I talked to him one day as I was nearing the end of my high school education—and that was it. I entered the Marine Corps in 1990, as an enlisted aviation mechanic. For the next twelve years I worked through school, graduated from S——— I——— University in 2002, applied for my commission, and here I am today, a lieutenant leading Marines.

No, my dad never got that far, and I'll tell you how I learned that. After I was already a Marine, I was stationed in Hawaii, my dad came and visited, and we were having dinner at a friend's house. The subject came up that my dad was a medically retired lance corporal. At the time I was a corporal myself, so everyone at the table got very curious, naturally. We all asked, "How did you become a medically retired lance corporal?" He looked right back at us and said, "I stepped on a land mine in Vietnam." Then tears come to his eyes—which was hard, very hard, to see. Since coming to Iraq, I can sense a little bit of kinship there, between us, and maybe it will open up a little more when I get back.

I don't think I could compare the two wars at all. Or at least I haven't really analyzed what the comparison is. I don't have any ideas of what to think about there. But I can definitely relate to my dad's . . . well, there are some things that I would prefer not to talk about when I get back home. So I definitely can relate to him there. Maybe I can talk to him about it, and maybe that'll open up and he'll talk to me a little more about what brought him to tears that day when we were at my friend's house.

Now I talk to him pretty regularly. I've called him a couple of times at work. The first time I did it, my mom said that it made his day. I've done it several times now. Look, I know Vietnam was a profound event in American history. And sometimes we're called to do things that are not necessarily the most popular decision, the popular choice, but as Marines, as servants of our country, we're called to do those things and sometimes what we think about it doesn't matter.

I am nervous to talk to you. Not nervous. I am reserved. Because I have many things to say. I remember everything. And what I remember is terrible. We still have many problems here. I was born in 1968. For those Vietnamese born during that time . . . things happened to us, but it is not good to talk about it. I can give you background. Please do not record me. My father fought in the southern army. He was an important man. He was wounded in 1974. He never left his bed again. He died in 1976. Now I cannot get a job here in Saigon. I don't know if it's because of my father. Maybe. Maybe it's because I'm from the countryside. I speak English, but I can't get a job. And now I'm not so young. I work for the veterans sometimes, when they come. I love the veterans. I love to talk to them. The U.S. veterans. I have veteran friends in many states. They are such good guys. It's important they come back here.

I think I like them because they remind me of my father.

Acknowledgments

During the composition of this book, several people provided me with especial insight, aid, or encouragement. They are Heather Schroder, Dan Frank, Roger Hodge, Lewis Lapham, Allan Jenkins, Philip Caputo, Amber Hoover, Dixon Gaines, Margot Meyer, Fred Nicolaus, Ted Genoways, Matt Gross, Theodore Ross, and Markus Taussig.

Thank you to GQ's Devin Friedman, who first suggested I write about my father and Vietnam. Although GQ did not ultimately publish the piece, I am grateful to Devin, John Jeremiah Sullivan, and Joel Lovell, all of whom helped me with multiple drafts.

Thank you to Doug Fix. My father and I traveled to Vietnam in November 2003, and a year later Doug and I retraced that trip. Doug was also a Vietnam veteran, my first writing teacher, and in all likelihood the reason I became a writer. Doug died while running a marathon on September 23, 2006. He is irreplaceable not only to me but to his wife, children, and grandchildren. His spirit and example have been a part of everything I have written, but his presence in these pages, however invisible, is especially profound. I would like to believe this book would have pleased him.

Thank you to Major Maria Pallotta, United States Marine Corps, without whom I could not have embedded with the Marines in Iraq in July 2005. This book is different, stranger, and, I hope, stronger because of that experience.

During my most recent trip to Vietnam in April 2005, made to cover the thirtieth anniversary of Saigon's fall for The Virginia Quarterly Review, I became part of a minor international incident when my traveling partners and fellow journalists Morgan Meis and Joe Pacheco were arrested and deported for interviewing a dissident artist without having first sought government permission. It was the first expulsion of foreign journalists to have occurred in Vietnam in more than five years, and the only thing that prevented me from sharing Morgan and Joe's fate was the fact that I had become sick and decided to stay at our hotel while they interviewed the artist. Which is to say that I would like very much to thank my Vietnamese friends, as well as my other friends who live in Vietnam or travel there regularly, but doing so could bring them unwanted attention. I would like these friends to know that this book could not have been written without their conversation, companionship, and generosity. I would also like to wish the men and women of Vietnam's intelligence apparatus continued happiness and independence, and to them offer my sincere and friendly hope that those so afflicted will one day be able to retrieve their heads from their asses.

Thank you to the staff of the Chancery Hotel in Ho Chi Minh City, where the bulk of this book was written.

Thank you to the Hawthornden International Retreat for Writers in Scotland and the staff of Hawthornden Castle, where a draft of this book was completed.

Thank you to Jason Wilson and Jamaica Kincaid, who were kind enough to select a part of this book for *Best American Travel Writing 2005.*

Thank you to all who spoke to me about their fathers and the war.

Thank you to my brother, Johno, fellow traveler in Spaceship Bissell, who sometimes has trouble understanding my compulsion to disclose highly personal family information in the pages of national magazines but who accepts this compulsion with what eventually becomes exasperated grace. Thank you to my mother, Alexandria Thomas, and my stepmother, Carolyn Bissell, for understanding why I needed to write this and supporting me throughout. Thank you to Donald Brandt, my stepfather: I hope you knew that I always considered myself lucky to have two such extraordinary fathers. I miss you. I love you.

Thank you, finally, to Nathalie Chicha, who has my love, shares my life, and for and alongside whom I write.

Bibliography
(Occasionally Fortified with Thoughts Toward Recommended Reading)

Addington, Larry H. *American's War in Vietnam: A Short Narrative History.* Bloomington: Indiana University Press, 2000. Among the best short histories of the war available.

Adler, Bill. *Letters from Vietnam.* New York: Ballantine, 2003.

Anderegg, Michael, ed. *Inventing Vietnam: The War in Film and Television.* Philadelphia: Temple University Press, 1991.

Anderson, Kent. *Sympathy for the Devil.* New York: Bantam, 1999. (Reprint of the 1987 edition.) A curiously underknown and terrifyingly convincing novel of the war.

Anton, Frank, with Tommy Denton. *Why Didn't You Get Me Out?: A POW's Nightmare in Vietnam.* New York: St. Martin's Press, 2000. (Reprint of the 1997 edition.)

Appy, Christian G. *Patriots: The Vietnam War Remembered from All Sides.* New York: Viking, 2003. Possibly the best book about the war to be published in more than a decade, and without question its finest oral history.

Baker, Mark. *Nam: The Vietnam War in the Words of the Men and Women Who Fought There.* New York: Cooper Square Press, 2001. (Reprint of the 1981 edition.)

Bao Ninh. *The Sorrow of War: A Novel of North Vietnam.* Translated by Phan Thanh Hao. New York: Riverhead, 1996. (Reprint of the 1995 edition.)

Bilton, Michael, and Kevin Sim. *Four Hours in My Lai.* New York: Penguin, 1993. (Reprint of the 1992 edition.)

Bizot, François. *The Gate.* Translated by Euan Cameron. London: Harvill Press, 2003.

Borton, Lady. *Ho Chi Minh: A Portrait.* Hanoi: Youth Publishing House, 2003.

A beautifully designed and interesting book that nevertheless soft-pedals on every single controversial fact regarding Ho's life and politics.

Broyles, William, Jr. *Brothers in Arms: A Journey from War to Peace.* New York: Alfred A. Knopf, 1986.

Bui Tin. *From Enemy to Friend: A North Vietnamese Perspective on the War.* Translated by Nguyen Ngoc Bich. Annapolis, Md.: Naval Institute Press, 2002.

Burkett, B. G., and Glenna Whitley. *Stolen Valor: How the Vietnam Generation Was Robbed of Its Heroes and Its History.* Dallas: Verity Press, 1998.

Butler, David. *The Fall of Saigon: Scenes from the Sudden End of a Long War.* New York: Dell, 1986. (Reprint of the 1985 edition.) A book it is hard not to ingest in one emotionally paralyzed sitting. Butler has the humility to include letters written to his wife in the last month of Saigon's siege in which he assures her that the city will not fall. As is obvious from the text, a major source for the first part of this book.

Caputo, Philip. *Means of Escape: A Memoir.* New York: HarperCollins, 1991.

———. *A Rumor of War.* New York: Holt, Rinehart and Winston, 1977.

Chandler, David P. *Brother Number One: A Political Biography of Pol Pot.* Boulder, Colo.: Westview Press, 1999.

Chomsky, Noam. *At War with Asia.* Oakland: AK Press, 2005. (Reprint of the 1970 edition.) My second favorite passage: "Others regard 'Khmer socialism' as being a step toward an egalitarian and modern society, within the specific context of Cambodian history and culture. I do not have enough information to attempt a judgment." My favorite passage: "My personal guess is that, unhindered by imperialist intervention, the Vietnamese would develop a modern industrial society with much popular participation in implementation and direct democracy at the lower level of organization, a highly egalitarian society with excellent conditions of welfare and technical education." The passage with which it is impossible to take issue: "Perhaps someday they [U.S. war planners] will acknowledge their 'honest errors' in their memoirs, speaking of the burdens of world leadership and the tragic irony of history. Their victims, the peasants of Indochina, will write no memoirs and will be forgotten. They will join the countless millions of earlier victims of tyrants and oppressors."

Clark, Johnnie. *Guns Up!,* rev. ed. New York: Presidio Press, 2002.

Clausewitz, Carl von. *On War.* Edited and translated by Michael Howard and Peter Paret. New York: Alfred A. Knopf, 1993.

Coll, Steve. *Ghost Wars: The Secret History of the CIA, Afghanistan, and Bin Laden, from the Soviet Invasion to September 10, 2001.* New York: Penguin Press, 2004. An amazing and deeply sobering history, the reading of which should be the duty of every American.

Dallek, Robert. *Flawed Giant: Lyndon B. Johnson, 1960–1973.* New York: Oxford University Press, 1998.

————. *An Unfinished Life: John F. Kennedy, 1917–1963.* New York: Little, Brown, 2003.

Dang Nghiem Van, Chu Thai Son, and Luu Hung. *Ethnic Minorities in Vietnam.* Hanoi: The Gioi Publishers, 2000.

Downs, Frederick. *The Killing Zone: My Life in the Vietnam War.* New York: W. W. Norton, 1993. (Reprint of the 1978 edition.) One is hesitant to criticize Mr. Downs (he lost his right arm during combat), but sentences such as "Never again would I trust any dinks" and "It turned out most of us liked to kill other men. Some of the guys would shoot at a dink much as they would at a target" make it very, very hard to sympathize with him.

Duiker, William J. *The Communist Road to Power in Vietnam,* 2nd ed. Boulder, Colo.: Westview Press, 1996.

————. *Historical Dictionary of Vietnam,* 2nd ed. Lanham, Md.: Scarecrow Press, 1998.

————. *Ho Chi Minh: A Life.* New York: Hyperion, 2000. Although I was not aware of it at the time of my first journey, this book, despite being dedicated to "the Vietnamese People," is banned in Vietnam because of the information on pages 199 and 200, which concern Ho's probable wife, Nguyen Thi Minh Khai; her lover; and Ho's possible role, glancingly treated by Duiker, in their arrest and execution by the French.

Duong Thu Huong. *Novel Without a Name.* Translated by Phan Huy Duong and Nina McPherson. New York: Penguin Books, 1996. (Reprint of the 1995 edition.) Written by a woman who led a PAVN Communist Youth Brigade of forty volunteers to South Vietnam. She was one of her brigade's three survivors. Almost all of Huong's work has been banned by the Vietnamese government.

Elliott, David W. P. *The Vietnamese War: Revolution and Social Change in the Mekong Delta, 1930–1975,* 2 vols. Armonk, N.Y.: M. E. Sharpe, 2003. Written by a U.S. Army veteran of the war who later worked for the Rand Corporation in Vietnam, this two-volume monster is, at 1,547 small-print pages, quite possibly the most elaborate examination of the war's development and consequences. Despite its zeroed-in focus on only one area of Vietnam, it is also tremendously enthralling. Highly recommended to any reader looking to understand how the war affected average Vietnamese and incomparable for its evenhandedness and emotional sobriety.

Ellsberg, Daniel. *Secrets: A Memoir of Vietnam and the Pentagon Papers.* New York: Penguin, 2003. (Reprint of the 2002 edition.) Better written and more entertaining than it has any right to be. Here is Ellsberg's take on *The Pentagon Papers* themselves: "[I]t was not any individual page or revelation, or even a small set of them, that was very important. It was the overall detailed documentation of our involvement over the years and the repetitive patterns of internal pessimism and desperate escalation and deception of the public in the face of what was, realistically, hopeless stalemate. It was the total lack of a good reason for what we were doing anywhere in the whole story." Strangely, Ellsberg broke no existing law in leaking the *Papers* to *The New York Times,* but as his lawyer explained to him, "Well, let's face it, Dan. Copying seven thousand pages of top secret documents and giving them to *The New York Times* has a bad ring to it."

Engelmann, Larry. *Tears Before the Rain: An Oral History of the Fall of South Vietnam.* New York: Oxford University Press, 1990. A splendidly discordant oral history, made all the more so by the many revealing inconsistencies within its shared memories. A major source for part one of this book.

Fall, Bernard. *Hell in a Very Small Place: The Siege of Dien Bien Phu.* Cambridge, Mass.: Da Capo Press, 2002. (Reprint of the 1966 edition.)

———. *Last Reflections on a War.* Mechanicsburg, Pa.: Stackpole Books, 2000.

———. *Street Without Joy.* Mechanicsburg, Pa.: Stackpole Books, 1994. (Reprint of the 1964 edition.)

Fenton, James. *All the Wrong Places: Adrift in the Politics of the Pacific Rim.* New York: Atlantic Monthly Press, 1988. Contains one of my favorite accounts of the fall of Saigon: Mr. Fenton, a poet and Englishman, personally looted the U.S. Embassy. And this: "I went as a supporter of the Vietcong, wanting to see them win. I saw them win. What feeling did that leave me with, and where does it leave me now? I know that by the end of my stay in Saigon I had grown to loathe the *apparatchiks* who were arriving every day with their cardboard suitcases from Hanoi. I know that I loathed their institutional lies and their mockery of political justice. But as the banners went up in honor of Lenin, Marx, and Stalin, I know too that I had known this was coming. Had we not supported the NLF 'without illusions'? Must I not accept that the disappearances, the gagging of the press, the political distortion of reality was all part of a classical Stalinism which nevertheless 'had its progressive features'? . . . We had been seduced by Ho. My political associates in England were *not* the kind of people who denied that Stalinism existed. We not only knew about it, we were very interested in it. We also opposed it. Why then did we also support it? Or did we?"

FitzGerald, Frances. *Fire in the Lake: The Vietnamese and the Americans in Vietnam.* New York: Back Bay Books, 2002. (Reprint of the 1972 edition.)

Gaiduk, Ilya V. *The Soviet Union and the Vietnam War.* Chicago: Ivan R. Dee, 1996.

Gannon, Kathy. *I Is for Infidel: From Holy War to Holy Terror: 18 Years Inside Afghanistan.* New York: PublicAffairs, 2005.

Greene, Graham. *The Quiet American.* New York: Penguin, 1977. (Reprint of the 1955 edition.)

Grossman, Dave. *On Killing: The Psychological Cost of Learning to Kill in War and Society.* New York: Little, Brown, 1996. (Reprint of the 1995 edition.)

Guillon, Emmanuel. *Cham Art: Treasures from the Da Nang Museum, Vietnam.* Bangkok: River Books, 2001.

Halberstam, David. *Ho.* New York: Alfred A. Knopf, 1971.

Hammes, T. X. *The Sling and the Stone: On War in the 21st Century.* Saint Paul, Minn.: Zenith Press, 2004.

Harrison, James P. *The Endless War: Vietnam's Struggle for Independence.* New York: Columbia University Press, 1989.

Hayslip, Le Ly, with Jay Wurts. *When Heaven and Earth Changed Places: A Vietnamese Woman's Journey from War to Peace.* New York: Plume, 2003. (Reprint of the 1989 edition.)

Hedges, Chris. *War Is a Force That Gives Us Meaning.* New York: PublicAffairs, 2002.

Heinemann, Larry. *Black Virgin Mountain: A Return to Vietnam.* New York: Doubleday, 2005. Weirdest—and perhaps most revealing—moment: A Vietnamese veteran of the war tells Heinemann that he read Whitman, Twain, Fitzgerald, and Hemingway and gave lectures on them to North Vietnamese troops on their way to the front. "Then," Heinemann writes, "Professor Lien asked in all earnest seriousness what Vietnamese literature had the United States Army taught *me* during the war."

Henderson, Charles. *Goodnight Saigon: The True Story of the U.S. Marines' Last Days in Vietnam.* New York: Berkley, 2005.

Herr, Michael. *Dispatches.* New York: Vintage, 1991. (Reprint of the 1977 edition.) My favorite line from a book containing nothing but indelible lines: "But once in a while you'd hear something fresh, and a couple of times you'd even hear something high, like the corpsman at Khe Sanh who said, 'If it ain't the fucking incoming it's the fucking outgoing. Only difference is who gets the fucking grease, and that ain't no fucking difference at all.' " I have no idea what that means, but goddamn.

Hersh, Seymour. *My Lai 4: A Report on the Massacre and Its Aftermath.* New York: Vintage, 1972. (Reprint of the 1970 edition.)

Hitchens, Christopher. *The Trial of Henry Kissinger.* London: Verso, 2001.

Isaacs, Arnold R. *Vietnam Shadows: The War, Its Ghosts, and Its Legacy.* Baltimore: Johns Hopkins University Press, 1997.

Jamieson, Neil L. *Understanding Vietnam.* Berkeley: University of California Press, 1993. Probably the best book to read before traveling to Vietnam for the first time. Find Nguyen Dinh Tu's "Fare Thee Well" dispatch in full here.

Jomini, Antoine-Henri de. *The Art of War.* Translated by G. H. Mendell and W. P. Craighill. Philadelphia: J. B. Lippincott and Company, 1862.

Kaiser, David. *American Tragedy: Kennedy, Johnson, and the Origins of the Vietnam War.* Cambridge, Mass.: Belknap Press, 2000. A major source of information for the Johnson administration's dramatis personae. Here is this book's shattering ending: "Johnson [in July 1965] had a 65 percent approval rating. The Gemini program, the next step on the way to the moon, had just completed a spectacular mission, including a space walk. The economy had been steadily expanding for four years and five months. . . . One U.S. dollar bought four Deutschmarks and 360 Japanese yen. The Interstate Highway system was well on its way to completion. *The Sound of Music* was the most popular movie of the year. America's colleges—with the sole exception of the University of California at Berkeley—were filled with well-dressed, industrious, and obedient undergraduates, and in June, in a cover story on the Palisades, California, high school class of 1965, *Time* announced that American youth seemed to be on the verge of a new golden age. No one knew that a whole era of American history was over."

Kaplan, Robert D. *Soldiers of God: With Islamic Warriors in Afghanistan and Pakistan,* rev. ed. New York: Vintage, 2001.

Karnow, Stanley. *Vietnam: A History,* rev. ed. New York: Penguin, 1997.

Kimball, Jeffrey. *The Vietnam War Files: Uncovering the Secret History of the Nixon-Era Strategy.* Lawrence: University Press of Kansas, 2004.

Kissinger, Henry. *Ending the Vietnam War: A History of America's Involvement in and Extrication from the Vietnam War.* New York: Simon and Schuster, 2003. A disgustingly evasive book from a thoroughly disgusting statesman.

Lamb, David. *Vietnam, Now: A Reporter Returns.* New York: PublicAffairs, 2002.

Langguth, A. J. *Our Vietnam: The War, 1954–1975.* New York: Simon and Schuster, 2000.

Laurence, John. *The Cat from Hué: A Vietnam War Story.* New York: Public-Affairs, 2002.

Le Duan. *Selected Writings: 1960–1975.* Hanoi: The Gioi Publishers, 1997.

Lind, Michael. *Vietnam: The Necessary War: A Reinterpretation of America's Most Disastrous Military Conflict.* New York: Touchstone, 2002. (Reprint of the 1999 edition.) Lind writes that it "was necessary for the United States to escalate the war in the mid-1960s in order to defend the credibility of the United States as a superpower, but it was necessary for the United States to forfeit the war after 1968, in order to preserve the American domestic political consensus in favor of the Cold War on other fronts." The thought occurs whether American soldiers on their way to Vietnam would have appreciated knowing that their lives were on the line for "credibility." Lind has much to say about the totalitarian regime of Ho Chi Minh, but who is totalitarian when, by Lind's reasoning, ten or fifteen thousand lives are regarded as an appropriate sacrifice to an abstraction? As Lind argues, "if one rejects the false morality of pacifism, then such grim calculations are unavoidable." Change only a couple of Lind's words, and one finds oneself staring at the airtight logic of a Marxist-Leninist starving out peasants for the proletarian commonweal. The biggest problem with Lind's thesis is that, in his view, had the United States not chosen to fight in Vietnam, its reputation would have suffered and something he calls the "bandwagon effect" would have inspired similar insurgencies all over the world. So the United States chose Lind's necessary path and fought. Its reputation suffered, and many insurgencies (by Lind's own admission) were inspired anyway—and not by American inaction but rather by the far more distressing example of American defeat.

Logevall, Fredrik. *Choosing War: The Lost Chance for Peace and the Escalation of War in Vietnam.* Berkeley: University of California Press, 1999. A fascinating source of information about the Diem years and a surprisingly gripping read.

Macdonald, Dwight. *Discriminations: Essays and Afterthoughts.* New York: Da Capo Press, 1985. (Reprint of the 1974 edition.)

Mangold, Tom, and John Penycate. *The Tunnels of Cu Chi.* New York: Berkley, 1986. (Reprint of the 1985 edition.)

Mann, Robert. *A Grand Delusion: America's Descent into Vietnam.* New York: Basic Books, 2001.

Mao Tse-tung. *On Guerrilla Warfare.* Translated by Samuel B. Griffith II. Champaign: University of Illinois Press, 2000. (Reprint of the 1961 edition.)

Maraniss, David. *They Marched into Sunlight: War and Peace, Vietnam and America, October 1967.* New York: Simon and Schuster, 2003. A beautiful, wrenching, horrible book. Much of my information concerning napalm was taken from here, as were some of the details concerning NLF privation. One of the few books about the war that manages to convey an admirably unbroken empathy for all.

Marr, David G. *Vietnam 1945: The Quest for Power.* Berkeley: University of California Press, 1995.

Mason, Robert. *Chickenhawk.* New York: The Viking Press, 1983.

McMaster, H. R. *Dereliction of Duty: Lyndon Johnson, Robert McNamara, the Joint Chiefs of Staff, and the Lies that Led to Vietnam.* New York: Harper-Collins, 1997.

McNamara, Robert S., with Brian VanDeMark. *In Retrospect: The Tragedy and Lessons of Vietnam.* New York: Vintage, 1996. (A revision of the 1995 edition.)

Military History Institute of Vietnam. *Victory in Vietnam: The Official History of the People's Army of Vietnam, 1954–1975.* Translated by Merle L. Pribbenow. Lawrence: University Press of Kansas, 2002.

Moïse, Edwin E. *Tonkin Gulf and the Escalation of the Vietnam War.* Chapel Hill: University of North Carolina Press, 1996. Incredibly well researched and skillfully, even movingly, told.

Moore, Harold G., and Joseph Galloway. *We Were Soldiers Once . . . and Young: Ia Drang: The Battle That Changed the War in Vietnam.* New York: HarperPerennial, 1993. (Reprint of the 1992 edition.)

Murphy, Edward F. *Semper Fi—Vietnam: From Danang to the DMZ, Marine Corps Campaigns, 1965–1975.* New York: Presidio Press, 1997.

Népote, Jacques, Xavier Guillaume, and Anita Sach. *Vietnam*. Hong Kong: Odyssey Publications, 1999.

Nghia M. Vo. *The Bamboo Gulag: Political Imprisonment in Communist Vietnam*. Jefferson, N.C.: McFarland and Company, 2004.

Nguyen Cao Ky, with Marvin J. Wolf. *Buddha's Child: My Fight to Save South Vietnam*. New York: St. Martin's Press, 2002. Vietnam's current leaders could doubtless do wonders for themselves and their country if they bothered to address the past with General Ky's hard-won, exile-honed honesty. Here are the final lines of this extremely fascinating book: "My biggest mistake was allowing the wrong man the opportunity to lead a guaranty of defeat. For this I beg forgiveness of those who fled into exile, of those who remained, and from those then unborn."

———. *How We Lost the Vietnam War*. New York: Cooper Square Press, 2002. (Reprint of the 1979 edition.)

Nguyen Khac Vien. *Vietnam: A Long History*. Hanoi: The Gioi Publishers, 1993.

Nguyen Phu Trong. *Viet Nam on the Path of Renewal*. Hanoi: The Gioi Publishers, 2004. Trong, one of Vietnam's foremost political scientists, has this to say about the collapse of the Soviet Union (which "had a glorious and honorable history"): "For a long time, the Communist Party of the Soviet Union made the mistake of taking over and performing the role of the State and almost turned itself into a state by doing tasks of the State, thus failing to bring into full play the role of the State itself." Uh, yeah.

Nixon, Richard. *RN: The Memoirs of Richard Nixon*. New York: Simon and Schuster, 1990. (Reprint of the 1978 edition.)

Oberdorfer, Don. *Tet!: The Turning Point in the Vietnam War*. Baltimore: Johns Hopkins University Press, 2001. (Reprint of the 1971 edition.)

O'Brien, Tim. *If I Die in a Combat Zone Box Me Up and Ship Me Home*. New York: Broadway Books, 1999. (Reprint of the 1975 edition.)

———. *The Things They Carried*. New York: Penguin, 1991. (Reprint of the 1990 edition.)

Olson, James S., and Randy Roberts. *My Lai: A Brief History with Documents*. Boston: Bedford, 1998.

O'Nan, Stewart, ed. *The Vietnam Reader: The Definitive Collection of American Fiction and Nonfiction on the War*. New York: Anchor, 1998.

Pham, Andrew X. *Catfish and Mandala: A Two-Wheeled Voyage Through the Landscape and Memory of Vietnam*. New York: Farrar, Straus and Giroux,

1999. A wonderful travelogue of contemporary Vietnam, by one of its most thoughtful sons-in-exile.

Philpott, Tom. *Glory Denied: The Saga of the Vietnam Veteran Jim Thompson, America's Longest-Held Prisoner of War.* New York: W. W. Norton, 2001. In telling the story of Thompson, a man both tormented and tormenting, Philpott manages in this oral history to relate the horror of the war as it was felt by its warriors, its captives, its captors, and its families. Inarguably the best book about Vietnam's American prisoners of war.

Pike, Douglas. *Viet Cong: The Organization and Techniques of the National Liberation Front of South Vietnam.* Cambridge, Mass.: MIT Press, 1966.

Reporting Vietnam: American Journalism 1959–1975. New York: Library of America, 2000. The reporting from South Vietnam in its last days by Paul Vogle, Malcolm Browne, Keyes Beech, Philip Caputo, and Bob Tamarkin can all be found here.

Sachs, Dana. *The House on Dream Street: Memoir of an American Woman in Vietnam.* Emeryville, Calif.: Seal Press, 2003. (Reprint of the 2000 edition.) There is so much to love in this book, from its nauseating description of Sachs's first run-in with the Vietnamese delicacy of embryonic duck eggs, to its patient and evocative portrait of mid-1990s Hanoi, to its recounting of Sachs's attempt to make hamburgers for her Vietnamese hosts, to its uncommonly moving love story between Sachs and a working-class Vietnamese man whose heart she breaks. One of the best books available on contemporary Vietnam.

Santoli, Al. *Everything We Had: An Oral History of the Vietnam War by Thirty-three American Soldiers Who Fought It.* New York: Ballantine, 1982. (Reprint of the 1981 edition.)

Shawcross, William. *Sideshow: Kissinger, Nixon, and the Destruction of Cambodia.* New York: Cooper Square Press, 2002. (Reprint of the 1979 edition.)

Shay, Jonathan. *Achilles in Vietnam: Combat Trauma and the Undoing of Character.* New York: Touchstone, 1995. (Reprint of the 1994 edition.)

Sheehan, Neil. *A Bright Shining Lie: John Paul Vann and America in Vietnam.* New York: Random House, 1988. The saddest and most consuming book—it is both *The Iliad* and *The Odyssey*—I have read about the war. Any war.

Short, Philip. *Mao: A Life.* New York: Henry Holt, 2000.

———. *Pol Pot: Anatomy of a Nightmare.* New York: Henry Holt, 2005. Both of Short's biographies of Asia's murderous supremos are excellent. To read one right after the other, however, is not advisable. This writer lost an entire week to drawn shades and hours of stunned, thoughtless banjo picking in their back-to-back aftermath.

Shultz, Richard H., Jr. *The Secret War Against Hanoi: The Untold Story of Spies, Saboteurs, and Covert Warriors in North Vietnam.* New York: Harper-Collins, 1999.

Snepp, Frank. *Decent Interval: An Insider's Account of Saigon's Indecent End, Told by the CIA's Chief Strategy Analyst in Vietnam.* Lawrence: University Press of Kansas, 2002. (Revised version of the 1977 edition.) One of my favorite books about the war and one I mined thoroughly for part one of *The Father of All Things.* Due to what Snepp condemns as, at best, wishful U.S. thinking about Saigon's chances for holding out in the war's final days, he lost his Vietnamese-Chinese girlfriend, as well as "a child I believe to be ours," after the Communists conquered the city. This was not Snepp's only debit. The CIA sued its erstwhile officer, and won, after the 1977 publication of *Decent Interval,* which the CIA claimed had been written in violation of agency protocol. Snepp, whose case went as high as the U.S. Supreme Court, was ultimately forced to forfeit all proceeds of *Decent Interval* from now until the sun burns out. Unavailable for years (except in pirated editions on the streets of Saigon), this reissued edition continues to garnish the CIA strongbox.

Sorley, Lewis. *A Better War: The Unexamined Victories and Final Tragedy of America's Last Years in Vietnam.* New York: Harcourt, 1999.

Spector, Ronald H. *After Tet: The Bloodiest Year in Vietnam.* New York: Free Press, 1993.

Summers, Harry G. *The Vietnam War Almanac.* New York: Ballantine Books, 1999. (Reprint of the 1985 edition.) Despite its combative (and unrevised) tone, a terrific source of information concerning the war, in particular its military hardware.

Taubman, William. *Khrushchev: The Man and His Era.* New York: W. W. Norton, 2003.

Taylor, Keith Weller. *The Birth of Vietnam.* Berkeley: University of California Press, 1983. As dry as rice powder, but an immensely helpful study of pre-colonial (and even pre-recorded-history) Vietnam.

Templer, Robert. *Shadows and Wind: A View of Modern Vietnam.* New York:

Penguin, 1999. Gets off to a rough start with its frankly *unbelievably* unsympathetic tone toward returning American veterans but evolves to become a deeply felt and insightful examination of the postwar(s) culture and economy of Vietnam.

Thompson, Leroy. *The Counter-insurgency Manual: Tactics of the Anti-guerrilla Professionals.* London: Greenhill Books, 2002.

Tran, Barbara, Monique T. D. Truong, and Luu Truong Khoi, eds. *Watermark: Vietnamese American Poetry and Prose.* New York: Asian American Writers' Workshop, 1998.

Truong Chinh. *Selected Writings.* Hanoi: The Gioi Publishers, 1994.

Truong Nhu Tang, with David Chanoff and Doan Van Toai. *A Viet Cong Memoir: An Inside Account of the Vietnam War and Its Aftermath.* New York: Vintage, 1986. (Reprint of the 1985 edition.)

Van Tien Dung. *Our Great Spring Victory: An Account of the Liberation of South Vietnam.* Translated by John Spragens, Jr. Hanoi: The Gioi Publishers, 2000. (Reprint of the 1977 edition.)

Vo Nguyen Giap. *How We Won the War.* Philadelphia: RECON Publications, 1976.

Walton, C. Dale. *The Myth of Inevitable U.S. Defeat in Vietnam.* London: Frank Kass, 2002. Did I mention that this book is nuts?

Wicker, Tom. *JFK and LBJ: The Influence of Personality upon Politics.* Chicago: Ivan R. Dee, 1991.

Wolff, Tobias. *In Pharaoh's Army: Memories of the Lost War.* New York: Vintage, 1995. (Reprint of the 1994 edition.) In my opinion, the best combatant's memoir to have emerged from the war. So finely written as to be almost cruel.

Young, Marilyn. *The Vietnam Wars: 1945–1990.* New York: HarperCollins, 1991.

Index

Permissions Acknowledgments

About the Author

Tom Bissell was born in Escanaba, Michigan, in 1974. After graduating from Michigan State University, he worked as a Peace Corps volunteer in Uzbekistan and then as a book editor in New York City. Since 2001 he has been a full-time writer and traveled widely in the Canadian Arctic, Central and Southeast Asia, and covered the wars in Afghanistan and Iraq. His first book, *Chasing the Sea,* was published in 2003 and was followed shortly thereafter by *Speak, Commentary,* a humor book he coauthored with Jeff Alexander. In 2005 he published the story collection *God Lives in St. Petersburg,* and for it was awarded a Rome Fellowship by the American Academy of Arts and Letters. He is a contributing editor for *Harper's Magazine* and *The Virginia Quarterly Review.* His work is often anthologized and has been published in several languages. After nine years in New York City, he currently lives in Rome, Italy, and is working on a travel book about first-century Christianity and a novel set in Michigan's Upper Peninsula.

A Note on the Type

This book was set in Minion, a typeface produced by the Adobe Corporation specifically for the Macintosh personal computer, and released in 1990. Designed by Robert Slimbach, Minion combines the classic characteristics of old-style faces with the full complement of weights required for modern typesetting.

Composed by North Market Street Graphics, Lancaster, Pennsylvania
Printed and bound by Berryville Graphics, Berryville, Virginia
Designed by Wesley Gott